Knowledge by Ritual

Journal of Theological Interpretation Supplements

MURRAY RAE
University of Otago, New Zealand
Editor-in-Chief

Knowledge by Ritual

A Biblical Prolegomenon to Sacramental Theology

DRU JOHNSON

Winona Lake, Indiana
EISENBRAUNS
2016

Printed in the United States of America

www.eisenbrauns.com

Library of Congress Cataloging-in-Publication Data

Names: Johnson, Dru, author.
Title: Knowledge by ritual : a biblical prolegomenon to sacramental theology /
  Dru Johnson.
Description: Winona Lake, Indiana : Eisenbrauns, 2016. | Series: Journal
  of theological interpretation supplements ; 13 | Includes bibliographical
  references and index. | Description based on print version record and CIP
  data provided by publisher; resource not viewed.
Identifiers: LCCN 2015043623 (print) | LCCN 2015042029 (ebook) | ISBN
  9781575064321 (PDF) | ISBN 9781575064314 (pbk. : alk. paper)
Subjects: LCSH: Sacraments. | Rites and ceremonies. | Knowledge, Theory of
  (Religion)
Classification: LCC BV800 (print) | LCC BV800 .J59 2016 (ebook) | DDC
  264.001—dc23
LC record available at http://lccn.loc.gov/2015043623

The paper used in this publication meets the minimum requirements of the American
National Standard for Information Sciences—Permanence of Paper for Printed Library
Materials, ANSI Z39.48-1984.♾™

To my mother and father, Patricia and Kenneth,
who instilled in me a profound reverence for the human body, personal history,
and the work of the Divine in the world.

Contents

PART III: THE BIBLICAL CASE FOR RITUAL KNOWING

PART IV: THEOLOGICAL IMPLICATIONS OF RITUAL KNOWING

Acknowledgments

This volume came about—like many such monographs—through the effort of many people and much guidance. However, this work simply would not have ever happened without a gracious grant from the Institute for Advanced Studies—Shalem Center in Jerusalem (now The Herzl Institute) through the John Templeton Foundation. Not only did the Institute provide me workspace and a scholarly community, even more, Yoram Hazony especially contributed to my work through his encouragement, mentorship, and friendship. Yoram and others at the Institute welcomed me into the work they have been pioneering in the field of philosophy and the Hebrew Bible. This includes Joshua Weinstein, from whom I have learned so much and who has sharpened my thinking on many fronts. Also, my officemate in Jerusalem, Miryam Brand, assisted me regularly in navigating Israeli culture, Judaism, and thorny biblical matters. Jeremiah Unterman urged me to analyze my own presumptions about the biblical texts and offered countless opportunities for seeing the text in a new way. As well, the conversations with Ofir Haivry, Sam Lebens, and others continually challenged and sharpened my thinking. The community of scholars gathered by The Herzl Institute provided a much-needed sounding board and correction, which formalize much of this book.

I would also like to thank the John Templeton Foundation, which is committed to funding such diverse areas of research and The King's College, who was extremely gracious to allow me research leave as a new professor. My colleagues there, especially Noel Rabinowitz, have been a regular well from which I could draw wisdom. My wife, Stephanie, and children Claudia, Olivia, Benjamin, and Luisa were overly indulgent in moving, yet again, overseas and spending four months in Jerusalem. This was no small sacrifice on their part and to them, I am especially grateful.

I would also like to acknowledge and thank the many people involved in preparing drafts and editing: Abigail Salvatore, Heather Cate, and Rebecca Au for helping to clean up early drafts and Celina Durgin for jumping in to edit the final draft. Of course, all the typographic and grammatical errors found in this volume—and I am certainly there are several hiding from me—are no one's fault but mine. Thanks to Carrie Orteza for her help with the bibliography. Ísabella Jordan deserves no modest praise for her triumph in reconciling the footnotes with the bibliography and creating the indexes. A very special thanks goes to Kenneth and Landreth Johnson for painstakingly creating the figures and diagrams used throughout.

Finally, I am particularly grateful to those who offered constructive feed-back to papers, chapters, and entire drafts of this book. Ryan O'Dowd has been instrumental in getting me to see some shortcomings in the content. The reviewers of the JTI Supplement Series and the series editor, Murray Rae, offered many insightful comments, all of which shaped the final draft. Michael Rhodes offered incisive comments on a final draft. As well, several conference series helped me to craft these chapters: the Ritual in the Biblical World and the Senses and Culture program units in the Society of Biblical Literature; Harvard Divinity School's Ways of Knowing Conference (2014); and the Philosophical Investigations of the Hebrew Scriptures, Talmud, and Midrash conferences in Israel. I am also privileged to have students who teach me and I heartily thank those who endured the epistemology classes and Hebrew literature classes at The King's College and Covenant Theological Seminary. Their critical engagement shaped some of the ideas presented herein.

Abbreviations

Ancient Works

b.	Babylonian Talmud
LXX	Septuagint
MT	Masoretic Text
NT	New Testament

Reference Works

AB	Anchor Bible Commentary
AMA	*American Mathematical Monthly*
ARS	*Annual Review of Sociology*
BBRS	*Bulletin for Biblical Research Supplements*
BBS	*Behavioral and Brain Sciences*
BDB	F. Brown, S. R. Driver, and C. A. Briggs. *Hebrew and English Lexicon of the Old Testament.* Oxford, 1907
BN	*Biblische Notizen*
BO	Berit Olam
BS	*Bibliotheca Sacra*
BZAW	Beihefte zur Zeitschrift für die alttestamentliche Wissenschaft
CBR	*Currents in Biblical Research*
CB	*Clinical Biomechanics*
CC	Continental Commentary
CCS	Cascade Companions Series
CD	*Church Dogmatics*
CI	*Critical Inquiry*
CL	Cultural Liturgies
COQG	Christian Origins and the Question of God
CP	*Cognitive Psychology*
CTHP	Cambridge Texts in the History of Philosophy
EBC	Expositor's Bible Commentary
ET	*Expository Times*
FP	*Faith and Philosophy*

FAT	Forschungen zum Alten Testament
FPS	Foundations of Philosophy Series
FRLANT	Forschungen zur Religion und Literatur des Alten und Neuen Testaments
HBM	Hebrew Bible Monographs
HTR	*Harvard Theological Review*
JAAR	*Journal of the American Academy of Religion*
JBL	*Journal of Biblical Literature*
JEP	*Journal of Experimental Psychology*
JEPHPP	*Journal of Experimental Psychology: Human Perception and Performance*
JHTR	*Journal of Head Trauma Rehabilitation*
JPSP	*Journal of Personality and Social Psychology*
JSOT	*Journal for the Study of the Old Testament*
JTS	*Journal of Theological Studies*
LHBOTS	Library of Hebrew Bible/Old Testament Studies
LHD	Library of History and Doctrine
LNTS	Library of New Testament Studies
MSP	*Midwest Studies in Philosophy*
OTL	Old Testament Library
OTT	Old Testament Theology
PCN	*Psychiatry and Clinical Neurosciences*
PS	*Philosophical Studies*
PSPB	*Personality and Social Psychology Bulletin*
RC	*Religious Compass*
RTR	*Reformed Theological Review*
SBibLit	Studies in Biblical Literature
SECT	Studies in Epistemology and Cognitive Theory
SHS	Scripture and Hermeneutics Series
SSS	*Social Studies of Science*
TD	*Tradition and Discovery: The Polanyi Society Periodical*
THOT	Two Horizons of the Old Testament Commentary
TPS	Theology and Philosophy Series
TWOT	*Theological Wordbook of the Old Testament*
UF	*Ugarit-Forschungen*
VT	*Vetus Testamentum*
WBC	Word Biblical Commentary
WUNT	Wissenschaftliche Untersuchungen zum Neuen Testament

Preface

In my previous work, *Biblical Knowing: A Scriptural Epistemology of Error*, I laid out a case for viewing biblical epistemology as most concerned with a social process.[1] That process places an explicit emphasis on listening to an authority in order to know. Hence, much of the Torah and Gospel narratives centered on Israel listening—or, more often, not listening—to the prophet who was authenticated to her and then following the prophet's directions in order to see what was being shown to her. Participating in this process brought Israel to know something that she could not otherwise know. If Israel listened *and* acted in accordance to YHWH's commands, then she knew. Knowledge, then, became a necessary product of this process.

Because *Biblical Knowing* was meant to demonstrate the primacy of listening to the proper prophetic voice, it purposefully neglected other constituent factors that ensued listening. In other words, as Israel learned to listen to Moses, now what? This book intends to pick up on the "now what" of biblical epistemology. There are myriad actions to take (e.g., keep the Sabbath), rites to perform (e.g., sin offering), ideals to uphold (e.g., justice for the foreigner), and more. If knowing well is contingent on listening to the proper authority, then our prime concern centers upon the authorities to whom we listen. But the rituals of Israel presume that the authority and authentication of Moses' voice have already been established. If Israel is ready to obey, then the question shifts to what she should be doing. Even then, a more basic question remains: How do animal sacrifice, bathing, or celebrating festivals bring Israel to know anything at all?

The answer will specifically aim first at describing the *how* before the *what*. I will not aim to flesh out all of *what* an ancient Israelite would come to know through ritual participation. *What* Israelites came to know through their rituals, as I will later argue, is at least partially off-limits to us for historical reasons. I will end this book with a venture into what Christians might know through the rite of Communion, but that analysis is available through current access to the practice of the Lord's Supper.

---

1. Dru Johnson, *Biblical Knowing: A Scriptural Epistemology of Error* (Eugene, OR: Cascade Books, 2013). For a briefer and more accessible version of this volume, see Dru Johnson, *Scripture's Knowing: A Companion to Biblical Epistemology* (CCS; Eugene, OR: Cascade, 2015).

In the coming chapters, I want to show what the Israelite Scriptures of the Hebrew Bible and New Testament presume: *that rituals bring participants to know something about the world that they could not have known otherwise.*[2] Rites teach them how to see the world. As I showed in *Biblical Knowing*, scientific episte-mology has turned to very similar explanations for how the scientific commu-nity arrives at knowledge of the world. Scientists are now wrestling with their older and mythic positivist self-identification, where data are collected and logically organized as scientific facts. Despite this Modernist anachronism, many are slowly coming to recognize that science could more easily be de-scribed as:

> Participation in a system of authoritative voices who train appren-tices through embodied rituals, relying upon trusted testimony in order to see the world differently than they could have otherwise seen it apart from skilled participation.

For instance, a trained astronomer can no longer look at the night sky as I do. The rituals of science have transformed her. She looks at the exact same sky that I look at, the exact same data as it were, but she sees something that I cannot see. I am logically separated from her knowledge of the sky *because I have not participated in the community and rituals of astronomical science.* Though it might not be immediately obvious how mine is a logical separation from her knowledge, I will address the logic of ritual fully in chapters two and five.

Biblical Knowing focused on listening to authenticated authorities. This book (*Knowledge by Ritual*) will examine the rationale behind the actions that biblical authorities prescribe in order for Israel to know well. In this sense, the present work intends to complement the former work. As well, I will discrimi-nate here among being insensitive to what one is seeing, recognizing, and dis-cerning. The biblical goal of the epistemological process is wisdom or discern-ment. As I have previously argued, wisdom is not knowledge-content that is applied to life. This caricature is aptly captured by those who artificially di-chotomize knowledge and wisdom—knowing what is true (knowledge) versus knowing what to do (wisdom). The biblical goal of wisdom does not reduce to a product to be had and applied. Often in Scripture, wisdom is skillfully seeing, discerning how the particulars cohere to a whole, how the glinting flashes of the night sky tell a cosmological story from creation to present. It is seeing differently, which coalesces with our actions.

In the following pages, I will show that the path to discerning wisdom is much like that of the path to being a discerning scientist or analyst of any va-

---

2. In this work, I consider the Christian texts of the New Testament as produced by Jewish authors in a majority Jewish population and often for the sake of a Jewish audi-ence. While they might not be considered "Scripture" to Judaism today, they are best categorized (and clearly view themselves) as a part and parcel extension of the Israelite God's plan from the beginning.

riety. Seeking out accredited authorities and embodying their prescribed rituals imbues discernment, the epistemic prize of the Hebrew Bible.

A Prolegomenon

I will argue in the coming chapters that sacramental theology can suffer from the temptation to over-determine the symbolic nature of ritual. The function of signs, signals, and symbols has consumed too much of the discussion. Here, I am attempting to offer some new and foundational questions with which to approach sacraments. Because sacraments are also rituals, they succumb to many of the same types of inquiry we bring to all rituals, religious and not. This book is a prolegomenon in that the epistemic function of ritual ought to cause a reappraisal of method in sacramental theology. Indeed, I will argue that any system of Christian theology begins on specious footing if its epistemological tenets are not grounded in the embodied, social, and ritual nature of knowing found throughout the biblical texts.

Although I am orienting this volume toward sacramental theology, I shelve the discussion of sacraments as rites until Part IV of this book. The reason for conflating sacraments and rituals will be made explicit later. For now, the salient features of ritual will not diminish the examination of practices that we might deem sacred. In fact, annexing particular parts of the rituals of Israel and Christianity as sacred is problematic and deserves further treatment beyond this work. Although I think there are good reasons for thinking about rituals as sacraments, highlighting their sacred and punctiliar function, there are other considerations. For instance, what makes the practice of baptism (i.e., pouring water on or submerging someone) sacred as opposed to the practices of catechesis, filling the baptismal fount (or pool), preparing the words of consecration, or getting dressed in baptismal garb, etc.? This question, unfortunately, goes beyond what I can address in this book. Though I will offer some ways in which all of these practices appear to be sacred within the ritual logic of the Hebrew Bible and New Testament, a particular and fuller theological account of the sacredness as a concept is needed.

Structure of the Book

This book will build an argument that Israelite rituals function as means to an epistemological end, one among several possible goals of ritual participation. The stronger version of this argument will be that all knowing requires ritual participation and hence, Israelite epistemology portrayed in the Hebrew Bible and New Testament is commensurate with folk and scientific epistemology.

Part I describes recent attempts in Anglo-American approaches to epistemology and ritual theory. We will consider why the various schools of epistemology are not only insufficient to account for what is happening in the development of Israelite knowledge, but also insufficient to account for the fostering of scientific knowledge. Moreover, recent suggestions in the new field called Analytic Theology offer exciting inroads, broadening epistemological theory to include literary analysis. However, the shortcomings of such an approach cannot overcome the intricacies created by ritual's primacy in human knowledge.

In ritual theory, there seems to be general agreement that rituals have a direct relationship to beliefs and knowledge, but theorists typically do not have the philosophical vocabulary to sufficiently describe the nature of that relationship. Moreover, Catherine Bell's work has questioned the entire lot of working assumptions in the field of ritual studies.

In light of these strengths and weaknesses in epistemology and ritual theory, we will offer a methodology for thinking about Israelite ritual as a normative means of knowing. A brief review of the central findings from *Biblical Knowing* is included here.

Part II lays out the argument for viewing rituals as epistemologically necessary, clarifying how ritual participation moves the agent from recognition to discernment and how that process dovetails with the biblical ideal of wisdom. Here we will directly engage the strongest arguments for embodied knowledge, including analogical reasoning and metaphor as functions of the embodied person and society. The test of this project's success relies on ritual's ability to plausibly, though not exhaustively, explain the rigorous arts of logic and mathematics formed through the body.

Part III analyzes the biblical evidence, demonstrating that from the Eden narrative forward, prescriptive and embodied practices have always been part of the biblical ideal of proper knowing. Prescriptive acts reflect the biblical priority of listening to the authoritative voice of Israel's authenticated prophets (e.g., Moses, Ezekiel, Jesus, etc.). Embodied participation reflects the creaturely nature of knowing that eschews strong notions of disembodied knowledge, such as our standard caricatures of Neo-Platonism found in various types of Gnosticism.

Finally, Part IV will focus on the practical implications of such a view. How does one who wants to reflect the biblical norms of epistemology participate in ritual and to what end? Even more, does theological discourse itself need to reflect a ritualized epistemology?

In sum, my aim is to show the confluence of thought regarding the epistemic function of rituals in scientific inquiry, ritual theory, and the biblical literature. My primary interlocutors in this task will emerge repeatedly. Michael Polanyi's epistemology of scientific inquiry, Catherine Bell's critique of ritual theory, and Jonathan Klawans's recent work on ritual in the biblical texts will be examined extensively in the coming chapters. To demonstrate the commensurability between these thinkers and their divergences, the philosophical examination of embodied knowing will include the constructs from nonverbal psychology, phenomenology, neuroscience, and analogical reasoning. Even the foundations of mathematical operations must be considered as related to embodied knowing. I will therefore argue for knowing as a type of movement: an embodied process that 1) begins with insensitivity to a present pattern in reality, 2) comes to a distinct recognition of that pattern, and 3) persists through discernment of the transcendence of that pattern.

The radical claim of this book will be that a similar presumption about knowledge appears both explicit and supposed throughout the biblical literature. In fact, the biblical authors force modern readers to rethink their basic conceptual scheme of knowledge in order to reconcile the body's primary role in biblical accounts of knowing.[3]

As a result, sacramental theology that has regard for the guiding authority of Scripture must reckon with this principle: *we practice the rite to know*. Moreover, it is not that rituals imbue knowledge, but that human knowing is *ritualed*, inaugurated in embodied rites that imbue the skill of discernment in community. Although science popularizers pit science against religion, I will show that the two fields' views about knowing profoundly resemble one another.

For Christian theology, respect for ritualized knowing does not entail commanding a systematic pattern of identical practices for all Christians. Israel's theology of rites resists egalitarian approaches to participation. Rather, the biblical literature esteems the cultivation of polyphonic discernment through disparate participation within community. This unequal distribution of ritual participation need not be viewed as unfair to some, but offers higher degrees of confidence for the whole of Israel. Like scientific understanding, diverse involvement in rites strengthens the community's discernment.

---

3. I am certainly not the first person to suggest this connection between ritual and understanding in the Scriptures. Though I will argue that he misunderstands the ritual nature of early Jewish Christianity, Ofir Haivry argues for the primacy of ritual over generalization from a single principle as the defining arc of the Hebrew Bible and Judaism "Act and Comprehend," *Azure* 1 (Summer 5756/1996): 5–42. Abraham Joshua Heschel argues for something similar regarding ethical motivation, "It is the act that teaches us the meaning of the act." *God in Search of Man: A Philosophy of Judaism* (New York: Farrar, Straus & Giroux, 1955), 404. Additionally, I discovered Clemens Cavallin's work just before going to press. Although helpful in many ways, I believe my thesis here, and the biblical evidence, would challenge the notion of abstraction from rituals as developed in that book. *Ritualization and Human Interiority* (Copenhagen: Museum Tusculanum Press, 2013).

Introduction
Overcoming Ritual's Negative Connotations

> But we have seen that those who are responsible for ecclesiastical decisions are only too likely to have been made, *by the manner of their education*, insensitive to non-verbal signals and dull to their meaning. This is central to the difficulties of Christianity today. It is as if the liturgical signal boxes were manned by colour-blind signalmen.[1]

Let us be sober about this task: ritual is a by-word in the English-speaking world. Ritual is an act most closely associated with rote behavior and sometimes superstition, even magic! It is deemed primitive, something which humankind has progressed beyond and has left in its evolutionary rear-view mirrors,[2] the ape-end of the rope in Nietzsche's analogy of the overcoming man (*übermensch*). Jonathan Klawans reminds us that sacrifice was not always a by-word, even up into the last decades of the pre-Christian Roman Empire.[3] Sallustius, the philosopher-friend of Roman Emperor Julian (ca. fourth century), vigorously defended animal sacrifice as a noble action that connected Romans with "the ancients" and, as opposed to prayer, did not risk being "merely words."[4]

Mary Douglas' analogy of "colour-blind signalmen" highlights this insensitivity to the embodiment of religious life. Her words did not shock her audience in 1970 and alarm even less so now. I want to resuscitate those sensibilities, to see in color that which has been obscured by the verbal sensibility that has supposedly dominated nonverbal articulation in the Western imagination. I qualify verbal with "supposedly" because I am not convinced that the verbal

---

1. Italics mine. Mary Douglas, *Natural Symbols: Explorations in Cosmology* (2nd ed.; New York: Routledge, 1996), 44.
2. Friedrich Nietzsche, *Thus Spoke Zarathustra* (eds. Adrien del Caro and Robert B. Pippin; trans. Adrien del Caro; CTHP; New York: Cambridge University Press, 2006), 5–7.
3. Jonathan Klawans, *Purity, Sacrifice, and the Temple: Symbolism and Supersessionism in the Study of Ancient Judaism* (Oxford: Oxford University Press, 2006), 10.
4. "Besides, without sacrifices prayers are words only; but accompanied with sacrifices they become animated words; and words indeed corroborating life, but life animating the words." Sallustius, *On the Gods and the World* (trans. Thomas Taylor; London: Edward Jeffery and Mall, 1793), XVI.

encounter with God and the verbal theology that proceeds from it are as verbal as they might initially seem. I want to suggest that a verbal docetism lingers in the church, permitting wordy theological discussions where meaning seemingly inheres to the words and ideas themselves.[5] In reality, I will suggest that the body imbues those verbal discourses with meaning. The discourse *seems* verbal, but it is not.

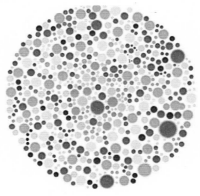

Figure 1

Douglas aptly diagnosed one side-effect of this verbal docetism: the church has become "insensitive to non-verbal signals and dull to their meaning." Just as color-blindness makes us insensitive to the number "6" in Figure 1, a figure easily noticed in the color version of the image, the habituation of meaning through verbal discourse can only make us insensitive to the prescribed rites of Israel and Christianity. The religious life of Israel easily reduces to a doctrinal life, which becomes incapable of inculcating the knowledge of the signals in the signal-box or even the meaning that those symbols are meant to communicate.

Some take ritual to be meaningful apart from verbal description. However, a pendulum-like swing to ritual practice as a reaction to the excesses of verbal analysis can end in two equal errors. First, the strict interpretation of all the ancient ritual signals in Israel's signal-box allows the appearance of understanding while possibly misunderstanding the function of the rite. For instance, suggesting that rites are fundamentally symbolic usually entails a desire to decode the symbols. The meaning of a rite becomes accessible when one fully understands the strict encoded meaning underlying the blood, the animal, the movement of the priest's hands, or hyssop waving, for instance. If the rite is *encoded*, understanding the rite becomes a matter of *decoding*.

---

5. Docetism being the early church gnostic movement that posited Jesus was not human incarnate, but like a phantasm, merely "seemed" (δοκέω) to be human. Justo L. Gonzalez, *A History of Christian Thought: From the Beginnings to the Council of Chalcedon* (3 vols.; Nashville, TN: Abington , 1970), I:130.

A second error can be found when one understands the meaning of ritual as pure social-construction. For the usual reasons, this is the default position of most ritual theorists in anthropology. A well-known version of this idea is that rites are constructed to solve a social problem. If a human condition makes someone epidemiologically unacceptable in a community (e.g., leprosy, moral corruption, etc.), a rite is constructed in order to allow the community to welcome the exiled member back in. Some wings of anthropology have also looked at what the ritual meant *to the participants alone*. This approach is not without its merit, offering phenomenological insights into the act, but it risks misunderstanding what we can know through ritual participation—something of which the participant might not be aware. It can also miss what the biblical text plainly reports: rituals are made by God and are practiced between God and his people.

Even more, merely identifying ritual meaning as socially-constructed tends toward localizing the ritual's meaning, which might be altered by localization. For instance, the Torah envisions foreigners participating in the rituals of Israel from the outset (e.g., Lev 19). The Scripture itself, which is our only access to Israel's rituals, supposes that meaning and learning are not so local and Hebraic as to exclude outsiders from other nations. Though all learning occurs at a locale, the Torah might presume that meaning can transcend the local act of the rite. This claim requires support and I will return to it in chapters eleven and twelve.

Regarding the strict interpretation of ritual signals and symbols, the temptation to do a theologically rigorous analysis of Israelite ritual overwhelms most who analyze rites. To name the symbols and express their direct and unambiguous connection to beliefs seems almost mandatory in order to discuss the knowledge such rituals bring. Honestly, how could we ignore the pregnant meaning of repeated actions and items in the Israelite ritual arsenal?

The ritual applications of blood—pouring it from the arterial flow of animals, smearing it on doorposts, dabbing it on ears and toes, sprinkling it on people, splashing it on the altar, and so on—almost demand that we figure out the conceptual world of blood among ancient Semites, a world that requires blood to be ritually used in such diverse ways. The exclusion of items in the rituals—the skins and entrails of sacrificed animals, the man with crushed testicles, and so on—make us hunger for a well-reasoned system upon which we can figure out why some things are excluded while other actions and items are allowed. Moreover, the strategic use of water, ash, fatty meat portions, and more equally compel us to find a code language amongst the items. They appear to be more than what they physically are; they appear as signs signifying something else.

> Blood signifies life.
> Water signifies cleansing.
> Laying the hand on a head signifies the transfer of sin.

Much of sacramental theology has sought after this exact line of reasoning. Accurate or not, notions about symbolic meaning can create a facile façade of analysis untrue to the rites and participants. In the coming chapters, I will scrutinize notions that presume ritual symbols signify a single belief about reality and then collectively gain meaning through performance.

So troubling was Israelite ritual for post-temple Jews that the Rambam[6] struggled to explain to the Jewish community why they should perform the rites of Israel. In other words, why obey the ritual scripts of Torah when they could not interpret the signals? Of the Rambam's varying views of sacrifice, he continually affirmed that rituals have a purpose[7] and God alone knows this purpose (or, possibly Solomon knows too).[8]

Many explanatory panaceas about the meaning of Israelite ritual have since ensued, among them Mary Douglas' own incisive contributions to the discussion. These explanations share a common concern to identify the actors/agents of the rite, the symbolic artifacts involved, the connective narratives and teaching, and then to give a theological interpretation of the meaning of the symbols and actions. Although I will add some primitive ideas to this approach in the following pages, I want to argue on the whole that these types of explanations are unnecessary in order to understand that ritual is an integral part of coming to know—*to be able to discern fine particularities and tell why it is so.* In fact, even the scientist in training cannot name why the actions and instruments bring her to know reality scientifically *while she learns to study the world.* Scientists train themselves through prescribed rituals, practice using their instruments, attune to their trainer's instruction, and trustingly look at what is being shown. For instance, it is through this process that a novice biologist comes to recognize the dynamic relationship between salinity and tonicity in cellular biology. After enough embodied practice of the rite, she cannot only recognize, but she can discern more subtle distinctions and name how she came to know them.

In the following chapters, I will contend that Israelite ritual, as conceived by the texts of the Hebrew Bible and New Testament, functions in a nearly identical way to scientific ritual. Each ritual act is prescribed by an authenticated authority and embodied through guidance in order to know something about reality (e.g., one's covenant relationship with YHWH, the historical significance of an event, etc.). Importantly for Israel and for the scientist, apart

---

6. I.e., Rabbi Moshe ben Maimon, known in the West as Maimonides.

7. Regarding Deut 32:47, "'It is not in vain, and if it is in vain, it is only so through you.' That is to say, the giving of these commandments is not a vain thing and without any useful object; and if it appears so to you in any commandment, it is owing to the deficiency in your comprehension." Maimonides, *Guide to the Perplexed*, III/26.

8. "Note this, and understand it. The repeated assertion of our Sages that there are reasons for all commandments, and the tradition that Solomon knew them, refer to the general purpose of the commandments, and not to the object of every detail." Maimonides, *Guide to the Perplexed*, III/26.

from participation in the ritual to the degree required they are both logically separated from skilled discernment.

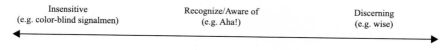

| Insensitive (e.g. color-blind signalmen) | Recognize/Aware of (e.g. Aha!) | Discerning (e.g. wise) |

Figure 2

    The central conviction of my thesis is this: Ritual participation forms us to recognize and then discern as one of its central functions. Because humans are ritualized creatures, we will always have embodied understanding of the world even where our understanding appears to be solely verbal (i.e., verbal docetism). Conversely, I am not attempting to describe in full *how* a particular ritual develops a discrete way of understanding of the world. I only hope to demonstrate that this is the presumption of the authors of Scripture: that ritual shapes and disposes knowers to recognize and develop discernment (Figure 2). Accordingly, these are the two phases of the process on a continuum: from *insensitive to recognizing*, and then from *recognizing to discerning.*

    Recognition means that I am able to identify "what it is." Discernment means first recognizing; but also seeing beyond the superficial features. Stated otherwise, discernment allows me to speak of its significance, historical context, or the implications of its presence in various contexts.

    As an example, if we asked a child to identify what she sees in Figure 3, she might offer possibilities that suggest she cannot even recognize the reality to which the picture refers: "It is a rocket." She has not been acculturated to seeing such shapes as planes. The drawing might not fit in the category of "plane" to her, as it does not look like any plane that she has ever seen. But if she had been raised in a ritualized practice, by which she were regularly exposed to many drawings of different planes, she might be able to recognize this drawing as a sketch of a particular plane: the MiG-25. However, we must be able to assess what I see in this picture as well: "A MiG-25, an answer to the West, and a testament to the engineering ethos of Soviet-era superpower competition."

    My ability to discern a MiG-25 as historically symbolic of nation-state's engineering prowess, through exposure to a simple two-dimensional sketch, must be explained by more than mere rote memory. One can recognize a sketch of a MiG-25 apart from other planes through repeated and scripted encounters. However, one cannot *discern* the significance of the MiG-25 within the Soviet arsenal by mere exposure to pictures of the MiG-25. Hence, it is necessary to describe how a ritual practice can enable recognition, along with other practices, can also foster discernment. Again, recognition means I can correctly assert, "That is a MiG-25 Foxbat," but discernment allows me to speak of its significance, historical context, or the implications of its presence in the skies over N.A.T.O. member countries.

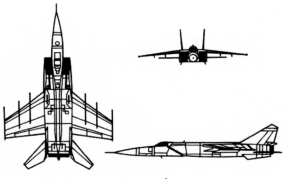

Figure 3[9]

This analogy could easily distract, as there are many relations between line drawings, planes, and Cold War history to explore. I employ it to help us distinguish between knowing what something is—basic recognition—and then discernment that transcends the instance—seeing the instance as one piece in a larger historical/conceptual fabric. I will show that the Hebrew Scriptures argue that embodied rituals factor most significantly in moving us along the continuum from not knowing, to familiarity, recognition, and then discernment (Figure 2).

Theological Attempts to Derive Ritual Meaning

Regarding the theological interpretation of ritual, two aspects must be considered at a methodological level: the hermeneutics of symbolism and the focus of sacramental theologies.

Interpreting symbolic meaning can become problematic when we treat rituals as if they were something akin to parables. Parables are devices meant to have patent symbolic meaning. And, the symbols are directly and logically related to each other, representing the reality to which the parable points. So when Jesus teaches about a man who did not count the cost of building the tower ahead of time (Luke 14:28–33), we realize that the man, the tower, and the failure to anticipate costs are all directly symbolic of another reality where

---

9. This drawing of a MiG-25 was taken from the U.S. federal government's aircraft recognition training manual. Stahlkocher (Wikimedia user), Foxbt_d1.gif, image [cited 5 Nov 2005]. Online: http://upload.wikimedia.org/wikipedia/commons.

those elements are logically related to each other. The logic of that parable could be shown this way:

World of the Parable	:: Actual World
Man	:: Disciple
Building costs	:: Costs of discipleship (financial and other)
Tower (carrying plan to completion)	:: Following Jesus (all the way to the end)

In parables, part of the strategy of symbolism is to show the relationship in the fictional world of the parable to an identical relationship in the actual world. So the primary goal is to decode the symbols—figuring out who is the prodigal son, the unworthy servant, or the naïve tower-builder—in order to understand the real world being described. In other words, the parable's encoded symbolism directly represents something else.

Many interpret biblical rituals this way too, supposing that rituals are just living parables. They are symbols in relationships. Under this view, the primary goal is to decode the ritual symbols and then the hidden world of ancient Israelite theology will be revealed to us. However, this all presumes that the ritual is the outward expression of the inner thought life of Israel's prophets, or even YHWH Himself.

As an example of this type of strict interpretation, we might be tempted to assign various meanings to the blood-bath ritual of a cleansed house in Leviticus 14:49–53. After a house has been declared clean, the priest uses two birds along with water, hyssop, scarlet yarn, and cedar wood to ceremonially cleanse a house. One bird is killed and bled into a bowl of water and the other live bird is dipped into the bowl along with the listed items. The priest sprinkles the house seven times with the hyssop, cedar, yarn, and the live bird and then releases the blood-bathed live bird into the air.

One might naturally ask what this rite means and for whom is it written. In other words, to whom would such a ritual have meaning and can we access that meaning?[10] This question gets at the "what can be known" aspect of ritual rather than the "how it can be known." I contend in the coming chapters that this ritual meant something to the ancient Israelite, however, that meaning is obscured to us. The *what* is not obviously available to us, in the text, though the *how* is. If we cannot know *what* it meant to them, then the tension of the methodological problem becomes palpable to us: our desire to decode the ritual meaning cannot overcome the historical gap between us and the rites *as they were performed*.

In order to explain the ritual, one solution has been to examine the significance of the symbols—birds, blood, water, vessel, hyssop, and so on. Is this a small-scale re-enactment of the Passover (e.g., the blood and hyssop)? Does

---

10. There have been convincing attempts to answer such question, but this is not our goal. See Mary Douglas's attempt to explain the analogic of the scapegoat in Leviticus 16: *Leviticus as Literature* (New York: Oxford University Press, 2000), 247–51.

this rite allude to priesthood itself (e.g., the sprinkling of blood-water)? After answering such questions, we could then imaginatively think about the ritual as a whole and *what* we would come to know by participation in it. The symbols and their meaning might be put into logical relationship with each other. Maybe this could even be stated propositionally: the uncleanliness of this house has been taken away like the flight of this bird from this place. In this caricature of ritual knowledge, we could make other inferences:

In order to have cleanliness, there must be some *taken-awayness* of uncleanliness. Metaphysical constructs can now evolve:

> Uncleanliness is a pollutant of sorts that must be absorbed and then directed away from the thing meant to be clean.

Finally, a theology of symbolic ritual knowledge can be built by imaginatively decoding the ritual's symbols and relations:

> Israel's theology held to a metaphysical substance (*ousia*) of sin so that sin permeated through discrete channels of daily life and remained as a substance called "uncleanliness." This substance acted as a metaphysical pollutant, changing the disposition of a normatively good and useful thing like a goat or a house into an unusable whole (i.e., the scapegoat or unclean house). The unclean substance played a spatially inverse role to the Holy of Holies where the substance is removed in layers and humans are given special access based on their proximity to uncleanliness, their tribe, and their clan in the nation of Israel.

This trite and provisional example works within very reasonable assumptions in that it represents a commonsense approach to the elements as symbols and the logic of performance of Israelite ritual. Methods such as these seek to derive some essential meaning of a rite that can be built into a larger and transcendent theological position, a position based on a metaphysical view of the cosmos that is expressed in the symbols and actions of the rite.

To the contrary, I will maintain that this approach to understanding the relationship between Israel's knowledge and her participation in ritual is an insufficient guide to understand the epistemological role of ritual. Even though I quite like my own example above, ritual theorists now decry the assumption that rituals can be understood by such a naïve parsing of the events. Explanations that reduce ritual participation to the expression of belief have now been shown wanting.[11] Ritual theorists have also often myopically focused too heavily on the act itself rather than dynamics of ritual preparation and follow-up.[12] Moreover, the as-

---

11. Catherine Bell, *Ritual Theory, Ritual Practice* (New York: Cambridge University Press, 2009), 47–54.

12. Gillian Goslinga, "On Cakti-Filled Bodies and Divinities: An Ethnographic Perspective on Animal Sacrifice and Ritual in Contemporary South India," in *Sacred Killing: The Archaeology of Sacrifice in the Ancient Near East* (eds. Anne Porter and Glenn M. Schwartz; Winona Lake, IN: Eisenbrauns, 2012), 33–56.

sumption that rituals correspond directly to discrete beliefs about the cosmos is no longer safe.[13] These matters will be taken up in the coming chapters.

In tandem with the recent sea change in ritual theory, it is important that we recognize the Scripture's focus on ritual as an epistemologically formative act.[14] At the sunset of expeditions to explain the exact theological meaning of biblical rituals by merely decoding the symbols, we still find plenty of work to be done. Nevertheless, I am required here to explain how participating in ritual brings Israelites to recognize and then discern something about their world, but not what it brings them to recognize. The former is our present task. The latter task will be taken up in part in chapter thirteen.

Sacramental Theologies: Protestant, Catholic, and Orthodox

Given what I offer above, neither Protestant nor Roman Catholic sacramental theologies will be untouched by this critique. Because we find within sacramental theologies a tendency to presume that rituals are symbolic stand-ins for or signifiers of some other reality, this analysis will have hard questions for all sacramental theologies. Considering their broad differences or caricatures help us to distinguish, but deficiencies still pervade all Christian traditions.

Historically, Protestants have tended to make the Eucharist, for example, a strictly mental event in memorialism or spiritual event in Lutheran and Reformed versions. Calvin's view that Communion by the Holy Spirit unites us to Christ in the heavens is a good illustration of the functional nature of sacraments. Calvin's robust view of the sacrament includes a pedagogical sense of the ritual, meant to dispose us in a particular way through the nature of the relationship between the sign and signified as we perform the rite:

> I hold then . . . that the sacred mystery of the Supper consists of two things—the corporeal signs, which, presented to the eye, represent invisible things in a manner adapted to our weak capacity, and the spiritual truth, which is at once figured and exhibited by the signs.[15]

Though beneficial to represent another reality to us, notice that it is our "weak capacity" that keeps us from the invisible things.

Protestants have emphasized what Communion does, functionally speaking, for the individual and the church, which has sometimes been a reaction over and against the Roman Catholic account regarding what the bread and wine are, ontologically speaking. However, strict interpretation of Baptism and

---

13. Anne Porter, "Mortal Mirrors: Creating Kin through Human Sacrifice in Third Millennium Syro-Mesopotamia," in *Sacred Killing*, 191–216.

14. See chapter two of this volume for a fuller account of the recent history of ritual theory scholarship.

15. Jean Calvin, *The Institutes of the Christian Religion* (trans. Henry Beveridge; Edinburgh: Calvin Translation Society, 1845–46), 4.17.11.

Communion as the only two Christian sacraments has often led to theologies maneuvering to make sense of only these two.

The traditional Roman Catholic approach has been to argue from the other end. What the sacramental elements *are*, ontologically speaking, informs us about what they functionally *do* for the church. Vatican II theologians extended this thinking by returning to the ancient fount of their theology, known as the *Ressourcement Movement* or *Nouvelle Theologie*. The innovative thought that sprung from this new era of Catholic theology still focused on the nature of the sign, signals, and symbols. Arguing for the sacramental impulse in all humanity, Edward Schillebeeckx distinguishes Christ as the "primordial sacrament" of God on the basis of his complete transparence from his interior to his exterior:

> The inward man manifests itself as a reality that is in this world through the body. It is in his body and through his body that man is open to the "outside," and that he makes himself present to his fellow men. Human encounter proceeds though the visible obviousness of the body, which is a sign that reveals and at the same time veils the human interiority.[16]

> Jesus' human redeeming acts are therefore a "sign and cause of grace." "Sign" and "cause" of salvations are not brought together here as two elements fortuitously conjoined. [Jesus'] Human bodiliness is human interiority itself in visible form.[17]

I will argue in the coming chapters that biblical sacramentality is not an accommodation to our weak minds that needs a symbolic representation of the invisible world (à la Calvin) or interiority that needs to be made exterior (à la Schillebeeckx). Instead, sacramental theology must be able to account for what rituals are meant to *do*, epistemologically speaking.

In the Eastern Orthodox tradition, Alexander Schmemann has championed an approach to sacramentality similar to what I am suggesting here: for the sake of seeing the same world differently. He describes the Eucharist as a liturgy, involving the enterprise of the church, but then:

> The liturgy of the Eucharist is best understood as a journey or procession. It is the journey of the Church into the dimension of the Kingdom. We use this word "dimension" because it seems the best way to indicate the manner of our sacramental entrance into the risen life of Christ. Color transparencies "come alive" when viewed in three dimensions instead of two. The presence of the added dimension allows us to see much better the actual reality of what has been photographed. In very much the same way, . . . our *entrance* in-

---

16. Edward Schillebeeckx, *Christ the Sacrament of the Encounter with God* (New York: Rowman & Littlefield, 1963), 15.

17. Ibid., 16.

to the presence of Christ is an entrance into a fourth dimension which allows us to see the ultimate reality of life.[18]

For Schmemann, who wants to resist the expected descent into mysticism, sacramentality changes our view, which will be a familiar description to the biblical accounts of knowing. Though Schmemann references both Scripture and philosophers throughout his work, he does not show how his account is biblical or philosophical in the sense that it directly comports with components of either.[19] That is the task of this present work.

Epistemology and Ritual in Scripture

In chapters two and three, I will lay out my considerations and methodology for approaching the biblical texts. Further, I will engage methods and conceptual approaches from philosophers, biblical scholars, and ritual theorists. However, I presume at the outset that the question of my task's validity, which could appear entirely foreign to the Scripture's use of ritual, has already been raised in the reader's mind. To alleviate some of the pressure concerning this task's biblical validity, I briefly mention some of these biblical episodes, which force us to reckon the relationship between ritual and knowledge. I will examine these more closely in Part II, but we can briefly look now at a common epistemological thread in the Israelite description of rituals.

Genesis 15: Doubt Answered by Ritual

In Genesis 15, the great promise of progeny and land are restated to Abram. First, YHWH foretells numerous children, as many as the stars. Abram trusts God for this incredible feat and his trust is counted to him as righteousness— whatever this may mean. God offers an immense pledge, Abram responds in trust, and God reciprocates in recognition of Abram's trust. After this comes an extensive promise of land, what turns out to be the Fertile Crescent, revealed to be Abram's inheritance. Abram responds in vocal disbelief stated in epistemic terms: "How will I know that I shall possess it?" (Gen. 15:8). God's answer to the question should instantly challenge many modern assumptions about

---

18. Alexander Schmemann, *For the Life of the World: Sacraments and Orthodoxy* (New York: St. Vladimir's Seminary, 1973), 26–27.

19. James K. A. Smith takes a very similar approach to sacramentality and employs Schmemann's epistemologically oriented discussion of sacrament, "worship is epiphany of the world." *Desiring the Kingdom: Worship, Worldview, and Cultural Formation* (3 vols.; CL; Grand Rapids, MI: Baker Academic, 2009), I:143. Though he shows how this view can be informed by philosophical exploration, his task does not include much interaction with Scripture. In many ways, this book will give biblical theological support to some of Smith's work.

knowledge. His answer presupposes a known ritual: bring me animals. Abram then understands that he is participating in a covenant-making rite, although the reader later learns of divine modifications to the ritual, where Abram is subdued from full participation.[20] The exact nature of the ritual, bizarre as it might seem to us, is not important for our task.

We must notice, however, that Abram's incredulity ("How will I know?") about YHWH's promise is answered with a ritual. In case we were in doubt that the ritual has an explicitly epistemological purpose, YHWH mirrors Abram's doubt in his words of pronouncement during the rite: "Knowing, you shall know (ידע תדע) . . ." (Gen 15:13). We do not need to investigate how cutting animals in half and arranging them produces knowledge in Abram in order to know that the biblical author presumes that some kind of knowing happens through participation in the rite.

Ceremonial Knowledge: Sabbath, Pesach, and Sukkot

While much of epistemological discussion in the past decades still centers on knowing facts (e.g., "knowing that 'H$_2$O is the chemical depiction of water'"), the Hebrew Bible commands that festivals be celebrated for epistemological reasons. Notably, this knowledge cannot be stated as a fact about the world. For instance, Leviticus ends its commands for festivals by indicating that Israel should keep the practice of sleeping in booths during Sukkot *"in order that the generations may know* (למען ידעו) that I made the sons of Israel live in booths when I brought them out of the land of Egypt" (Lev 23:43). Deuteronomy reinforces the epistemological thrust of the festival, emphasizing that Sukkot is for Israel's children who, *"have not known* (לא ידעו) . . ." (Deut 31:13).

This example alone broaches a fundamental question about the fact-knowing view of epistemology: If Israel were meant to know facts—consecration by God, sanctification, and that Israel once lived in booths—then why perform the prescribed actions of Sabbath rest or booth-living? If these are mere facts to be known, why cannot they verbally pass along the facts?

This might plausibly mean that God intends Israel to know something *about* the fact that God consecrated her through the practice of rites, festivals, etc. There is some way in which Israel needs to discern that information beyond mere recognition, some insight to be gained only by performing the festivals and Sabbaths. By doing these things, Israel sees her history differently, just as the skilled insight of the astronomer sees the night sky differently than

---

20. Even if this is not an idealization of a Hittite-vassal treaty, as Kline believes it to be, the treaty elements are clearly present. However, Abram's non-participation in passing through the pieces of animal appears to be a ritualization of a treaty where normally, both parties would pass through. Meredith Kline, *By Oath Consigned: A Reinterpretation of the Covenant Signs of Circumcision and Baptism* (Grand Rapids, MI: Eerdmans, 1975), 17–21.

I do. In brief, the festival rites presume that mere verbal knowledge of the fact is less desirable and possibly insufficient. The knowledge desired by YHWH requires embodied participation in order to see the history of Israel in the correct light. Merely *knowing that* Israel was made to live in booths does not bridge the gap between what Israel now knows and what her generations need to know—the present and future significance of this historical reality.

We can now see that at least some rites of Israel have a clear epistemological impetus (e.g., Gen 15:13) and goal (e.g., Lev 23:43). These instances demand that we answer whether or not all Israelite rituals have a functional role in proper knowledge of the world. If all Israel's rites do not have an epistemological function, then how do we distinguish the epistemologically oriented rituals from the others? The answer to this question will come in Part II.

Remembering to Know

In the opening chapters of Joshua, God commanded Israel to set up twelve stones from the Jordan river as a sign (אות) that begs questions from Israelite children: "What is the meaning of those stones?" To answer their questions, God instructs Israel to "make them know (הודעתם), saying 'Here the Israelites crossed the Jordan river'" (Josh 4:22). Again the miracle of crossing the Jordan had a wider epistemological audience than even the children of Israel, as the text goes on to say that God dried up the Jordan "*in order that* all the peoples of the earth *shall know* (למען תדע) how mighty is the hand of YHWH" (Josh 4:24).[21]

This language, "make them know," in reference to Israel's children, only has one counterpart in the historical texts of the Hebrew Bible. Deuteronomy 4:9 contains a similar call to instruct the children: "Only take care, and keep your soul diligently, lest you forget the things that your eyes have seen, and lest they depart from your heart all the days of your life. *Make them known* (הודעתם) *to your children* and your children's children."[22] Likewise, the prescription to not forget what YHWH had done for Israel included keeping the Torah rituals. Just as important to keeping Torah, Deuteronomy specifically warns Israel to avoid rituals that might syncretize Israelite rites with the worship of foreign deities (Deut 4:15–20). Then, as if to seal the connection, the idea of foreign ritual negatively affecting the children's knowledge is explicitly linked again (Deut 4:25) and the epistemological thrust of this section is summarized (Deut 4:39–40):

---

21. In Part II, I will deal with the question of how the knowledge of Israel and the nations differs in quality and kind.

22. There are only a handful of occurrences of the hiphil of "know" (ידע) regarding children (either ילד or בן) in the Hebrew Bible: Deut 4:9; Josh 4:22; Ps 78:5; 103:7; 145:12; Isa 38:19; Ezek 16:2; 20:4; 22:2.

Know therefore today, and lay it to your heart, that YHWH is God in
heaven above and on the earth beneath; there is no other. Therefore you shall keep his statutes and his commandments, which I
command you today, that it may go well with you and with your
children after you . . .

Passages like these command our attention about how our children's
knowledge relates to encounters with memorial stones and the active avoidance of foreign worship. While memorial stones are not generally thought of
as ritual, they do affirm the need for an embodied encounter that directly relates to how Israelites know their own history for the sake of discerning their
future. Historical report is not a sequence of facts, but remembering by embodied encounter. Already we can see the need for a more robust definition of
ritual, which will receive full treatment in Part II.

Testing to See

One last episode from the Hebrew Bible will be instructive in developing the
view that not all acts of knowing are of the same quality. First, the narrator of
Judges directly addresses the relationship between knowing and doing at the
fore of the book. Because a new generation arose who "did not know YHWH or
the deeds that he did for Israel," that generation performed rituals to other
gods (Judg 2:10). By the logic of Deuteronomy's epistemology, one plausible
reason this next generation did not know was because their parents did not
practice the Torah rituals with them. Their insensitivity to YHWH fostered
false worship, which created a devolving knowledge of YHWH by the end of
the book.

Minimally, we can see that the author of Judges opens the book by linking
together embodied action and knowledge. Maximally, it is not until later that
we find out another key factor in their devolution according to the Tanakh:
Israel had not been practicing the rituals of Torah. According to Nehemiah,
Sukkot had not been regularly practiced "from the days of Jeshua the son of
Nun" (Neh 8:17). Passover reportedly fades and ceases during this time as well
(cf. 2 Kgs 23:22; 2 Chr 35:18). If so, the two most overtly epistemological rituals
of Israel languished already by the time of the Judges.

Second, and more specifically in Judges, God tests Israel and the Israelites
test God in order to know something about each other. These tests point to a
distinction already made—between tests as discovery of one's recognition versus discernment. Judges states that God "might test (לנסות)" Israel because she
did not know the wars of prior generations (Judg 3:1–2). The purpose of the
test is stated unambiguously, "to know whether they would listen to the commandments . . ." (Judg 3:4). Setting aside the Judeo-Christian-Islamic presumption of God's omniscience, the text portrays God as needing to *recognize* something about Israel that is foundational for discerning what kind of people they

were. God is in the position of the pedagogue who subjects his pupils to examination in order to recognize patterns in their behavior (e.g., Are they the kind of people who will generally trust Moses through their parent's instruction?).

Looking at Israel from God's vantage, which rituals this new generation practiced allows the audience to see Israel's location on the epistemological spectrum: insensitive, able to recognize, or having discernment. The narrator suggests that the presence of the Philistines and Canaanites in the land tests Israel about her ritual practices, not theological beliefs. Whether or not Israel will perform rites foreign to the Torah marks their ability to recognize.

These divine tests are not unique to Judges. We see the same epistemological goal stated in the Akedah—the binding of Isaac. Genesis 22 tells us that God was intent to test Abraham: "After these things it happened that God put Abraham to the test (נסה)" (Gen 22:1). When Abraham prepared to kill Isaac, the angel of YHWH announced that recognition was achieved: "Do not raise your hand against the boy . . . for now I know (ידעתי) that you fear God" (Gen 22:12). The implications are patent: God needed to recognize something about Abraham and it required a ritual *in order for God to know*. Without indicting the extent of God's knowledge, we can see how the text reports YHWH's epistemological process to us.

Ritual Epistemology in the Hebrew Bible

By way of brief review before moving on, the above passages were meant to demonstrate the variegated use of ritual for epistemic purposes in the Hebrew Bible:

1. God answered the need to know by a covenant cutting ritual (Gen 15).
2. Ceremonies, including Sabbath-keeping, require embodied participation so that Israel may know something about that which appears to be a plain fact (e.g., God made Israel live in booths) and not the fact in and of itself (e.g., Lev 23:42–43).
3. Knowledge imbued to Israel's children directly relates to which rituals they participate in: those prescribed by Moses or foreign cult.
4. Prescribed embodied encounters with memorials create the opportunity to know beyond verbal fact-knowing.
5. Testing—that is, physically putting someone to the test—allows the examiner to recognize something about the examinee.

Much more analysis will be offered, including that written by the earliest Jewish followers of the Jesus movement in the New Testament. These examples are meant to offer a basic motivation for this work, but demand further investigation.

Disparate Participation and Equal Knowing

One final comment is required about unequal participation in biblical rituals. Perusing the rituals of Scripture, it becomes obvious that some rites are for specific individuals (e.g., Abram, Gen 15; the red heifer rite, Num 19), the whole family (e.g., Sukkot), and genders (e.g., a mother's purification sacrifice). What are we to make of this disparity if the rites are for the purpose of knowing? Does this establish a *separate but equal* epistemic system? I will address this matter more fully in chapter eleven, but let me briefly offer two points to guide our thinking about disparate ritual participation.

First, ethical preparation for rituals is just as important as the cult of sacrifice. If this is the case, then the life of the whole family, young and old, imbues itself into the actual participation in the sacrifice event, for instance. In saying that not everyone has equal access to the rite, we might miss the import of year-long ritual preparation only to myopically focus on the killing event at the Temple. So any discussion of disparate ritual participation must take the preparatory aspect of the family into account. I examine this further in chapter two.

Second, all effective communities for the sake of knowing rely upon disparate participation in order to know well. It is not a deficit to the community, but an advantage. Scientists do not have direct access to all the performed rituals that led to the culmination of their scientific knowledge. In fact, even in a single laboratory, scientists do not perform all the rituals meant to dispose them to know. Lab workers, graduate students, and colleagues often perform the laboratory rituals, which necessarily means that a matrix of witnesses with diverse participation is usually built up around any single cluster of experimental data. This becomes an advantage only if those polyphonic witnesses bring their diverse experiences, records, and testimonies of the rites to the community of knowers in order that they can have confidence in what they have seen—that it was interpreted correctly. Hence, there is no reason from the outset to have a negative disposition toward the fact that the Scriptures codify a non-egalitarian performance of Israel's rites, both in the Hebrew Bible and New Testament. Again, I will address this further in chapter eleven.

Preliminary Definition of Ritual

Several priorities should now be obvious, even with such a terse walk-through of these biblical employments of ritual. First, ritual and knowledge are not casually, but instead integrally related to each other at many points in Scripture. Hence, we cannot discuss a biblical view of epistemology without significant treatment of ritual's role in knowing. Second, a binary view of knowing—we either know or we are ignorant—will not be sufficient. For instance, sometimes "to know" simply means "to be aware of" and at other times it denotes "wise and skilled discernment."

While the biblical authors describe a gradation of knowledge on a continuum (see Figure 2), they often employ monolithic vocabulary (e.g., "to know") to describe diverse instances of knowing or even use sense language (e.g., "to see") to denote wisdom. We must be responsive to those differences, discernible by considering the context of their utterance, and provide a coherent structure for thinking about the differences in the biblical use of epistemic terminology.

The most common Hebrew term for "know," *yada* (ידע), can mean "to recognize," "to discern," or even "to have sexual relations." For each epistemological text encountered, we must distinguish these different uses to determine what kind of knowing is being described. In all, I am attempting to answer: What processes in Scripture lead to knowledge and how? And even then, what quality of knowledge is expected to come by participation in the ritual? These differences will need a structure able to distinguish them.

Third, I have broached the problem of variegated passages describing ritual above. Are festivals rituals, or are they ceremonies? What is the difference? In order to aid us into the initial chapters, I will offer this tentative definition of ritual as we are discussing it here, with a view to justifying a more robust definition in Part I. For our immediate purposes, ritual, ceremony, and rite will be roughly synonymous and defined as: *A practice that is scripted (usually by an authority) and performed by a subject.* Or more simply, *rituals are something scripted and something done.*

What then is a sacrament? Traditionally, all sacraments would be considered rituals, but not all rituals are sacraments. Defining a sacrament apart from a ritual becomes a matter of tradition. Protestants tend to insist that sacraments are those rituals specially instituted by Jesus the Christ. Hence, marriage is affirmed, but not instituted and therefore not a sacrament. Roman Catholic theology defines sacraments in relation to a broader view of sacramentality. As one introduction to Catholicism plainly puts it, "The idea of sacrament is that some person, word, event, thing, can mediate an experience of God."[23] Because a thing can become sacred and mediate God, the Roman Catholic priesthood, in the ilk of Levitical priests, must mediate between the sacrament and the people, as the *cohanim* did for Israel. Orthodox teaching has leaned into the mystical aspects of rituals to define the sacraments, officially calling them "holy mysteries." But even this approach to sacraments entails some epistemological aspect to the rite. Because the tradition determines the definition of "sacrament," this volume will restrict its discussion to ritual as prolegomenal to any particular approach to sacramental theology.

Finally, the attempts to capture human activity within a global definition of ritual have been traditionally problematic. While I do not intend on offering a singular definition of ritual that can distinguish the slaughter of an animal

---

23. Richard Chilson, *Catholic Christianity: A Guide to the Way, the Truth, and the Life* (New York: Paulist Press, 1987), 296.

for meat from the Levitical sin offering—also a slaughter for meat—there are aspects of the practice that must be necessarily constitutive of the ritual act *in se*. These will be clarified where it is necessary to do so.

Part I

Epistemology, Ritual Theory, and Methodology

Chapter 1

Why Standard Theories of Knowledge
Are Insufficient

This discussion would be remiss if it did not immediately engage the world of philosophical epistemology. How a person knows accurately has captivated the long-time interest of Modern philosophy.[1] Below, I tersely assess recent suggestions for a combination of epistemological approaches. These combinations attempt to arrive at an epistemology able to account for both the breadth of human experience and the description of knowledge found in Scripture. In sum, I argue that Analytic epistemology, narrative analysis, phenomenology, or any flat combination thereof comes up short. Instead, scientific epistemology fares far better where it can be sensitive to the claims of phenomenology. Also, the analytic method of theology (i.e., Analytic Theology) should be employed to show that ritual is not restricted to the domain of religion, but is a normatively human way of knowing. Because we are creatures, we are *ritualed* (or *traditioned*, if you like)[2] and any attempt to describe knowing apart from our embodied history and prescribed rituals will only artificially describe knowledge—describing more about what we would like to be epistemologically true *about us* than can be actually described in the history of human knowing. This includes the history of human knowing recorded in the Scriptures.

---

1. By "modern" I mean from ca. 1640 C.E. to the present.

2. Gadamer's notion that we are all "historically-effected consciousnesses" (*wirkungsgeschichtliches Bewußtseinen*) dovetails nicely with what I am trying to propose. We are all ritually-effected consciousnesses (*wirkungsrituell Bewußtseinen*). We could replace the term "history" with "ritual" and get the point: "Whether we are aware of it or not, the efficacy of history is at work. When a naïve faith in scientific method denies the existence of effective history, there can be an actual deformation of knowledge." Hans Georg Gadamer, *Truth and Method* (trans. Joel Wensheimer and Donald G. Marshall; 2nd ed.; New York: Continuum, 2012), 300.

Biblical Epistemology

In order to assess the various approaches to epistemology, I begin with my previous findings in *Biblical Knowing*.[3] Although they may not represent the totality of Scripture's epistemological vision, they act as the implicit presumptions of this work and the measuring stick for other methodologies. These are the six immovable convictions of biblical epistemology in Scripture as found in that work:

1. *Knowing is a process, not an event.* Though we often conceive of knowledge as a "fact to be discovered," every *Eureka!* or Aha! moment is the fruit of a process. Biblical knowing is extensively concerned with good process, which rightfully yields proper knowledge.
2. *Knowing requires guidance.* A person's initial attempts at knowing require an authority—a coach who already possesses the skill of discerning. That authority guides the knower to see that which is being shown to her, and they are both bound to each other throughout the process. The knower does not *come to know* if the authority does not commit to the process, and vice versa.
3. *Knowing is performed.* The body is not accidental to one's knowledge, but at the very least, instrumental or the analogical basis for what is known. This includes knowing abstract constructs (e.g., the quadratic equation), knowing facts ("the sky is blue"), and knowing persons somewhat and/or intimately (e.g., "know" occasionally means "to have sex with").
4. *Knowledge always results from participation in the process.* Even erroneous knowledge is still a type of knowing. Error can happen by not listening to one's teacher or guide,[4] by listening to the wrong authority, or by not embodying the guide's instructions to the degree required. Either way, submitting to a process is requisite in the initial stages of knowing. Particularly for this book, the processes of concern are the rituals of the Pentateuch that are overtly framed with the effect "in order that you know."
5. *There is no brute knowledge.* All knowing is a way of seeing the world and seeing must be skilled. Extended examples of seeing and appropriately interpreting miracles were offered as paradigmatic cases. In

---

3. Dru Johnson, *Biblical Knowing: A Scriptural Epistemology of Error* (Eugene, OR: Cascade, 2013). For the full context of this description along with more detailed exegetical analysis, see Andrew M. Johnson, "Error and Epistemological Process," (Ph.D. diss., University of St Andrews, 2011).
4. In chapter eight of this work I distinguished two degrees of error. Failing to acknowledge the authenticated prophet's authority is a first-order error (e.g., Pharaoh's response to Moses in Exod 5–14). The failure to embody the instructions of the prophet to the degree required is a second-order error (e.g., the manna episode in Exod 16).

order to grasp their significance, even the brute witnessing of miracles required a guide both in the Hebrew Bible and New Testament. An extended discussion was also required to evince how a child could even "see" that "the sky is blue"—a simple fact which requires quite a bit of epistemological process in order to understand in the most primitive sense.

6. *Knowing is knowing.* Scripture does not employ a dichotomy of religious (special) versus natural (general) epistemology. Hence, scientific epistemology is an extension of the normative epistemological processes described in Scripture with one major caveat: authentication of authorities is divinely-driven in Scripture, whereas authentication elsewhere follows the mores of trusted networks of licensing and sanctioning authorities (e.g., as the Federal Aviation Administration authenticates airline pilots in the United States).

In summary, to know in the Scriptures is to submit to a process whereby an Israelite listens to the authority authenticated to her, performs the instructions prescribed by that authority, and comes to know that which is being shown to her.

Beyond these six aspects to biblical knowing, a distinction must be made concerning the differences between degrees of knowing described in Scripture. As mentioned in the introduction, a gradation of knowing exists where the biblical authors were happy to employ monolithic vocabulary (e.g., "to know") to describe variegated ends, or sense language (e.g., "to see") to denote wisdom. What is the best structure for thinking about the differences?

That structure, best defined by a continuum, begins with not knowing (or, unable to see), continues to recognition of some pattern, and extends indefinitely into discernment (or, wisdom). We move from insensitive—not acculturated to see that which is there—to able to recognize and then to discerning (See Figure 1.1). The first task on this continuum is to move *from* being a "color-blind signalman" *to* "able to recognize."

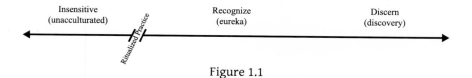

Figure 1.1

Part of this task, then, will be to examine and distinguish which point on the continuum best matches the passage under consideration. For instance, God acting "so that the nations will know" appears to describe the nations' recognition or awareness more than their discernment. Yet, booth-living during Sukkot (i.e., the Levitical festival of booths) seems to develop a new view of an already recognized history, hence the beginnings of discernment.

Overall, this analysis must situate different instances of knowing by means of ritual. This requires an assessment of the knowers described in texts, whether they are being portrayed to us as insensitive, needing to recognize something, or—having recognized something over and over—if the reader is expected to see discernment being fostered in them. Now we must turn briefly to current trends in epistemology and assess if they fit with what Scripture depicts as normative knowing.

Analytic Epistemology

In *Biblical Knowing*, I argued that the major branches of analytic epistemology (i.e., the Standard View, Naturalized Epistemology, Virtue Epistemology, and Reformed Epistemology) all had deficiencies in addressing the biblical description of proper knowing.[5] This inability is no fault of those epistemological theories *per se*, but exists primarily because they are unable to accommodate Scripture's central emphasis on knowing 1) under proper authorities and 2) through one's body. Because Scripture tends to depict proper knowing as beginning in a sociological affair, epistemologies that concentrate synchronically on a single knower justifying a single belief in a single proposition are far too estranged from actual instances of knowing in Scripture. For instance, if Abram or Israel are explicitly intended to know something vital to their livelihood through ritual, then reducing our discussion of biblical epistemology to "Subject *knows that* P (where P is the proposition: e.g., "God intends to give the cradle of civilization to Abram")" appears disjointed from the structure of these stories (Gen 15:7–21).

Recent attempts within analytic philosophy have opened up examinations of religious experience, but notably, they diverge from the typical style of synchronic propositional analysis in order to do so.[6] Paul Moser's *The Elusive God* is but one commendable example that focuses on knowing as personal, and employs an "argument from volitional transformation" rather than facts that can be suitably justified; though one can entail the other.[7] Howard Wettstein's *The*

---

5. With the advantage of a few years' reflection, I would make the case of Analytic epistemology's deficiency in this region less dogmatically now. Johnson, *Biblical Knowing*, 149–80.

6. A notable example of an analytic philosopher attempting to work within the terms of contemporary analytic epistemology, yet re-writing the terms is Terence Cuneo, "Ritual Knowledge," *FP* 31 (2014): 365–85.

7. "It would thus be purposive knowledge as suitably grounded commitment to loving and obedient discipleship toward an authoritative personal agent with definite expectations of us for the sake of divine–human reconciliation. It thus wouldn't be mere well-grounded intellectual assent to true propositions, but would rather be inherently *person*-relational and *will*-changing." Italics in the original. Paul K. Moser, *The*

Significance of Religious Experience spends a very profitable chapter analyzing ritual, even hinting at the epistemological function of ritual and its role in "transformation." He concludes that rituals, specifically the rituals of Judaism, are "training in awe."[8] Wettstein's essay on ritual presents a good example of movement away from strict propositional analysis in examining ritual. Indeed, his argument for thinking about ritual as training is funded by both biblical repetition of the phrase "*y're Adonai*" (ירא יהוה) and the liturgical development of Deuteronomy in the synagogue. Like Moser, an emphasis on transformation dominates Wettstein's discussion and propositional analysis remains noticeably absent from his analysis:

> Ritual plays a major role in effecting and sustaining the transformation. Consider the practice of saying blessings: on eating and drinking, on smelling fragrant spices, herbs, plants, on seeing lightning, shooting stars, vast deserts, high mountains, a sunrise, the ocean, on seeing trees blossoming for the first time of the year, on seeing natural objects (including creatures) of striking beauty, on meeting a religious scholar, on meeting a secular scholar, on seeing a head of state, on hearing good news, on hearing bad news.[9]

Many contemporary epistemologists who want to foster a useful understanding of ritual are going to struggle in their current constructs if they do not give equal attention to the two types of knowledge, according to most analytic epistemologists, primary to understand in ritual epistemology: skill (know how) and acquaintance (know who). Analytic epistemology that emphasizes knowledge[10] as a discrete instance of *knowing-that-something-is-true-or-*

Elusive God: Reorienting Religious Epistemology (New York: Cambridge University Press, 2008), 96–97.

8. Howard Wettstein, *The Significance of Religious Experience* (New York: Oxford University Press, 2012), 206.

9. Ibid., 206.

10. Contemporary analytic philosophers in the Anglo-America tradition have most often tended, *though not entirely*, toward knowledge being constituted by a subject who knows that a proposition is true and can be logically justified. Truth and justification have to be meted out according to the particular theory of knowledge involved. Though many epistemologists today would not reduce knowledge to propositions alone, Richard Feldman begins his primer on epistemology by distinguishing the different types of knowledge and justifies his exclusive focus on propositional epistemology: "The most reasonable conclusion seems to be that there are (at least) three basic kinds of knowledge: (1) propositional knowledge, (2) acquaintance knowledge or familiarity, and (3) ability knowledge (or procedural knowledge). . . . Furthermore, many of the most intriguing questions about knowledge turn out to be questions about propositional knowledge." Richard Feldman, *Epistemology* (FPS; Upper Saddle River, NJ: Prentice Hall, 2003), 12.

false, or its deflation into psychological pragmatism[11] leaves the field without the requisite tools to analyze ritual for its epistemic features.

Phenomenology

I have also previously suggested that an analytical approach to biblical epistemology is not unwarranted. Nevertheless, such epistemologies must reconcile with the fact that biblical scholarship has found the topic of knowledge in Scripture most aptly captured by phenomenology.[12] This poses an initial problem. After all, who really wants to read a thoroughgoing phenomenological description of biblical knowing? Apart from the dense and unfriendly style typical of Continental philosophers, useful descriptions of knowing must do justice to the clear and palpable phenomenological elements implicit in biblical knowing. Below are the least controversial marks that one's thinking functions more in phenomenological and less in discrete propositional terms. Phenomenological descriptions of knowledge would exhibit:

1. a continual return of our attention to the subject who acts,
2. notions of inhabitation or indwelling as ultimate constraints and categories in philosophy,
3. a heightening of embodiment as integral to meaning,
4. a rejection of the representational model of knowledge in favor of direct engagement with reality,
5. and the insistence on *the other* having some epistemic/moral authority on *the I*.[13]

At the end of the day, we are left with that which the biblical texts unashamedly report, these same motifs found in phenomenological thought. There is a socio-prophetic role in knowing where authorities are established and the intended knowers either submit to or reject those authorities. Knowing is a diachronic process, not a punctiliar moment in the narrative's logic, although it often comes to heightened points of illumination (e.g., Gen 2:23; Exod 14:31; Deut 4:35, Mark 8:29–33). Knowledge requires the embodiment of instructions given by the authenticated authorities. The biblical picture of proper knowing is relayed to us through phenomenological depiction, subjects in processes and relationships which lead them to know an objectively real

---

11. Quine might hold to the most extreme form of Naturalized Epistemology, ultimately usurping epistemology with psychology and arguing for a pragmatic approach to epistemology: what we know is found out in the engineering payoff of the construct. W.V.O. Quine, "Natural Kinds" in *Ontological Relativity and Other Essays* (New York: Columbia University Press, 1969), 114–138.

12. Johnson, *Biblical Knowing*, 181–201.

13. Ibid., 199–200.

world.[14] This also helps to explain why biblical scholars most often engage Continental thinkers when they examine texts philosophically.

The problem with reverting to phenomenology as our main guide to biblical knowing is that there tends to be a lack of clarity, often intentionally so. As a (possibly) real example, anyone who has been forced to read about the significance of *mise en abyme* in medieval shield heraldry and its implications for authorial intent has felt the pinch of phenomenology's peculiarity in writing style. Even more, *I* might think that *I* know what Merleau-Ponty means when he says, "Our body is not in space like things; it inhabits or haunts space," but I can appreciate why this does not feel like an explanation to my colleagues in analytic philosophy.[15] Consequently, a raw phenomenological analysis of ritual will not suffice, both for reasons of clarity and possibly problems of comprehensive fit with Scripture's epistemological aims. However, tropes of phenomenological thinking will certainly aid in this analysis.

Literary Analysis

Among the various schools of literary criticism (New Criticism, Reader-Response Criticism, Structuralism, etc.), narrative criticism has come into recent favor with theologians who want to work from the stories of Scripture. Literary analysis provides a particularly useful tool in that narratives have discrete structures to them and narrative logic constrains the range of meaning. Hence, narratives have premises that are worked out within their own logic to necessary conclusions. Narrative logic intrigues us as humans too because unlike a syllogism, where premises also can be worked out to a necessary conclusion, the narrative conclusion can surprise us even when it flows perfectly from the narrative logic.[16]

Eleonore Stump has made a recent proposal that analytic philosophers and theologians ought to take the study of narratives more seriously and integrate them into their propositional approach to knowledge. In *Wandering in Darkness*, she makes forceful claims about how analytic approaches are blind to the central stories of Israel. Epistemologies that only look at the synchronic and analytic ideals of knowing have "hemianopia," or occluded vision, of the reality they wish to study.[17] So Stump surmises: "Theories of knowledge that

---

14. Johnson, *Biblical Knowing*, 199.

15. Maurice Merleau-Ponty, *The Primacy of Perception* (Chicago: Northwestern University Press, 1964), 5.

16. For an excellent and bloody example of an unexpected resolution flowing from the narrative logic, cf. 1 Kgs 21:17–19; 22:35–38.

17. Eleonore Stump, *Wandering in Darkness: Narrative and the Problem of Suffering* (New York: Oxford University Press, 2010), 25.

ignore or fail to account for whole varieties of knowledge are correspondingly incomplete."[18]

Stump's work and her impetus are ground-breaking and speak prophetically to her peers, especially those few who have overemphasized the explanatory power of analytic philosophy to their own detriment. However, her suggestions for combining the analytic task with narrative theology might not go far enough for our purposes. Mainly, we need a methodology that can pursue both the social and embodied task of knowing. Narrative theology is an attempt to account for the social nature—a narrator brings the audience to know something—but on most accounts, narratives do not necessarily require the body.[19] Despite this, merely combining analytical and narratival analyses will not provide a sufficient explanation of ritual epistemology. This requires an account that can explain why knowers must listen to the authority (the narrator) and must also perform what that authority instructs in order to know what she is showing us (entering the narrative, as it were).

Synthetic and Analytic Theology

I intend to describe how ritual is necessary in the epistemological process, developing this transcendent idea of biblical epistemology while maintaining fidelity to the particular texts of interest. We seek to overcome the retreat into creatureliness. This kind of retreat maintains that everything is so historically concrete that no transcendent concepts are viable. This retreat into creatureliness is often caught by that broad-net term: Postmodernism. I also want to avoid the opposite error of maintaining a view so utterly transcendent that every time the view descends from the heavens and encounters the realities described in Scripture, it crumbles in our hands: a caricature of Scholasticism.

My approach will be philosophically synthetic, able to appropriate the language and categories that most approximate what we find in Scripture. This means that we will be moving back and forth between synchronic and diachronic modes of analysis, analyzing particular instances in the context of how they function in the larger story of the canon. Where appropriate, we will employ the language and constructs of phenomenology, analogical reasoning, ritual theory, literary criticism, anthropology, and analytic philosophy.

A synthetic approach finds common epistemological ground outside of the biblical texts. In this case, I examine many aspects of biblical rituals with their counterparts in the laboratory of scientific epistemology. If the ancient Hebrews had a veracious account of knowing, then we should expect that it could

---

18. Stump, *Wandering in Darkness*, 59.

19. I will later argue that reading narrative, like tracking multiple narratives in our lives, is an embodied task. For the time being, we can assume that narrative approaches to knowing insufficiently deal with the embodied and historical nature of the task.

withstand comparison to modern accounts of knowing.[20] Philosophers of science have offered an embodied, social, and historical view of scientific epistemology that is worth considering in tandem with biblical epistemology, possibly even as an extension of it.[21]

I will also strive for the rigor and precision (as much as is warranted) best exemplified in analytic theology. Oliver Crisp informs us, "For the analytic theologian, clarity and precision of argument, coupled with attention to possible objections to one's position, will be very important considerations, as they are in analytic philosophy."[22] However, we need to define "clarity" carefully.

William Wood's review of the Analytic Theology project highlights the possibility that clarity is not at stake as much as rhetorical virtues that differ from field to field:

> There is a certain naïve triumphalism at work here [in *Analytic Theology*]. Somehow I doubt that continental philosophers or theologians cheerfully prize writing that is vague, wordy, incoherent, rigor-free, and unclear. Moreover, what counts as clear, parsimonious, and rigorous writing will vary according to the community for which one writes ... Note, too, that someone with continental commitments might reasonably call analytic writing "thin" instead of "clear," and might reasonably call densely allusive continental writing "rich" instead of "obscure." Rhetorical virtues do not transcend disciplinary socialization. Analytic philosophy is not the unmediated language of thought.[23]

One lingering concern here is the presumption of "precision" which can presumptively go unexplained within analytic circles. Precision appears to

---

20. We are assuming here that James Barr et al. were correct in their contention that the Hebrew mind evinced in the Scriptures of Israel functions the same as the Greek mind and the modern mind. There is no ancient mentality that presumably would cut us off from meaningful interaction with their thinking through the text. In other words, they know like we know. For the original argument for a dichotomy between the Hebrew and modern mind, see Johannes Pedersen, *Israel, Its Life and Culture* (2 vols.; Oxford: Geoffrey Cumberlege, 1959), I:124; Thorlief Boman, *Hebrew Thought Compared with Greek* (LHD; London: SCM, 1960). For the historically decisive counter-argument, see James Barr, *The Semantics of Biblical Language* (Oxford: Oxford University, 1967); Michael Carasik also has an excellent analysis of the debate in the introduction to *Theologies of the Mind in Biblical Israel* (SBibLit 85; Oxford: Peter Lang, 2005).

21. Most notably, Marjorie Grene's philosophy of biology, *The Knower and the Known* (London: Faber & Faber, 1966); Michael Polanyi's scientific epistemology, *Personal Knowledge: Towards a Post-Critical Philosophy* (Chicago: University of Chicago Press, 1974); and Thomas Kuhn's social history of scientific knowledge, *The Structure of Scientific Revolutions* (3rd ed.; Chicago: University of Chicago Press, 1996).

22. Oliver D. Crisp, "On Analytic Theology," in *Analytic Theology* (eds. Oliver D. Crisp and Michael C. Rea; New York: Oxford University Press, 2009), 44.

23. William Wood, "On the New Analytic Theology, or: The Road Less Traveled," *JAAR* 77, no. 4 (December 2009): 949.

mean "discretely precise," so that a syllogism is generally viewed as more precise than a narrative. Or, a proposition is more precise than a parable. Why should this be so? There appears to be a presumption that the arguments which are more open, traceable, and defeasible are the most precise ones. But if this captures the sentiment of what analytic philosophers mean by "precise," then the definition is clearly skewed toward their own particular methodology.[24] However, the definition of precision ought to be based on that which explains best. If so, then the precision of a given analysis is co-relative to its ability to aptly explain. Scientists regularly speak of theories as being better because they have more explanatory power. The most precise explanation can aptly relate the parts to the whole, even when those relationships can only be explained symbolically or metaphorically and are strictly untraceable to direct observation.

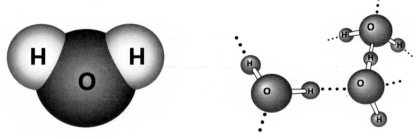

Figure 1.2   Figure 1.3

For instance, no one has ever seen a water molecule unmediated with her own eyes. She relies upon representations to mediate a two-dimensional image to her eye, which she then has to mentally (imaginatively) reconstruct into three dimensions (See Figure 1.2). Even then, it is impossible—so they say—to separate out just one molecule. Hence, water molecules are seen in clumps due their unique bonding structures (See Figure 1.3). To know what a water molecule is, educators employ verbal symbolism as well (e.g., H_2O). In order to relate the relative size and bonding of the atoms within the molecule—what the molecule looks like—chemists describe it as the Mickey Mouse structure. To help students understand the bonding visible in the mediated image (See Figure 1.3), educators use the analogical construct of "attraction." Thus, when a chemist says that she understands what water is and how it functions chemically, she tugs upon networks of analogical images and constructs at many granularities and can therefore say why the mass of the oxygen molecule—at the atomic granularity—relates to surface tension of "water" at the granularity of human observation.

---

24. Wood, "On the New Analytic Theology," 949, 957.

The editors of *Analytic Theology* anticipated these objections regarding precision and include them in the twin introductions, in analytic style. Michael Rea states the objection most clearly:

> The problem with analytic philosophy is that it prioritizes clarity and precision at the expense of everything else, and it ignores the fact that sometimes, in order to attain wisdom and understanding, we have to rely substantively on metaphor and other literary tropes. Analytic philosophers are unwilling to step outside the box of what is cognitively familiar—their own "well-understood primitives," reasoning in accord with the canons of logic, and so on—for the sake of wisdom, philosophy's traditional prize.[25]

Oliver Crisp emphasizes that method does not guarantee palatable outcomes, and so we cannot blindly advocate results from a rigorous process *just because the process is rigorous*:

> Of course, adoption of an analytic theological method is no guarantee that the conclusions for which a particular theologian argues are true. An analytic theologian might end up holding doctrine that is unorthodox, or even heretical, and have argued for this in an impeccably analytic fashion. But this should not be terribly surprising. After all, one can have a valid argument with a false conclusion.[26]

Even here, Crisp seems to implicitly argue that precision means "precise" in the strictly analytical form, as the fruits of precise thinking on such matters might be undesirable yet logically valid conclusions. In this move, Crisp leaves room for cleaving the rigorous process of analytic method from the contextual reality of a particular theological matter we might be analyzing.

The question persists: Does "precise" include "understanding the part's relation to the whole"? Virtue epistemologist Jonathan Kvanvig argues that meaningful knowledge can only come *as a whole*. Precision can only be considered in cases like the chemist's, where "understanding" maintains a mediating position between the parts and the whole. Addressing the matter of propositional epistemology that centers on subjects knowing discrete facts, Kvanvig argues that such approaches may atomize content meant to be understood holistically. Further, most or all knowable content is only interpretable as a whole because that is the way our minds are structured: "[E]xperience conveys information only en masse, and the individuation into propositional form often imposes structure rather than conforming to it."[27] Kvanvig asserts that

---

25. Rea, "Introduction", 18.

26. Crisp, "On Analytic Theology," 46.

27. I do not adhere to the totality of Kvanvig's argument for information as "chunks." This quote is Zagzebski's summary of Kvanvig's critique. Linda Trinkaus Zagzebski, *Virtues of the Mind: An Inquiry into the Nature of Virtue and the Ethical Foundations of Knowledge* (Cambridge: Cambridge University Press, 1996), 44. Jonathan L. Kvanvig, *The*

breaking knowledge down to propositions, which epitomizes precision of the analytic sort, does not reflect the things that we are actually concerned to know about:

> An epistemology sensitive to the representational structure of the mind will begin the tasks of structural epistemology from a differ-ent point than that of asking when a particular person knows or jus-tifiably believes an individual proposition. . . . The point I want to emphasize is the remoteness of such issues [atomization into prop-ositions] from the central epistemological concerns that arise from the social perspective.[28]

It should now be clear that precision risks being upheld as an artificial idealization of understanding without a more rigorous definition. This nar-rower notion of "precision" might even be the vestiges of imported cross-talk with engineering (i.e., precision engineering). However, if we are to truly un-derstand how rituals bring Israel to know her world, then we will attempt to arrive at an understanding that looks more like the chemist's rigorous knowledge of water than the logician's knowledge of rhetorical form. We will see this scientific version of precise knowledge borne out in the rituals of the Hebrew Bible explored in Part III.

Chapter 2

What Is a Rite and What Does
It Have to Do with Knowledge?

"But also all journeys have a secret destination
of which the traveler is unaware."[1]

As I write this from Jerusalem, the whole city prepares to celebrate Pesach (Passover) next week. In Jerusalem, the Pesach celebration can take on divergent Judaic elements[2] along with Israeli peculiarities,[3] all of which are rooted in the historical commandment to celebrate (Exod 12:43–51). The Samaritans will celebrate Pesach a few weeks from now on Mount Gerizim. The Samaritans will slaughter dozens of Pesach lambs, separating the parts of the lamb devoted to YHWH from the parts consumed by the people on Passover.

Is Pesach a ritual? Or, is it a sacrament, holiday, or ceremony? What defines a ritual so that Samaritan Pesach and a Creole witch doctor's animal sacrifice can be analyzed under the same definition? Even more, what definition of ritual can clarify the difference between the public slaughters by the *cohanim* (the priests) on Mount Gerizim from the private slaughterhouse killing that provides the symbolic bone for the Jewish Pesach?[4]

In this chapter, I consider definitions offered by ritual theorists themselves on how we should understand Israelite ritual, of which we only have textual reports. Moreover, I must clarify what ritual theorists propose concerning knowing *through* rituals, as no explanation of an overarching episte-

---

1. Martin Buber, *The Legend of Baal-Shem* (trans. Maurice Friedman; New York: Routledge, electronic, 2005), 23.

2. Different traditions and geographically located peoples within Judaism will celebrate Pesach variously, some even celebrating for different durations. E.g., Ashkenazi, Sephardi, Ethiopian, etc. Region of origin differences will also provide variety: United States, Russia, Eastern Europe, Spain, etc. At the very extreme, Samaritans celebrate on an entirely different calendar.

3. E.g., Pesach celebrated as a national holiday, grocery markets emptied of leavened bread, the agricultural connectedness of the holiday to the land, etc.

4. Some Jewish Seder traditions replace the bone with an alternative bone (i.e., goat) or vegetable (i.e., beets).

mological framework can be found in their work. I also examine what counts
as a ritual and why, attempting to sufficiently answer the questions posed
above. Because this topic intersects ritual studies, epistemology, and biblical
studies, I begin with Catherine Bell's paradigm-shifting analysis of ritual studies. She offers an incisive critique of ritual practice and ritualization that help
to navigate the choppy waters of ritual studies in the past century.[5] I then construct a working definition of Israelite ritual that attempts to stay within the
spirit of Bell's insights, basically describing how ritual functions epistemologically within Israelite society according to the Hebrew Bible.

Catherine Bell's Critique of Ritual Theory

Bell's 1992 work *Ritual Theory, Ritual Practice* "changed the framework for understanding the nature and function of ritual."[6] Without rehearsing all the
ways in which this might be true, we will take her core observations as directive for this present work:

> [T]he problems we face in analyzing ritual, as well as the impetus
> for engaging these particular problems have less to do with inter-
> preting the raw data and more to do with the manner in which we
> theoretically constitute ritual as the object of a cultural method of
> interpretation. The implicit structure of ritual theory . . . has im-
> posed a powerful limit on our theoretical flexibility, our divisions of
> human experience, and our ability to perceive the logical relations
> inscribed within these divisions.[7]

How we conceive of ritual largely relies upon our anthropological imagination. Are we thinkers who act, or are our thoughts and acts co-mingled beyond separation? Or, are we something else entirely? The problem, for Bell,
goes even deeper into the discourse of ritual theory. She describes three
movements that have allowed an artificial discussion of ritual to persist:

1. Ritual is separated as an activity, distinct from concepts in the mind.
2. Ritual is presumed to be a cultural medium meant to reintegrate beliefs and behaviors, actions and concepts.
3. Ritual performance is then integrated with the theorists' concepts by
   analysis of the integrative aspect of the ritual.[8]

From these three movements, a discourse has been created that allows the
theorists to propose masterful analyses. However, Bell warns: "It is possible

5. Catherine Bell, *Ritual Theory, Ritual Practice* (New York: Oxford University Press, 2009).

6. Diane Jonte-Pace, foreword to *Ritual Theory, Ritual Practice* by Catherine Bell (New York: Oxford University Press, 2009), vii.

7. Bell, *Ritual Theory, Ritual Practice*, 16–17.

8. Ibid., 47–55.

that the whole structure of the theoretical discourse on ritual primarily serves to solve the problems posed for scholars by their reliance on a distinction between thought and action."[9]

Although she is addressing the study of contemporary rituals that can be directly observed by anthropologists, the majority of her criticism can be retrofitted for what the Hebrew Bible describes as a normatively *ritualed* life, which is then carried into the earliest Christian communities.

First, Bell takes issue with Durkheim's view that rituals symbolically represent beliefs. For the Durkheimian approach, primacy is placed on the mental activities of the religious practitioner, which then have a corresponding expression in ritual. Hence, the dangerous assumption develops that "beliefs could exist without ritual; rituals, however, could not exist without beliefs."[10] Bell continues to describe how ritual is objectified. In some cases, rituals are treated as a text (or textualized), studied independent of thought. Theorists could surmise that rites are performed acts, not functions of thinking. This creates the thinking-acting dichotomy that clearly prioritizes the thinking side of the dichotomy.[11] Bell argues most incisively against the danger of domestication, or subordination, of ritual. Ritual theorists cannot merely apply their constructs to rituals and test them for fit without considering the ways in which their theory contorts the very rite studied.

> Yet the more subtle and far-reaching distortion is not the obvious bifurcation of a single, complex reality into dichotomous aspects that can exist in theory only. Rather, it is the powerful act of subordination disguised in such differentiations, the subordination of act to thought, or actors to thinkers. Indeed, no matter how provisional or heuristic, a distinction between thought and action is not a differentiation between two equally weighted terms. . . . To perceive this is to grasp differentiation itself *as an activity* and, therefore, to begin to appreciate the strategic activity of theory-making in general.[12]

Archaeologist Anne Porter iterates the difficulty of understanding ancient ritual as a vivified conduit of internal beliefs. In looking at the hard cases of funerary remains found *in situ*, Porter contends that it would not make sense to construct "a one-to-one relationship between mortuary deposit and belief," a theology of meaning constructed from sacrificial remains and the corresponding texts.[13] To do so might imply that the artifacts and the texts of a culture's rituals are simply the ritual expression of a system of beliefs.

---

9. Ibid., 47–48.

10. Quoting Edward Shils, "Ritual and Crisis," in *The Religious Situation* (ed. Donald R. Cutler; Boston: Beacon, 1968), 736.

11. Bell, *Ritual Theory, Ritual Practice*, 45–47.

12. Ibid., 48–49.

13. Anne Porter, "Mortal Mirrors: Creating Kin through Human Sacrifice in Third Millennium Syro-Mesopotamia," in *Sacred Killing: The Archaeology of Sacrifice in the An-*

Basically, if ritual is primarily conceived of as a symbolic expression of a belief in the mind of the participant, then it is fundamentally a thinking man's game where actions represent thoughts directly. Bell argues that such a conflated and binary approach foists more into the ritual than it seeks to understand what actually happens in and through ritual. And for this present work, such a view excludes what the Scriptures plainly report, that at least some of Israel's rituals—if not all of them—are meant to form knowers and not merely express what is believed or known.

Two notable movements in scholarship have recently buffeted this thinking-acting dichotomy, a dichotomy characterized by a psycho-centric anthropology of action.[14] First, the feminist critique no longer tolerated the diminution of the body as an inferior constituent in human thought. For both Hebrew Bible and New Testament scholars, the body has always held sway in the reasoning of the noblest characters. As an easy example from the biblical literature, the natural reading of epistemological texts indicates that wisdom has a feminine character (e.g., Prov 8). Moreover, Lady Wisdom is attractive: meant to be more physically desirable than Dame Folly, the adulterous woman of Proverbs 7. Noticeably, wisdom is *not* portrayed as the mind (*nous*) and folly the body (*soma*), but two desirable embodied women—wisdom and folly—compete for the audience of young men.[15]

Second, Mark Johnson and George Lakoff's groundbreaking studies of metaphor and analogical reasoning definitively argued that abstract concepts can be built up through an embodied experience. Both scholars have gone on to argue persuasively that no necessary connection exists between triangularity or the concepts of calculus to a naïve Platonic view of ideas and forms.[16] These concepts, even mathematical relations, were not ideas given by the heavenly realms. They don't exist *up there*, rather, the most abstract conceptual schemata are derived from *down here*: our own bodies.

In all, by the late twentieth century, the human body as the conceptual center of epistemology had a rigorous and growing defense. The feminist critique along with the rise in analogical thought as the ground for human reason caused a broad re-appraisal of the body as integral to thought. I will discuss the role of the body and reason further in Part III.

---

cient *Near East* (eds. Anne Porter and Glenn M. Schwartz; Winona Lake, IN: Eisenbrauns, 2012), 191–216.

14. For a helpful summary of body talk in scholarship: Caroline Bynum, "Why All the Fuss about the Body? A Medievalist's Perspective," *CI* 22, no. 1 (Autumn 1995): 1–33.

15. The insights of Phyllis Trible, among many others, have been particularly helpful here. *God and the Rhetoric of Sexuality* (Minneapolis: Fortress, 1986).

16. George Lakoff and Mark Johnson, *Metaphors We Live By* (Chicago: University of Chicago Press, 1980); Mark Johnson, *The Body in the Mind: The Bodily Basis of Meaning, Imagination, and Reason* (Chicago: University of Chicago Press, 1987). For precise examples from mathematics, see: George Lakoff, *Women, Fire, and Dangerous Things: What Categories Reveal about the Mind* (Chicago: University of Chicago Press, 1989), 353–69.

If the body itself provides the concepts of reason and we do not accept the thinking-acting dichotomy, what then is the relationship between ritual acts and beliefs? Stated otherwise, if participants are not primarily thinkers, for whom thoughts and actions are extricable from each other, how are rituals a kind of thinking, rather than mere expressions of thought? Two problems immediately present themselves: 1) delineating ritual from ordinary activity and 2) showing how "rituals form knowers" better fits the reality of ritual than "rituals merely express beliefs." First, we must describe rituals so that we can differentiate what is normal non-ritualed human activity and what is special ritual activity. For instance, anthropologists often note the difficulty in determining whether ancient skeletal remains are merely ordinary interment, sacred graves, or instances of human sacrifice.[17]

In Woolley's renowned 1934 discovery of the great royal cemetery in Ur (Mesopotamia), Woolley supposed that all the slaves and soldiers who were buried with the royalty and entered the tomb peaceably. In his imaginative reconstruction of the burial—just forty-four years prior to the Jonestown mass suicide—Woolley pictured over one hundred servants submissively drinking their compliant death in cups of poison. Just as was the case with Jonestown, the violence of the situation might have been worse than Woolley suspected. Baadsgaard, et al., have since shown through Computer Axial Tomography (CAT) scans of the servants' skulls that a Sumerian battle-ax was probably used to kill the members of the royal entourage *from behind*.[18] In this instance, a technological advance can contextualize the sacrificial practices at work. But when archaeologists find a child's remains under the corner foundation of an ancient house, it is less clear how and why the body was placed there. In other words, both among archaeological finds and anthropological study today, what counts as ritual must be considered with care.

But this problem of differentiating rituals from ordinary human activity does not evaporate by observing current rather than ancient rituals or actual, rather than textual accounts of ritual. Today, omnivores like me participate—either directly or by proxy—in slaughtering animals and interring human remains as often as did the ancients. What makes a modern slaughterhouse different from the slaughter activities at the Herodian Temple in Jerusalem? Saying that one is formal and the other informal does not resolve the ambiguity. Bell answers this problem by developing the view of "ritualized practice," which is meant to overcome some of the objectifying and dichotomizing of ritual found in much of ritual theory.

---

17. This is the topic of Glenn M. Schwartz's introductory chapter in *Sacred Killing*, 1–32. Almost all of the authors in that volume struggle to determine whether or not interred remains are instances of sacrifice.

18. Aubrey Baadsgaard, Janet Monge, and Richard L. Zettler, "Bludgeoned, Burned, and Beautified: Reevaluating Mortuary Practices in the Royal Cemetery of Ur," in *Sacred Killing*, 125–58.

Second, I must convincingly offer a comprehensive view of human know-ing that aptly critiques the long-held theories that "rituals merely express beliefs." I am rejecting this view, but need to show why my view that "rituals form knowers" fits the biblical data with higher fidelity than an epistemology that claims such as: ancient Semites have justifiably true beliefs about the world and express those beliefs in rituals.

Below, I want to explore Bell's answer to the first difficulty, discerning ritual from normal action. For the second difficulty, I will lay down the frame-work for an exploration that will extend into Parts II and III of the book: the distinguishing marks regarding the Hebrew Bible's use of ritual. Building upon Bell's treatment of practice, ritualization, and oversight, I suggest that the bib-lical assumption about ritual requires it to be scripted, prepared and practiced, logical, and most importantly, formative (not merely expressive).

Practice

Practices are the things we do, but rites must intentionally do something to us. As highlighted in the example of Woolley's interpretation of the funerary practices at Ur, the problem of discerning why something is done cannot al-ways be determined by observation. A society's rituals often look like all their other behaviors. The Lord's Supper, within its original setting, is in part a meal of bread and wine. The pedestrian nature of the food and actions involved does nothing to denote it as a ritual. The same could be said about baptism and bathing, temple sacrifice and butchering animals, or praying to God and pray-ing to a king. Definitions of ritual that try to find the universal tendencies in these practices will usually violate the particularity of the practice in order to maintain the universal aspect. Attempts to identify ritual's essence as its rou-tinization, communication, performance, symbolism, or political empower-ment end up needlessly excising the rite from its context.[19]

Bell avoids this universalizing tendency and opts for the internal ac-knowledgment of the continuity and discontinuity with societal norms in the ritual itself. In other words, how is this practice a critique of the acts with which it is continuous? In biblical terms, how is *this* pile of stones different from the myriad piles of stones (Josh 4:6)? How is *this* meal different from all of our other meals (Exod 12:27)? How is living *in a booth* different than living *in a house* (Lev 23:43)? As Bell puts it: "What do these activities do that other activi-

19. Though he is referring to something slightly different, to definitions of "place" apart from "space," Craig Bartholomew recently coined this similar and general prob-lem under the phrase "the problem of abstraction in relation." Specifically, our abstrac-tions need an intellectually honest way of maintaining a connection to the relation from which they were abstracted. *Where Mortals Dwell: A Christian View of Place for Today* (Grand Rapids, MI: Baker Academic, 2012), 184.

ties cannot do?"[20] We must notice that by switching the conversation away from the essential nature of ritual, rites become necessarily instrumental towards several possible ends. I will contend that in the Hebrew Bible one of those ends is explicitly epistemological.

Ritualization

Bell assesses practices through the lens of ritualization. She defines ritualization this way:

> [R]itualization is a matter of various culturally specific strategies for setting some activities off from others, for creating and privileging a qualitative distinction between the "sacred" and the "profane," and for ascribing such distinctions to realities thought to transcend the powers of human actors.[21]

Under this arrangement, for instance, habituation is a strategy of some rituals, but not a function of ritual itself. This returns the discussion of ritual back to its situational context, as the local context determines the particular strategy employed. For instance, the lack of evocative and graphic elements in the cannibalistic ritual of Christian communion might be a strategy for reinforcing the symbolic nature of the meal. Although it is described in cannibalistic terms, its reduction of flesh to bread and blood to wine are a strategy for marking it off from the real practices of cannibalism or flesh-eating of any type. Despite its symbolism, the similitude between wine and blood is not entirely accidental, but a strategy derived from the situation.

Oversight: Seeing but not Sighting

Bell's study of the epistemological function of ritualization lacks an overarching epistemological structure. Nevertheless, two key movements within her thinking will be helpful for us to consider: practice as oversight and the ritualization of the body. First, ritual oversight means that a practice cannot see *how* it is doing *what it is doing.*[22] Basically, participation in the ritual practice creates new questions that the ritual does not answer, transforming the participant's insights to a new horizon.

At this point, the centrality of the body most naturally re-enters the discussion. Bell and others suggest that embodied participation creates a trans-

---

20. Bell, *Ritual Theory, Ritual Practice*, 74.

21. Ibid., 74.

22. Polanyi will describe this as the apprentice's trust in the master while embodying the steps in his scientific epistemology. *Personal Knowledge: Towards a Post-Critical Philosophy* (Chicago: University of Chicago Press, 1974), 55–56.

formed participant in a way that leaves the thinking-acting dichotomy clearly impotent to address ritual:

> [T]he molding of the body within a highly structured environment does not simply express inner states. Rather, it primarily acts to re-structure bodies in the very doing of the acts themselves. Hence, required kneeling does not merely *communicate* subordination to the kneeler. For all intents and purposes, kneeling produces a sub-ordinated kneeler in and through the act itself. . . . [R]itualization is not the mere display of subjective states or corporate values. Rather, we see an act of production—the production of a ritualized agent able to wield physically a scheme of subordination or insub-ordination.[23]

Because ritualized agents are transformed by their participation, there exists a blindness to exactly how the process is transforming them. Anyone who has taught understands well that students rarely appreciate how various classroom teaching rituals are meant to shape them and not merely impart knowledge to them. I regularly have students who cannot discern why I ask them to write a limerick that summarizes a passage of Scripture. There is an oversight; the rite is not what they expect to be done in a college class on Scripture. But if practiced well, the translation of history into a specific form of rhyme can produce a new type of student, one who makes contact with the textuality of Scripture in a way previously off-limits to her. Again, as Martin Buber put it: "But also all journeys have a secret destination of which the traveler is unaware."[24]

Rituals in Context

With these now in view—practices, ritualization, and oversight—Bell maintains that studies which focus only on the elements of precision and performance of a ritual (e.g., Rappaport)[25] do not fully capture what is happening *in* ritual.[26] The body as the source of meaning, the social context in which a practice is strategically ritualized, and the fresh production of a ritualized agent through her participation requires that rites always resist de-contextualization: "no ritual style is autonomous."[27]

Bell's critique will surface again in the coming pages. However, this summary of her analysis provides enough conceptual leverage upon which I can

---

23. Italics in the original. Bell, *Ritual Theory, Ritual Practice*, 100.

24. Buber, *The Legend of Baal-Shem*, 23.

25. Roy A. Rappaport, *Ecology, Meaning, and Religion* (Richmond, CA: North Atlantic Books, 1979).

26. She is referring to performance criticism of ritual, but others could fall under Bell's critique as well. Bell, *Ritual Theory, Ritual Practice*, 101.

27. Bell, *Ritual Theory, Ritual Practice*, 101.

examine how the Hebrew Bible reflects what Bell has proffered. The Hebrew Bible has a rigorous discussion of ritualized practices which mean to form ritualized agents who can see their reality differently. In the end, I will argue that the texts of the Hebrew Bible and New Testament picture rituals as bridges spanning the logical gap between what Israel does not know and what she needs to know.

Distinguishing Marks of Israelite Rituals

Taking into account all that Catherine Bell has offered in her critique, I must now sketch out the most essential features of Israelite ritual according to the Scriptures. Bell herself advocates that a more fruitful way of approaching the study of ritual will account for what rituals mean from within a culture's *emic* understanding rather than imposing *etic* universal categories.[28] Hence, I will ask the question: How do the Israelite Scriptures describe the strategic use of rituals to distinguish the rite from normal actions and to produce ritualized Israelites themselves? Ritual in the Hebrew Bible and New Testament will be distinguishable, therefore, as: 1) scripted, 2) prepared and practiced, 3) logical, and 4) formative. Though these aspects may describe all ritualized practice, we are restricting our sights to what is described in paradigmatic texts of the Hebrew Bible and New Testament.

Scripted

All performances of ritual will be unique expressions. No matter how precisely performed according to instruction or improvised, Israelite rituals will follow a script. In fact, prescription on the basis of a prophet's authority is a hallmark of Israel's ritualized practices. Performance criticism of ritual has been helpful on this front. Roy Rappaport highlights the scripted aspect of performance based on who encodes the ritual sequence: "I take the term 'ritual' to denote *the performance of more or less invariant sequences of formal acts and utterances not entirely encoded by the performers.*"[29] If we can discern a ritual from normative activity, then scripted practices distinguish actions that are performed apart from sociological or physical pressure.[30] But scripts of ritual can emerge through mere repetition, and so we need to be able to delineate emergent scripts of process from scripts intended to form knowers.

---

28. Ibid., 74.

29. Roy A. Rappaport, *Ritual and Religion in the Making of Humanity* (Edinburgh: Cambridge University Press, 1999), 27.

30. Even if the rites are performed under such pressures, it need not be normative for our thinking on the matter.

As an example, if we begin to regularly butcher animals for meat, then we expect that our butchering practices will eventually become predictable. Safety practices will be adopted and liturgies of behavior will emerge from the repetitive nature of the task itself. Anyone who has ever worked a manual labor job is familiar with the rituals that naturally emerge from the repetition and exertion needed for the task. However, the script of ritual butchering in Leviticus distinguishes itself, bypassing both the practices that emerge through repetition and the physical need for the food itself.

For instance, anthropologists have studied the ritualized practices in laboratories using high-powered lasers. In such work environments, where the chance of mutilation and death are high, scripted practices quickly emerge—often called safety procedures—to ensure pursuit of happiness for all involved. As Sims wryly observes, "There is surely no more useful skill in the practice of scientific research than the knack for not accidentally killing oneself with the laboratory equipment."[31] In the case of such scripts, Sims examined the striking similarity between these safety rituals and Levitical practices. If a ritual practice emerges merely by seeking efficiency in a repetitive environment or safety of the participants, then the intent of that script to form the knower is in question.[32] However, I only want to consider scripts that do not appear to emerge from a repetitive practice, but that overtly intend to form the knower in a particular way—to produce a ritualized agent.

Hesse, et al., review the importance of associating scripts with ritual, citing the aspects of ritual which needs to be present in order for them to certify the rites prescribed. Hence, ritual scripts, written or oral, will emphasize:

1. The repetitive nature of ritual,
2. The notion of ritual as performance,
3. The accompanying implication of the participation of both actors and observers in rituals,
4. The maintained formal traditions that are included in rituals, and
5. The limits on individual expression that are set by the ritual form.[33]

---

31. Benjamin Sims, "Safe Science: Material and Social Order in Laboratory Work," *SSS* 35, no. 3 (June 2005): 333.

32. No doubt that one could argue, as I would, that these naturally emergent scripts of process also do teach us about creation writ large. Working at a shipping company, we had to move thousand pound freight canisters on a roller-deck floor all night long. Many scripts of process emerged, which were eventually codified into my training as a new employee. However, following those scripts actually hindered me, for a while, from understanding both the rationale of the ritual and the laws of inertia that could prevent me from being crushed. The rituals that emerged were basically a litany of "do this" and "do not do that or you'll lose your foot, get killed, etc." These did not teach me what others had learned, but they did keep me alive long enough to see why the list of rituals had emerged.

33. Brian Hesse, Paula Wapnish, and Jonathan Greer, "Scripts of Animal Sacrifice in Levantine Culture-History," in *Sacred Killing*, 220.

Following the Patriarchal period, Moses is the sole prescriber of Israel's rites and ensuing prophets follow his prescriptions. Failure to comply with the scripts of sacrifice to the degree required end in the ritual act being prophetically condemned. For example, an operative question in the stories of the Hebrew Bible is: How closely ought we to follow the script? We will discuss this further in the biblical exegesis of Part III. However, the narratives do indicate clear instances of the failure of Israelites, both in waiting for exact prescriptions and in following them. In the absence of an exact ritual script, both the Israelites (Exod 32) and the king of Israel (1 Sam 15) are upbraided by the prophets for their failure to wait and their performing of unscripted sacrifices. The implication of both accounts—the golden calf and Saul's offering of animals devoted to the ban—points to the participants not merely inventing a script, but possibly following another known script. On the whole, the feast of Exodus 32 and Saul's sacrifice appear to be socially reasonable acts, indicating that they follow some kind of accepted script or norm. However, after the ritual scripts of the Torah are codified, failure to heed the directions, or the prophet who gave them, becomes a capital crime (e.g., Lev 10; Num 16).

Later, the prophets chastise Israel for performing rites while their lives defy the Torah's instructions as a whole. Namely, oppressing the poor (e.g., Amos 2:6–8; Mic 6:6–8) and syncretism (e.g., Amos 5) become primary means of contravening their ritual performance. The Pentateuch advances scripts of Israel's rituals robust enough for prophetic indictment from any of the instruction found within the Torah. Stated otherwise, neglecting the practice of the principled ideals of Torah—love, justice, etc. (Lev 19)—creates sufficient reason to abrogate an Israelite's ritual performance, turning rites into vain practices. As it later turns out in the Hebrew Bible, Israel's performance of the Torah's instruction as a whole mediates the efficacy of the ritual parts.

If ritual is requisite for knowing, the notion that rites are scripted is consistent with the epistemological process found in the Hebrew Bible and New Testament.[34] Moses, the authoritative voice that was authenticated to Israel, also scripted her ways of knowing beyond his lifetime, particularly her ritualed ways of knowing. Adherence to those Torah rites, and their transmogrification in the New Testament, is considered tantamount to listening to the voice of Moses and Jesus respectively. Because the prophetic voice plays the pivotal role in Israel's epistemology, ritual scripts act as the prophetic guide. Hence, biblical epistemology centers upon whose scripts Israel is performing.

Prepared and Practiced

A ritual's "center of gravity" must be understood as plotted along a multitude of centers of gravity, on either side of the act itself, and in

---

34. The question of who prescribes these ritual scripts and how are they authenticated is taken up in Johnson, *Biblical Knowing*, 22–86.

and around the humans, converging on the ritual from the past and the future and many dispersed points in the present. These centers of gravity taken together express, quite literally through the everyday biographies of humans and ritual objects, one *particular* instantiation or perhaps orchestration of the relationship between the collective of devotees and the divinity.[35]

Gillian Goslinga reveals that, even in her own work, ritual study has often become too focused on the sacrificial act itself. Even in our literary texts of ritual, which require our imaginative reconstruction of the rites, we often become over-interested in the killing of the animal, the casting of blood, or burning of the carcass. This does a disservice to the emphasis in the Torah, which stresses sacrifice as an event that begins in the home and daily life of Israel.

Goslinga herself overlooked the preparation for sacrifice until she personally studied a goat-killing rite in India by a priestess who channeled her father. While interviewing the subjects involved over the year prior to the sacrifice, the preparation of the rite became overwhelmingly important to her understanding of what she saw in the actual sacrifice—a rite which visibly consists of chopping off a live goat's head and then drinking the blood directly from the arterial flow. The gruesome nature of the act is fascinating, at best, to the observer. Nevertheless, Goslinga emphasizes that it is the detailed preparations throughout the year leading up to the ritual that make sense of the terse and seemingly violent act.

So too with ancient Israel, who is given scripts of sacrifice, but also scripts of normal agricultural and subsistence life in the land. Which sheep is led to the slaughter actually requires a diachronic discerning process of attentiveness to one's flock. A subsistence-based agrarian hamlet in the Levant simultaneously lives out many overlapping scripts of farming, husbandry, multigeneration family relations, internal dispositions, home management, participation in the local economy, and much more, all of which culminate in the sacrifice of an animal or grain on behalf of that home and family. Hence, Jonathan Klawans concludes: "Rituals—sacrifice included—are multivalent entities whose levels of meaning cannot be reduced to any single idea or purpose."[36]

Considering that the ritualized practices of Israel might have an epistemological function, we cannot casually separate out the rite from the intricate system of political, economic, and theological relations from which it emerges. Because of the inextricable nature of ritual, we will always have to consider each performance as not only unique and new, but also complex: a nexus of history, place, and persons. As Jonathan Foer illustrates concerning our contemporary and synchronic view of animals as food:

---

35. Goslinga, "On Cakti-Filled Bodies and Divinities," in *Sacred Killing*, 43.

36. Jonathan Klawans, *Purity, Sacrifice, and the Temple: Symbolism and Supersessionism in the Study of Ancient Judaism* (Oxford: Oxford University Press, 2006), 68.

Food . . . is not *food*. It is terror, dignity, gratitude, vengeance, joyfulness, humiliation, religion, history, and, of course, love. . . . Perhaps there is no 'meat'. Instead, there is *this* animal, raised on *this* farm, slaughtered at *this* plant, sold in *this* way, and eaten by *this* person—but each distinct in a way that prevents them from being pieced together as a mosaic.[37]

Without being unhelpfully romantic, I do presume that ancient Israelites who embodied the Torah would have been more disposed to think in terms of "*this* animal, raised on *this* farm," at least, more so than most of us modern urbanites (especially in the United States). The view of food as a mosaic—a collage of activities that begins in mating/birthing and ends in butchering/cooking—might be more immediately graspable to them than us.

A rite is a nexus of events contiguously construed together, and yet we normally focus our examinations on what happens at the temple, for instance. But *what happens at the temple* is predicated upon a series of events and biographies that culminate at the temple. The preparation as ethical practice will be examined in full in chapter eleven.

Formative, not Merely Expressive

An essential aspect of some and possibly all Israelite ritual is that the rite forms the participants.[38] Although rites and symbols can express a relationship, the "scripted" aspect of Israel's rituals defy a bare notion that rites express beliefs. Again, returning to Bell's conviction that the thinking-acting dichotomy has created an artifice in ritual studies, she is rightfully cautious when the researcher interprets the actions in light of the beliefs that the actions are meant to express. Along with Bell, I am suspending that view for both similar and divergent reasons. I affirm Bell's general critique, but also add the primacy of ritual script as a distinctive of Israelite rituals. If the Israelites believe that their rites come directly from YHWH through Moses—where YHWH and Moses' voices are sometimes blurred beyond recognition—then the rites cannot merely express beliefs for them.[39] Rather, the rites qua *script directly*

---

37. I originally came across this passage in Hesse, Wapnish, and Greer, "Scripts of Animal Sacrifice," 217. Jonathan Safran Foer, *Eating Animals* (New York: Back Bay Books, 2010), 5, 11.

38. I will eventually need to substantiate this claim in Part II.

39. Ryan O'Dowd and others maintain that there is a steady progression throughout Deuteronomy that creates an intentional blur between the words of YHWH and of Moses. Robert M. Polzin, among others, also takes this view. "Deuteronomy" in *The Literary Guide to the Bible* (London: Collins, 1987), 92–101. See also Stephen K. Sherwood, *Leviticus, Numbers, Deuteronomy* (ed. David W. Cotter; BO; Collegeville, Minn.: Liturgical, 2002), 228–229. Ryan O'Dowd, *The Wisdom of Torah: Epistemology in Deuteronomy and the Wisdom in Literature* (FRLANT 225; Göttingen: Vandenhoeck & Ruprecht, 2009), 29.

from YHWH form them to see the world differently, and only from such formations can Israelites express what they believe. This reorientation is fundamental for understanding Scriptural epistemology and will act as an affront to many traditional epistemological inroads in contemporary philosophy.

In other words, we do not generally find in Scripture the sentiment that "because we *believe* these things, we therefore *do* these things."[40] Such a sentiment epitomizes the thinking-acting dichotomy. While we do find things believed by Israel and stated clearly in Scripture (e.g., the Shema), those statements about God, Israel, and creation found in Deuteronomy 6 are couched between substantial instruction on how to perform rituals (Deut 4) and an explicitly embodied appreciation of YHWH's grace and election (Deut 7–9).[41]

Logical

> The total effect of sacrifice depends on social understandings of the
> perceived effect and a collective judgment of its accomplishments
> in achieving its intended goals.[42]

Participation in the rituals as a reasonable act beyond mere social pressure (i.e., doing it because it is what *we do*) requires an existing universe of discourse within which the ritual practices make sense and accomplish their ends. Or, as Frank Gorman says, "The 'world' of ritual is a world of meaning, a world of symbols; it is the world of meaning and significance within which the ritual is conceptualized, constructed, and enacted."[43] We do not have to understand in detail this "world," and neither do we need to explain the exact dimensions of its universe of discourse. But in order to affirm the common logic of ritual action, we must acknowledge there is a world of discourse operative where the actors, actions, and communities *act reasonably.* As the Rambam (i.e., Maimonides) argues in his *Guide for the Perplexed*, ritual actions do not need to be logically traceable to the participant as long as they trust the one who orchestrates the ritual for their benefit (i.e., God).[44] We must scrutinize

---

40. I will maintain that the New Testament authors tended to presume the Hebrew Bible's disposition toward the role of ritual more than they discussed it. Here, we follow the heuristic that silence generally confers continuity in thought and action.

41. Nathan MacDonald argues extensively that even specific and simple beliefs, such as "YHWH our God is one" are often Modernistic impositions onto Deuteronomy 4—more than could have been present for the Israelite reader of the text. *Deuteronomy and the Meaning of "Monotheism"* (FAT 2/Reihe 1; Tübingen: Mohr Siebeck, 2003).

42. Baadsgaard, et al., "Bludgeoned, Burned, and Beautified," 125.

43. Frank H. Gorman, Jr., *Ideology of Ritual: Space, Time and Status in the Priestly Theology* (LHBOTS 91; Sheffield, England: JSOT Press, 1990), 15.

44. Although Maimonides vacillates on the purpose of following the Torah in the absence of reasons throughout the *Guide*, he regularly returns to the idea that God's

several aspects of the term "logical" with regard to ritual participation. First, can the Hebrew Bible's system of rituals live up to the philosophical standards of classical logic? Second, is ritual participation a means of arguing by symbolic logic? Third, how does ritual employ narrative logic? Moreover, throughout this entire discussion of logic, the problem of traceability will persistently plague us: Can we trace the logic of the rite?

Logical and Complete System of Ritualization

> Those who despise ritual, even at its most magical, are cherishing in the name of reason a very irrational concept of communication.[45]

By accusing those who despise ritual with the charge of irrationalism, Douglas indicts the supposedly logical systems of reason that want to avoid the mysteries associated with ritual. She knows, as do many philosophers, that communicating truth does not happen in a rigid logical framework, but at the nexus of sociological agendas, the body politic, individual insights, and more. To reduce the complex of circumstance and agency to a paradigm supposing the singular flow of information from one rational agent to another irreparably distorts reality for the sake of maintaining the paradigm.

If the purpose of Israel's rites is to communicate something to her, individually or *en masse*, then the universe of discourse of that communication, its grammar, and its logic need to be coherent. However, they do not need to be complete. In order for logic to be logical, most people generally presume that it must be internally rigorous and complete. We will consider some examples of scholars who have examined the logic of ritual participation; however, we must first ensure that we are not holding ritualized logic to an unfair standard.

First, Kurt Gödel conclusively demonstrated that for any closed system of logical discourse, and universe of discourse, there exists a set of relationships within that discourse that are true, but cannot be proved from within the system. Gödel's incompleteness theorem proved to be the death knell of Logical Positivism. This specific form of positivism earnestly sought to root all empirical observations in an unshakable foundation of logically connected and axiomatic truths. Yet, Gödel had shown conclusively that the true statements—statements such as "1+1=2"—one would need in order to prove all the true relationships within this set of relationships could not be found within the system. In order to be logically consistent within a formal system, it would need to borrow rules from outside the system. Hence, in order to prove all the true statements, one either has to trust (have faith) that they are true or go outside

---

authoritative voice through Moses is a sufficient reason to follow the Torah. He cites Deut 32:47 in support: "for it is not a vain thing for you." Maimonides, *Guide for the Perplexed*, III/26. Cf. III/32 and III/46.

45. Mary Douglas, *Natural Symbols* (2nd ed.; New York: Routledge, 1996), 53.

the set in order to get the needed rules that would complete the logical relationships within the set. Thus Gödel decided that all formal systems (e.g., a set
of numerical and logical relationships) are either incomplete or inconsistent.

The implications of this finding and the conclusiveness with which it was
demonstrated deflated the positivist projects *du jour*. Specifically, Logical Positivism wanted to put all objective and inductively gathered scientific data in
deductively logical relationships with the most rigorous and fundamental
truths (i.e., axiomatic statements) in a complete and logical system. Stated
otherwise, complete logical description of what was both *true* and *provable*
would be the glue of the map of human knowledge. Once Gödel showed that
the map would always and necessarily be incomplete in its logical formulation,
the quest to logically secure all knowledge in a closed map fell apart. It was not
a devastating discovery for the hard sciences as a whole, but for those who
wanted to build a system of logically mapped data that did not ultimately rely
upon faith (or trust), Gödel showed that all such systems require such faith.

Gödel's work created new ways of doing mathematics, contributed to the
collapse of the Logical Positivism movement, and caused epistemologists to
look elsewhere for the foundations of epistemic confidence. W.V.O. Quine
seized upon the implications of Gödel's incompleteness theorem, employing
them in the realm of epistemology. Essentially, it was once thought by epistemologists that we might be able to have an airtight system of logical truths
that were deductively-mathematically related. More importantly, given
enough calculating power and time, it was presumed that we could exhaustively prove those internal relations of true statements with mathematical cer-
tainty. Gödel's finding seemed to demonstrate otherwise.

Likewise, for any system of theological relations there will always be true
ideas that lie outside of our deductively logical ability to prove that they are
true. This does not open the door to relativism, but rather shows that we must
find warrant for our trusted beliefs in places other than a closed set of deductively logical relationships.[46]

Peter Hicks suggests that in constructing a Christian epistemology, we
must not feel compelled to have an airtight set of logical relations as the foundation for our trusted beliefs, as there is no natural or philosophical standard
requiring this.[47] Nevertheless, our most trusted beliefs cannot directly contradict or violate other core convictions.[48] In other words, there must be tracea-

---

46. Alvin Plantinga has shown to the satisfaction of many analytic philosophers
why warrant acts as valid justification. *Warranted Christian Belief* (Oxford: Oxford University Press, 2000).

47. Peter Hicks, *Evangelicals and Truth: A Creative Proposal for a Postmodern Age*
(Leicester, England: Apollos, 1998), 143–46.

48. This is not the coherence theory of truth—that which posits truth to be coherent to the logical scheme within which it is found—because we need not posit an idea of
truth as something external to human understanding (an extra-biblical notion of
truth). To understand truth as it is used in Hebrew Scripture (אמת/אמונה) means that

ble reasons that justify our claims to know reality truly, but just as with scientific knowledge, those reasons are not justified merely by their logical relations to uncontroversially true axioms.[49]

For instance, I might have justified reasons for believing that my home-built airplane can fly, which I could list: previous experience flying in a similar model airplane, understanding the physics of lift, a community of trusted aeronautical engineers behind the plane's design, seeing other similar airplanes flying, etc. However, what does *not* ultimately justify my trust in the plane is my confidence that all my beliefs about the plane's ability to fly are rooted in logically connected axiomatic truths. Hence, I can trace out the justifiable reasons for my beliefs about the plane's flight-worthiness without needing an airtight justification. Though I do not need to put them in particular deductive relationships, the reasons I trace out cannot violate one another. For instance, I cannot logically trust that the plane can fly if most planes of the same model have failed to fly.

Returning briefly to the notion of precision previously posited, the justification for truth claims might be warranted, not by indubitable logical relationships, but by embodied insight into the relations between the particular to the whole—instance-to-context knowledge. For example, I might claim to know that "anesthesia makes humans numb." My justification, then, cannot be an appeal to the traceable logic of the statement in direct connection to all other logical statements we could make about anesthesia and humans. Rather, my statement is *justified* when it acts as a request for others to embody the actions and attempt to see what I see. This is called repeatability in most versions of the scientific method. Though repeatability is embodied and emplaced by its nature, the confirmation of its truth is not strictly traceable by the logic alone. I should be able to locally repeat your experiment in order to see what you see. If I do, this justifies your statements about what you observed in your version of the experiment in your local lab.

We will later return to the idea that logic itself derives from an embodied existence when we explore Lakoff's suggestion that all mathematico-logical operations are built from concepts solely derivable from *being a body* and *being in the world*. For now, we only need to recognize that for the ancient Israelite, reasons might exist to participate in ritual beyond rote obedience and we have no compelling basis to hold ritual logic to a higher logical standard than science, mathematics, or even deductive logic itself.

Not only must we presume a logical structure to ritual, but also, that the structure could conceivably be demonstrated. As an example of this view,

---

which has high fidelity to objective reality, requiring truth to be assessed in degree by knowers who are soberly subjecting their interpretations to reality and others for confirmation. See further in chapter four, "The Biblical Idea of Truth and Its Consequences for Ritual."

49. Axioms are more technical versions of statements such as "something cannot be true and not-true at the same time," "the whole is greater than the part," etc.

Mary Douglas takes her readers on a fascinating tour of the logical inferences from beliefs in witchcraft and evil.[50] Christian communities such as the Brethren Church, she argues, emphasize dichotomous theology that engenders community behavior. By imbuing their theological constructs with insider/outsider divisions, Douglas argues that this leads quite naturally to other heightened dichotomies: saint/sinner, spirit/flesh, spontaneous/formal, and in ritual, sign/signified.[51]

Whether or not one agrees with her analysis, her methodology shows a logically traceable relationship between beliefs in the existence of evil, for instance, and how that belief becomes a compelling force more broadly in theology and ritual practice. Douglas attempts to demonstrate that in societies where a strong belief in witchcraft exists, those societies tend to follow an organizational ideal that compiles opposites and forms a string of binary categories about the world. Unfortunately, she does not explore the genesis of such beliefs in light of Bell's critique. Nevertheless, her insights are fruitful in seeing the consistency of theo-logic in a community's rituals. For instance, insider/outsider motifs create the tendency for shunning. In such a society, where witchcraft represents to them strict ritual forms deemed evil, the strict establishment of any external forms of ritual worship within the Brethren community thus becomes suspect of possible influence from the occult world.

Douglas' examination fascinates us, in reference to logical relationships, because she is able to demonstrate how communities diversely exhibit the same theological impulses. Douglas' particular insights are suggestive, but her method reveals a type of logical relation between theological claims and ritual behavior, traceable to anyone who follows her interpretive insights. Stated otherwise, animistic witchcraft and Christian Brethren communities maintain their ritual life for similar reasons which can be adequately argued.

I will not argue for the particular reasons for Israelite ritual on the whole, but rather, I consider if the texts of the Hebrew Bible and New Testament evince an appreciation for the participant qua knower—an Israelite who needs to participate in order to know and needs to know something about why they are participating. Rituals ought to make sense in structure, impetus, and aims.

Analogic in Ritual

Above, I contended that participation in a system of ritual is logical, not rote, although these are not mutually exclusive. Now I want to consider how the ritual itself *incarnates* logic, for lack of a better term. In other words, if knowing occurs by means of reasonable argument or instruction (or both), then how do embodied actions *reason* with the participant?

---

50. Douglas, *Natural Symbols*, 115–31.
51. Ibid., 121–22.

Analogical reasoning is the form of reasoning that necessarily involves our embodied knowledge in order for certain ideas to be logical to us. For instance, if we hear that "Judy's career path is taking off," then we know that this is a good thing, in general. However, analogical reasoning forces us to think about how we can make any sense of this sentence at all. The phrase "career path" and "taking off" both require another notion to mediate the meaning to us. Particularly, we would need to understand what a path is, which we only know because we have physically vectored from one place to another, point A to point B. Because we understand "path" as a function of our embodied experience alone, we can analogically employ the concept of "path" and apply it to other things that go forward in time, like a career. Notice that there are also embodied notions of time and progress built into the term "career path." The same goes for "taking off," which has a decidedly different analog after the space race than prior to it. "Taking off" could mean leaving, as in "Joey is taking off," or as in "leaving the earth's atmosphere." In this context, "taking off" most probably tugs upon our experience of something that has been stagnant for a long time and then suddenly moves in a progressively positive direction (i.e., a rocket launch). However, Mark Johnson would want to remind us that all of these meanings require an embodied situatedness that knows the meaning and maps the analog over to the current statement in order to make that sentence reasonable.[52]

Mary Douglas, Catherine Bell, and others have suggested that rituals reason with the participant through "analogic"—the building up of hierarchical matrices of overlapping embodied meaning in condensed symbols.[53] "[R]ather than affirming clear and dogmatic values to impress them directly into the minds of participants, ritual actually constructs an argument, a set of tensions."[54] As opposed to the discrete symbols of a linear and symbolic logic, the condensed symbols of ritual have multiple points of contact with each other and with reality, some symbols being subsumed into others. Playing off the analogical work of George Lakoff, Bell summarizes why ritual creates both matrices and hierarchy:

> This ritual logic is a minimalist logic that generates a "sense" of logical systematicity while simultaneously facilitating subtle shifts in the ability of some symbols to dominate others. . . . In sum, ritualization not only involves the setting up of opposition, but through

---

52. By embodied experience, I only mean that we have waited for a launch and then seen it take off. Anticipation and eventual rapid progress is the analog and witnessing it in a rocket launch is sufficient to have an embodied schema of it.

53. "All communication depends on use of symbols, and they can be classified in numerous ways, from the most precise to the most vague, from single reference signs to multi-reference symbols. I ask you here to be interested in a variation, within the class of multi-reference symbols, which runs from the most diffuse to the most condensed." Douglas, *Natural Symbols*, 10.

54. Bell, *Ritual Theory, Ritual Practice*, 195.

the privileging built into such an exercise it generates hierarchical schemes to produce a loose sense of totality and systematicity. In this way, ritual dynamics afford an experience of "order" as well as the "fit" between this taxonomic order and the real world of experience.[55]

Again, I affirm with Bell the body's potential to be the actual source of meaning: "Through these operations whole systems of ritual symbols and actions can be generated by means of a small number of oppositions (male/female, within/without) or reduced to a few pairs that appear fundamental."[56] Distinct from Bell, this current exploration of analogic is not contingent on oppositions being fundamental, but necessarily relies upon the conviction that the body is the place from which ritual meaning comes. Even in instances where words of ordination accompany the rite, the meaning is still analogically derived.

Douglas argues that socialization builds the analogical interpretation into the ritual. Beginning in childhood, social truths such as "human feces are bad" or "front is good" color our analogic as well.[57] How our parents and cultures socialize us will then affect our understanding of our bodies, and thus, our analogic. When it comes to the social training about body and society, the relationship with a natural kind of symbol becomes complicated and organic. Thus, Bell contends:

> Natural symbols will not be found in individual lexical items. The physical body can have universal meaning only as a system which responds to the social system, expressing it as a system. What it symbolizes naturally is the relation of parts of an organism to the whole. Natural symbols can express the relation of an individual to his society at that general systemic level.[58]

We need not describe all of these symbolic systems accurately in order to understand the primacy of analogic in ritual understanding. The importance of this premise will be seen not only in religious ritual, but its extension to the rituals performed for scientific understanding as well.

In *Leviticus as Literature*, Douglas provides us with a vivid example of what this type of analogic could look like to the Israelite participant. It is not consequential that we trust her interpretation, but that we imagine there to be something roughly equivalent to it operative in ritual participation. Her analysis of Yom Kippur's scapegoat demonstrates how she thinks this type of matrix of hierarchical meaning could operate.[59] Eschewing the common and rabbinic

---

55. Bell, *Ritual Theory, Ritual Practice*, 104.

56. Ibid., 103.

57. Douglas, *Natural Symbols*, 80.

58. Ibid., 91.

59. Up to this point, I have been using the phrase "ritual participation" as if every single Israelite participated in every rite. However, much of ritual participation is rep-

notion that the *azazel* (i.e., the scapegoat) is released to a dismal fate, op-pressed by the sins of Israel, Douglas prefers to look at the meaning within the analogical matrix of Israel's ritualed life. Hence, "Surely the two goats . . . par-allel the two pairs of birds treated in the same way in the rites of cleansing from leprosy."[60]

One bird is killed and one released, both for leprosy and house cleansing. One goat is killed and the other released for the Day of Atonement. Both rites are performed in the same place: at the gate to the tent of meeting. Douglas concludes that these similarities, along with several others related to rites that cleanse the body (Lev 14:14–16), force us to consider the scapegoat as a con-densed symbol of Israel leaving Egypt. She highlights the overlapping similari-ties between the rites in order to demonstrate that the "sent out" aspect of the rite takes priority in a hierarchy of meaning. Hence, the goat "sent out" re-minds us of Israel sent out of Egypt, but also Ishmael and Esau as well. Analogi-cally, this forces participants to question, why are these things sent away? Her initial answer is that "[T]he teaching says something about degrees of puri-ty."[61] Douglas goes on to show more of the matrix containing the overlapping meaning of "uneven pairs": breeding cattle, mixing seed in a field, or sewing two fabrics together. Of these, she concludes: "The pairs are not so much une-ven as different; respecting their difference is symbolic of completion and to-tality."[62] The scapegoat is thus interpreted primarily as "sent out for the sake of completion," and not primarily as "tyrannized by the sins of Israel."

Once more, we are contending methodologically with Douglas that the logic within such actions lies not in a linear relation between belief and ex-pression through ritual. Rather, an analogical system creates reasons for ritual and coming to know through that participation. Whether or not we agree with Douglas' analysis, the supposition that Israel's analogic is traceable must be presumed in order to proceed. As well, the specific analogical matrix does not need to be traceable to us today. Despite the Rambam's concerns about not knowing the linear logic of the rite, the analogic necessarily must have been traceable to the ancient participant to some degree.

Narrative Logic in Ritual

A related matter to the logic of ritual regards the possibility that rituals follow a narrative structure where 1) a conflict is posited, 2) a plot develops with

resentative. On Yom Kippur, the representative function of Israel's High Priest could not be clearer. We will discuss the significance of representative and direct participa-tion in Part III.

60. Mary Douglas, *Leviticus as Literature* (New York: Oxford University Press, 2000), 248.
61. Ibid., 249.
62. Ibid., 251.

heightening tension, and 3) the tension culminates at a climax, eventually coming to resolution. Narrative, in this naked form, has a logical structure similar to a syllogism. Narratival premises (i.e., conflict and its subsequent plot tension) work to a conclusion, which follows necessarily from those premises. While narratives can be resolved in surprising ways, they cannot be resolved outside of the narratival logic.[63]

For instance, Yom Kippur could be conceived of as a conflict (i.e., the sins of Israel), which is addressed through the tensioning plot (i.e., the various aspects of the rite), coming to culmination in the climax and resolution (i.e., the offering of one goat and sending out of the other).[64] In this case, there would be an implied continuing action: the wandering of the scapegoat.

I want to, at the least, attend to the possibility that rites have such a structure. The implications of this structure weigh heavily in any examination of Israelite ritual. As with narrative criticism, the conflict and resolution are in a necessary and logical relationship. Thus, narratival analysis requires the correct identification of the elements (conflict, tension, resolution) in order to understand what is being taught through the story. Narrative criticism affords the analyst the ability to organize the particularities of a story into a rough hierarchy. As queer theologians and others have noticed, the story of Sodom (Gen 19) focuses on the conflict/resolution logic of hospitality, not homosexual rape.[65] While homosexual practice is clearly problematic from a canonical perspective, it might play a lesser role in the hierarchy of the logic imbued in the narrative. Less controversially, the Passion narratives of the Gospels include the brutal particularities of Roman execution methods. But the narrative logic does not direct our focus upon Roman execution. Narrative logic helps us to sort discrete items in the narrative, and more importantly, give them some sort of systematicity.

Although I will not employ narrative analysis to the ritual texts, we must consider that such an analysis might have had more explanatory power regarding the focus of the rite. If we had real access to the rites described in the

---

63. We are not discussing here whether or not the ritual texts (e.g., Leviticus) are narratival, but whether or not performing the rite itself has a narrative structure. See: Brian D. Bibb, *Ritual Words and Narrative Worlds in the Book of Leviticus* (LHBOTS 480; New York: T&T Clark, 2009).

64. In saying that rituals might follow a narrative structure, we can do so without also presuming what Catherine Bell critiqued in prior ritual theory (i.e., it is unnecessary to presume here that rituals are the practices invented to resolve a conflict merely because a conflict can be resolved within a ritual). Bell, *Ritual Theory, Ritual Practice*, 47–54.

65. Choon Leong Seow, "Textual Orientation," in *Biblical Ethics and Homosexuality: Listening to Scripture* (ed. Robert Lawson Brawley; Louisville, KY: Westminster John Knox, 1996), 21–24. See also: William Loader, *The New Testament on Sexuality* (Grand Rapids, MI: Eerdmans, 2012), 28–30.

biblical texts, such an analysis might instruct us on how to organize the particularities, the logic, and the hierarchy of the rite.

Conclusions

Thus far, provisional reasons have been given for approaching the rites of Israel, maintaining that rituals are best understood as 1) scripted, 2) prepared for and performed, 3) logical, and 4) formative for an Israelite's knowledge. The category "symbolic" is noticeably absent from my list of attributes above. I do not want to deny any symbolism of the elements and actions in Israelite rituals. However, symbolism has been well-studied and interpretations abound. With Roy Gane, I would like to suggest that these rites are not mere symbolism, as the actions and artifacts of ritual do not always seem to have a clear meaning in themselves.[66] Returning to our opening example of Pesach, is Passover week a ritual or a ceremony, or both? It should now be clear that this poses a false dichotomy. Two better questions might be: How do the various practices of Pesach distinguish themselves from daily Israelite behavior? And, how does this ritualized behavior shape the participants' views of themselves in relation to their community and God? These two questions will be pursued further in the ritual logic of the Torah and beyond (Part III).

Though ritual theorists have offered several universal definitions of ritual[67] that try to answer to the question "What is ritual for?"[68] I am skirting the

---

66. Roy E. Gane, *Cult and Character: Purification Offerings, Day of Atonement, and Theodicy* (Winona Lake, IN: Eisenbrauns, 2005), 7–8. Though Gane cites Catherine Bell as an influence on his own ritual theory, he sometimes appears to also imbibe in, or flirt with, the very style of thinking she critiques: the thinking-acting dichotomy.

67. Universalized definitions of ritual and sacrifice range from metaphysical to political. As an example of metaphysical: "Sacrifice . . . is defined not as an act of willful loss or appeasements made in fear, but as a means to create sacred spaces, imbue houses with sacred power, create bonds between people, and act as a supernatural link to the ancestors." Sharon Moses, "Sociopolitical Implications of Neolithic Foundation Deposits and the Possibility of Child Sacrifice," in *Sacred Killing*, 58. Fritts Staal's nihilistic definition: "Ritual is pure activity, without meaning or goal." "The Meaninglessness of Ritual," *Numen* 26, no. 1 (1975): 9. Nerissa Russell offers the most utilitarian definition: "the most useful definition of sacrifice is ritual slaughter." "Hunting Sacrifice at Neolithic Çatalhöyük" in *Sacred Killing*, 87. A transactional view: "offering of something of value either in appeasement or homage to a higher power(s)." Elizabeth Carter, "On Human and Animal Sacrifice," in *Sacred Killing*, 97. Rites as instrumental in sociopolitical shifts of power is most famously espoused by Meyer Fortes: "Ritual mobilizes incontrovertible authority behind the granting of office and status and thus guarantees its legitimacy and imposes accountability for its proper exercise." "Ritual and Office in Tribal Society," in *Essays on the Ritual of Social Relations* (ed. Max Gluckman; New York: Manchester University Press, 1966), 86.

problems associated with those approaches in favor of Bell's suggestion that the local texts of ritual and the practices themselves might have the right to define the rites.

> Rather than impose categories of what is or is not ritual, it may be more useful to look at how human activities establish and manipulate their own differentiation and purposes—in the very doing of the act within the context of other ways of acting.[69]

Hence, we will consider first and foremost what the Scripture deems as ritual and how those authors depict rites as differentiated for epistemological purposes—in order that Israel might know.

---

68. Glenn Schwartz lists the following "global or universal theories": 1) gifting, 2) nourishment for the deity, 3) devotion, 4) communion, and 5) averting other acts of violence. "Archaeology and Sacrifice," in *Sacred Killing*, 3–7. René Girard's renowned suggestion fleshes out the problematic actions associated with averting violence. Namely, the violence is redirected in rituals of all societies. *The Scapegoat* (trans. Yvonne Frecero; Baltimore: John Hopkins University Press, 1986).

69. Bell, *Ritual Theory, Ritual Practice*, 74.

Chapter 3

How We Will Proceed:
Cautions and Liabilities of This Study

Having established some basic context and conceptual vocabulary, this study aims to clearly demonstrate that Israelite rituals, as conceived of and discussed in the Jewish Scriptures, have an epistemological goal. It is not my aim to describe the goal of ritual participation in detail, even where the text is explicit about the goal: "In order that you may know X."[1] Even if we agree that rites are meant to communicate *something* to Israel, I will restrict this examination mostly to the function that ritual plays in communicating that knowledge.[2] Basically, God is the authoritative voice that instructs Israel so that she might see what he or his prophet is showing her. Ritual becomes the embodied practice that shapes Israel *so that she can recognize and discern.* In the same way that one must learn to be a skilled user of the instruments and ideas of scientific inquiry prior to making discoveries, Israel must be skilled in rituals to discern what she is being shown. For instance, I can look down the same microscope as the pathologist, but I am in no way equally disposed to discern what she sees in that same microscope slide. I will argue that ritualized practice disposes one to recognize in order to finally discern.

The goal of this study is *not* to arrive at the discourse of knowledge that Israel was meant to know by participating in sacrifice. Rites do not convey information, or as Bell clarifies, "One is never confronted with 'the meaning' to

---

1. Projects like those undertaken by Frank H. Gorman, Jr. envision the Priestly literature of the Hebrew Bible as "doing theology." Gorman espouses an entangled framework of epistemic goals that he then unfolds and articulates for the reader. "The rituals depicted in the texts, however, present a means by which the Priests thought their world of meaning and significance could be enacted, actualized, and realized. The Priestly ritual texts, thus, embody the Priests' thinking 'theologically'; the rituals proper present ways of 'doing' theology." *Ideology of Ritual: Space, Time and Status in the Priestly Theology* (LHBOTS; Sheffield, England: JSOT Press, 1990), 229.

Gorman gives a four-part answer to his own question, "What is communicated?" Each of these essentially acts as an epistemic goal for ritual participation: 1) status of individuals, 2) status of society, 3) status of the cosmos, and 4) the status of God in relation to the individual, community, or cosmos. *Ideology of Ritual*, 37–38.

accept or reject; one is always led into a redundant, circular, and rhetorical universe of values and terms whose significance keeps flowing into other values."[3] To the contrary, we suggest that the theological matrix meant to be known via the ritual life of Israel is lost to us. Jonathan Z. Smith makes the stronger claim that we do not even have access to the rites of Israel through the Torah, but rather "scattered, theoretical reconstructions of what may have happened." Smith declares, "You cannot perform a single biblical ritual on the basis of what is given to you in the text. If you can't perform it, then by definition it is not a ritual."[4] Because the rites of Israel must be practiced in order to know, and we cannot embody Israel's rhetorical universe—her life, land, or logic of ritual—we are separated from Israel's precise knowledge. Our access to her ritualed life is vestigial—even in the ritualized versions of Israel's rites in modern Christianity and Judaism. Although we need not pursue knowledge content exhaustively, I must show that the Scriptures certainly frame Israel's participation in epistemological terms, even more, as instrumental in disposing Israel to know. For if a ritualed life is part of how Israel knows reality—theologically and otherwise—then the continuation of ritualed life in Christianity bears the same functions. In other words, if rituals brought Israel to know something, then the modified rituals of Israel practiced apart from a temple, pilgrimage, and priesthood can also bring us to know what YHWH is showing us today. Another study would have to take on this task in full, as this prolegomenon means to offer the tools for such an analysis. In brief, the remainder of this study will establish that:

1. ritual fits into a epistemological process depicted in Scripture,
2. ritual is portrayed within Scripture as having a necessary epistemological function,
3. ritual's epistemological function is fully commensurate with biblical epistemology, and,
4. current scientific epistemology offers a comparable framework.

---

2. Bell, *Ritual Theory, Ritual Practice*, 106.

3. Jonathan Z. Smith, whose comments were quoted by Jonathan Klawans, *Purity, Sacrifice, and the Temple: Symbolism and Supersessionism in the Study of Ancient Judaism* (Oxford: Oxford University Press, 2006), 52. Other projects, such as Gruenwald's, take issue with the idea of ritual theory being able to cover the gamut of activities in Scripture. He prefers instead to posit that each rite has its own discrete ritual theory embedded within it. Unfortunately, the critique of ritual theory waged by Catherine Bell does not seem to have penetrated Gruenwald's analysis. And so, its value is more potential and idiosyncratic than actual for my purposes here. Ithamar Gruenwald, *Rituals and Ritual Theory in Ancient Israel* (Atlanta: Society of Biblical Literature, 2003), 1–7. Gerald A. Klingbeil, in a wide-ranging and helpful book on biblical ritual, spells out the many possible functions of Israelite ritual. The "communicative dimension" appears most in common with my thesis in that ritual can communicate subltly things not directly symbolized by the elements and actions of the rite itself, such as social standing. *Bridging the Gap: Ritual and Ritual Texts in the Bible* (BBRS; ed. Richard S. Hess; Winona Lake, IN: Eisenbrauns, 2007), 212–14.

We are compelled, regardless of our broader theological views, to consider how Israel's rituals functioned toward knowledge for a variety of reasons. However, I would like to consider one already discussed in Maimonides. The Rambam's overriding concern was the absent-minded performance of ritual, from which participants could not trace the reasonableness of the rite.[5] His concern is funded, as is mine, by the presumption that rituals teach us something. If rituals are simply magic, then Israel should enchant YHWH by rote performance. I want to go further and suggest that the Scriptures themselves speak directly against a mere rote performance of rites.

If Israelites should learn through participation, then the present task requires me to show how ritual might confer a disposition to know. In current psychological studies of nonverbal behavior, a truism exists that nonverbal behavior must be commensurate with verbal communication. When a conflict between our verbal and nonverbal communication occurs (i.e., Your words say "yes," but your body says "no."), the nonverbal is considered more veracious. In most cases, so-called "body language" trumps "verbal language."[6]

I am suggesting that this observation in psychology extends back to the practices of Israel. At some level, there must be commensurability between her nonverbal ritualized practices and her articulated knowledge of the world. Again, I am not seeking to expound the knowledge, but to consider how rites dispose one to know. Recent work in nonverbal psychology has even suggested that embodied acts shape thinking, and hence, the notion that nonverbal behavior merely expresses thought is under fire. "[T]he assumption that language functions to express thinking and abstract ideas and that nonverbal communication does not, and indeed cannot be used for this sort of thing, may also be incorrect."[7] In sum, embodied actions can form *and* express abstract thinking, but the fact that the two are inextricably linked for psychologists should be impetus enough for considering the present thesis.

Cautionary Warnings

Even in the tentative description of ritual above, a narrower methodology must be further justified. In the essay, "Studying Ancient Israelite Ritual:

---

4. Maimonides, *Guide to the Perplexed*, III/26.

5. Although Beattie critiques some methodological assumptions of Mehrabian's original research and Mehrabian's argument for two distinct languages, nonverbal and verbal, he supports the truism because of its veracity in the research that ensued because of it. I find Beattie's critique compelling and it integrates nicely with this project. However, for us folk psychologists, the two-language distinction is readily understood by everyone. Geoffrey Beattie, *Visible Thought: The New Psychology of Body Language* (New York: Routledge, 2003), 36; Albert Mehrabian and Morton Wiener, "Decoding of inconsistent communications," *JPSP* 6 (1967): 109–114.

6. Beattie, *Visible Thought*, 36.

Methodological Considerations," Wesley Bergen posits four cardinal cautions which directly confront this present study. They are worth enumerating here with response.[8]

Texts, not Rituals

First, Bergen rightly notes that there are no rituals to study. Or as James Watts puts it, "texts are not rituals and rituals are not texts."[9] This striking problem must be confessed at the outset, as we have no access to the actual embodied rituals of Israel. We have texts and scant archaeology, but mainly texts. In a time when anthropologists are claiming that a more intimate and less clinical approach is preferred to study the embodied nature of ritual, I face the opposite problem here: no rituals at all.[10] In light of this, Bergen suggests humility about the claims we can make and the recognition that we are not studying rituals, but texts about rituals (Figure 3.1).[11]

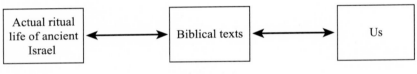

Figure 3.1

I hope to partially bridge the gap between text and history by considering two current embodied ritual practices that might provide fruitful links. These links are only helpful inasmuch as they demonstrate without imposing or pre-

---

7. Wesley Bergen, "Studying Ancient Israelite Ritual: Methodological Considerations," *RC* 1, no. 5 (2007): 579–86.

8. James W. Watts, *Ritual and Rhetoric in Leviticus: From Sacrifice to Scripture* (New York: Cambridge University Press, 2007), 29.

9. Gillian Goslinga offers an insightful view into South Indian rites namely because she removed the clinical distance and acknowledged the blur between observer and ritual participant: "This essay is intended, therefore . . . not as an analytic, etic interpretation of what sacrifice is and what it does, but as an emotive, sensory experience in which relationships between observer and participant, archaeologist and material, believer and unbeliever, worshiper and worshiped shift even as we read." "On Cakti-Filled Bodies and Divinities," in *Sacred Killing: The Archaeology of Sacrifice in the Ancient Near East* (eds. Glenn M. Schwartz and Anne Porter; Winona Lake, IN: Eisenbrauns, 2012), 33.

10. This reality causes Watts to open his study of Israelite ritual with a series of questions that point to the textuality of Israelite ritual study: Why did P write about these rituals? What did P think the rituals meant? Do P's descriptions reflect actual practice? What did these rituals mean in ancient Israel? How did these rituals function in ancient Israel? Watts, *Ritual and Rhetoric in Leviticus*, 27–29.

suming beyond our purview of inference. Some Israelite practices continue in new ritualized form, both in Judaism and Christianity. Additionally, if this thesis explains human knowing in a more profound way, then I should expect to see the epistemological motifs in Scripture extend not only to religious ritual today, but to other practices as well. Hence, I will examine the ritualized practices of science for the possibility of kinship.

Language, not Rituals

Second, Bergen warns that the language of ritual experience might separate us from the essential core of rites. "Do words ever really convey either the emotions or the physical responses to ritual?"[12] Moreover, problems persist in understanding the words that we do have in the texts. "['Tame'] is usually translated as 'impure', but what does this mean when applied to a bodily discharge? Is it like 'yucky' or more like 'evil'?"[13] While language, linguistics, and hermeneutics all represent major challenges to understanding Israel's rituals, this challenge is tautological in that this is not a unique challenge concerning rites. This challenge is equally present when I try to understand the meaning of my daughter's words today. While the ubiquitous nature of hermeneutical challenges does not make them any less real, they also should not pose a terminal difficulty for any study of ritual.

Despite the philological challenges of all studies, I am not attempting to define key sacrificial terms and coordinate the terms through a matrix of meaning (e.g., whether or not *kippur* [כפר] means something more akin to "atonement" or "purgation").[14] Instead, I am focusing on how the Scriptures themselves conceive of ritual as part of the Israel need to know described throughout the Hebrew Bible.

Culture Loss

Third, cultural associations are almost entirely lost to us. "In our society, the problem is compounded because we react in horror to the killing of animals, yet happily consume meat in quantities unheard of in the ancient world."[15] This complication in understanding the meaning of the ritual has some spillover into my procedure. I will argue that rituals help to shape analogical meaning, embodied in order to see what is being shown. However, if the analogs—

---

11. Bergen, "Studying Ancient Israelite Ritual," 582.

12. Ibid., 582.

13. An excellent example of overcoming such linguistic challenge is Jay Sklar, *Sin, Impurity, Sacrifice, Atonement: The Priestly Conceptions* (HBM; Sheffield, England: Sheffield Phoenix, 2005).

14. Bergen, "Studying Ancient Israelite Ritual," 583.

the real life and palpable referents of the analogy—of the meaning are lost to us, our cultural distance will mitigate our access to that meaning.

Again, if this study was seeking the meaning of the rite itself, this challenge poses severe limitations. Direct implications flow, however, for how we are to understand knowledge itself. This is complicated by the semantic range, where sexual intercourse and knowing Israel's history are described by the same verb: *yada* (ידע). Because of the culture of intellectualism in the West, my students often have trouble explaining how the word for "know" could span the range it has in Biblical Hebrew. Conversely, when I teach in rural parts of East Africa, students generally connect so naturally to the agrarian culture of the biblical texts that I often gain insights by having them explain to me how they understand the texts. However, Bergen's caution acts as sufficient warning to not be naïve about our lexical *and* cultural understanding that we bring, the possibility of ideas etic to the texts.

Tradition Bias

Fourth, different traditions read Israel's ritual texts with varying priorities. We will arrive at divergent understandings of ritual depending on whether we believe that the Talmud or the apostle Paul is the authoritative interpreter of the Hebrew Bible. How can I ameliorate this caution other than to fully disclose below what takes priority in my interpretation? In brief, I want to allow the logic of ritual participation to unfold canonically in the Scriptures, which I will present in Part III. Hosea, Amos, Jesus, Paul, and the author of the Hebrews epistle will all be heard in Part III, where the Torah (i.e., Pentateuch) will be allowed to set the logic of the enterprise. Hence, primacy is given to the Torah and, even then, to Deuteronomy as interpreter of the Tetrateuch.

The Problem

With Catherine Bell's critique of ritual theory and Bergen's more precise warnings in mind, how shall I proceed? Both Bell and Bergen, among others, have recognized the value of ritual studies combined with increased understanding of the body (socially, physically, analogically, and theologically). This study skirts only some of the warnings above by not seeking to understand exactly what the rituals meant, but how they are used in epistemological process. Even then, I do not presume that knowing is the only outcome of ritual, but one of several outcomes.

Additionally, in focusing my study on the epistemological function of rites, I am also avoiding metaphysical questions such as:

Where is sin and where does it go once atoned?
Are rites theurgic or magic?
Is atonement transactional, and if so, is it *quid pro quo*?

These questions and others of similar kind focus on what rituals do *for* the practitioners. Although we all want answers to such questions, I will not pursue a cosmological explanation of ritual and its metaphysical relations. I am most interested in the sentiment, sometimes expressly stated and other times implied, that Israel should perform in rites "so that you may know X." Once more, it is beyond the scope of this volume to argue for the content of X, but the goal is rather to understand the functional relationship between the rite *and* its stated outcome: "so that you may know." In future research, I will pursue how Christian rituals appropriate much of the same epistemological content imbued by ancient Israelite rituals.

To state the problem directly, these biblical texts reveal that at least some rituals are specifically epistemological. Yet, if rites express beliefs and beliefs can be directly expressed in symbols, then the most natural course of examination would seek to map those beliefs to the actions, actors, and symbols in order to determine the theological meaning. I have already argued that this direct-expression approach is infeasible because it creates an artificial discourse premised upon the thinking-acting dichotomy where mental life is expressed externally.

Methodology

In the introduction, I considered a handful of examples in Scripture where knowledge was a central concern and rituals were employed epistemologically. I will revisit those examples and present more, building a case canonically from Genesis forward. Although this approach has had some detractors, I want to allow the Hebrew Bible and New Testament texts to unfurl the use of rituals for epistemological purposes and delimit my analysis to that unfolding description. This style of biblical theology allows for constructs to be posited in nascent form and developed without giving priority to later interpreters wherever possible.[16] In this sense, we are blinding ourselves to what will be

---

15. Methodologically, I recognize Barr's warning: "The possibility of biblical theology remains, even for its own practitioners, a very precarious thing." James Barr, *The Concept of Biblical Theology: An Old Testament Perspective* (London: SCM, 1999), 229. Hence, this study is guided by Watson's call to lower the "lines of demarcation" between biblical studies and systematic theology. Francis Watson, *Text and Truth: Redefining Biblical Theology* (Grand Rapids, MI: Eerdmans, 1997), 1–29. See also Ted M. Dorman's critique of the Barthian aspects of Watson's proposal that go unstated: "The Future of Biblical Theology," in *Biblical Theology: Retrospect and Prospect* (ed. Scott J. Hafemann; Leicester, England: Apollos, 2002), 250–66. And finally, the warning of F. F. Bruce is ever-present: "This is not to say that the tracing of patterns is illegitimate, but that it should not be pressed beyond the plain sense of the biblical narrative and language. It is better to think of recurring patterns of divine action and human response . . . all the more so because such recurring patterns were recognized by the biblical authors themselves, in

later developed. By way of illustration, Pesach's significance will not be found in its Christian form (i.e., communion), but as the rite that Israel is command-ed to celebrate—a command that preceded the liberation it means to recount.

Examining Biblical Texts

In my previous work, *Biblical Knowing*, I employed a heuristic for refraining from over-emphasizing texts as epistemological. For example, only a quick search of the term "know" is required to see that the word pervades the can-on. However, not all employments of the term are equal. At times, knowing is described through sensory language (i.e., "to see")[17] or the term "to know" is used innocuously, providing no real insights into biblical epistemology. Some previous studies have used the statistical density of epistemic vocabulary as the basis of their selection of texts, but I will not.[18]

Consequently I rely upon a three part heuristic for determining the legit-imate extent of a passage's epistemological insights: presence, relevance, and persistence. First, epistemological language must be present in a passage ei-ther explicitly or implicitly. For instance, a passage might speak about ritual without epistemological language in the immediate context, but if the passage acts as a premise *of* or inference *from* the epistemological rhetoric in context, then it meets the criterion of presence.

Second, the epistemological language must be relevant. Mere presence of terms will not suffice. The passages where knowing is discussed, but not de-veloped in any significant way, may take part in a larger philological argu-

---

both Testaments." *This is That: The New Testament Development of Some Old Testament Themes* (Exeter, England: Paternoster, 1968), 14.

16. My approach is meant to be commensurate with Nicholas Perrin's solution to the polarities of traditional biblical theologies and Bakhtin's social matrix of language meaning at the nexus of external reality. If biblical unity can be resolved, then dispar-ate texts can speak univocally, even if approximately, of similar constructs. "Dialogic Conceptions of Language and the Problem of Biblical Unity" in *The Practice and Promise of Biblical Theology* (ed. Scott J. Hafemann; Minneapolis: Fortress, 1991), 212–24; M. M. Bakhtin, *The Dialogic Imagination: Four Essays* (ed. Michael Holquist; trans. Caryl Emerson and Michael Holquist; Austin: University of Texas, 1981), 252–4. This "dialogic nature of language" allows us to be co-readers of the biblical texts just as first century Jews saw themselves as co-readers of the Hebrew Bible. See also, Craig Bartholomew, "Story and Biblical Theology" in *Out of Egypt: Biblical Theology and Biblical Interpretation* (eds. Mary Healy, et al.; SHS; Grand Rapids, MI: Zondervan, 2004).

17. See further, Yael Avrahami, *The Senses of Scripture: Sensory Perception in the He-brew Bible* (LHBOTS 545; New York: T&T Clark International, 2012), 223–75.

18. Douglas Yoder, "Tanakh Epistemology: A Philosophical Reading of an Ancient Semitic Text" (Ph.D. diss., Claremont Graduate University, 2007), 94. Sometimes, the philological density of a term in a particular passage or text is significant (i.e., זקר [zaqar] in Deuteronomy), but not always.

ment, but not one which we will discuss here. For instance, the term "know" is used strategically three times in the literary structure of Genesis 4. Clearly, knowing is present in that chapter. However, the author uses the term to mean "procreate" and so there is no obvious relevance of the idea of knowing, despite the repeated presence of the term.

Third, the terms and constructs of epistemology must be persistent in the logic of the texts examined. A simple allusion to knowledge as a state of affairs is less interesting than a persistent interest that a character ought to know something in a particular way. The idea of persistence also demands that I analyze instances of knowing and ritual in terms of their character context. Noticeably, the content of what YHWH and/or Jesus know is of much less interest to biblical authors than what Israelites or resident aliens know.

Narrative context will often determine our degree of confidence. Generally, when biblical authors speak of YHWH's knowledge—and God is the subject—we have the least degree of confidence about what is known and how. Conversely, first and second person accounts where God is not the subject generally yield the highest degree of confidence. The descriptions in such cases are generally more rich and persistent than when the divine character is the subject. For instance, there is not a concerted effort to show the reader exactly how the nations will "listen and know" (Jer 6:18) about YHWH and Israel, apart from the contexts of judgment (e.g., Ezek 30:26) or eschatology (e.g., Ezek 37:28). Israel and Israelites as the prime characters of these epistemological texts become the natural objects of character development, which includes their epistemological development.

To sum up, I will concentrate this examination on passages where the development of epistemological categories or process can be legitimated. I proceed fully aware of the following:

1. We have no direct access to the knowledge that Israelites possessed by practicing the same rituals.
2. We have no access to the Israelite rituals as practiced *in situ*.
3. If Mary Douglas is correct, then Scripture associates the symbolic meaning of rituals to the social body of Israel. We do not have access to that social body within which the symbols find their meaning.
4. We only have access to a text, which prescribes the process of ritualized practice with modest interpretation, but no clear statement of the precise epistemic goal. For Christian theology, we also have direct access to a rich nexus of ritual practice from which we can look for analogous content and structure today.

Ritualized Practice in Scientific Epistemology

What is the epistemological goal of ritual more generally? I cannot neglect the fact that participation in ritual intends to teach something, even if an objective observer can identify no precise content. As a terse illustration, the epistemological goal of ritual might be akin to the goal of a scientific training ritual. The ritualized practice of using an oscilloscope is not knowledge content that can be analyzed, but rather, a skilled knowing that enables a one to extend her observation of reality to the electrical "world of discourse." The rituals of oscilloscope adjustment and electrical observation are only interesting inasmuch as they dispose one to see reality from that perspective.

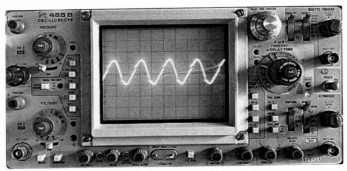

Figure 3.2[19]

It would be a mistake, however, to focus one's pursuit of electrical understanding to the content of oscilloscope use (e.g., memorizing all the rules for using an oscilloscope). Rather, the rituals of oscilloscope use merely dispose one to see electrical signals symbolically (see Figure 3.2 for a symbolic representation of an electrical wavelength). Similarly, that which is discerned by means of the oscilloscope cannot be reduced to factitive knowledge either. Michael Polanyi laid the groundwork for the sober depiction of a scientist's knowledge as ineffable, but real and rigorous nonetheless. He called this "tacit knowledge," that which is only known to the scientist herself, because she is practiced in seeing it.[20] Frederick Grinnell laments the compression of the scientist's tacit understanding into an "announcement of discovery," which deflates the history, habits, and location that allowed the practiced scientist to discover it in the first place:

> Textbooks usually present facts without clarifying where and how
> they arise. . . . *The consequence is that practice becomes invisible.* The
> more common the knowledge, the more anonymous will be its
> source. Years of research are compressed into one or several sen-

19. Gdirwin (Wikimedia user), RAV4_Tach_750rpm.JPG, image, 17 Oct 2009, http://commons.wikimedia.org/wiki/File:RAV4_Tach_750rpm.JPG

20. Michael Polanyi, *Personal Knowledge: Towards a Post-Critical Philosophy* (Chicago: University of Chicago Press, 1974), 90–91.

tences. At the same time, the adventure, excitement, and risks of real-life discovery disappear.[21]

Anyone who has learned to use a measuring instrument like the oscilloscope knows that, after time, one embodies the tool almost as an extension of oneself in order to see the relevant signals. The ritualized practice disposes one to see the signal, but even then, one must interpret the signal. If it is agreeable that seeing a signal—a point of knowing—on an oscilloscope requires practiced seeing, then it appears reasonable to also scrutinize the rituals that foster and enable such sight.

I want to pursue the idea that the Hebrew Scriptures use ritualized practice for a similar effect. *The epistemological goal is not to inculcate Israel with a non-verbal symbolic logic of rites that reflect beliefs (or beliefs that should be held).* Rather, Scripture describes a ritualed life of Israel which produces persons trained to see—properly disposed to interpret reality accurately. This approach could also help to explain the epistemological status of Israel in the eschaton as portrayed by prophets, a topic to which we will return in chapter ten.

---

21. Italics in the original. Frederick Grinnell, *Everyday Practice of Science: Where Intuition and Passion Meet Objectivity and Logic* (New York: Oxford University Press, 2009), 6.

Part II

The General Case for Ritual Knowing

Chapter 4

The Biblical Idea of Truth
and Its Consequences for Rituals

The Nature of Biblical Truth

"The sky is blue."

If I believe the above sentence is true, the reasons for its truth must be explored before discussing how the biblical literature develops ways of discovering truly. Specifically, I need to consider if my own presumptions about truth might be running interference, blocking me from the biblical conception of truth. When I aver in undergraduate classes that the biblical authors cannot conceive of a simple notion of "absolute truth," some students immediately go into epistemic arrest. Many of them have been taught their whole lives that absolute truth—sometimes known as "capital-T Truth"—is the ideal and everything else is "little-t truth." Not only does this idea of truth risk importing very dangerous notions into the biblical world, but it also does not make sense of the epistemological task. I will eventually show that this view does not make sense in *any* epistemological structure that can account for religious and scientific knowledge without reducing them both to mere caricatures.

Several philosophical theories of truth attempt to give the most reasonable view in assessing whether a proposition such as "The sky is blue" is true or false. The most popular in religious circles, the correspondence theory of truth, generally maintains that a proposition is true when the reality to which it refers actually is the case (Figure 4.1).[1] The proposition represented by the sentence, "The sky is blue," is true *if and only if* (*iff*) the sky is actually blue. Other theories of truth work out the same problem, but use a different metric for truth than correspondence. Coherence theories seek to situate the truth of a proposition in a larger logically connected scheme, within which it is coherent. Truth means making sense in a given web of knowledge. For coherence

---

1. According to a recent survey, approximately 62% of philosophers, largely from the Anglo-American tradition, believe in some kind of correspondence theory of truth ("The overall list included 62 departments in the US, 18 in the UK, 10 in Europe outside the UK, 7 in Canada, and 5 in Australasia."). David Bourget and David J. Chalmers, "What Do Philosophers Believe?" *PS* 170, no. 3 (September 2014): 465–500.

theory, "a true proposition is one that coheres appropriately with certain other propositions."[2] Then there are pragmatic views of truth (i.e., it is true if it works), which have the admirable quality of being inextricably tied to reality, but also bring some ethical baggage. The traction needed to define "it works" has a slippery history.[3]

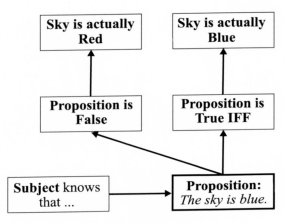

Figure 4.1

What must be observed in these approaches to truth is that the proposition functions as the centerpiece of truth or falsity. True and false are posited as opposite ends in binary relationship and are applied to an idea or state of affairs, *disembodied and independent of the knowing subject* (Figure 4.1).

In this chapter, my two goals are to re-orient us to the biblical notion of "truth" and then propose an epistemological process where rituals move the knower toward recognizing and then discerning through the body. After seeing how biblical authors used truth conceptually, we are left without recourse to a merely binary conception, where we know something to be either true or false. Rather, we always and constantly know something more *truly* or less so. Truth is fidelity. Obviously, discussions such as this cause many readers epistemological duress, especially if they have assimilated various and popular definitions of truth from recent philosophical thinking. Even more, this can make for an uncomfortable conversation for those who have simply mapped those contemporary views of truth directly onto their reading of Scripture.

---

2. Robert Audi, *Epistemology: A Contemporary Introduction to the Theory of Knowledge* (3rd ed.; New York: Routledge, 2011), 288.

3. See discussion on Naturalized Epistemology in Dru Johnson, *Biblical Knowing: A Scriptural Epistemology of Error* (Eugene, OR: Cascade, 2013), 169–71.

However, any view of truth that hopes to accurately reflect the biblical construct must wrestle with the fact that the term for truth (אמת) in the Hebrew Bible modifies:

> actions (e.g., treatment toward a servant,[4] anointing,[5] walking,[6]), statements,[7] and
> things (tent pegs,[8] roads,[9] seeds,[10]).

Similarly, in the New Testament, truth (ἀλήθεια) describes people,[11] actions,[12] statements,[13] realizations,[14] and itself becomes nominalized as a metaphor for the faithful instruction of God: "the truth."[15] In fact, truthfulness becomes a supreme quality of important statements according to Jesus himself: "Truly I say to you (ἀληθῶς λέγω ὑμῖν)," describing his speech as truly guiding, not as statements of truth.[16]

How is a tent peg true in the same way that reports or actions are true? We must begin this discussion by frankly admitting the semantic distance between the modern English "true" and the ancient Hebrew *emet* (אמת). Yoram Hazony explores this problem in *The Philosophy of Hebrew Scripture*, and I will follow him closely here where he concludes about true speech:

> [W]e could say that *emet* and truth are simply two different things. What prevents us from reaching this conclusion is not only the traditional translation of *emet* as truth . . . it is also the fact that *emet* is the only term available to describe the truth of speech in the Bible. Thus if we were to dispense with the term *emet* as referring to the truth of speech, we would be left without any way in which biblical Hebrew could express the idea that something that someone said or thought was true![17]

True, in Scripture, does not refer to the tradition of truth that posits the statement itself as independent of our reality. For instance, Scripture does not

---

4. Gen 32:10.
5. Judg 9:15.
6. 1 Kgs 2:4.
7. Deut 17:4.
8. Isa 22:23.
9. Gen 24:38.
10. Jer 2:21.
11. E.g., Jesus, Matt 22:16; teacher, Mark 12:14; worshipers, John 4:23.
12. E.g., practicing truth, John 3:21; standing in truth, John 8:44; sanctifying in truth, John 17:17.
13. Mark 5:53; Luke 4:25; Acts 26:25.
14. Matt 27:54; Mark 14:17.
15. Rom 1:25; 2:8.
16. Luke 12:44.
17. Yoram Hazony, *The Philosophy of Hebrew Scripture: An Introduction* (New York: Cambridge University Press, 2012), 338, n. 36.

seem to contain a persistently developed notion that it is true that "Jesus is the Christ" independent of whether or not anyone knows this to be the case. Hazony incisively shows what many philologists and biblical scholars have observed for some time—that Scripture does develop a notion of truth as a function of reliability. Despite whatever denotations and connotations we have packed into the word "true," should not the *emic* meaning of "truth" in the vernacular of the Scriptural authors have some sway with those of us doing theological work?[18]

Without rehearsing his entire argument here, Hazony's critique of the slip and grip between our notion of truth and Scriptural lexicography is worth considering in detail. Scripture employs *emet* similarly to the narrower sense in which "true" is used in carpentry today.[19] A true cut (or maintaining a true course in a ship) is one that reliably "is what it ought to be": "[I]n the Hebrew Bible, that which is true is that which proves, in the face of time and circumstance, to be what it ought; whereas that which is false is that which fails . . . to be what it ought."[20]

This view cannot be confused with the correspondence theory of truth precisely because the truth of the something is not synchronic or independent of the thinker. This runs counter to the correspondence theory of truth, where discerning the proposition "Jesus is the Christ," and saying "Jesus is the Christ," are equally true because there is an independent proposition that at-

---

18. James Barr pursues the problematic insistence by both theologians that there is a "fundamental meaning" of a Hebrew word root (e.g., אמן). Their debate then proceeds by arguing for this fundamental meaning, and according to Barr, commits several hermeneutical fallacies in the process. See "'Faith' and 'Truth'" in James Barr, *The Semantics of Biblical Language* (Oxford: Oxford University Press, 1967). See also: A. G. Hebert, "'Faithfulness' and 'Faith,'" *Reformed Theological Review* 14, no. 2 (June 1955): 33–40; T. F. Torrance, "One Aspect of the Biblical Conception of Faith," *ET* 68, no. 4 (January 1957): 111–114. To be sensitive to Barr's critique, this analysis must proceed with an affinity to sentences bearing theological meaning within larger contexts, both narratival and rhetorical. This means that support for a theological position cannot be asserted solely based on individual terms (e.g., ידע, ראה, שמע, etc.). Rather, support must be demonstrated from the linguistic context from which those terms gain their meaning. It might be further argued that the larger narrative structures often bear the ultimate theological meaning, as pithy truisms do not occur in a narratival vacuum. The conflict, narrative tension, characters, and plot movement toward resolution all can play on the words and meaning to such a degree that the story becomes the ultimate context for the lexical stock, thereby nullifying the notion of "lexical stock" itself. Something similar has been argued in "The Narrative Approach to Paul" where the *dianoia* (i.e., interpretive framework) applied to the Hebrew Bible and Gospel narratives constrain the rhetorical meaning of the Paul's letters. Bruce W. Longenecker, "The Narrative Approach to Paul: an Early Retrospective," *CBR* 1, no. 1 (October 2002): 94–103.

19. Because I can appeal to the carpenter's sense of "true," we do maintain one sense of the biblical denotation in the semantic range the English word "true."

20. Hazony, *The Philosophy of Hebrew Scripture*, 201.

tains truth upon the objective reality that "Jesus actually is the Christ." This is how correspondence theory might construe the matter. Rather, Hazony contends, "We find, therefore, that to adopt the biblical account of truth and falsity has the following consequence: that the truth and falsity of speech is found to be dependent on the truth and falsity of the object [or person] to which this speech refers."[21]

Two factors then become central aspects for biblical truth: diachronic proofing and interpretation. Hazony uses the phrase "proves, in the face of time and circumstance" to mean that truth, by its very nature, cannot be determined in a singular instance. Truth can only be interpreted through a process of attending to something's veracity—its reliability. In addressing the question of how a tent peg and speech can both be considered diachronically true, the matter of interpretation becomes primary. Faithfulness of the peg to do what it ought to do—to hold down the tent in sun and storm—is the hallmark of its *emet*. So it goes with speech; its veracity, fidelity, or faithfulness to interpret that to which it speaks is its truth, like the carpenter's true cut or the ship's true course.

This notion, that truth captures the fidelity between what is and what ought to be, makes sense of the cognate terms of *emet*. One of the few Hebraisms to persist in English religious language, *amen* is from the root term *emet*, as well as *emunah*, often translated both from the verb and adjective as "faithful." To propose that truth is more like veracity or faithfulness does have currency in modern English. However, it is the conceptual barrier that truth is a thing in and of itself that often distances us from the biblical meaning.

Although Hazony does not explore the matter of speech as interpretation, it must be resident in his thinking in order for speech to be true in the biblical sense. The problem of espousing brute sight also has implications for brute speech as well. When speech is referred to as "true," this indicates that it reliably interprets actual events or objects. Many statements can be offered, but the true one interprets best. Notice that in this last statement, "the true one interprets best," true does not refer to the offered statement *in se*, but the interpretation of the offerer. Just as with maps, the truest map serves its purpose best (e.g., to guide tourists to landmarks, to reveal water systems, to navigate highways, etc.). However, *the map itself is not true* in the biblical sense. Rather, the instruction of the cartographer by instrumental means of the map is true. Hence, truth will always have an epistemologically prior function, speaking to the relationship between knowers and the referents of what they are interpreting, that which they recognize and discern. To extend this example, we do not consider a water table map false merely because it does not lead tourists to local landmarks. Water table maps are not true to the aims of local tourism as tourist maps are not true to aquifer locations, but that does not make those

21. Ibid., 205.

maps fundamentally true or false. Again, the biblical sense of truth generally accounts for a thing doing what it ought to do per the context and *in situ*.[22]

This is why I argued in *Biblical Knowing* that, in this sense, a tent peg cannot be true/false *in se* any more than a proposition can be true/false *in se*.[23] The biblical sense of truth has the advantage of parsimony over the propositionally based views of truth, not requiring the existence of *ad extra* entities such as propositions in order to evince truth.

For instance, Deuteronomy discusses the possibility of a true report of adultery in the land. Specifically, in discussing how to deal with disobedience, Deuteronomy raises the matter of a report first and then its veracity. "If it is told," (נגד in the *hophal*) is followed by "and if the truth was established" (Deut 17:4). The relationship between that which was told and that which is true is not resolved by an extra and intervening proposition "Mr. X was adulterous," which is then determined to be true or false. The truth of the report is established by how well the reporter has interpreted the actions of the one reported. This veracity, the establishment of the truth of the matter, is necessarily a diachronic affair, unable to be true in an instant. On this theme, Hazony summarizes: "On the biblical conception, then, it would seem that the truth or falsity of the spoken word [i.e., interpretation] cannot be known until it has proved itself reliable in the course of investigation, which is to say, in the course of time."[24] As a term and concept, "true" functions epistemically and diachronically, not ontologically and synchronically.

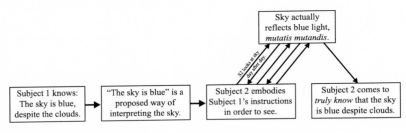

Figure 4.2

Essentially, Hazony argues for situating truth between the dialectic of persons and things—interpretation of events by persons over time. This requires an epistemological process robust enough to distinguish a non-binary version of truth from falsity. On this account, which we take to be foundational for understanding biblical epistemology, suggestions about absolute truth find no

---

22. I am not suggesting that there is no correspondence between reality and the guidance that disposes us to see it truly. Rather, I am arguing that traditional correspondence theory does not do justice to what biblical authors seem to be doing with truth as a term and concept.

23. Johnson, *Biblical Knowing*, 154–66.

24. Hazony, *The Philosophy of Hebrew Scripture*, 205.

home unless we make our true knowing contingent upon an absolute Being's will. We arrive at true statements, such as "The sky is blue," through diachronic knowing, embodied in order to be known (Figure 4.2). Just as a carpenter's cut can be true to a line, our knowing can be true to a correct understanding of matters great and small. In the Hebrew Bible and New Testament, a correct understanding conforms to the way YHWH intends Israel to know.

However, if a truth is absolute—X is true without reference to anyone's understanding of it, even God's understanding—then what can we say about such a truth? What would an absolute truth even look like that could be reasonably discussed without appeals to our active interpretation? Philosophically speaking, absolute here means "without reference to," in contrast to the idea of being relative to other truths.

As an analogy, Max Black demonstrated something similar with the notion of absolute position in space (the notion that there is a position in space independent of everything else).[25] Black offered a thought experiment presuming that there were two spheres in absolute space, meaning that they existed completely independent of anything. He then demonstrates that any attempt to describe one sphere will inevitably refer to either the other sphere or some location relative to the spheres. Without discussing the relative positions between the two spheres, they are indiscernible, possibly even the same sphere when described absolutely. In this experiment, Black succeeds in showing the absurdity of our attempt to have meaningful discussion about those two spheres, despite whether or not they exist in an absolute position in space. Merely trying to discriminate one from the other becomes an impossible task. A thin notion of absolute truth may turn out to be equally indiscernible and therefore inconsequential to a biblical view of understanding

To discuss without discernment a supposedly true thing apart from its context either brings talk of nonsense or the need to contextualize (i.e., "Sphere A is to the left of Sphere B"). But discussing the context defeats the purposes of designating it absolute. Or, "absolute" becomes an *ad hoc* faith position in the discussion of the spheres. While there might be such realities, they appear to us as wholly uninteresting at the very least, and more likely, indiscernible from other realities.[26] And as I have attempted to show, discernment is the very ideal of biblical knowing.

Another advantage to discussing truth in terms of the biblical vocabulary is that ethics and knowing are no longer separable. In order to know, and to know truly, we must hear another person's interpretation. We must indwell their vision of the thing, their lens for looking at the same reality, to see how true their interpretation is. Scientists call this repeatability. Hence, biblical knowing is fundamentally ethical, dictating what we ought to do in order to

25. Max Black, "The Identity of Indiscernibles," *Mind* 61 (April 1952): 153–164.
26. For a summary of why such "truths" are not helpful, or even accurate understandings of said truths, see Johnson, "Broad Reality and Contemporary Epistemology," in *Biblical Knowing*, 149–80.

discern finer and finer particularities. We will return to the relationship between knowing and ethics in Part IV.

Two Distinct Epistemological Stages

We often say "I don't know" in a binary sense opposed to "I do know." While admissions of ignorance often have a genuine basis, I want to argue that good knowing is depicted in Scripture on a continuum (Figure 4.3), moving from *insensitive-to-something's-presence* (unacculturated) to *able-to-recognize* (eureka) to *discernment* (discovery).

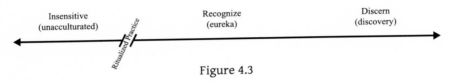

Figure 4.3

A working example for this conceptual continuum is second-language learning. Although this could easily extend to a culturally-specific language (e.g., Mineiro-Brazilian Portuguese, stock broker shop-talk, the ever-acronymistic military vernaculars, etc.), we will restrict our discussion to known languages. At the time of writing, I am currently living in Jerusalem and meeting with a Hebrew tutor. When I first begin to hear a new language, such as Israeli Hebrew, it is a cacophony of phonemes. Individual words rush together making them indistinguishable from each other. When we do not know a language, we are completely unacculturated to it. That language sounds to us like a wall of noise: flat, without contour or shape, and a barrier to communicating (Figure 4.4). We are insensitive to the lively acts of communication surrounding us, not because we are numb, but because we are unskilled and therefore, unknowing.

What makes us able to hear words and phrases rather than verbal static? When we submit ourselves to the disciplined practices of language learning, then we can begin to recognize units within the walls of sounds. Even though there are many language-learning systems, from private tutoring to software, what is central to my thesis is that they are systems. Language learning systems script practices which require the learner to submit to the system designer and embody their rituals of learning in order to hear the language and truly interpret what it means. These systems all have their own sets of rituals, but their rites are scripted, following a pattern in order to dispose the learner's ear to hear the new language.

Figure 4.4

After embodying these rites—repeatedly listening to the language, hearing words being defined in our native language, etc.—we can eventually begin to recognize, picking out a word or phrase on the streets. However, at the point when we are gaining the skill to recognize, we are heavily focused on the particular words and phrases, trying to break them down, but not yet seeing how they fit in the whole. We are not fluent hearers, but rather struggling to make sense of the flood of linguistic particularities that we are learning. When someone asks us "מה שלומך?", we are focused on the particulars of the words, trying to recognize them:

מה *means* "what"

שלום *means* "peace"

ך at the end of a noun *means* "your"

After enough practice of hearing, we can eventually discern what is meant. But our practice is not private, for the ability to recognize requires correction from an authoritative guide external to us, keeping us on the true course, and scripting our language learning rites. By saying "What [is] your peace," this person is actually asking, "How are you?" The particular words have moved from our central focus into a subsidiary background as our focus shifts to the meaning of the words themselves and the context in which they were stated.

As an example of recognizing in the visual field, Esther Meek has shown how computer-generated autostereogram images (known under the trademark "3D Magic Eye") can demonstrate to us the difference between unacculturated ignorance, recognizing, and discerning.[27] When first confronted with the wall of visual static in an autostereogram, there are nothing but particu-

27. I first discovered this apt illustration through philosopher Esther L. Meek, who has used 3D Magic Eye images in her epistemology classes for years as an artifact to show how scripted practices guide the knower to see what is already there.

lars on which to focus (Figure 4.5). Even the patterns in the static are deceptive, as they are not constitutive of the actual embedded image meant to be seen in three dimensions.

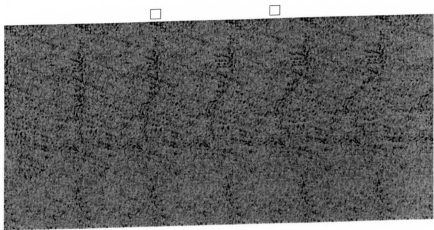

Figure 4.5

One could conceivably stare all day and never see the image there in the autostereogram. However, seeing can be enabled by instructions, rites which one can embody in order to see the embedded image—to move from unacculturated to recognizing. These instructions below are taken directly from the makers of the commercial autostereograms. In their scripts, they use two boxes above the image in order to ritualize the practice of looking for the novice. It is also worth noticing that the instructions, if taken literally, are nonsense. They must be embodied and in the act of submissively embodying them, the directions make the act logical:

> Hold the center of the printed image *right up to your nose.* It should be blurry. Focus as though you are looking *through* the image into the distance. *Very slowly* move the image away from your face until the *two squares* above the image turn into *three squares.* If you see four squares, move the image farther away from your face until you see three squares. If you see one or two squares, start over!

> When you clearly see three squares, hold the page still, and the hidden image will magically appear. Once you perceive the hidden image and depth, you can look around the entire 3D image. The longer you look, the clearer the illusion becomes. The farther away you hold the page, the deeper it becomes. Good Luck![28]

---

28. "3D Viewing Instructions," Magic Eye Inc., [Cited September 29, 2015]. Online: http://www.magiceye.com/faq_example.htm.

Through ritualized practice, we can come to recognize what was before us the whole time, to see what was already there in the picture. The practice is ritualized because it is a differentiated practice, of sorts, from regular observation. Normal looking will never get us to cross the logical gap that separates us from seeing the image embedded here. The instructions indicate that this is not normal looking, but a queer sort of "looking through" by embodying crossed eyes. The scripted practices are the only way to see what is already there. After embodying the rite, we begin to see something beyond the static of particularities. Our focus moves beyond the surface image of fuzziness and dots to the image beyond. Similarly, Polanyi describes the scientist's skill of looking beyond the particulars in order to see the present but unknown object:

> The admonition to look at the unknown really means that we should *look at the known data, but not in themselves, rather as clues to the unknown; as pointers to it and parts of it.* We should strive persistently to feel our way towards an understanding of the manner in which these known particulars hang together, both mutually and with the unknown. By such intimations do we make sure that the unknown is really there, essentially determined by what is known about it, and able to satisfy all the demands made on it by the problem.[29]

With enough embodied effort and submission to the scripted rite, we come to see in three dimensions. The visual static has become subsidiary to our new focus on the image of a shark, that although it is presented on a two-dimensional plane, it has three-dimensional depth to it (Figure 4.6).

At the point where we can see the shark and look around inside the depth of field, we can affirm that ritualized practice (and only ritualized practice) has led us to recognize that which was beyond the particulars of the surface image.[30] Further, we were logically separated from seeing the shark apart from embodying the rite (See Figure 4.7). This is a prime example of recognizing. However, we cannot yet affirm discernment, for that lies beyond recognizing. But in this instance, we can now see how one moves from insensitivity to recognition through the practice of ritual. Yet how do we distinguish the ability to recognize from discernment, which is not bridged by a logical gap but a gradation? Generally, we test people by showing them novel instances, subtler in detail, to assess their range of discernment. Assess your own skill of recognition with a different example (Figure 4.8).

---

29. Italics in original. Polanyi, *Personal Knowledge*, 127.

30. What about cases of accidental discovery? For instance, my wife claims to have seen the three dimensional image in autostereograms purely by accident. While this is possible, and some discovery is clearly a product of accident, it is not normative. Further, if I had asked my wife to teach me how to see the image upon her accidental discovery, she could not merely instruct me to look at it by accident. She would have scripted some actions that approximated the conditions of her discovery.

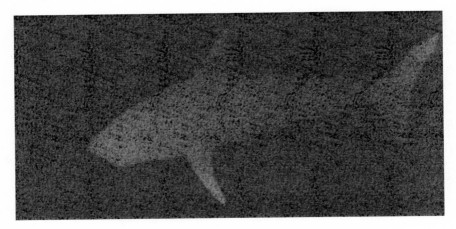

Figure 4.6

Figure 4.7

With a novel instance (Figure 4.8) and practiced rites, we should be able to embody those same rites time after time, disposing us to see what is already there in the image. After the skill of recognition is acquired, the quest to discern the meaning can begin. For instance, you must be able to recognize the shark in these images in order to discern why there are only sharks in these images. Like a medical student who has learned how to recognize a malignant tumor, that skill is only the beginning of what she needs to know in discerning the implications of finding a malignant tumor.

Figure 4.8

Returning briefly to our discussion of truth, we are now in the position to see how disjointed a propositional conception of truth is to the epistemological process, especially if this process truly describes the scientific epistemology as well. Ritualized practices do not dispose us to see *the truth*, rather, they dispose us to *see truly*. Again, this fundamental shift in our concept of truth must be made in order to make sense of Scripture's language of truth. A true road (דרך אמת) does not lead us to truth, but leads us truly to our destination. In the same way, a well-calibrated microscope does not allow us to view truth, but to truly view (and interpret!) the reality at the bottom of the lens.

From Recognition to Discernment

Before continuing on, the movement from insensitive to discerning is worth describing in more detail. First, under this view, knowing is habituated and shares sympathies with virtue epistemology's notion that knowing consists of diachronically acquired epistemic habits.[31] Knowing cannot happen at an instant but is proved over the course of time. As someone becomes skilled in discerning, she can then more readily interpret. For example, my children found several pottery shards on a slope of Mount Zion in Jerusalem. When we saw these fragments, we could not interpret whether they were replicas, contemporary pottery, or ancient shards. After hours spent on the internet comparing photos of ancient pottery, we felt even less confident that we could ever determine their origins. However, when we showed one jar handle fragment (Figure 4.9) to an antiquities dealer, he immediately interpreted the

---

31. Though virtue epistemology often still relies upon a propositional notion of truth and/or analysis. See my critique: Johnson, *Biblical Knowing*, 171–73.

piece: "This is from the Mamluk period" (ca. 1200 C.E. Islamic period). After taking the piece to several other experts, they all confirmed the same thing and did so instantly. They recognized something that we were incapable of seeing, even with concerted and modestly informed effort.

Figure 4.9

Upon presenting these experts with another more unremarkable thick piece of pottery from the round belly of a large jar, more incisive recognition skills were required. After weighing the piece in their hand, inspecting it under white lights and a magnification lens, and one man even flicking it like a bell, their verdict placed it as a late Bronze Age piece (ca. 1200 B.C.E.). Both epistemic feats required interpretive recognition, but the latter had to weigh the particularities of the fragment more carefully—its color, density, and component elements.

The blur between recognition and discernment is relative to the epistemic act. After all, what exactly marks the boundary between able-to-recognize a tumor and skilled-discernment of its malignancy? Such liminal ideas are generally demarcated with licenses. For instance, everyone in a pathology lab has shown that they are skilled to discern different cancers. Nevertheless, if we had a tissue sample especially difficult to discern, certainly lab workers would point to someone who is more skilled than the average lab worker. Or, at the very least, there are generally skilled lab pathologists, but some are more skilled in particular types of interpretation.

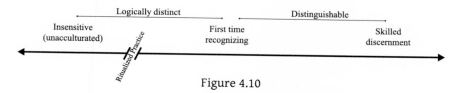

Figure 4.10

On the other hand, there is no blur between insensitivity (unacculturated for the task) to the first act of recognition, as those two are distinct from each other. Polanyi describes this initial movement (Figure 4.10), from not knowing to recognizing for the first time, as "illumination," as if we are seeing something for the very first time that has been there all along: "'Illumination' is then the leap by which the logical gap is crossed. It is the plunge by which we gain a foothold at another shore of reality. On such plunges the scientist has to stake bit by bit his entire professional life."[32] In the above examples of the autostereograms, "the logical gap is crossed" when we first are able to see the contours of the shark, its depth and fit to a known pattern.[33]

Additionally, the distinction between the first act of recognition and truly skilled discernment are clearly separated, not by logical space, but gradation. We do not need to be able to distinguish between a right and wrong interpretation, but at the least, be able to differentiate better from worse acts of discernment with reason.

Once we have recognized a pattern among myriad particulars, the process that then ensues as we learn to discern finer particularities is less dissectible. As well, expert discernment is more clearly distinguishable; where we can not only recognize that which is before us, but interpret its transcendent significance. The very thing we are interpreting moves from the focal to the subsidiary, taking part in a larger and coherent scheme of interpretation (e.g., that jar handle fragment is the McDonald's Big Mac® of the thirteenth century. It reveals the Qur'anic ideals of order implemented through foreign rule.).

Recognition

For clarity's sake, let us reiterate the cardinal features of recognition. First, in order for the individual to recognize a pattern among the mayhem of items, she must embody an act which focuses her beyond the particularities, and once she has recognized, she must learn to habituate the practice. We should be honest about embodiment here, where "looking" could effortlessly fall in

---

32. Polanyi, *Personal Knowledge*, 123.

33. I believe there is another dimension of recognition worth mentioning because of its notable impact on us: our awareness, upon recognizing a pattern previously unknown to us, of a human agent who put the image there for us to see.

the category of mental task. However, looking is an embodied task requiring muscular memory (i.e., ocular muscles) to shape the cornea in such a way as to focus. Further, any time cognition is required apart from bare consciousness, whatever that might be, we are speaking of embodied tasks. Second, and consequent to the act, who determines what specific actions should be taken? This is a matter of authoritative guides, those who know how to recognize and can help us to do the same.[34] In order to recognize, we must submit to the authoritative guide who is fiducially bound with us in this process that aims exclusively at our recognition.

Third, we must embody the practices to the degree prescribed by our guides until we come to that point that Polanyi called *illumination*, when we finally *get it*. We might not even recognize the pattern as a whole, but at the least, we recognize what Esther Meek calls "the profundity of the pattern."[35] Although recognizing a scheme can bring us to coherently see it, we never exhaust our knowledge of it. As with rocks, persons, the moon, and everything else, there is always a side obscured to us because we approach from a situated perspective. We must affirm one aspect, if no other, in the Kantian turn: that we never get exhaustive knowledge of a thing in and of itself (noumenal knowledge). However, because we are embodied, we know reality through the phenomena of our perspective. I would also add, opposing the commonplace rhetoric on this topic, that Scripture never espouses our embodied situatedness as a negative function. Rather, it asserts from the creation onward that our creatureliness is a fundamental and creational *good*, the way we are supposed to be. We must clarify that this ability to recognize is not merely visual, but true of all sorts of knowledge: mathematic, aural, narratival, etc.

Discernment

As we will observe in Part III, the biblical authors are not as particular with their use of epistemological vocabulary. At times, authors use "know" to refer to recognition, to discerning, and even to erroneous knowing at times. My task will be to consider the context under which the epistemological acts are being described in order to determine whether the original gap between not knowing and recognizing has been bridged. Or, are the authors portraying discernment in the characters of the text?

First, discernment requires habituation of the skill of recognizing, mastery of detection. With that embodied *habitus*, we can refine the knack for recognizing subtler distinctions in patterns. We can assess how we came to know and lead others to do the same. Second, and important for the social aspect of

---

34. I dealt with the problem of identifying better authorities (i.e., those who are authenticated within authoritative communities) in Johnson, *Biblical Knowing*, 40–43.

35. Esther L. Meek, *Longing to Know: The Philosophy of Knowledge for Ordinary People* (Grand Rapids, MI: Brazos, 2003), 126–38.

knowing, with discernment comes a liberty to apply the skill on our own. When we are coming to recognize, we need to be guided by some kind of authority. However, once we begin to habituate the skill, we can discover on our own. Considering that the world is ever-novel, good knowing necessitates the employment of the skill beyond the familiar to the unfamiliar.

Third, and as a consequence of the social aspect of knowing, we examine skilled knowers precisely with novel and more complex instances in order to assess their level of discernment. What is a test, but a process to assess whether or not you can recognize and/or discern the pattern? Tests of pattern recognition, such as the traffic sign exam for a driver's license, simply assess whether or not we have crossed the logical gap from insensitive to recognizing. But other exams, such as a board certification or Ph.D. defense, assess our ability to discern. We will see tests of individuals in Scripture which aim at both recognition (e.g., Gideon's fleece) and discernment (e.g., Abraham with Isaac, Jesus in the wilderness, etc.).

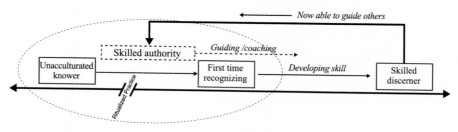

Figure 4.11

Generally, we want the discerning ones to train us, to act as our guides in learning to recognize (Figure 4.11). So the epistemological process actually perpetuates itself because it requires authoritative guides and eventually produces such guides. In the Hebrew Bible, and later in the New Testament, extreme emphasis is then placed on authenticating Israel's authoritative guides, for these are the only women and men who can ground the epistemological process of Israel, sparing it from religio-syncretistic relativism.

Finally, "knowing" is the more generic term in Scripture applied both liberally and specifically at times. However, there is a lexical group reserved for the idea of skilled discernment that goes beyond mere ability to recognize: wisdom or discernment (חכמה). As Michael V. Fox summarizes it, wisdom is the most "effectively transmitted knowledge" to the young and inexperienced through a "substitute experience."[36]

---

36. Michael Fox, *Proverbs 1–9: A New Translation with Introduction and Commentary* (AB; New York: Doubleday, 2000), 62.

Tacit Awareness

Although often missing from theories of knowledge, motivation to engage the epistemological process must be part of our discussion. A popular motivation theory in social psychology offers some observational insights for epistemology. Victor Vroom's expectancy view of motivation asserts that persons act through instrumental means because they expect to attain something of value through the process.[37] Students subject themselves to the instrument of undergraduate education because the conferred degree has a transcendent value (e.g., to aid in securing employment, to stroke one's ego, etc.). Similarly, we expect that persons subjecting themselves to an epistemological process would see it as the instrumental means to attain the valued knowledge. Expectation then figures directly into the coherent structure of knowledge, which encourages persons to participate in the process while not fully understanding how particular rites bring them to know that which they hope to know. Expectation is the glue that holds them in the process, even when they cannot identify how the process will bring them to know.

I once explained my experiences from boot camp to my son, namely the practice of precision marching (i.e., drilling) that involved hours of rather exhausting practice each day and much yelling from our drill instructor. My son then asked an apropos series of questions:

"How long were you in the military?"

"Seven years."

"So did you do a lot marching in the military? Did you march in combat?"

"No, the only time we marched was in boot camp."

"So why did you have to march so perfectly if you never did it again after boot camp?"

"Because the precision and unity of mind required to get sixty teenagers to march perfectly taught us a type of teamwork that we would not have known otherwise. We all went on to do different jobs after boot camp, but every job required a high amount of teamwork and close attention to detail. Whether you were an aircraft mechanic or security team member or an air traffic controller, we practiced marching so that we could know how unity and precision worked together, a transferrable skill which is easier to visually see when marching than when fighting in an infantry squad, but equally present."

---

37. Although it has been critiqued as being a frail construct, the modifications to the theory essentially maintain the central relationship between valence, expectancy, and instrumentality as key for measuring motivation in psychology. Victor Harold Vroom, *Work and Motivation* (New York: Wiley, 1964).

"Oh, so you knew when you were in boot camp that marching was going to make you better at your job?"

"No, actually I didn't know that at all."

He was perplexed at this point because he could not see why we participated in something of which we clearly did not see the benefit. He was not able to connect the fact that we must trust those who prescribe the actions that guide us. We usually cannot point to and name the logic of the rites that we embody until after we have come to recognition of the thing in question. Crucial to this, we must have a sense of progress toward knowing, a tacit awareness that what we do has epistemological efficacy, even if we cannot presently name precisely how it helps us.

This tacit awareness funds the motivation to participate in the process, not being part of the discovery itself, but compelling us because we are *on the way to discovery*. Two tensions give us impetus to continue in the process: confidence in our authoritative guide and a sense of progress. Continuing to embody rites, which force us to re-look at the unknown, without trusted guides or a sense of movement toward illumination is generally deemed foolishness.

Once more, we see that knowing is entangled with ethics, both in that we must have compelling reasons to furnish trust to our authoritative guide and then submit to their instruction. The breakdown of that fiduciary commitment between guide and knower is contingent on the knower's confident participation in the process.

Conclusions

I have presented in this chapter three distinct elements of epistemological process: 1) the nature of truth, 2) the acts of recognition as distinct from discernment, and 3) the tacit awareness that motivates a knower toward discernment. It should be clear that rituals will now be considered as true practices which dispose the participant to recognize some pattern which transcends the ritual itself. Through habituated practice, rites can enable discernment. In Part III, we will establish that the authors of Scripture are often overtly aware of the tacit awareness required to motivate ritual participants on the path to knowing. At times the biblical texts explicitly state the epistemic purpose of the rite: do this in order that you might know. In the next chapter, I consider how the body functions epistemologically to bring about recognition of patterns and lead knowers toward discernment.

Chapter 5

The Centrality of the Body
for Knowing

"Can one go more dangerously wrong than by despising the body?"[1]

Two problems confront a meaningful view of Israelite and Christian rituals. First, what role does the body play, if any, in epistemology? I will argue below that knowing—including reason and interpretation—is fundamentally an embodied act. Joel Green's basic proposition on this question is simple, but weighs heavily in any discussion:

> In order to make life events meaningful, we must conceptualize them and we do so in terms of well-worn paths in our brains—that is, imaginative structures or conceptual schemes that we implicitly take to be true, normal and good.[2]

By identifying "well-worn paths in our brains," Green is appealing to our embodied history, specifically the embodiment of habit that deepens those neural paths.

Second, the following discussion about the bodily, or somatic, nature of epistemology must reconcile the semantic range of the biblical and epistemic terms. "To know," just within the first four chapters of the Hebrew Bible, includes the ever-ambiguous knowledge of good and evil,[3] knowledge of nakedness,[4] and three instances of successful procreation.[5] At the very least, no epis-

---

1. Friedrich Nietzsche, *Nietzsche: Writings from the Late Notebooks* (ed. Rüdiger Bittner; trans. Kate Sturge; CTHP; New York: Cambridge University Press, 2003), 244.

2. Joel B. Green, *Body, Soul, and Human Life: The Nature of Humanity in the Bible* (Grand Rapids, MI: Baker Academic, 2008), 118.

3. The story does not dwell on knowledge as an object. Instead, it offers indications of the nature of the error in only one instance: Genesis 3:17. For further discussion on the content of "knowledge of good and evil," see chapter seven note eleven in this volume.

4. The fact of the first couple's nakedness is stated clearly by the narrator before the couple knows it (Gen 2:25). However, the word play between their unashamed nakedness (עֲרוּמִים . . . . וְלֹא יִתְבֹּשָׁשׁוּ), the serpent's shrewdness (עָרוּם), and their realization of nakedness (וַיֵּדְעוּ כִּי עֵירֻמִּם) indicates that the author is developing their understanding of nakedness, not that they were flatly ignorant of the fact before eating the fruit. In other words, they recognized something about themselves that was true all along.

temological theory that intends to take Scripture seriously can neglect the semantic range of the Hebrew term *yada* (ידע). Though "know" can mean sexual intimacy in the Hebrew lexicon, occurrences as such are rare.[6] But no matter how rare, knowing qua sex made sense in the Semitic context so much so that authors used it without comment or explanation, if only sparsely.

How then should we incorporate this lexical information? Michael Carasik and Gerhard von Rad offer the most parsimonious view that "to know" connoted the idea of "coming closer to" for the ancient Israelite.[7] The sexual connotation of "know" (ידע), "is right in so far as the verb *yd'* ('to know') never signifies purely intellectual knowing, but rather an 'experiencing,' a 'becoming acquainted with' . . ."[8] Though we cannot make too much of semantic overlap based on vocabulary alone, Klawans points out that the term "sacrifice" (קורבן) also has a sense of "coming closer to." Thus, sacrifices allow the offerer to come close to YHWH through temple rituals. The use of this specific term (קורבן) cannot be entirely disregarded concerning YHWH's proximity to the tabernacle and thus, to Israel.[9]

More immediately, I must clarify how acts of the body are epistemically functional. There are many divergent ways in which we could understand the notion of the "epistemic body." In this present work, I do not mean to speak of the body's knowledge itself, how the body knows things of which the person is unaware. For example, when a child is severely malnourished over months, the developing body will redirect nourishment away from the extremities. The brain and the organs will benefit most during that time of deficiency. Similarly, a pregnant woman's body, when malnourished, will redirect nutrients to her child instead of the mother. These fairly amazing epistemic feats are accomplished on behalf of the persons without them ever being aware. It is an epistemic feat because the body must register the levels of nutrients coming in and make an inductive inference based on the trajectory of supply. It is *as if* the body is saying, "Based on our current inventory, we need to rewrite our distribution plans accordingly." After more than a few days of starvation, the body induces a trajectory based on the current levels of deficiency and acts accordingly. If not necessary to productive life, then those parts of the body

---

5. "And the man knew his wife" employs ידי to euphemize sexual intercourse, which does not always refer to procreatively successful intimacy (cf. Gen 19:5).

6. Michael Carasik, *Theologies of The Mind In Biblical Israel* (SBibLit 85; Oxford: Peter Lang, 2005), 20. There are four instances out of 174 in the Pentateuch where ידי is employed to mean "sexual intimacy."

7. Ibid.

8. Gerhard von Rad, *Genesis: A Commentary* (OTL; Louisville, KY: Westminster John Knox, 1972), 79.

9. Jonathan Klawans, *Purity, Sacrifice, and the Temple: Symbolism and Supersessionism in the Study of Ancient Judaism* (Oxford: Oxford University Press, 2006), 69.

are excised from the distribution routes.[10] When one pauses to think about the inductive inferences involved in this kind of bio-chemistry, it is difficult to assess what to make of it. The throwaway explanations that "evolution or a creator *just* designed our bodies thus" appear thin at these very moments. However, these are different, though intriguing matters, which I cannot deal with here. My concern regards those practices of the body that involve cognizant participation.

Below, I first address the history of the mind-body schism through the Nietzsche-Overbeck critique of Christianity and the malingering Hebrew-Greek mind problem. Nietzsche viciously attacked European Christianity for its narrow and Neo-Platonist eschatology. Namely, Christian theology meant to ameliorate all the woes and ills of this world by being world-fleeing, and thus body-fleeing, in its outlook. The implications of this critique are pursued below. The Hebrew-Greek mind debate centers on the proposal that ancient Semites were not able to objectively conceptualize their world. Further, they supposed that the Hellenistic age yields to us the best epistemology because only then did humanity conceptualize chairs qua chair, a spiritual object apart from the individual instances of chairs. I want to show that Nietzsche was at least partly correct in his critique and reiterate the consensus in scholarship that those who uncritically reiterate the Hebrew-Greek mind distinctions are incorrect.

Extending Nietzsche's somatically oriented approach and countering the Hebrew-Greek mind proposal, I argue that knowledge must always be somatically rooted because:

1. we extend ourselves cyborgically into both the objects and the concepts that we use,
2. the constructs we reason with and the logic of our reasoning are both formed through the body,
3. our habits shape our thought due to our neuro-plasticity, and
4. our judgments about the world external to us do not require non-embodied abstract ideas.

By taking the body seriously and preferring the most parsimonious explanation of human reasoning and knowing, we can make sense of the biblical notions of knowing, and in the next chapter, current scientific epistemology. As well, we end up with epistemologically robust reasons for knowing as a functional outcome of ritual participation.

---

10. One might argue that even though the autonomic nervous system can keep us alive without complex thought or language, the entire brain is not necessary to keep us alive. However, the brain benefits from the nutrient redirection nonetheless.

Mind-Body Schism

Part of the difficulty with centering epistemology in our body can be attribut-
ed to a latent notion of the mind-body schism. Why would we presume, for
instance, that our mathematical concepts do not originate in our embodied
engagement of reality? I will address the body's role in mathematics below,
but if that question causes duress, then the mind-body duality might be the
source of that distress. There exists an entire framework that assumes human
knowledge to be mental, which is then unmindfully associated with extra-
physical faculties. Without joining in the arguments for and against body-mind
dualism I must challenge the most basic presumption that our thinking and
abstract concepts happen in the mind and our actions happen in the body.
First, neuro-science is not convinced that this thinking-acting dichotomy remains a tenable position.[11] Second, even if we were to hold firmly to dualism,
the idea that thinking happens in the mind as opposed to the body is unnecessary.[12] Third, a purely mental description of epistemology does not do justice
to the reality of knowing depicted in Scripture, contemporary life, or science.
Therefore, I will scrutinize this assumption, looking at it historically and the
ever-lingering effects of the thinking-acting dichotomy.

---

11. For summary of the debates, see Malcolm Jeeves and Warren S. Brown, *Neuroscience, Psychology, and Religion Illusions, Delusions, and Realities about Human Nature* (West
Conshohocken, IN: Templeton Foundation, 2009). Additionally, in social psychology,
nonverbal behavior studies have resisted the notion that body and mind occupy two
realms of being. Similar to Catherine Bell's critique of the thinking-acting dichotomy in
ritual theory, Geoffrey Beattie has recently argued against the currents regarding verbal and nonverbal psychology. Specifically, the view that there are two languages—
verbal and nonverbal—and nonverbal language is that of the heart, separable from our
rational thought and expressing that which cannot be said verbally. "So the argument
goes that we express relationships nonverbally because these types of communication
are less subject to voluntary control, and therefore presumably more honest, and yet at
the same time are more nebulous. We send out signals and yet remain unaccountable
for their expression." Geoffrey Beattie, *Visible Thought: The New Psychology of Body Language* (New York: Routledge, 2003), 22. Although Beattie argues that nonverbal gestures
can and do express abstract thought as well—apparently appealing to the thinking-
acting dichotomy—he demonstrates that gesturing actually shapes how verbal language is intended. They are not two languages, but one: "There is no such thing any
longer as being merely a good listener. You will have to watch speakers that much
more carefully if you really want to understand what others are thinking." Beattie,
Visible Thought, 180. In other words, our acting is shaping our speaking. While we cannot dwell on the point, it is worth noting that embodied cognition and abstract thought
are connected in nonverbal psychology.

12. Alan J. Torrance, "What is A Person?" in *From Cells to Souls—and Beyond: Changing Portraits in Human Nature* (ed. Malcolm Jeeves; Grand Rapids, MI: Eerdmans, 2004),
199–222.

Nietzsche and Overbeck: World-fleeing Theology

The critique to re-evaluate the body's role in knowing is not novel. While we could root this dichotomy of thinking-mind/acting-body in the Hellenistic philosophies, we will pick up the discussion in the mid-nineteenth century. In fact, it was the centerpiece of Nietzsche's critique of the Christian West, but also Franz Overbeck's critique too—his best friend and historical theologian. Nietzsche laments about the creation of the soul as the center of human thinking in his private notebooks:

> The human body, in which the whole most distant and most recent past of all organic becoming regains life and corporeality, through which, over which, beyond which a tremendous, inaudible river seems to flow: the body is a more astonishing idea than the old 'soul'.[13]

Later in that same notebook, in a section titled "What has been *spoiled* by the church's misuse of it," Nietzsche follows a similar line of reasoning used by Franz Overbeck.[14] Nietzsche lists the items *spoiled* and shows how their abuse

---

13. Nietzsche, *Writings from the Late Notebooks*, 27.

14. What happened when Jesus did not actually return? According to Overbeck, that world-fleeing mentality was transformed into asceticism in the church, which is just another type of world-fleeing. Theology, which is a questionable enterprise for Overbeck, resulted in the church trying to justify itself to different cultures. This is what he refers to as the Alexandrian shift in the church. Again, Overbeck sees this move into formal exposition of doctrine as having a fundamentally negative effect on the spirituality of the early church. The "apologetic theology" of the church was the final nail in the coffin for any hope of a faithfully spiritual church. Clement of Alexandria is symptomatic of this apologetic bent, where he tried to reconcile the Greek philosophers to Old Testament theology. How could the church recapture its essential world-fleeing mentality when the apologists were constantly seeking to tie the world to the church in arguing from pagan context to justify the religion?

From there, the church entered a "paganizing" phase where art, beauty and all cultural phenomena were recaptured for the life of the church. Ecclesiastical ritual absconded true spirituality. The "world-denying" character of Christianity is even used to fund the martyrdom of Christians, being another avenue of denying identification with the world.

In what appears ironic, Overbeck mirrors Nietzsche's early attitude toward the explanatory power of art beyond explication. Propositional analysis cannot capture the essential faith without remainder. He says in a lecture on John's Gospel, "In every century where Christian faith has been a living faith, church history is full of holy poetry." Franz Overbeck, *On the Christianity of Theology* (trans. John Elbert Wilson; Eugene, OR: Pickwick, 2002), 25. For Overbeck, the subduing of the arts for ritual and instantiation of Alexandrian doctrine runs counter to the world-fleeing spirit of the church. But Overbeck believes that the nature of the world-fleeing church must be unapologetically (in both senses of the word) expressed. That expression, since it is attempting to express the essentials of the spirituality, will have a heightened sense of "holy poetry."

does not mitigate their proper use: ascesis, fasting, monasticism, the festival, lack of courage, and death.[15] Particularly of interest here, he cites these practices as used by Christians for world-fleeing purposes (sans the festival, which Nietzsche finds contradictory to Christian morality). By world-fleeing, Nietzsche means to describe a Christian theology of his day, where the goal of humanity is to go to heaven or find some state of it on earth. It is, in essence, Christian escapism. Nietzsche's point, following Overbeck, is that all of these rites have "natural usefulness," wrongfully commandeered by Christianity, misappropriated in order to fund projects of pity and escapism. This old idea of a soul plagued Nietzsche in that it held humanity's naturally embodied rituals hostage to Christian and other-worldly idealizations. While Overbeck believed that these rites became expressions of world-fleeing mentality specifically after the *nonfulfillment* of Jesus' return, Nietzsche merely rebukes the church for their improper use.

But their general trajectory is the same: Overbeck argues that asceticism is merely the transferred expression of a world-fleeing desire. Nietzsche felt that ascesis was the body's tool for the "service of *educating the will.*"[16] Fasting and cloister are aspects of the monastic life that Overbeck deems the retreat from the apostolic spiritualism.[17] Nietzsche acquires them to hone our enjoyment of the bodily senses and respite respectively. Both scholars had in mind a direct line of argument against the mind-body schism, which stems from the Alexandrian attempt to place thinking in the mind and acting in the body.

Any attempt by the church to affirm the world is seen as an attempt to rob Christianity of its very soul. "The matter is different only when one realizes that world-denial is the inmost soul of Christianity, that for Christianity the world is no longer a possible and worthy place for religion." *On The Christianity of Theology*, 98. Not even the Reformation is spared from his rebuke where Overbeck says, "It allowed the use and enjoyment of a world it could not annihilate." *On The Christianity of Theology*, 97. Overbeck commends a new theology: critical theology. "Critical theology will prevent such theologies from dragging through the world an unreal thing they call Christianity, from which has been taken its soul. Namely the denial of world." *On The Christianity of Theology*, 107.

15. Nietzsche, *Writings from the Late Notebooks*, 201.

16. "[A]scesis: one no longer really dares to point out the natural usefulness of ascesis, its indispensability in the service of educating the will. Our absurd world of educators (which has in mind the 'efficient servant of the state' as a regulating model) believes it can make do with 'instruction', with dressage of the brain; it lacks even the concept that something else must come first—education of the will-power." Ibid., 200–201.

17. "We must emphatically deny . . . that original Christianity's expectation of the early return of Christ after its factual nonfulfillment in the church only stepped into the background, and so we also especially deny that the world-fleeing character of original Christianity disappeared in the ancient church. Otherwise one must forever remain with the unsolvable enigma that a belief whose whole view of the world depended on its physical fulfillment was not dashed to pieces on its nonfulfillment." Overbeck, *On the Christianity of Theology*, 95.

The Hebrew-Greek Minds Problem

This divide between action in the body and abstract thinking in the mind also maintains roots in the Hebrew-Greek mind debate of last century. Though that debate ended in academia with a fairly definitive loss for those who maintained the Hebrew-Greek dichotomy, it certainly engendered a legacy of thought patterns that extends to today.[18]

The mid-twentieth century debate focused on this question: Did ancient Israelites think like we do today? Those who answered no on this question were verbose. Johannes Pedersen posited that the Israelites, like other ancient cultures, had no embedded construct for thinking and therefore, had no language to discuss a construct which they did not hold. Instead, the Israelite mind could only address things directly perceived. According to this view, the Israelite could not conceive of water qua water, but only of water in a river or puddle. Thus, the Hebrew mind did not abstract:

> The Israelite does not occupy himself with empty nor with sharply defined space images. His logic is not the logic of abstraction, but of immediate perception. It is characteristic that the problems treated in the Old Testament are problems pertaining, not to thought, but to life, and that what they seek are not logical results.[19]

For Pedersen, the Hebrew mind is marked by the complete fusion of concepts so that a man can only conceive of action and outcome as a unity, not a cause and effect which demands further investigation. For the Israelite, "there is no such thing as 'good intentions'" because, "the intention or will is identical with the totality of the soul which creates action":[20]

> For the Israelite—as for primitive peoples generally—the mental processes are not successive, but united in one, because the soul is always a unit, acting in one. But no more are the action and its result to be distinguished from each other or from the mental activities; they are implied in the actual mental process.[21]

This inability to abstract, argues Pederson, means that Israelites could not think as we do. Their thoughts are mired, fused in body and action whereas ours can freely range in the abstract world of ideas.

---

18. The dichotomy is so resilient that even the most current research exploring the body, mind, and senses in biblical epistemology still feels obligated to give a thorough refutation of the two-minds problem. See Michael Carasik, *Theologies of the Mind In Biblical Israel* (SBibLit 85; Oxford: Peter Lang, 2005), 1–11; Yael Avrahami, *The Senses of Scripture: Sensory Perception in the Hebrew Bible* (LHBOTS 545; New York: T&T Clark International, 2012), 22–31.

19. Johannes Pedersen, *Israel, Its Life and Culture* (2 vols.; Oxford: Geoffrey Cumberlege, 1959), I:124.

20. Ibid., I:132.

21. Ibid., I:124.

In a similar comparative study, Thorlief Boman develops the contrast between Israelite and Greek thinking using a dynamic/stative dichotomy.[22]
Where Israelites could only think in terms of dynamic action, Greeks har-
nessed the ability to think of bodies and properties as stative concepts now
domesticated by their minds. His examination of Hebrew language looks at
elements such as the verbs that describe inner mental states as movement
(e.g., "*turn* my attention to," "a thought is *coming*," etc.). In making the case,
Boman argues that Hebrew thought was fundamentally psychological while
Greek thought was logical. Logical, in this sense, consists of the ability to place
"ourselves objectively and impersonally outside the matter and ask what is the
strict truth about it."[23] As for the psychological Hebrew mind, "In our psychic
life, thinking and understanding are inseparable." And, "when we would understand a matter psychologically, we familiarize ourselves with it and
through sympathetic pursuit of its development we try to grasp it as a necessity."[24] Thinking, for Boman, is abstract and objective. Yet the Hebrews are associated with somatic ideas of thought from embodied experience. This might
seem like an advance toward our thesis, but Boman's use of "familiar" and
"acquaintance" for Hebrew thought is to show why it is not really thinking at
all, but reacting to environment.

James Barr's unfavorable appraisal of these two-mind constructs was definitive. He groups the two-mind proposals by the following properties: 1) contrasts Greek thinking as stative and Hebrew as dynamic, 2) contrasts Greek
thinking as abstract and Hebrew as concrete, and 3) contrasts the Greek conception of man as a duality and the Hebrew as unitary being. All of this is
based upon the nature of *language*, the philology of mind in the extant texts of
the Hebrew Bible.

Barr's basic rejoinder aims at the faulty claim that two distinct mentalities
can be derived from the languages of the people represented. If Hebrew represents the "verb" mentality and Greek the "noun," does that dichotomy reflect
their mentality *per se* or the nature of the texts? Barr argues for the latter,
pointing out the phenomenological aspect of the extant texts: "The typical
vehicle of Hebrew thinking is the historical narrative or the future prediction,
both forms of literature in which the verb is likely to be of great significance."[25] His second major critique points to the vague nature of the comparison itself. Boman et al. have constructed a theory of mentality that includes
their own European mentality and Indo-European language group as the contrast to the Hebrew mentality and Semitic language group. This creates an
ineffectual comparison to which Barr raises one penetrating implication. "[I]f
the Greek language can be somehow correlated with certain abstract or static
features of Greek thought, how is (say) the Albanian language, which is also

---

22. Thorlief Boman, *Hebrew Thought Compared with Greek* (LHD; London: SCM, 1960).
23. Ibid., 193.
24. Ibid., 193.
25. Barr, *Semantics*, 15 (see introduction, n. 20).

Indo-European, related with these features?"[26] In short, the two minds analysis is not self-reflected on the analysts themselves, and therefore, it is incomplete.

Later, Julian Jaynes would provide the evolutionary fuel for this discussion in his *The Origin of Consciousness in the Breakdown of the Bicameral Mind*.[27] The basic premise focuses on the two parts of early man's brain (i.e., bicameral) where one side fires off commands to the other side and it obeys. This work in and of itself enters biblical criticism right at the level of bicameral functions, so that the right side of the bicameral brain is the center of processing voices. Bringing this analysis to the Hebrew text, Jaynes argues that the Hebrew Bible offers the reader a history of the developing mind. Beginning with guidance by hallucinogenic voices from divine beings (e.g., Exod 3), the early human bicameral mind operates by voice. Hence, Moses does what the other hemisphere of his brain, known to him as YHWH Elohim, tells him. Only when consciousness later arises in human beings does the visual command guide humanity and seeing then becomes metaphorical for knowing. Where we find the ancient person of scripture "hearing" God, according to Jaynes, we are reading about the bicameral human. When humankind reaches consciousness, then we read about people "seeing" what is going on. We cannot review the inherent problems of Jayne's position here, other than to say that one must accept much more than *merely* the concept of a bicameral mind, which most scholars do not, in order to bear fruit from such an analysis.[28]

Indeed, the basic question needs to be taken up: Did ancient Israelites, as described in the Hebrew Bible and New Testament, think and therefore know like we do? Moreover, do we share *any* mentality with ancient peoples so that our constructs and language can map onto theirs in a productive way? An affirmative answer is required *without hesitation* in order to do any broad-ranging analysis of ancient texts. After this, we must then go along with Barr and Carasik to affirm that the biblical languages refer to the same epistemological constructs we have today *mutatis mutandis*.

If we do share mentality communicated by language, then how does one go about translating the language of Scripture into the common epistemological referents that we share today? Carasik prescribes the study of lexical use within narratives in order to gain an understanding of overlapping language and constructs. For instance, when we say, "He thought X," we grasp that some biblical authors would state this differently. Some would have understood the heart (לבב) to be the center of thoughts and intent. In looking at those narratives, we do not expect to see language about *thinking*, but rather the actions of one's heart. Through building up matrices of *the use of* specific

---

26. Barr, *Semantics*, 18.

27. Julian Jaynes, *The Origin of Consciousness in The Breakdown of The Bicameral Mind* (Toronto: University of Toronto Press, 1976).

28. For a critique of Jaynes, see David R. Crownfield, "Consciousness and the Voices of the Gods: An Essay Review," *JAAR* 42, no. 2 (1978): 193–202; Carasik, *Theologies*, 1–14.

language with reference to what we call mentality (i.e., epistemology),[29] we can then come to appreciate what writers intended to portray. Carasik is not suggesting that this would be a method for finding hidden beliefs about mentality, but that it becomes the framework to justify any conclusions we may draw from the texts.

The purpose of this brief review of two discussions, Nietzsche-Overbeck and the Hebrew-Greek mind problem, is to show that the thinking-acting dichotomy appears to be the predisposition in many corners of academic discourse. Though Catherine Bell might have clearly shown the weaknesses in the thinking-acting dichotomy as a background assumption of ritual theory, we cannot presume that the fruit of her critique can be felt in biblical studies, theology, and certainly not epistemology. This should not be taken as a rejection of Greek thought, as I do not believe that this dichotomy actually captures Hebrew or Greek thought aptly. Instead, I want to suggest below that what the Platonic tradition parceled out to the eternal and heavenly realms could be found here in our earthly bodies. We do not lose the benefits of the Hellenistic tradition on my account; only seek to better explain them apart from the heavenly forms.

Though these debates have continued in corridors of academia, it was not until the end of the twentieth century that the body took center stage in various academic discourses, creating an implicit argument that complicates a naïve view of the mind-body schism. As previously mentioned, it was the rise of feminist critiques, analogical reasoning, and recent nonverbal psychology that gave compelling reasons to regard the body as integral to thinking, to what had previously been considered the domain of abstract Greek thought. We are not merely thinkers who act, but our thinking is shaped by our action and our acts are types of thinking. Now, we must consider further how phenomenology and neuroscience give us insights and tools for understanding ourselves beyond the mind-body and thinking-acting dichotomies.

Cyborgic Extension of the Body

> Our brains care so much about the fine details of our embodiment that they are ready and willing to recalibrate those details on the spot, again and again, to accommodate changes (limb growth, limb loss) and extensions (prosthesis, implants, even sports equipment).[30]

Andy Clark claims that any time we pick up a pen to write or grab a bat to swing, we have assumed a cyborgic position. By cyborg, I mean nothing more

29. Carasik reveals that what he means by mentality is actually something like knowing, thinking, and remembering. *Theologies*, 11.
30. Andy Clark, *Natural-Born Cyborgs: Minds, Technologies, and the Future of Human Intelligence* (Oxford: Oxford University Press, 2003), 190.

than extending some human capability into a non-human object, even an abstract object.[31] By this extension, we conceive of ourselves and the object together. In fact, it no longer is an object *to us*, but part *of us* as the writing or swinging subject. I will address how actions shape our thinking below, but more immediately, I must engage the phenomenological issue of extending ourselves into the world, a topic that Polanyi views as fundamental for good scientific practices. The practice of assimilating a tool as if it were an extension of our own bodies, what Andy Clark terms "nonpenetrative cyborg technology," is well rehearsed by those who speak of the body as central to knowing.[32] Polanyi exemplified this cyborgic extension of our presence, what he calls "the pouring of ourselves into the subsidiary awareness of particulars," with the use of a hammer or a blind woman's use of a stick:

> Our subsidiary awareness of tools and probes can be regarded now as the act of making them form a part of our own body. The way we use a hammer or a blind man uses his stick, shows in fact that in both cases we shift outwards the points at which we make contact with the things that we observe as objects outside ourselves.[33]

Cyborgic extension of myself into a guide stick marks a definitively divergent approach to knowledge that, as Polanyi notes, neither conflates nor dichotomizes skill knowledge ("knowing how") and factual knowledge ("knowing that").[34] As Clark observes throughout, by nature of our humanness and neural plasticity, the stick becomes transparent to the blind woman's task of knowing the terrain. It has become part of her, or more accurately, she has extended herself to include the stick. After Polanyi but well before Clark, Merleau-Ponty makes a similar observation:

---

31. Or, Andy Clark says it more fluidly: "We see some of the 'cognitive fossil trail' of the cyborg trait in the historical procession of potent cognitive technologies that begins with speech and counting, morphs first into written text and numerals, then into early printing (without moveable typefaces), on to the revolutions of moveable typefaces and the printing press, and most recently to the digital encodings that bring text, sound, and image into a uniform and widely transmissible format. Such technologies, once up and running in the various appliances and institutions that surround us, do far more than merely allow for the external storage and transmission of ideas. They constitute, I want to say, a cascade of 'mindware upgrades': cognitive upheavals in which the effective architecture of the human mind is altered and transformed." Ibid., 4.

32. Ibid., 28.

33. Polanyi, *Personal Knowledge*, 55–56.

34. More specifically, "We may think of the hammer replaced by a probe, used for exploring the interior of a hidden cavity. Think how a blind man feels his way by the use of a stick, which involves transposing the shocks transmitted to his hand and the muscles holding the stick into an awareness of the things touched by the point of the stick. We have here the transition from 'knowing how' to 'knowing what' and can see how closely similar is the structure of the two." Ibid., 55–56.

A woman may, without any calculation, keep a safe distance between the feather in her hat and things which might break it off. She feels where the feather is just as we feel where our hand is. If I am in the habit of driving a car, I enter a narrow opening and see that I can 'get through' without comparing the width of the opening with that of the wings . . . . The blind man's stick has ceased to be an object for him, and is no longer perceived for itself; its point has become an area of sensitivity, extending the scope and active radius of touch, and providing a parallel to sight.[35]

Likewise, the pen in our hand becomes a "transparent technology" to the task of writing a letter (e.g., consider the difference, from the drawer's perspective, between the two pencils in Figure 5.1). However, Clark reminds us of the implications, "All three items, the pen, the hand, and the unconsciously operating neural mechanisms, are pretty much on a par. And it is this parity that ultimately blurs the line between the intelligent system and its best tools for thought and action."[36]

Figure 5.1[37]

Further, the above concept of cyborgic extension is not merely conjecture. There are tangible experiments which can immediately reveal their veracity to the reader. Ramachandran and Blakeslee write about easy-to-do experiments that simulate phantom limb syndrome to those who have all their limbs. The

35. Maurice Merleau-Ponty, *Phenomenology of Perception* (trans. Colin Smith; New York: Routledge, 1962), 126–7.

36. Clark, *Natural-Born Cyborgs*, 29.

37. "Konstruktionsplan" Allgemeiner Deutscher Nachrichtendienst - Zentralbild (Bild 183). Heinz Himhorf (photographer), Bundesarchiv_Bild_183-1989-0523-016,_Konstruktionsplan.jpg, image, 23 May 1989, http://commons.wikimedia.org.

results, which can be repeated at home, demonstrate that we can extend our sense of touch to someone else's nose and our sense of pain to a table.[38]

In terms of prior ritual theory, the thinking-acting dichotomy encounters a much more serious objection from neuroscience: the objects we use transparently become equivalent to the neuro-biology that extends our bodies through them. If the use of external objects shapes our thinking about reality, then the notion that "rites merely express beliefs" becomes almost unsustainable on any account. Rather, it might be the case that ritualized practices shape our neurobiology through the benefits of super-plasticity in the human brain.[39] For as I am performing a ritual, for instance, the performance and objects I employ might be actively shaping what I would refer to as "my beliefs."

Embodied Construct and Logic Formation

Not only do we extend ourselves into the objects we employ, it is equally possible that our embodied experience of reality has provided the abstract constructs and logic required to conceptualize reality. In other words, not only do we extend ourselves through physical objects, but into abstract objects as well. Again, Polanyi will argue that the scientist must extend themselves into formulae and constructs in order to have a coherent grasp of them:

> I generalized this structural analysis [re embodying tools] to include the recognition of signs as indications of subsequent events and the process of establishing symbols for things which they shall signify. We may apply to these cases also what has just been said about a tool. Like the tool, the sign or the symbol can be conceived as such only in the eyes of a person who *relies on them* to achieve or to signify something.[40]

Once we have grasped the impetus and construct of a formula or equation, we can use it as a heuristic, extending ourselves into its symbols and relations as we do with physical tools. So too can we extend ourselves into constructs,

---

38. With the help of friends, two chairs and a table, you can do these experiments yourself at home. V. S. Ramachandran and Sandra Blakeslee, *Phantoms in the Brain: Probing the Mysteries of the Human Mind* (New York: William Morrow, 1998), 59–60.

39. Clark notes: "Such neural plasticity is, of course, not restricted to the human species; in fact, some of the early work on cortical transplants was performed on rats. But our brains do appear to be far and away the most plastic of them all. Combined with this plasticity, however, we benefit from a unique kind of developmental space: the unusually protracted human childhood." *Natural-Born Cyborgs*, 85.

40. "*This reliance is a personal commitment which is involved in all acts of intelligence by which we integrate some things subsidiarily to the centre of our focal attention. Every act of personal assimilation by which we make a thing form an extension of ourselves through our subsidiary awareness of it, is a commitment of ourselves; a manner of disposing of ourselves.*" Italics in the original. Polanyi, *Personal Knowledge*, 61.

such as the tonicity of biological cells or quiescence in electrical fields. When we grasp the principle, we can employ it transparently to the task of discovery. As a simple example, conceptually grasping how the quadratic equation functions—not just being able solve for a particular integer in the equation— allows one to employ the equation as a heuristic. We extend our sight to see the world *quadratic-ly*, as it were, opening up vistas into everything from the braking distance required by cars to the downdraft on a Ping-Pong ball.[41]

Two areas of research point to abstraction and thought as an embodied function and are worth bringing to bear on this discussion: 1) phenomenology and 2) analogical reasoning.

Phenomenology

In *Phenomenology of Perception*, Maurice Merleau-Ponty offered a view of the body as the basis of knowing and gave veracious, though sometimes linguistically veiled, reasons for taking the body seriously—a view deeply commensurate with Michael Polanyi's scientific epistemology.[42] Merleau-Ponty supposed that our thoughts neither reduce to an embodied stimulus reaction nor arise to a mentalism, but reside in between. Our thoughts are neither merely our neural connectives firing nor merely objects floating free of our biology. We incorporate the reality that surrounds us into our sense of self (i.e., cyborgic extension) and we inhabit the objects of this world in order to know them. Our body is not an object *to us*, our body *is us*, the fundamental reality to which all else is estimated:

> The body therefore is not one more among external objects, with the peculiarity of always being there. If it is permanent, the permanence is absolute and is the ground for the relative permanence of disappearing objects, real objects.[43]

If even partially correct, the notion of body/mind in regards to thinking/acting must be recontextualized in its entirety to account for Merleau-Ponty's description of perception. The question of *coming to know* is taken up quite clearly in Plato's *Meno*, where Socrates discusses the enigmatic situation of looking to know something when we do not know what it is.[44] How are we

---

41. For more examples, see "101 Uses of the Quadratic Equation," https://plus.maths.org/content/101-uses-quadratic-equation-part-ii (Accessed April 7, 2015).

42. "Particularly striking, however, is the convergence between the arguments of Polanyi in Personal Knowledge and of Merleau-Ponty in the Phenomenology of Perception." Marjorie Grene, *The Knower and the Known* (London: Faber & Faber, 1966), 14.

43. Merleau-Ponty, *Phenomenology of Perception*, 80.

44. *Meno*, 80d–e.

not just mad men and women groping hopelessly into the unknown? Knowing as an embodied process might help rescue us from Meno's paradox.

In reviewing the problem of explicit knowledge raised by this Platonic dialogue, Marjorie Grene sees Polanyi and Merleau-Ponty in accord. Specifically, they both esteem the centrality of an embodied perspective for knowing, one which allows us to grope toward the unknown and effectively excises the possibility of knowing by discrete mental and abstract ideas with no relation to our body:

> In other words, as Polanyi and Merleau-Ponty seem to agree, this single question [How do you know that which you do not know?] asked by Plato at the very start of inquiry into the nature of knowledge already puts paid to the centuries of effort in which men have sought to formulate canons of wholly *explicit* truth. Instead, we must admit as essential to the very nature of mind the kind of groping that constitutes the recognition of a problem.[45]

Exploring that which we know, and that which we suspect we do not know, we have a sense of the movement toward resolution that cannot be reduced to mentally explicit knowledge. Even the concept that we call "progress" can be derived from embodiment, the sense that we are moving toward resolution. As Esther Meek once admitted of her own philosophical struggles, "I needed to know that nobody gets from point A to point B, even in a deductive syllogism, apart from human effort."[46] Even performing logic is an embodied act, a performance.

For Merleau-Ponty, our creaturely situatedness and persistence in history is the basis of our ability to grope—recognizing problems and groping toward solutions. Our "habit-body," as he calls it, is conditioned to the reality in which it is situated. Hence, when a leg is amputated, the habit-body must re-situate according to the "body at present" that is now missing a limb.[47] Because we are habituated bodies—humans formed in part from the very physical acts and conventions we act out—we cannot merely acknowledge the explicit fact that our leg is now gone. Our bodies, not our minds alone, shape our thinking through those "well-worn paths" in our neurology—a neurology that extends to the tips of our fingers and toes. Phantom limb syndrome exemplifies this state in that the body habitually considers the leg to be there—we still feel pain and movement in a limb that no longer exists. This might seem philosophically uncontroversial; however, Merleau-Ponty then shows how this fundamental shift in the body's relation to knowledge—that our bodies do not mediate knowledge to us, but that our knowledge is embodied—has a spillover effect:

---

45. Grene, *Knower and the Known*, 24.

46. Esther L. Meek, *Longing to Know: The Philosophy of Knowledge for Ordinary People* (Grand Rapids, MI: Brazos Press, 2003), 64.

47. Merleau-Ponty, *Phenomenology of Perception*, 2–10.

> The acquisition of habit as a rearrangement and renewal of the cor-
> poreal schema presents great difficulties to traditional philosophies,
> which are always inclined to conceive synthesis as intellectual syn-
> thesis. It is quite true that what brings together, in habit, compo-
> nent actions, reactions and 'stimuli' is not some external process of
> association. Any mechanistic theory runs up against the fact that
> the learning process is systematic; the subject does not weld to-
> gether individual movements and individual stimuli but acquires
> the power to respond with a certain type of solution to situations of
> a certain general form.[48]

For instance, our most keen and intellectualized discoveries about reality are not products of intellectualism—the deduction of propositional knowledge from discrete premises. Rather, those discoveries stem from the human ability to inhabit relationships, frame good questions from an apt perspective, and grope historically toward resolutions. Charles Taylor reinforced this point in his renowned essay "Overcoming Epistemology," showing how a wide swath of philosophers and scientists have failed to see the implications of a phenome-nology of which they might have tacitly approved, where thoughts are mental and actions are physical:

> A proper following through of Merleau-Ponty's arguments would, if
> they were valid, show a wide range of approaches in these sciences
> to be mistaken—those which involved applying mechanistic or du-
> alistic categories to thought or experience, as Merleau-Ponty him-
> self clearly saw.[49]

For us, ensconced in Modernism and Post-Modernism, the ambiguity of these arguments strike us most flatly when it comes to verbal language, the very medium I am using right now. If all knowing is embodied, and abstract explicit knowledge is a misleading ideal, then how are these words on this page conveying a meaningful argument? Again, Polanyi, Merleau-Ponty, and Taylor[50] have a view of the rich use of language, but one where speech is personal (i.e., claims are claimed by persons) and *post hoc* (i.e., we say because we know). For Taylor, our language is a tool to express our "grasp of the world":

> What you get underlying our representations of the world—the
> kinds of things we formulate, for instance, in declarative sentenc-
> es—is not further representation but rather a certain grasp of the
> world that we have as agents in it. This shows the whole [Enlight-
> enment] epistemological construal of knowledge to be mistaken.

48. Merleau-Ponty, *Phenomenology of Perception*, 126.
49. Charles Taylor, *Philosophical Arguments* (Cambridge, MA: Harvard University Press, 1995), 27.
50. Ibid., 12.

Merleau-Ponty says it more abstrusely:

> Speech is the surplus of our existence over natural being. But the
> act of expression constitutes a linguistic world and a cultural world,
> and allows that to fall back into being which was striving to outstrip
> it.[51]

Polanyi clarifies, describing the scientist's ability to say what she knows:

> Now that I have spoken at some length of the ineffable, it is easier
> to see why this is neither impossible nor self-contradictory. To as-
> sert that I have knowledge which is ineffable is not to deny that I
> can speak of it, *but only that I can speak of it adequately*, the assertion
> itself being an appraisal of this inadequacy.[52]

Our language comes to us as a tool to express what we know, but the process of groping in discovery admits that we are bodies situated and engaged
with reality. Knowledge, under this description, cannot be explicit, exhaustive,
or abstracted in the sense that it is "mental apart from the body." Speech is
both an embodied process and a tool. As a ritualized practice, we innovatively
perform with speech which, for many, becomes a way of thinking and reasoning. Like a laser pointer or any other apparatus, speech also allows us special
appeal to express particular embodied knowledge that we already know.

Analogical Reasoning

The concept of discovery as a form of groping leads us directly into a more
recent field of somatic epistemology. George Lakoff and Mark Johnson began
this revolution with their book *Metaphors We Live By*.[53] They argued incisively
that all of the images and schemas required in order to understand the world
around us are built up through layers of metaphor. These metaphors are ultimately rooted, however, in our embodied experience of the reality to which
they refer. Further, the basic concepts that we take for granted are derived
from our experience. For example, metaphor derived from experience appear
when we speak of theories as buildings, where we express theories in metaphorical terms of their *foundation*, their *support*, a theory is *shaky*, we must *construct* an argument, our argument *stands/falls*, our *framework*, etc. Or, the "ideas
are plants" metaphor describes ideas in terms of: *fruition, budding, offshoot, fertile, ripening, branching, flowering*, etc.

Lakoff and Johnson's continuing work, which developed into a theory of
analogical reasoning, is of specific interest to us. To repeat what was said in

---

51. Merleau-Ponty, *Phenomenology of Perception*, 177.

52. Italics mine. Polanyi, *Personal Knowledge*, 90–91.

53. George Lakoff and Mark S. Johnson, *Metaphors We Live By* (Chicago: University
of Chicago Press, 1980).

Part I: Analogical reasoning is the form of reasoning that necessarily involves our embodied knowledge in order for certain ideas to be logical to us.

Recalling the claim, "Judy's career path is taking off," we know that this is a good thing, in general. However, considering that sentence as a form of analogical reasoning helps us to think about how we can make any sense of this sentence at all. Importantly, the sentence's meaning did not inhere to the sentence *in and of itself.* It required my own embodied analog to be logically mapped onto the particular person (Judy) and situation (career) in order to make any sense whatsoever. *Hence, a logical gap between my understanding and the meaning intended exists as long as I do not have the requisite embodied experience.*

We discover the truth of this constantly with children or with people learning our local culture, inside jokes, etymology of particular words in a foreign language, etc. Our only recourse, when they do not have the experience to make the analogies reasonable, is to compare the concept to something known by experience. Because the meaning does not inhere logically to the sentence, then explicit meaning solely deduced in the intellectual realm now appears as a concept without embodied analogs. Even basic propositions, such as "the sky is blue" or "Obama is the U.S. President," require significant amounts of being-in-the-world and logical mapping of concepts in order to cohere.

Most people will notice the common-sense appeal of the above description. We have immediate access to its veracity. Try to describe anything without tugging upon someone's ability to apply their experience analogically to the terms and conditions. However, as with most philosophically rigorous works, the real test of the description is mathematics. George Lakoff and Mark Johnson both go on to produce separate works arguing that even the operations of logic and mathematics derive from the same source: our bodies.

First, Johnson develops the concept of image-schemas, which are not images, but patterns of action or shape, or both. For instance, the "compulsion schema" is derived from physical force: pushing or being pushed. However, that image-schema can be analogically mapped onto many other dimensions, including deductive logic itself: "In the epistemic realm this movement *just is* an inferential pattern, for, if something *must* be true, then we are forced to infer that it *is* [true]—no other conclusion will do."[54] Physical pushing provides the necessary image-schema to understand the concept called "logical necessity." Likewise, the balance image-schema can only derive from our embodied knowledge of balance and analogically mapped on to other ideas, such as equations (i.e., two sides in an equation must balance by logical necessity).[55]

> In sum, we are now in a position to begin to explain how our notion
> of abstract (purely logical) rationality might be based on concrete

---

54. Mark S. Johnson, *The Body in the Mind: The Bodily Basis of Meaning, Imagination, and Reason* (Chicago: University of Chicago Press, 1990), 63.

55. George Lakoff, *Women, Fire, and Dangerous Things* (Chicago: University of Chicago Press, 1990), 363.

reasoning that makes use of image-schematic patterns and meta-phorical extensions of them. Our acts of reasoning and deliberation are not wholly independent of the nonpropositional dimension of our bodily experience. We can, and do, abstract away from this experiential basis, *so that it sometimes looks as though we are operating only with a priori structures of pure reason*; however, the extent to which we are able to make sense of these extremely abstract structures is the extent to which we can relate them to such schematic structures as connect up our meaningful experiences.[56]

Johnson offers a much richer account and defense of his position than I can rehearse here. However, his work should be considered in detail by anyone advancing an embodied epistemology or antagonistic to it. Johnson demonstrates in *The Body in the Mind* that the nature of inference itself should be considered as logically rooted in our embodied engagement of reality.[57] For instance, we all know compulsion because we have been pushed physically, or we have pushed other things. However, on the flip side, *we must also answer how we understand logical necessity apart from an embodied knowledge of compulsion.*

By the end of Johnson's treatise, it is wearisome to imagine anything that does not somehow find its origins in a core set of image-schematic patterns built and applied analogically from human experience. It also helps to explain the reverse, a topic which Johnson does not address: namely, that we have genuine difficulties understanding those things for which we have no experience-based analogies. Think of quantum mechanics and how its empirically recorded functions defy our concepts. We describe quantum phenomena in ways that sound like nonsense to the average observer (e.g., indeterminacy, super-position, and quantum entanglement, which Einstein officially and aptly called *spukhafte Fernwirkung* or, "spooky action at a distance").[58] These evidence-based descriptions all come across as logical nonsense to us *because we do not have image-schemata from which we can analogically reason with many of the observations of quantum mechanics.*

---

56. Italics mine. M. Johnson, *Body in the Mind*, 64.

57. We mean "logical" here in the sense that there is an internal logic to the embodied experience. As Lakoff says elsewhere, "Each of these schemas is understood in terms of direct experience. Each of them has an internal structure, that is, there is a "logic" of each schema. Entailment is characterized in terms of truth, which is, in turn, characterized in terms of understanding. When made fully explicit, the result would be a cognitive semantics that covers the subject matter of predicate calculus. The resulting logic would apply to any subject matter that can be understood in terms of these schemas. Such a logic would cover pretty much the same subject matter as classical logic, but it would have an experientialist rather than an objectivist interpretation." Lakoff, *Women, Fire, and Dangerous Things*, 366.

58. Albert Einstein, "To Max Born," 3 March 1947, Letter 84 in *The Born-Einstein Letters: Friendship, Politics, and Physics in Uncertain Times* (ed. Diana Buchwald and Kip S. Thorne; trans. Irene Born; New York: Macmillan, 2005), 155.

Second, beyond concepts and logical necessity, George Lakoff dedicates an entire chapter to clarifying how mathematics itself, or at least calculus, can be derivable from embodied image-schemata. Relying partially on previous work from mathematician Saunders Mac Lane, Lakoff begins by tackling the presumption that mathematics, as a field, must *uniquely* deal with *transcendental truth*, whether Platonic or something else. Using the Zermelo-Fraenkel axiom of choice (ZFC), Gödel's incompleteness theorem, and Hilary Putnam's critique of supposed sets in mathematics, Lakoff concludes: "it follows that there can be no unique body of truths that we can correctly call 'mathematics.' That result is itself a truth of mathematics, *whatever* plausible referent that term has."[59] Hence, mathematics is plural, not "subsumed in any one big model or by any one grand system of axioms."[60]

Third, and following Mac Lane, Lakoff argues that the grand question of mathematics dealing with transcendental truth is stymied by one simple "nontrivial" question: "Why does mathematics have the branches it has?"[61] Basically, of the various matters dealt with (e.g., real numbers, Euclidean geometry, linear space, etc.), nothing internal to the discourse of mathematics itself can decide or explain which one of these fields should be dominant, or at times, how one could employ one branch of mathematical explanation over the other. Mac Lane reverts to human activity itself for the explanation:

> In our view, such a Platonic world is speculative. It cannot be clearly explained as a matter of fact (ontologically) or as an object of human knowledge (epistemologically). Moreover, such ideal worlds rapidly become too elaborate; they must display not only the sets but all the other separate structures which mathematicians have described or will discover. The real nature of these structures does not lie in their often artificial construction from set theory, but in their relation to simple mathematical ideas or to basic human activities. *Hence, we hold that mathematics is not the study of intangible Platonic worlds, but of tangible formal systems which have arisen from real human activities.*[62]

Lakoff then takes Mac Lane's suggested areas of human activities and connects them to the image-schemata on which he and Johnson have written prolifically.[63] He then concludes, "What this list is intended to show ... is that basic ideas in mathematics are understood in terms of basic concepts in cogni-

---

59. Lakoff, *Women, Fire, and Dangerous Things*, 360.

60. Saunders Mac Lane, "Mathematical Models: A Sketch for the Philosophy of Mathematics," *AMA* 88, no. 7. (1981): 470.

61. Lakoff, *Women, Fire, and Dangerous Things*, 361.

62. Italics mine. Mac Lane, "Mathematical Models," 470.

63. Lakoff lists over a dozen mathematic operations where there is a commensurate image-schema, such as (e.g., math function-image-schema): correspondence-link, equality-balance, operator-agent, prime-part-with-no-other-parts, etc. Lakoff, *Women, Fire, and Dangerous Things*, 363.

tion, as revealed by empirical studies in cognitive semantics."[64] In other words, the basic concepts of math come from basic cognition, which Lakoff and Johnson have shown to be rooted in embodied experience.

In the end, mathematics appears as a collection of models because it does not deal with an underlying Platonic reality, but with the cognitively encountered reality of experience. Mathematics is not reducible to one grand scheme and for any given human experience, there are various mathematical ways to model that discrete event. It is not my present concern to convince the reader of the Lakoff/Mac Lane view of mathematics. However, I am concerned to show a grand sweep of scholarship that is arguing persuasively for the centrality and priority of the body in knowing reality, even mathematically. That scholarship does not reside in just one field, but everywhere the body is a natural object of study, included now in the philosophy of mathematics.

Habit and Plasticity

> The human brain is nature's great mental chameleon. Pumped and primed by native plasticity, it is poised for profound mergers with the surrounding web of symbols, culture, and technology.[65]

If we extend ourselves into objects which we employ as tools, both physical and heuristic, then the repetition of such cyborgic extension in our practices must have a measurable and biological effect. Notably, the super-plasticity of the human brain, as compared to any other creature, means that our brains are discretely capable of being shaped by ritualized practices of all sorts, more than any other animal.[66] This plasticity is not only a pediatric function of the developing child's brain, but continues throughout the life-span of humans.[67] Bringing together Merleau-Ponty's idea of a habit-body and what is now known of our super-plasticity, we understand why new research is revealing that humans are *rituled* beings by their physical constitution.[68] In essence, we are now in the position to assert that rituals, far from being expressions of beliefs, provide structure and shape our way of seeing the world. We can also now understand better what Catherine Bell describes as the "ritualized agent,"

---

64. Ibid., 363.

65. Clark, *Natural-Born Cyborgs*, 197.

66. Ibid., 85.

67. "This line of work indicates that an important activity-dependent component in synaptic development remains as a lifetime capacity. Biological systems often conserve useful mechanisms; this appears to be another example of a mechanism that had an important developmental role that was then utilized in mature forms of plasticity (learning)." Steven R. Quartz and Terrence J. Sejnowski, "The neural basis of cognitive development: A constructivist manifesto" *BBS* 20, no. 4 (1997): 541.

68. E.g., Cristine H. Legare and André L. Souza, "Evaluating Ritual Efficacy: Evidence from the Supernatural," *Cognition* 124 (2012): 1–15.

who is molded by practices in a constructed environment.[69] Bell is worth re-peating on this point:

> [T]he molding of the body within a highly structured environment does not simply express inner states. Rather, it primarily acts to re-structure bodies in the very doing of the acts themselves. Hence, required kneeling does not merely *communicate* subordination to the kneeler. For all intents and purposes, kneeling produces a sub-ordinated kneeler in and through the act itself. . . . Ritualization is not the mere display of subjective states or corporate values. Ra-ther, we see an act of production—the production of a ritualized agent able to wield physically a scheme of subordination or insub-ordination.[70]

We can now see why merely describing how kneeling expresses subordi-nation, a supposed inner-mental state, is distracting at best and misleading at worst. Rather, kneeling disposes her through her body to see something that she could not have otherwise seen. The logic of ritual is embodied and analogi-cal. Hence, Douglas regularly reminds her readers that "analogic thought is not a handicap" as opposed to deductive logic.[71] She reiterates that ritual cate-gories do not fit exact dimensions, but this slight misfit actually bolsters their epistemic strength:

> [T]he nonfit plays an essential part in extending scientific theory. Not only in science, the models of everyday thought also have areas of poor fit with their examples. Learned habit and the support of the speech community protect the analogy that does not fit very well by restricting the range of interpretation.[72]

Both Bell and Douglas argue that ritualization sets up a series of hierar-chical oppositions, which in turn, create logical structures that dispose the participants to see that which the rites direct their attention toward.[73] As a simple example, the repetitive practice of the sin offering might dispose an Israelite to see something about their own attitudes and behaviors in regards to Israel's covenant. Both scholars contend that analogical meaning is deferred rather than resolved in discrete propositional knowledge—what is known makes sense within the context. "Not only is 'meaning' never arrived at; it is never present in any sense at all. However, in such a system of endless deferral of reference, meaning may never be given *but is always implied*."[74] This subjec-

---

69. Catherine Bell, *Ritual Theory, Ritual Practice* (New York: Oxford University Press, 2009), 107.

70. Italics original. Ibid., 100.

71. Mary Douglas, *Leviticus as Literature* (New York: Oxford University Press, 2000), 21.

72. Douglas is relying on Mary Hesse's scientific epistemology here. Ibid., 22.

73. Bell, *Ritual Theory, Ritual Practice*, 104. E.g., Douglas, *Leviticus*, 247–51.

74. Italics mine. Bell, *Ritual Theory, Ritual Practice*, 105.

tive appreciation of insight is not purely subjective in the sense that its meaning has no basis, but is contextually immediate to the rite. Again, "Learned habit and the support of the speech community protect the analogy . . . It is a relational theory. Each thing has its meaning only in the relations it has within a set of other things."[75] Bell concludes:

> This orchestrated deferral of signification never yields a definitive answer, a final meaning, or a single act—there is no point of arrival but a constant invocation of new terms to continue the validation and coherence of the older terms.[76]

The goal then is not a body of knowledge, so to speak, but ritualized bodies—agents who are disposed to interpret. Bell suggests that this can be done through "ritual mastery," where habitual practices are transformed and impressed on ritual agents' bodies, which can then be extended analogically out into new ways of thinking. For instance, baptism takes the normal human practice of washing and ritualizes it into a "privileged ritual experience."[77] This experience, when habituated through the body of persons, which includes their super-plastic brains, will inevitably shape their conceptual view of the cosmos (e.g., uncleanliness is a construct that differentiates that which is wanted from that which is unwanted). This construct of uncleanliness, impressed upon the habit-body through repeated ritualized practice, can then be extended to other things (e.g., weeds are unclean plants because the term differentiates that which is wanted from that which is not).[78]

The implications of this combination—habit and plasticity—are profound. If correct, it means that as humans, *we do not get to choose whether our thinking is shaped by ritual or not.* Rather, we must assess which ritualized practices we ought participate in and hence, allow to shape our plastic habit-bodies. As Merleau-Ponty presaged, our efforts will inevitably shape our habit-bodies:

> If habit is neither a form of knowledge nor an involuntary action, what then is it? It is knowledge in the hands, which is forthcoming only when bodily effort is made, and cannot be formulated in detachment from that effort.[79]

Merleau-Ponty's emphasis on "bodily effort" should not be missed. Rote performance is still effort, which entails intention and a modicum of attention to script and performance. Later in chapter eleven, I will argue that ritual preparation and practice are tightly entwined. Hence, the performer is not merely

---

75. Douglas, *Leviticus as Literature*, 22–23.
76. Bell, *Ritual Theory, Ritual Practice*, 106.
77. Ibid., 116.
78. "Weeds are unclean" is not a real belief (that I am aware of), but represents an example as to how the analogical construct could be extended.
79. Merleau-Ponty, *Phenomenology of Perception*, 126–7.

shaped by the rite itself, but everything that leads up to the rite and flows from it.

Embodied Judgment and Critical Appraisal

Thus far, I have addressed the critique of Nietzsche and Overbeck in the theological neglect of the body. Second, the debate about Hebrew and contemporary minds was resolved last century. Yet, it persists in more subtle forms. However, for me to read the Hebrew Bible and presume to understand most anything in it also presumes a common human mentality. Third, I have shown that cyborgic extension is not only natural to human behavior, but a feature of our abstract thinking as well. Fourth, I argued that all concepts including logic itself could be plausibly linked to our embodied experience of reality. And lastly I discussed the implications of habituating ritualized practice on a superplastic body. In this final section, I merely want to discuss the problem of precise judgments that are made apart from discursive verbal argument. In short, we can and do judge precisely by means of nonpropositional logic once we habitually practice the prescribed rites.

> This ineffable domain of skilful knowing is continuous in its inarticulateness with the knowledge possessed by animals and infants, who, as we have seen, also possess the capacity for reorganizing their inarticulate knowledge and using it as an interpretative framework.[80]

We know through our bodies both internally and externally, a dichotomy which is quickly losing its utility. We know concepts through analogical employment of experience. We can extend ourselves into tools in order to better explore and understand. Yet there are other things we come to know which are much less articulable, possibly ineffable, but certainly critical nonetheless.

Thomas Nagel claimed in his famous essay that there is something that it is like to be a bat. And if there is *something*, even if we cannot say exactly what that *something* is, then that *something* cannot be reduced to a mere mechanism of chemicals in the human brain.[81] In a similar way, there is something that it is like to know a perfect golf swing, a resolved family conflict, or an impending sense that a team project is about to fall apart. These *somethings*, whatever they might be, are a type of knowing that we have because we have habitually practiced, recognized, and can now discern patterns of complex realities. They are muscle and habituated brain (habit-body) attentiveness that dispose us to discern those *somethings*. We are no longer concentrating on the particulars of our knees during the golf swing. We do not have to get caught up in every lit-

80. Polanyi, *Personal Knowledge*, 90.
81. Thomas Nagel, "What Is It Like To Be A Bat?" in *The Mind's I: Fantasies and Reflections on Self and Soul* (Toronto: Bantam Books, 1982), 391–402.

tle argument in a personal squabble with our child. We can now see how those particulars take part in a focal pattern, discernible only through habituation which has disposed us to see.

Because we can discern the developing pattern, we can then say something about what we know. However, our speech will not exhaust that which we know. Polanyi's notable example concerns the common practice of riding a bike. Something that can only be known by habituated practice impressed upon the habit-body. Polanyi appeals to why the knowing articulation of bicycle balance is unhelpful in balancing a bike:

> A simple analysis shows that for a given angle of unbalance the curvature of each winding is inversely proportional to the square of the speed at which the cyclist is proceeding. But does this tell us exactly how to ride a bicycle? No. You obviously cannot adjust the curvature of your bicycle's path in proportion to the ratio of your unbalance over the square of your speed; and if you could you would fall off the machine, for there are a number of other factors to be taken into account in practice which are left out in the formulation of this rule.[82]

Knowing the articulated formulation of balance is actually useless to the person balancing a bike, and that only pertains to balance. Many other activities going on in the body while riding a bike create a cacophony of formulations just to describe riding a bike. But this point is uncontroversial.

What Polanyi goes on to suggest is that all appraisals, either within our own bodies (e.g., balance) or of events external to us, are equally dependent on our habit-bodies knowing prior to and apart from articulation. The articulation of that which we know is a *post hoc* affair. For instance, much of experimental science relies upon observation as the primary tool of discovery. The central question in experiment design is always: What will be measured and how will that measurement be made? Polanyi, a research chemist himself, reminds us repeatedly that the scientist *herself* brings a habituated body to the act of observation. The critical judgments and identification of what is significant in an observation solely depend upon the scientist *herself*, who has been practiced and habituated to see what is before her. The non-habituated scientist cannot discern enough to make a scientific observation. Or, as Polanyi says it, "Any process of enquiry unguided by intellectual passions would inevitably spread out into a desert of trivialities."[83]

82. Polanyi, *Personal Knowledge*, 50.

83. Ibid., 135. "I want to show that scientific passions are no mere psychological by-product, but have a logical function which contributes an indispensable element to science. They respond to an essential quality in a scientific statement and may accordingly be said to be right or wrong, depending on whether we acknowledge or deny the presence of that quality in it. . . . The excitement of the scientist making a discovery is an intellectual passion, telling that something is intellectually precious and, more par-

As an example, we "read" data and critically evaluate it apart from articulation of our evaluations. In studies of data interpretation, raters assess and critically appraise electroencephalography (EEG) results (see Figure 5.2). These raters were then asked to articulate their appraisals verbally, but the verbal articulation entered the process as a tool post-judgment. In the Japanese study of EEG interpretation, all the participants were faced with the same data and were required to evaluate complex patterns on an EEG readout. The raters' initial disagreements concerning interpretation were only realized as they attempted to agree on a statement that captured their complex nonverbal analysis of the EEG readouts. Through refined definition and normalizing their language of articulation, they were able to improve their interpretations over time. Nevertheless, their critical and exacting analyses came prior to the articulation of their judgment or utterance of language in any sort.

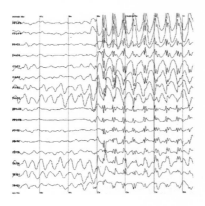

Figure 5.2

The dilemma confronts us clearly now. What epistemically differentiates the nonpropositional observations from the verbal statements of the observations? The articulation of what they know and critique is useful for the purposes of communication with each other about what they critically appraised, for confirmation, to aid in recall, and arriving at clear summaries. However, if the objection to knowledge being ineffable presumes that such knowing lacks rigor, analysis, and precision in critique, these rigorous analyses of EEG data all happen at the embodied phase of observation, before the raters can articulate what they have judged.[84]

---

ticularly, that it is precious to science. And this affirmation forms part of science." Ibid., 134.

84. In psychological research, experimenters are sensing, storing, and critiquing nonverbal stimuli that are prior to a propositional judgment concerning the nonpropositional analysis.

The observer-rater, in these experiments, must learn to critically judge and analyze very minute actions nonpropositionally before they are allowed to articulate what they observed. Importantly, the raters are then statistically scrutinized against each other for inter-rater reliability. The rigor, calculus, critique, and rater's skill are all honed nonpropositionally before the rater becomes skilled at organizing the observable behavior into something that looks to us like propositions.[85]

The nonpropositional observation in research, from which the rater's articulation emerges, is not another *kind* of knowledge. They are experiences formed in their habit-body and integrated with other nonpropositional experiences and judged for their fit in the pattern emerging, none of which needs to be articulated and cannot be articulated until after the findings are condensed into an observational statement.

While there is a wealth of research that supports the critical judgment involved in nonpropositional rating, one such experiment highlights what I am contending. In the following, a head trauma assessment (TEMPA) relies on raters who make qualitative decisions based on watching the limb movement of patients.[86] These assessments, in particular, are not symbolically quantified, but are judged with only the rater's inarticulate observations and compared to other raters once the observation is articulated by a metric. Again, the statistically measurable reliability between raters speaks to the quality of critique and analysis without the use of articulation. It is not until the proposition is posited that raters confirm their own experiences.[87]

Those who observe and rate nonverbal behavior must be fluent in understanding stimuli such as eye tracking while observing certain spatial movements. The rater of the head trauma assessment must be fluent in the "quality of limb movement." Again, deeming nonpropositional experience as a skill—so-called "know how" knowledge which is annexed apart from propositional knowledge—does not distinguish it sufficiently from propositional statements of knowledge.

---

85. Hideki Azuma, et al., "An intervention to improve the interrater reliability of clinical EEG interpretations," *PCN* 57, no. 5 (October 2003): 485–89.

86. TEMPA is a French acronym (*Test Evaluant la performance des Membres superieurs des Personnes Agees*) which translates in English to: Upper Extremity Performance Evaluation Test for the Elderly.

87. A. M. Moseley and M. C. Yapp, "Interrater Reliability of the TEMPA for the Measurement of Upper Limb Function in Adults with Traumatic Brain Injury," *JHTR* 18, no. 6 (2003): 526–31.

Contemporary Epistemological Discussion

I deal at length in *Biblical Knowing*[88] with the problems associated with dividing knowledge into know-how, know-who, and know-that. Nevertheless, I should briefly reconcile the propositional nature of much of analytic epistemology with what I have been describing above. If I could summarize the disparity, I would return to Nietzsche's statement at the fore of this chapter, "Can one go more dangerously wrong than by despising the body?"[89] While I understand that the field of analytic epistemology—though certainly not all analytic philosophers[90]—is generally attempting to assess knowledge by their extensive analysis of belief, justification, and truth, I am simply not convinced that they have taken the human body seriously enough.

By way of analogy, we can consider a prime biblical narrative that deals with human discovery and knowledge: Genesis 2:18–23. In this passage, man is diagnosed as "alone," which is "not good." This conflict sets the plot moving forward which will resolve in the discovery of man's proper companion: the woman. There are several ways in which we could assess what is happening epistemologically here, but let me juxtapose two caricatures for the sake of clarity: the habit-body approach and the analytic epistemology approach.[91]

The analytic approach, in general, will focus on the statement of the man at the end of the story and consider it a proposition: an idea that is either true or false.[92] In other words, the epistemic thrust of this passage centers on whether or not the man has veracious reasons for believing the proposition P: "This woman is my proper mate." This makes plain sense to those of us whose habit-bodies are practiced at thinking in terms of facts that are true, false, or ambiguous. Or to put it in our Western lingo: "It simply is the case that either P is true or P is not true." The epistemological analysis then focuses its effort on establishing good reasons, deductively logical reasons if possible, for the man believing P. Eleonore Stump has voraciously critiqued her analytic colleagues, saying that this singular approach risks being blind (*hemianopic*) to the reality portrayed in the text. She contends that the narrative must also shape our understanding of what is known by the man.

I agree with Stump that a narrative understanding enables us to better grasp the process by which the man came to know P. The narrative focuses not

---

88. [D.] Johnson, *Biblical Knowing*, especially 149–201.

89. Nietzsche, *Nietzsche: Writings from the Late Notebooks*, 244.

90. I have in mind here philosophers such as Eleonore Stump and Paul K. Moser who have been advocating for a much broader view of knowing to include narrative and the body. See further: Stump, *Wandering in Darkness*; Moser, *The Elusive God: Reorienting Religious Epistemology* (New York: Cambridge University Press, 2008).

91. We will pursue this narrative further in Part III.

92. Analytic philosophers disagree on exactly what propositions are and where they are, but they do agree that states of affairs can be represented by sentences which can be judged for their veridicality.

on the fact articulated by the man, but on how the man knew. Without revealing too much exegesis here, God then walks the man through the process of
recognizing that not just any companionship resolves his problem (i.e., the
animals that were successively presented to the man). God is presenting animals and the man is naming, a ritualized practice which appears to dispose the
man to eventually see his proper companion. At the end of the naming process, the text even emphasized that the man, after habitually seeing and naming, "did not find for himself" a proper companion.[93]

Then God constructs the woman from the dazed man's bone and "presents" her to the man. Here, we have an articulation that is not a proposition
in and of itself, but rather a statement pointing to *the pattern discerned by the
man*, reiterating a discovery based on their similitude: "At last, bone of my
bones and flesh of my flesh" (Gen 2:23). This term, "at last" (הפעם), has the
sense of repetitive actions within its connotation, meaning something akin to:
"This time from among the other times." How did the man know that this was
the proper companion? Rabbi Eliezer claims in the Talmud that the man must
have sexually approached all the animals and it was by the sexually-
experienced difference that woman's affinity was confirmed.[94] John Calvin
believed that God secretly revealed this truth to the man.[95] But the narrative
only stresses the initial conflict (i.e., man is alone and this is not good), the
tensioning of the plot (i.e., animals presented to the man which do not resolve
his aloneness), and the resolution (i.e., man recognizes that the woman is the
resolution to his aloneness). Or, as Karl Barth keenly points out, "The whole
story aims at this exclamation [At last!]."[96]

The point is, the story stresses that the man came to know by submitting
to a process whereby God prescribed a ritualized practice of noticing and naming, which according to the narrative, eventually disposed his habit-body to
see the woman truly as his companion.

> God leads the man through the process of coming to know some-
> thing and the man articulates that knowledge in its discovery. But
> what was the man meant to know: a proposition? The proposition
> that she is "bone of my bones" comes at a point of discovery, not to
> be confused with the thing discovered. In other words, it seems that
> because he now knows his proper mate via the epistemological pro-

---

93. Or as Cassuto effectively argues, "but (antithetic Wāw) as far as man was concerned, he did not find a creature worthy to be his helper and to be deemed his counterpart . . ., and hence to be called by a name." Umberto Cassuto, *A Commentary on the
Book of Genesis* (Jerusalem: Magnes, The Hebrew University, 1961), 133.

94. The, the Talmudic sages speculate: "This teaches that Adam had intercourse
with every beast and animal but found no satisfaction until he cohabited with Eve."
b. Yebam. 63a.

95. Jean Calvin, *Commentaries on the First Book of Moses, Called Genesis* (2 vols.; Edinburgh: Calvin Translation Society, 1847), I:134–35.

96. Barth, *CD*, III/1, 291.

cess, he could then articulate with language something about what he now knows. His knowledge appears to precede his utterance. His articulation gives the reader clues about what he now knows, upon which the narrator then rhetorically acts to stitch together the story with a matrimonial maxim (2:24–25).[97]

The real danger of practicing philosophical analysis apart from the habit-body lies in the risk of our ideas about knowledge free-floating from reality. For all the attempts to ground the truth of beliefs in logically rigorous foundations, the possibility that reality is missed or distorted when divorced from the body appears notably absent from those attempts. For Christian theology interested in reflecting the texts of Scripture, the absolute foundation of proper knowing through the habit-body cannot be sidestepped without the real threat of falling prey to Nietzsche's world-fleeing critique. Ignoring the epistemic body leaves no guarantee that our discussions will not merely center around concepts of other worlds, where knowing could be such and such if it were not for this pesky body always meddling in our epistemic affairs.

---

97. Johnson, *Biblical Knowing*, 26.

Chapter 6

The Scientific Use of Ritual
in order to Know

> The initial stage, the act of conceiving or inventing a theory, seems
> to me neither to call for logical analysis nor to be susceptible of it.
> The question how it happens that a new idea occurs to a man—
> whether it is a musical theme, a dramatic conflict, or a scientific
> theory—may be of great interest to empirical psychology; but it is
> irrelevant to the logical analysis of scientific knowledge.[1]

Karl Popper's assertion that the genesis of a theory evades logical analysis
opens the door to ask, "Why then do we gravitate toward certain theories and
how do we justify our attraction to a theory?" Or, what is a theory if not a certain way of *looking at* the observable phenomenon? Theories contain the possibility of discernment but are not discerning in and of themselves. As Popper
notices, theories do not derive from nowhere and wherever they originate
from we cannot deduce. In other words, how a scientist conceives of her particular task cannot be scrutinized by scientific investigation. Nevertheless, I
would like to consider whether or not theory—that way of disposing ourselves
to the observation—resides outside of the scientific enterprise. If it lies outside
the scrutiny of scientific inquiry, then how does science as a collective instill
theory-making in generations of scientists? I suggest that the ritualized practices of science form part of the theory generation, disposing scientists to see
the phenomenon from new vistas, similar to the way they learned the craft of
science in the first place.

In Part III, we will be looking more closely at the biblical material concerning ritual epistemology. Before considering the Scriptures in detail, we should
describe both how the process of scientific discovery and practices of scientists themselves appear to follow commensurable presumptions to those I
have espoused so far. Why science? First and most obviously, the scientific
enterprise has produced a body of knowers and technologies that attests to its
epistemological validity *prima facie*. Science, as a community of knowers, does

---

1. Karl Popper, *The Logic of Scientific Discovery* (New York: Routledge, 2005), 7.

not merely speculate about metaphysical possibilities, but has enabled physical realities that are presently tangible to us.[2]

Second, we are all roughly familiar with the epistemological tenets of scientific discovery, even if we only know the caricature of science. Indeed, for most of us, our only formal epistemological discussions occurred in primary and secondary schooling while learning the scientific method. We understand, even if barely, that scientists observe, measure, posit ideas about significant patterns, attempt to validate through statistical analysis, and repeat experimentation for the sake of confirmation.[3] In this sense, scientific epistemology is often the only epistemology instilled through formal education.

Third, despite our familiarity with scientific epistemology, it is often misunderstood, even by scientists themselves. Although philosophers of science have discredited the Modernist and Positivist views of the enterprise, there is a malingering narrative about science persists. That narrative resembles those mid-twentieth century positivist ideals. In the West, we have the lamentable reality of being able to obtain a doctorate of philosophy (Ph.D.) in a scientific field without ever having to wrestle through the philosophical view of science or epistemology. In other words, most working scientists with a Ph.D. are not ever required to study the "Ph" upon which their "D" is predicated. In a recent conference, I witnessed a physics professor lament openly in his paper the fact that most of his own colleagues at the Massachusetts Institute of Technology still believed that their primary duty was to collect facts through observation. These facts would then be put together with other facts, and from the larger collection of scientific data, our knowledge of the world could be deduced. However, Thomas Kuhn famously warned that the sober history of scientific discovery tells otherwise, "that a discovery . . . does not simply add one more item to the population of the scientist's world."[4] It sounded as if these researchers at M.I.T. were not required to read one of their most famous faculty, Thomas Kuhn, who meant to chip away at such a view.[5]

This thin view of scientists as clinical and objective collectors of fact has been in disrepute for over six decades. And yet, that image of science—an au-

---

2. Just dial a phone, swallow a pill, or watch a video to demonstrate the tangible fruits of scientific discovery.

3. This version of the scientific process is only viable in certain fields, so it is not indicative of what is and is not scientific. For instance, no astrophysicist can repeat the conditions of the Big Bang. Likewise, no anthropologists can repeat a sacrificial burial mound as an experiment. However, this does not mean that scientific process and discovery are not possible in these fields. We also do not need to concern ourselves with the logical problems of confirmation or inductive generalization. See further: Carl Gustav Hempel, "Studies in the Logic of Confirmation (I.)," *Mind* New Series 54, no. 213 (Oxford University Press, 1945): 1–26; Popper, *The Logic of Scientific Discovery*, 3–7.

4. Thomas Kuhn, *The Structure of Scientific Revolutions* (3rd ed.; Chicago: University of Chicago Press, 1996), 7.

5. Kuhn, *The Structure of Scientific Revolutions*, passim.

tonomous clinical exercise of one's rational faculties foisted upon the world—persists despite the definitive and now-classic arguments against it. We cannot survey the cultural phenomenon other than to act as a sounding board for those renowned and corrective voices from the twentieth century, scholars such as Kuhn, Polanyi, Popper, Grene, and Hanson.[6]

In brief, Polanyi began the critique by suggesting that science is not a mechanism, but a collective of skillful knowers and who trust each other. Science, by this definition, is a social fabric whose scrupulousness cannot be assessed by any one person. Polanyi is worth quoting at length here:

> Indeed, nobody knows more than a tiny fragment of science well enough to judge its validity and value at first hand. For the rest he has to rely on views accepted at second hand on the authority of a community of people accredited as scientists. But this accrediting depends in its turn on a complex organization. *For each member of the community can judge at first hand only a small number of his fellow members, and yet eventually each is accredited by all.*[7]

Additionally, the scientific enterprise is deeply humanistic, requiring embodied passions and heuristics in order to effectively proceed, not objective or dispassionate observers:

> Nobody has ever affirmed the presuppositions of science by themselves. The discoveries of science have been achieved by the passionately sustained efforts of succeeding generations of great men [and women!], who overwhelmed the whole of modern humanity by the power of their convictions.[8]

Most astonishingly, this social fabric called "science" requires extensive networks of trust to be mutually furnished and deeply imbued between scientists in order for the system to work, as it were. Or in biblical language, the system is fraught with faith:

> Science will appear then as a vast system of beliefs, deeply rooted in our history and cultivated today by a specially organized part of our society. We shall see that science is not established by the acceptance of a formula, but is part of our mental life, shared out for cultivation among many thousands of specialized scientists throughout the world, and shared receptively, at second hand, by many millions.[9]

---

6. Kuhn, *The Structure of Scientific Revolutions*; Michael Polanyi, *Personal Knowledge: Towards a Post-Critical Philosophy* (Chicago: University of Chicago Press, 1974); Popper, *The Logic of Scientific Discovery*; Marjorie Grene, *The Knower and the Known* (London: Faber & Faber, 1966); Norwood Hanson, *Observation and Explanation: A Guide to Philosophy of Science* (London: Allen and Unwin, 1972).

7. Italics mine. Polanyi, *Personal Knowledge*, 163.

8. Ibid., 171.

9. Ibid.

In what follows, I will demonstration the above claims. The enterprise of science seeks to form the novice scientist into a discoverer through the social and ritually practiced feats. I am not attempting to describe knowing in quiescent circumstances, nor do I want to appeal to truth untainted by human bodies and reason. Following the descriptive trends in Polanyi, Grene, and Kuhn, but also Naturalized Epistemology,[10] we want to sketch out a description of how a novice *actually* gains skilled discernment that disposes her to see the world scientifically.

Ritualized Practice in Scientific Training

I begin by suggesting a minimalist definition of scientific epistemology regarding the scientist herself, with close affinity to what Michael Polanyi describes in *Personal Knowledge*:

> Knowing, for the scientist, is developed through *practices* in which novices can submit to an authoritative knower *and* the reality external to her in order to *skillfully* discern patterns by *embodied participation*.[11] Once that skill has been formed in her, she is able to indenture the skill on her own for the process of discovery.

It behooves us now to take on a common example of discovery in the sciences in order to see what is being recognized and how ritualized practice enables the scientist to discern. We will look at various factors in turn while acknowledging that these exist in a dynamic relationship. First, I assess skilled knowing as the objective of a biologist. In this example, the novice must come to recognize the pattern of *tonicity* (i.e., the relationship between a cell's salinity and osmotic pressure) and how it is expressed in cellular biology.[12] Second, I will account for the matter of necessary dispositions of the novice: dual submission and dual commitment. Third, I account for the role of the authoritative guide. And finally, how does the scientist embody ritualized practices in order to recognize and then discern?

---

10. W. V. O. Quine, "Epistemology Naturalized," in *Naturalizing Epistemology* (ed. Hilary Kornblith; 2nd ed.; Cambridge, MA: MIT Press, 1997), 15–32.

11. Esther L. Meek, a current interpreter of Polanyi, summarizes his epistemology as "the responsible human struggle to rely on clues to focus on a coherent pattern and submit to its reality." Taking on board the loadedness of each term in this definition, it is an apt and pithy account of Polanyi's work. *Longing to Know: The Philosophy of Knowledge for Ordinary People* (Grand Rapids, MI: Brazos, 2003), 13–18.

12. More or less, tonicity is the pressure of osmosis between two solutions separated by a semi-permeable membrane (i.e., the walls of a cell). "A property of a solution that depends on the osmotic force exerted across the membrane as influenced by the differing concentrations of solutes in and out of the cell." "Tonicity," Biology Online [cited September 29, 2015] Online: http://www.biology-online.org/dictionary/Tonicity.

Skill Desired

Biologists must be able to recognize (and eventually discern) the features of a cell that make it especially susceptible to salinity (i.e., its tonicity). A pedagogue scripts a process by which the novice comes to know the cellular feature called "tonicity." When she can discern *tonicity* as a biological construct, this is not equivalent to knowing propositions about tonicity (e.g., P: "hypertonic cell membranes will evacuate water"). Rather, her discernment of tonicity as a construct is *enmeshed with* and comes at the end of an epistemological process involving an admixture of:

1. authoritative knowers,
2. submission to that authority,
3. cyborgically extending her habit-body through tools,
4. particular ritualized practices,
5. the conventions of technical vernacular, and then
6. actually enacting the ritualized practices in order to exhibit discernment in novel circumstances.

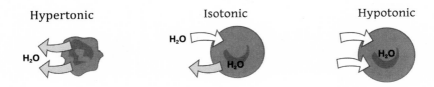

Figure 6.1

It becomes difficult to have an epistemological theory that takes the broadness of reality seriously and yet wants to begin at the proposition P: "Cells are hypertonic under conditions X, Y, and Z." In a broad epistemology, I want to describe the discernment by which a knower successfully recognizes that "Cells are hypertonic under conditions X, Y, and Z." Even more, I want criteria that enable me to affirm that the knower errs by claiming that, "Cells are hypertonic under conditions A, B, and C."

If a proposition's basic function in knowing is to be justified as a true, reliable or coherent belief, then I immediately face the mystery of the process that fruits into that kind of belief. This process cannot be argued for propositionally, but only somatically and historically. By somatic, I mean that the knower learned to map linguistic constructs onto their embodied observation of the cells. By historic, I mean to describe the process of 1) repeated submission to authoritative guidance, 2) extending oneself through instruments, and

3) observation of the cellular phenomenon itself, which ended in *recognizing that* "cell tonicity happens under conditions X, Y, and Z."[13]

Polanyi and others have challenged the scientist's own understanding of science as fact-generating against the reality that knowing is a skill, conferred from connoisseurs to novices, even within the scientific enterprise. Not only a skill, the logic of ritual practice that develops the skill need not be comprehensible to the novice practitioner, though it must be precisely known and scripted by the skilled guide.

> Science is operated by the skill of the scientist and it is through the exercise of his skill that he shapes his scientific knowledge. . . . I shall take as my clue for this investigation the well-known fact that the aim of a skillful performance is achieved by the observance of a set of rules *which are not known as such to the person following them.*[14]

Therefore, epistemologies seeking to explain the breadth of nonpropositional reality must adhere closer to an apprenticeship model than to a datum-centric model of knowing. When scientific process is thoroughly described, knowledge does not appear to be imparted as propositions. Rather, scientific knowing offers *a way of discerning reality* developed as a skill.[15] After all, no professional scientist has been trained to see only historical instances of hypertonic cells, but trained to know what are and what are not events of hypertonicity in the future. It does a biologist no good to know past events of hypertonicity without possessing the skill of discerning hypertonicity in future observations. All the while, she needs to simultaneously recognize that her construct of tonicity may eventually be revolutionized by a new way of seeing.[16]

---

13. For instance, how could one argue about the scientific construct of tonicity in cells unless one presumes it to be a historical reality that the term "tonic" has been the social convention for the same phenomenon in observation from the past up to the present? Justifying our knowledge of "tonicity" then presumes a grander historical perspective (i.e. the etymology of "tonicity") and a narrower history of this authoritative knower faithfully instructing the novice in the proper terms that map onto the physically observed reality. In other words, the linguistic convention called "tonicity" is only helpfully related to our knowledge of the actual reality of tonicity if the convention and the reality are stable throughout history or we can adjust for changes in either. Justification of our knowledge requires both this conceptual/actual stability and historical awareness that can account for changes.

14. Italics mine. Polanyi, *Personal Knowledge*, 49.

15. Kuhn depicts the historical role of a "paradigm" acting as a conceptual lens, a way of seeing the same data differently and inducing conceptual revolutions in scientific thinking in scientists themselves: "A paradigm governs, in the first instance, not a subject matter but rather a group of practitioners. Any study of paradigm-directed or of paradigm-shattering research must begin by locating the responsible group or groups." Kuhn, *The Structure of Scientific Revolutions*, 179.

16. See Polanyi on "Scientific Controversy" which is later developed in Kuhn. Polanyi, *Personal Knowledge*, 150–54; Kuhn, *The Structure of Scientific Revolutions*. See also

This shift from science as *data-collection* to science as *skilled discernment* is necessary in order to see the deficit in the positivist and clinical view of scientific epistemology that persists today. *Not only does scientific training focus on skills of discernment, but also, scientists develop these skills* within a social fabric. The in-groups of scientists authenticate who are the authoritative guides able to develop the same skills in others. Polanyi defines science socially, "as a vast system of beliefs, deeply rooted in our history and cultivated today by a specially organized part of our society."[17]

It should now be apparent that know-how, as a distinct type of knowledge apart from explicit knowledge of facts (i.e., know-that), is untenable in the practice of scientific discovery. Skilled seeing enables coherent scientific observation, which can then be articulated succinctly. Unfortunately, we often confuse succinct statements of scientific discernment with the knowledge itself. Grinnel is worth repeating on this point:

> Textbooks usually present facts without clarifying where and how they arise. . . . *The consequence is that practice becomes invisible.* The more common the knowledge, the more anonymous will be its source. Years of research are compressed into one or several sentences. At the same time, the adventure, excitement, and risks of real-life discovery disappear.[18]

What Grinnel presumes without saying is that those years of research rely entirely upon the fostering of skilled discernment in a social fabric called "the scientific enterprise."

Commitments Required

In order for the scientist in training to know what the skilled scientist already discerns, the process then entails a dual submission and dual commitment from the one seeking the skill. First, the scientist must submit to a teacher who guides her in the use of equipment that will allow her to recognize tonicity in cells. Or as Polanyi puts it, "To learn by example is to submit to authority. You follow your master because you trust his manner of doing things even when you cannot analyze and account in detail for its effectiveness."[19] Second, the scientist must submit to the cell's way of revealing this feature to her, a novice. Cells cannot talk, so she must embody practices that allow the cell to express itself to her, anthropomorphically speaking. She submits to the reality

---

Struan Jacobs, "Michael Polanyi and Thomas Kuhn: Priority and Credit," *TD* 33, no. 2 (2006–2007): 25–36.

17. Polanyi, *Personal Knowledge*, 171.

18. Italics mine. Frederick Grinnel, *Everyday Practice of Science: Where Intuition and Passion Meet Objectivity and Logic* (New York: Oxford University Press, 2009), 6.

19. Polanyi, *Personal Knowledge*, 53.

that she ultimately wants to discern because that reality might change her questions or reveal that her initial questions were ill-formed. The discernment that can enable the most basic scientific discovery entails this dual submission to both the authoritative guide and the external reality under examination.

There must also be a dual commitment on the novice's part. First, she must commit to focus on the salient features of the observation in such a way as to understand the immediate construct within its context. Her ear commits its attentiveness to her instructor, she cyborgically extends herself through the tools at her disposal, and she commits to the human effort to recognize. Second, she must commit to seeing the transcendent features beyond parochial teaching occasions, attempting to discern depth to the construct that goes beyond the immediate observation. There is a fiduciary binding between the authority, knower, and the discernment desired so that the novice is not just learning this instance of tonicity by rote, but she is committed to discern how this instance may relate to all future instances. Regarding the scientist committed to studying gulls, Marjorie Grene tells us about a requisite passion that seeks something beyond the immediate observation:

> As the sea-gull, . . . or the man are driven by their individual appe-
> tites, the man who happens to be a scientist is driven also by a drive
> continuous with instinct yet emergent as something profoundly dif-
> ferent from it: not an appetite consuming that which it is nourished
> by, but a passion which seeks intellectual satisfaction not only as
> what satisfies itself but with universal intent.[20]

Prior to any development of skilled discernment through ritualized practices, the novice must maintain the dual submission to the trainer and reality itself. Additionally, the novice must also maintain the dual commitment to the extension of her habit-body through the tools of discovery (physical and heuristic) and to embodying the construct in order to discern future and novel instances.

Authoritative Guidance

Given the description of epistemological process thus far, clearly our guides determine what can be known. In this example, there are three if not more guides: the experienced biologist, the cell itself, and the microscope. The microscope acts instrumentally to cyborgically extend the novice's vision to the cellular granularity. The crucial feature of an authoritative guide is authentication. In order to know cell tonicity, she must submit to an authoritative knower, a more experienced scientist. How can she be assured that she is being led to the correct construct of tonicity? The only answers are authentication and the fruits of ritualized practice itself: discernment. On the front end

---

20. Grene, *The Knower and the Known*, 216.

of the ritual, authentication provides tentative reasons to trust her authorities. After habituating the practice, her discernment of tonicity itself confirms the authority of her instructors. To reiterate Polanyi's point, the whole of the scientific endeavor is fraught with trusts (i.e., faith), from top to bottom.

Authenticating mechanisms are another part of the social fabric of science. Groups of scientists form institutions which accredit scientists, and through that accreditation, those scientists lead new scientists to discern the implications of constructs. However, authentication is a means to help justify why we would submit to a particular expert. On the other side of participation, authentication can act only as a means of recourse when we have been duped. There are various ways of authenticating scientists which cannot be explored here except to say that only authenticated scientists participate in what is properly deemed scientific discourse because of the problem of authentication. This is why scientists do not train in solitude, but work in a community. Indeed, we rarely trust scientists who work independently of accredited organizations and without authentication.

"Guide" is an apt term here for it shades the discussion out of the static world of propositions and into the reality of process or quest. The scientist is on a quest to discern tonicity and she embodies that quest. Polanyi espouses that the quest to discern is modeled by the proximal-distal nature of epistemology, that we move from near to distant in knowing.[21] When we set out to know something, we are confronted with the proximal particularities of the observation, such as the visual static of autostereograms of chapter four. By this I mean that in her first encounters with tonicity, the novice cannot necessarily distinguish what is significant and what is not in that novel observation. After all, it is not as if tonicity did not exist before we first recognized it.[22] As the novice submits to an authenticated guide, that guide helps the her to recognize that which is already before her in the observation—just as the three dimensional shark was "already there before us" in the autostereogram.

Our guide's directives (e.g. "Peak around borders of the cell membrane!") aid us in cyborgically extending ourselves to the task. Guides help us to extend ourselves through the tools of discovery, committed to look beyond the bare sensory input that may not make any sense to us in and of itself.

---

21. Michael Polanyi and Amartya Sen, *The Tacit Dimension* (Chicago: University of Chicago Press, 2009), 10–20.

22. In a similar sense, Mary Douglas points out the recognition of Hebrew parallelism amongst biblical scholars: "Bishop Lowth, who first discovered this rhetorical device [parallelism] in the eighteenth century, took it to be typical of the Bible, and to this day scholars associate it with Semitic languages . . . *The good bishop did not make a discovery that had been missed for two millennia, he invented a word.*" Italics mine. Mary Douglas, *Leviticus as Literature* (New York: Oxford University Press, 2000), 46–47.

Participation

With guides, submission, and commitment in place, ritualized practice then requires a committed attempt. The novice must participate, enacting the instructions of the guide and extending herself through the tools with a directed focus. Understanding the tonicity of cells allows her to see other related features of cells and the implications of this particular construct. The novice must commit to the practice, which means that she must balance on a three-legged stool in order to recognize cell tonicity: 1) dual submission (to our guide and reality), 2) dual commitment (to the current practice and beyond), and 3) embodiment of the instrument that disposes her to see the construct of tonicity in action.

Again, by embody we mean cyborgically extending herself—that her cognitive focus and the boundaries of her body extend beyond itself in the way she thinks about the world. Embodying the task means that she allows her gaze to extend beyond the upper reticule of the microscope and toward the cell itself at the bottom of the lens barrel. After all, it is not necessarily obvious as to how a microscope should be embodied in order to see at the cellular granularity. Most universities dedicate entire websites with videos to the embodiment of a microscope which can, when properly adjusted, dispose one to see.[23] However, the novice could become stuck staring at the top lens itself, never able to see the cell on the slide below. We must instead, look *through* the lens, in order to see and be guided toward discernment.

The novice, in respect to the microbe, acts like the blind woman who cyborgically extends herself through her walking stick, extending her gaze through the end of that stick as the stick becomes part of her space that she navigates. This is a difficult yet necessary concept to maintain as it is fundamental to knowing. Again, Merleau-Ponty attempts to describe this:

> We grasp external space through our bodily situation . . . . A system of possible movements, or "motor projects" radiates from us to our environment. Our body is not in space like things; it inhabits or haunts space. It applies itself to space like a hand to an instrument, and when we wish to move about we do not move the body as we move an object. We transport it without instruments as if by magic, since it is ours and because through it we have direct access to space. For us the body is much more than an instrument or a means; it is our expression in the world, the visible form of our intentions.[24]

---

23. E.g., Rice University's biology lab instructions for using a microscope [Cited September 29, 2015] Online:
http://www.ruf.rice.edu/~bioslabs/methods/microscopy/microscopy.html

24. Maurice Merleau-Ponty, *The Primacy of Perception* (Chicago: Northwestern University Press, 1964), 5.

More remarkably to the Western mind, the use of instruments requires embodiment even if no physical instrument is ever used. In this sense, mental heuristics and physical instruments both extend the knower's habit-body into contact with the phenomenon. So that embodying the microscope functions to extend the novice's eye down to the very cellular level they wish to observe.

> This reliance [on a tool or construct] *is a personal commitment which is involved in all acts of intelligence by which we integrate some things subsidiarily to the centre of our focal attention.* Every act of personal assimilation by which we make a thing form an extension of ourselves through our subsidiary awareness of it, is a commitment of ourselves; a manner of disposing of ourselves.[25]

Thinking about tonicity as a construct requires embodying the mental structure, where things can even be put in spatial relations to one another (Figure 6.1). As with the microscope in a lab, a trained biologist can use the construct *tonicity* as an instrument to further understand the relationship beyond the construct itself. In this sense, she must commit *herself* in order to discern. This means she must ritually practice the act of extending herself by focusing beyond her subsidiary awareness of the construct or tool itself to a focal awareness of what she is coming to know.

Because she can extend herself through these mental (i.e., tonicity) and physical tools (i.e., microscope), she can then see all sorts of implications beyond the immediate observation. Seizing upon Polanyi's view of the awareness of the implications that open on a horizon of knowing, Esther Meek has coined the phrase "Indeterminate Future Manifestations."[26] It is not that one can see exactly what will come from their new ability to discern. Rather, in committing to the epistemological process, she has a definitive sense or grasp of the proliferating possibilities.[27] It is only in participation, committing to the act of knowing, that she gains this necessary sense of the extended proliferation of implications beyond her immediate circumstance.

> Generality [i.e., inductively generalizing] is indeed but an aspect of profundity in science, and profundity itself, as we shall see, but an

---

25. Italics original. Polanyi, *Personal Knowledge*, 61

26. Esther L. Meek, "'Recalled to Life': Contact with Reality," *TD* 26, no. 3 (1999–2000): 72–83; Meek, *Longing to Know*, 159.

27. In a discussion with my local mathematician, Dr. Phillip Williams, he relayed to me the common mythos regarding Evariste Galois who—if alive today—would have to have the mathematic theory (i.e., group theory) that he himself invented explained to him. The proliferating implications of Galois' group theory have been played out in formal mathematics over the years. But Galois, who died young on the streets of Paris in a pistol duel, only constructed the foundational idea. Surely, however, he had a sense of these indeterminate future manifestations of group theory, which if explained to him today, would coherently fit together with his seminal thinking on the matter.

intimation that we are making a new, more extensive contact with reality.[28]

I have mentioned a series of great speculative discoveries which eloquently testified to the veridical powers of intellectual beauty, and have shown at the same time how frequently such discoveries may remain unrecognized by the most expert judges, and that no one—not even their authors—can even remotely discern at first what they imply.[29]

It is by committing and extending herself through the cognitive and physical tools of scientific inquiry that the novice first comes to recognize a single instance of tonicity. But through the habituated practice of this extension, she discerns it as a pattern with proliferating implications.

Ritualized Practices in Scientific Epistemology

I am now in a position to claim that ritualized practice, far from the restrictive domain of religion, applies more broadly to scientific practice. Looking is a normal human practice. We can gaze at the ocean from the shore, not attempting to discern patterns, but just to "take it in" as it were. But, I "look" at my children's faces in a different manner when attempting to discern if they understand my instructions, for instance. Looking *through a microscope* in order to recognize tonicity as a construct is ritualized *looking*. It is special, markedly different than other kinds of *looking at*, specifically for the sake of seeing *something we could not have seen otherwise*. It is also ritualized in the sense that there is a script to follow: the guidance of our instructor. Although the script of ritually looking *through* a microscope may appear to us as spontaneous, those who have ever taught understand that when we find better paths that lead people to extend their attention, we prescribe them over and over. In my courses, I have *spiels* on various topics which are meant to guide students toward discernment of a construct. We all have *spiels* for the sake of guiding others and these act as the scripts of the ritualized practices.

Biology professors also have *spiels*, no matter how variegated they may be, for getting students to attend to the relationship between cell salinity and osmotic pressure (i.e., tonicity). When guides script a practice, they ritualize the normal practice of looking. In my own undergraduate biology lab, the teaching assistants literally scripted the practice with step-by-step instructions for how to look at the cells while applying different solutions to the slide. The practices, ritualized by authoritative knowers who are authenticated to us, logically bridge the gulf between not recognizing the construct of cellular tonicity and recognizing. Even more, the goal is not merely to recognize tonicity's features

---

28. Polanyi, *Personal Knowledge*, 137.
29. Ibid., 160.

in a single instance, but to discern what kind of tonicity is at work in novel instances. Ultimately, for the trained scientist, these ritualized practices and the discernment formed into her habit-body will dispose her to discern many features at many granularities. The discernment gained through rites generates a sense of profundity and engenders future research questions.

This is, in essence, Polanyi's answer to Popper's mystery posed at the outset of the chapter. From where do theories generate? Theories generate from participation in the embodied practices of experimental science, where recognition of a construct's profundity offers avenues for pursuing its yet to be known future manifestations.

Conclusions

Good knowing requires the development of skilled discernment. I will argue in the coming chapters that the Scriptures take ritualized practice to be the primary means of developing skilled discernment. Israel participates in the rituals of the Torah so that she is disposed to recognize and discern particular patterns in reality. This epistemological process found in the Hebrew Bible and New Testament is not limited to religious epistemology, but appears to be part of normative knowing, even scientifically normative discernment.[30] Just as scientific discovery requires individuals passing along the skills of discernment through ritualized practices, Israel was also logically separated from discerning that which was required of her apart from ritual participation. The habit-body is the prior and fundamental reality of discernment.

Appendix

What about propositions in science? Even though we have not discussed propositions in the central tenets of scientific epistemology, they clearly have their place (e.g., P: "Cell A becomes hypertonic given conditions X, Y, and Z"). This sentence means to grasp onto something like an actual proposition that is believed by the scientist. As we have hinted at above, the inherent meaningfulness of a proposition is suspect outside of the epistemological process that culminated in its affirmation. In order to signify reality, a scientist who has an embodied observation, extending herself through her tools and constructs, in order to see what is being shown to her, must affirm a proposition.

Even though Quine does not formally extend his epistemology into the non-propositional realm, he is sympathetic to the social dimension as a necessary part of scientific knowledge. Quine puts the "observation sentence" uttered between scientists as the centerpiece of epistemology without which, the enterprise of science cannot know any-

---

30. We do not have the rituals of Israel to perform which might give us a sense of what Israel was meant to know under the Torah's fullest extent of ritual epistemology.

thing.[31] The very nature of an epistemic-social fabric is that scientists must be able to communicate what they know. They must be able to ask, "Are you seeing what I am seeing?" These propositions are then tools to authenticate privately observed experiences in a lab within the public forum of science. Propositions are not "knowledge" in se, but tools that help to convey what is known using conventional language amongst a community of language speakers (i.e. the language of a biology) in order to confirm similar private experiences.

Similarly, formulae and explanatory constructs are not knowledge, but can be embodied as tools to determine their fit to private experience. In this way, knowledge can only be public via propositional sentences, even if individuals share the exact same experience together. It is not until language is employed as a tool that confirmation of interpretation can be reckoned.

---

31. W. V. O. Quine, "Epistemology Naturalized," in *Naturalizing Epistemology* (ed. Hilary Kornblith; 2nd ed.; Cambridge, MA: MIT Press, 1997), 15–32.

Part III

The Biblical Case for Ritual Knowing

Chapter 7

Why Israel's Rites Are Epistemological
in the Hebrew Bible

Israel's rituals do many things. They impress the sense of locale and earthiness into the participants. They foster skilled practices: tending a fire to the heat required by burnt offerings, butchering animals, controlling the flow of arterial blood, measuring portions of grain, and much more. To know how to participate in a ritual is to know many things. Nevertheless, in the following discussion, I am only concerned to show that the Hebrew Bible considers *embodied practices* as generally required for knowing. More precisely, *ritualized practices* are prescribed for the sake of specific dispositions to interpret history, place, and new events correctly. In other words, not only is the body directly associated with knowing in general, even more, placing the body into a scripted rite expressly disposes Israelites to know.

Of course, contiguity of local and historical knowledge is a primary concern in the Hebrew Bible. How does the community of Israel ensure the continuation of skilled discernment? The focus upon an Israelite's ability to interpret her history accurately funds and shapes her interpretation of reality writ large. So much so, that in the Deuteronomic retelling of history, "remembering" (זכר) what has happened in the prior 40 years and that which has happened "today" (היום) are the predicates for discerning what will happen in the future. Similarly, the scientist requires good interpretation of prior local observations in order to cohere novel and distant observations. Remembering is done locally, in the body, through the rites of Israel. Whether in pilgrimages to the tabernacle and temple, gatherings at Mizpah, or the home-based rites, knowing is not instilled through universalized sutra, but through local collectives of skilled knowers.

Sometimes, the entire rite seems to aim at the skill of answering the climactic question, for instance, the Passover's question from the children: What are *these rites* (העבדה הזות לכם) to *you all?*[1] Stated less literally: What do these rituals mean to you all? Notably, this question does not aim at a theological statement of truth: "What does God mean by this rite?" This question exemplifies what I mean by the local focus of Israelite epistemology: *This* ritual, hap-

---

1. E.g., The Passover service appears to climax at the child's question (Exod 12:26).

pening *here* and guided by *you all*, means something *to you all* and the child is prompted by *this service* to ask for *your* guidance to recognize its purpose. Depending on how widely we can extend this principle to all Israelite ritual, it broaches the idea that rituals do not come loaded and encoded with as much meaning as we might think. In other words, the symbolism of the Passover service—the cleansing of leaven, the roasted lamb, etc.—could function just as much for the sake of being interpretive artifacts as anything else. In their local performance and interpretation, they gain meaning.

In what follows, I would like to present a tentative case for the Hebrew Bible being a ritually loaded text, from Eden to Exile and back. What is given at creation extends through Levitical ritual and beyond, aiming at multiple goals for Israel. However, I will restrict our exploration to the epistemological goal of ritualized practices. Starting with a general argument that knowing comes by performing scripted actions in the Hebrew Bible, I review the specific rituals that are cited in the Torah as epistemological, including animal sacrifices and calendric celebrations.

Israel is logically separated from that which she needs to know apart from participating in the scripted rights of the Torah. In chapter eight, I will demonstrate that this logic of rituals extends into the realm of tests, signs, memorial rites, and objects that function to trigger the memories of Israel's history in order to steer her into the yet-unknown world. I conclude with a discussion of counter-examples, where prophets appear to plainly set knowing in opposition to ritual. Chapter nine, then, explores the Jewish ritualization of Torah rites in the New Testament description of the early Jerusalemite Jesus movement.

Ritual Practices and Knowing: The General Case

Before proceeding into specific epistemic functions of rituals, I must first establish the case that the Torah explicitly considers knowing in general to be embodied and practiced. When a character in the Torah's stories must know something clearly, their ability to know is contingent upon embodied practices scripted for epistemic purposes.

Genesis 2

When described this way, it comes as no surprise that the Eden narrative is a prime, possibly paradigmatic, example of knowing. Many have noticed that epistemology is at the heart of one of the most central narratives to the Western world. What and how earliest humanity knows serves as the crux of the story which must be resolved by the demands of the narrative logic. However, the quest to know through embodied practice perhaps does not begin in Genesis 3, as is so often supposed. The man comes to know his mate in Genesis 2 by embodying a process through which he is disposed to see the woman as his proper mate. As the reader or hearer of the story, we have no access to how the man knew the difference, for all the animals could be "mates" in the most general sense. Technically speaking, after God presents the first animal to man, man is no longer alone. However, the sequential presentation of animals and their naming, both of which are embodied acts, seemed to prepare the man to recognize the woman as proper *to him*.[2]

A parallel idea exists in psychology where subjects are *primed* through repetition, a type of priming which has the effect of focusing their attention because they can process subsequent repetitive events more quickly.[3] For instance, if we are shown fifteen pictures of ducks in a row, we begin to process the sixteenth image differently because our brain is now in "duck viewing" mode. We begin to look more rapidly at features of similarity and parity, and more quickly. As a linguistic example of priming, the repeated use of prepositions primes our conversations for their absence:

Repetitive Priming:

> *At* what place would I find the car?
>
> *At* Fifth Avenue.

Priming Effect then allows the absence of preposition to be understood:

> [At] What place would I find the car?
>
> [At] Fifth Avenue.

Levelt and Kelter surmise from their results, "It is as if previous talk sets up a more or less abstract frame in the mind of an interlocutor, which is then used in the formulation of the next turn."[4] In the same way, previous ritualized practices dispose us to see new instances differently, to interpret them better. Thus, philosopher Howard Wettstein asserts about rote ritual practices: "One who regularly engages with prayer, for example, not only can come to take comfort in the familiar, but can also come to see, *in the repeated sentences, new depths*."[5] The same principles from ritual epistemology hold true: sequentially embodied practices shape us to see new instances differently from how we would have otherwise seen them.

I am not making radical claims about Genesis 2, but rather attempting to make plain what the narrative focuses upon: man comes to know woman as his

---

2. For a detailed account of the Gen 2 narrative as fundamentally epistemological, see Johnson, *Biblical Knowing*, 22–44.

3. E.g., Irving Biederman and Eric E. Cooper, "Size invariance in visual object priming," *JEPHPP* 18, no. 1 (February 1992): 121–133.

4. Willem J. M. Levelt and Stephanie Kelter, "Surface Form and Memory in Question Answering," *CP* 14 (1982): 78–106.

5. Howard Wettstein, *The Significance of Religious Experience* (New York: Oxford University Press, 2012), 208.

proper mate through a process that begins by embodying this ritualized practice scripted by YHWH Elohim. The climax and resolution of that text's conflict—"it is not good for the man to be alone" (Gen 2:17)—can be found together in the man's exclamation: "At last, bone of my bones and flesh of my flesh. She shall be called 'woman,' for she was taken out of man" (Gen 2:23).

> For unless we see God as someone guiding the man through the process of coming to know, then God's actions might appear haphazard. In other words, the man's "at last" (הפעם) makes sense of YHWH Elohim's "not good" (לא טוב) only if the man's naming (קרא) and his not finding (לא מצא) are directed by God for a specific epistemological effect: man knowing woman as his proper mate.[6]

The more radical claim retrojects my supposition beyond what the text says. I want to assert that the man is logically separated from knowing woman as his proper mate apart from his submitted and committed participation in this scripted practice of naming the animals.

Does Genesis 2 intend to describe a ritual for the sake of knowing? If I understand ritual to have an implicitly global meaning, then no. I contend that Genesis 2 depicts an epistemological process, which entails participation in a guided practice—scripted by YHWH—in order to see the woman as a mate befitting the man. Even though she fulfills the requirement of fittedness *apart from the process of naming and not finding*, he cannot see her as thus apart from being primed by the practice.

Genesis 3

If Genesis 2 has an implicit epistemological thrust, Genesis 3 could not be more explicitly epistemological. Previous commands about what should be eaten are now at the fore, notably, eating brings knowledge. Indeed the very first command to the man is not restrictive; rather, the practice of free-range eating appears to be normative. YHWH Elohim emphasizes the open nature of their freedom to eat in the infinitive absolute: "From all the trees, *eating, you shall eat* (מכל עץ הגן אכל תאכל)."[7] Then comes the differentiation of the practice, "but for the tree of knowledge of good and evil, you must not eat" (Gen 2:17). Notice the components present: authority, script, ritualized practices, and embodied

---

6. Johnson, *Biblical Knowing*, 40–41. Umberto Cassuto argues that מצא must be interpreted as reflexive for the man: "he *did not find* for himself." Umberto Cassuto, *A Commentary on the Book of Genesis* (Jerusalem: Magnes, The Hebrew University, 1961), 133.

7. Gen 2:16. This pattern is repeated in the Noahide covenant where the unrestricted command to eat creatures and grass (Gen 9:3) is given, and then constrained by the command to not eat blood (Gen 9:4–5). As well, the "fall" of Canaan is due to Ham's behaviors regarding nakedness (Gen 9:18–28).

actions, which end in knowledge. Presumably, eating the fruit from all the trees would have brought the man and woman to know something in particular, however, that arc is left unexplored because of what develops in Genesis 3. Historically, many have understood the original command—"eating you shall eat from all the trees"—as a sacred ritual. Jean Calvin interpreted their proper actions as sacraments of their knowledge. So he says regarding Genesis 2:9:

> He intended, therefore, that man, as often as he tasted the fruit of that tree, should remember whence he received his life, in order that he might *acknowledge* that he lives not by his own power, but by the kindness of God alone; and that life is not (as they commonly speak) an intrinsic good, but proceeds from God.[8]

Even here, Calvin's discussion of ritualized practice commends Catherine Bell's critique. Notice that, for Calvin, the practice is not a rite is that expresses the couples' beliefs, but rather brings about their acknowledgment. In a similar vein, Barth treats this passage as ritualized, mediating freedom to the couple: "As the tree of life was to mediate life to man as a reward for obedience by its enjoyment, so the tree of knowledge was to give man a right use of freedom by its avoidance."[9] And, "The tree of life is the symbol and sacrament of the eternal life promised to the perfectly obedient man and accruing to him as a reward."[10] For Barth, the practice of eating does not express belief. The practice *does* something to them, shaping and disposing their bodies through habituation.

The narrative does not focus on their avoidance of the prohibited fruit. Eating ritualizes the practice insofar as eating from all the other trees forms an implicit critique of the one tree—the tree of knowledge of good and evil—the content of which we must remain agnostic.[11] But it could not be stated more

---

8. Emphasis mine. Jean Calvin, *Commentaries on the First Book of Moses, Called Genesis* (trans. Henry Beveridge; 2 vols.; Edinburgh: Calvin Translation Society, 1847), I:55.

9. Karl Barth, *Church Dogmatics* (4 vols.; Edinburgh: T&T Clark, 1936–77), III/1, 285.

10. Barth, *CD*, IV/1, 59.

11. The story does not dwell on knowledge as an object. Instead, it offers indications of the nature of the error in only one instance: Genesis 3:17. For Gerhard von Rad, however, the phrase "good and evil" is "not at all used only in the moral sense, not even especially in the moral sense." Gerhard von Rad, *Genesis: A Commentary* (OTL; Louisville, KY: Westminster John Knox, 1972), 79. Even though he admits to the sexual and relational nature of knowing in the meaning of ידע, von Rad ends up espousing what later became a generally accepted interpretation of "knowledge of good and evil": "omniscience in the widest sense of the word." Moberly finds agreement with Barr and others when he argues that the text itself provides the meaning, namely "moral autonomy": "one decides right and wrong for oneself rather than in obedience to divine Torah." R. W. L. Moberly, "Did the serpent get it right?" *JTS* 39, no. 1 (April 1988): 23–24. In his recent book, Moberly choses to reflect more upon the "heart of the interpretation of this narrative" (i.e., YHWH's authority) instead of the content of knowledge. R. W. L. Moberly, *The Theology of the Book of Genesis* (eds. Brent A. Strawn and Patrick D. Miller;

plainly than here, knowing is predicated on the ritualized practices. The man and woman are logically separated from knowing good and evil apart from the embodied act of eating from that one tree. Reciprocally, they know something else—possibly something akin to covenant goodness, in terms of later Pentateuchal theology—by eating from all the other trees according to what was scripted and prescribed for their good in Genesis 2:16–17.

Indeed, the only diagnosis of error in the Eden narrative falls directly on these two aspects of knowing: authority to prescribe scripts and embodying the actions. YHWH Elohim's search and ensuing indictment aim exclusively at the man. This is clearer in the Hebrew where it is stated in all masculine singular (m.s.): "Because *you* [m.s.] listened to the voice of *your* [m.s.] wife and ate of the fruit of the tree, which I commanded *you* [m.s.], '*You* [m.s.] shall not eat of it'" (Gen 3:17). The woman, who was following the interpretive lead of the serpent, presumably had no authority to script actions and neither did the ser-

---

OTT; Cambridge: Cambridge University Press, 2009), 70–78. Barth recognizes both the moral agency of the term while holding onto the sexually laden context, but he does not allow that the grandeur of sin can be merely equated to sexual corruption. Barth, *CD*, III/1, 285–6. James Barr believes that "the power of rational and especially ethical discrimination is meant." *The Garden of Eden and the Hope of Immortality* (London: S. C. M., 1992), 62.

Westermann most clearly shifts the understanding away from knowledge as strictly objective toward knowledge as a skill, even if an ethical skill: "The expression 'to know good and evil' is to be understood as a whole. It would be misunderstanding to divide it into a verb 'to know' with an object 'good and evil.' It is a whole and as such describes a particular way of knowing. This way of knowing is not a knowledge of some thing, of an object, as it is very often explained; it is rather a functional knowledge. 'Good and evil' does not mean something that is good or evil in itself, but what is good or evil for humans, i.e., what is useful or harmful. . . . If 'the knowledge' is functional and concerned with mastering one's existence, then the meaning of 'good and evil' is explained. There is no question of an isolated object which is good or evil in itself." Claus Westermann, *Genesis: An Introduction* (Minneapolis: Fortress, 1992), 241.

"[T]here has been in my experience a tendency for students to accept uncritically the statement that the basic meaning of knowledge of good and evil is 'omniscience.'" Malcolm Clark, "A Legal Background to the Yahwist's Use of 'Good and Evil' in Genesis 2–3," *JBL* 88 (1969): 266–78. Methodologically, Malcolm Clark argues that prevailing views of the content of the knowledge of good and evil, specifically von Rad's, do not have to frame the discussion.

Following Clark's methodological lead, whatever "knowledge of good and evil" might mean, we must not restrict our work to the prior explanations in order to make sense of the narrative. Further, per Westermann, we are not constrained to working out knowledge as an object rather than a skill, disposition, or adeptness. The narrative does not require us to define knowledge in terms of objective content or skill because knowledge does not resolve the narratival tension. The tension of the plot resolves by listening to a prophetic voice, specifically the serpent's voice. Thus, we will not center our analysis on the content of the knowledge of good and evil, because the narrative appears to be ambiguous about its content.

pent, a matter to which we must return. And the man, following the woman who was following the serpent, had compelling reasons to embody YHWH's practices rather than the serpent's. Script and practice lead to knowing of particular kinds, and are differentiated in the Bible's inaugural narrative.[12]

If my thesis is correct, then we should also observe the result of ritualized practice shaping the participant so that they see the same phenomenon that they previously saw, but now differently. They have been transformed as knowers. This is exactly what we find as central to the narrative. The rhetoric of the story is established in the prior account of man and woman as husband and wife: "*naked* and unashamed (ערומים . . . ולא יתבששו)" (Gen 2:25). Most commentators agree that this use of "naked" (ערומים) begins the play on words in the next sentence: "And the serpent was the most *clever* (ערום) of all animals" (Gen 3:1). This play with double-meaning of *arum,* naked or clever, ends with the new vision received by the couple's eating the fruit: "their eyes were open and they *knew* that they *were naked* (וידעו כי עירמם)" (Gen 3:7).

Two points of interest here strengthen my argument. First, they did not "see" that they were naked, but rather, "knew" (ידע) that they were naked. Because they were previously naked, and their nakedness was not accidental—specifically juxtaposed against their lack of shame—this change in their knowledge must be directly related to their embodied action of eating. Second, their new knowing is not stative knowledge, facts about themselves or their world. Rather, their knowing enables them to see (recognize) their same bodies differently. Walter Moberly also understands this "seeing" as a function of listening and embodying a view of the reality: "When the woman looks again at the prohibited tree, seeing it with fresh eyes in the light of the serpent's words, all she can see is that everything about it looks desirable."[13]

Seeing the tree differently began with submitting to the serpent's authoritative interpretation of the tree and its effects, all of which turned out to be correct. Their eyes were opened (Gen 3:7), they did become like God (cf. Gen 3:22), and they did not die in that day.[14] Eating from that tree, based on the serpent's interpretation enables a new vision—a recognition which is neither

---

12. For an argument that Genesis 1–4 is the introduction to the theology of the Hebrew Bible, see: Brian G. Toews, "Genesis 1–4: The Genesis of Old Testament Instruction," in *Old Testament Theology: Retrospect & Prospect* (ed. Scott J. Hafemann; Leicester, England: Apollos, 2002), 38–52; William J. Dumbrell, *Covenant and Creation: An Old Testament Covenantal Theology* (Exeter, England: Paternoster, 1984), 65. For a summary of how Genesis is employed in canonical Old Testament theologies, see: Richard Schultz, "What is 'Canonical' about a Canonical Biblical Theology? Genesis as a Case Study of Recent OT Proposals," in *Biblical Theology: Retrospect and Prospect* (ed. Scott Hafemann; Downer's Grove, IL: IVP, 2002), 83–99.

13. R. W. L. Moberly, *The Theology of the Book of Genesis*, 80.

14. R. W. L. Moberly, 'Did the serpent get it right?' *JTS* 39, no. 1 (April 1988): 1–27; Stephen Geller, *Sacred Enigmas: Literary Religion in the Hebrew Bible* (New York: Routledge, 1996), 161.

anticipated nor desired. My goal here is to show a provisional case, demon-strating that the Hebrew Bible cares to generally describe knowing by per-forming ritualized practices. Here in Genesis 2 and 3, we have two instances where persons come to a discrete recognition ("At last, bone of my bones" and knowledge of nakedness) only through following scripted practices from YHWH Elohim and the serpent respectively.

As I have argued elsewhere, from the very outset of the Hebrew Bible, knowledge is not inherently desirable *in se*, as everyone comes to know some-thing through their practices.[15] The kind of knowing valued in the Hebrew Bible, however, follows the advocated process of identifying authorities au-thenticated to guide knowers, and then enacting the practices they prescribe.

Genesis 15

In Genesis 15, YHWH makes two substantial promises with two different re-sponses from Abram. Both promises, progeny and land, are repeated more specifically than when originally given in Genesis 12. No biological heir exists. However, Abram is promised multitudinous children. Abram is a "wandering Aramean," but he will be given "this land," which turns out to be the entirety of the Fertile Crescent. When Abram trusts (אמן) the former promise, it is counted to him as righteousness. When Abram hears the latter promise, he questions YHWH: "How shall I know that I am to possess it?" (Gen 15:8).

Directly at stake is Abram's recognition of the promisor's veracity. Our present task requires that we assess how YHWH brings Abram to see the same promise differently. Importantly, if my thesis holds true, then we should ob-serve an authority (i.e., YHWH) script a practice that Abram embodies in order to recognize something different regarding the same promise.

In this passage, we do not know the exact location: somewhere in Canaan. We do not know the social setting of this scene, except the scant and mysteri-ous actions of the Canaanite kings and Abram's various reactions to them.[16] We do know that Abram asks a question and YHWH answers by means of a ritual. This ritual somehow means to answer Abram's question, "How shall I know?" YHWH's answer may indicate that this ceremony was a part of the cultic mi-lieu within which Abram was familiar. Or, the rite somehow conveyed divine information to Abram that was exclusive or subjectively known by him. In other words, it might be the case that another person of similar social back-ground to Abram could have witnessed the ritual and still not have understood its meaning or implications.

A third option seeks to amalgamate the two above. It could be the case that Abram both understood some elements of the ritual from within his own

---

15. Johnson, *Biblical Knowing*, 67–73.

16. For instance, Abram accepts Melchizedek's tithe (Gen 14:17–20) while refusing offerings from the King of Sodom (Gen 14:21–24).

sociological locale, but through the peculiar and particular practices in this ritual, YHWH inheres new and exclusive understanding to these elements.[17] If this rite mimics ancient land-grant treaties, then it certainly seems to modify the formal structure of oaths. If nothing else, only YHWH seems to enter the treaty, passing alone between the animal pieces. This unique expression of the oath could also act to differentiate it from other land-grants and thereby make it a *ritualized* ritual practice. Whatever the case, the ritual itself definitively makes the reader aware of something particular to this scene, whether the rite is socially isolated or common in the patriarchal period.

Geography is another element of the narrative that plays a subversive role. In the foreground, it acts as the promise that evinces Abram's disbelief. In the background it lingers as a monumental promise that becomes elephantine once its full boundaries are revealed. Commentators differ on what is meant by the boundaries and the people groups mentioned. However, merely considering the preceding narrative (i.e., Gen 11–12) will yield a minimally obvious observation, namely that Abram has purportedly traveled the breadth of this avowed land from his call out of Ur in the East to Haran in the North to Egypt in the South and now Canaan in the West.[18] Per the prior story, he has personally traversed this land being promised.

While the issue of heirs is dealt with rather swiftly and ends on an epistemically positive note (Gen 15:1–7), the extent of this pledged land becomes the background to the more difficult belief on Abram's part. YHWH begins by offering a minimal description: "I give you this land." Once the extent of "this land" is known by the reader and related to Abram's own itinerary, his distrust becomes more reasonable, so to speak.

The conflict and resolution come tightly packed within the temporal setting of the discourse (day, dusk, evening).[19] The plot could be summarized this way: God promises, Abram does not trust the promise, and God answers his unbelief in a ritual. How is this ceremony and divine monologue an answer to

---

17. This could be similar to the rite of circumcision that is in use for different purposes in the Ancient Near East well before Abram, but is commandeered and made an exclusively revealed rite upon its practice within Abram's descendants.

18. Cf. Gen 11:31; 12:1; 12:8–9; 12:10.

19. Solar tracking indicates a break in the narrative events. Abram's lack of progeny at the fore of this passage is addressed when God brings Abram from his vision to the outside view of the stars (15:5). The night sky is presumably required in order to make the simile poignant. The next scene indicates that after Abram had finished preparing the slaughtered animals, the sun was setting (15:12). Then the revelation of the land to Abram's offspring is ensued by the narrator's note that the sun had just set (15:17). This comes directly before the scene of fire going between the pieces of cut animal. Solar tracking both acts as an indicator of the temporal setting (i.e. time passing in one evening), but also as a break in the action. Whereas Abram was just outside stargazing (15:6), the sun has now come up again and is almost setting from verse seven onward. Thus, there appears to be a break in the discourse time between these two events.

Abram's question? The answer must presume two things: that Abram has
asked an answerable question of God and that the ceremony and discourse are
indeed an answer to his question. Abram's question, "how shall I know (אדע)
that I shall possess it [the land]" is answered by YHWH: "Knowing, you shall
know (ידע תדע) that your offspring will be sojourners in a land that is not
theirs." We could summarize YHWH's response in three parts: 1) a prescribed
ritual (Gen 15:9–11), 2) a proclamation concerning descendants (Gen 15:12–16),
and 3) a ritual practice enacted with reification: "knowing, you shall know"
(Gen 15:17–21).

Again, we return to the previous question urged by the narrative: In what
way do these three parts comprise an answer to Abram's question? This ritual
practice must be familiar to Abram; otherwise, it is genuinely difficult to see
how it would have affected him epistemically and renders YHWH's words
empty ("Knowing, you shall know . . ."). We must remain agnostic about exactly how familiar Abram could have been with the specific ritual practice being
critiqued by this modified version of the ritual, or at least, not dogmatic about
his familiarity. Although similar rituals have been discovered, there are no
direct parallels to this ceremony in the Ancient Near East.[20] The divine discourse clearly intends to reassure Abram of what has already been promised
through:

1. direct and concrete language (e.g., "Knowing you shall know," in the
    infinitive absolute),
2. a definitive revelation of the generations and coming history of
    Abram's descendants, and
3. a socio-geographical description of the land that is being promised.

---

20. While Jeremiah 34:18 bears similitude (as does an Assyrian/Arpad treaty),
there is nothing that specifically fits what is described in Genesis 15. See John H.
Sailhammer, *Genesis* (EBC; Grand Rapids, MI: Zondervan Publishing, 1990), 130. Meredith
Kline argues that this ceremony must be taken as a self-maledictory oath (e.g., "Cross
my heart and hope to die, stick a needle in my eye."). Meredith Kline, *By Oath Consigned:
A Reinterpretation of the Covenant Signs of Circumcision and Baptism* (Grand Rapids, MI:
Eerdmans, 1975), 17–21. Whatever the veracity of Kline's claim, the narrative of Gen 15
states plainly that this ceremony is meant to be an epistemological process: "Know for
certain (ידע תדע) that" (15:13). Although adding many nuances and caveats, and not
addressing the epistemological issue, Gerhard Hasel concludes that at the very least,
"Yahweh binds himself in a promise to the patriarch." "The Meaning of the Animal Rite
in Genesis 15," *JSOT* 19 (1981), 69. McKeown sees it as resembling the formation of
woman while the man is likewise asleep. Nevertheless, its significance can be found in
the fact that it is an oath. James McKeown, *Genesis* (THOT; Grand Rapids, MI: Eerdmans,
2008), 93. Wenham is most succinct on a minimal meaning of the rite: "This act is then
interpreted as an enacted curse. 'May God make me like this animal, if I do not fulfill
the demands of the covenant.'" Gordon J. Wenham, *Genesis 1–15* (WBC 1; Waco, TX: Word
Books, 1987), 332. See also: Claus Westermann, *Genesis 12–36* (CC; Minneapolis: Augsburg
Publishing, 1985), 227–31.

Whatever else we would want to say, these three work together with the ritual in order to answer Abram's concern.

Finally, what are we to make of this cryptic ritual? Again, without going afield from the narrative itself, we can come to minimally sufficient conclusions that resolve the literary tension. Does Abram participate in this ritual as he does in other rites?[21] Although he passively attends the rite, portrayed in a state of "great dreaded darkness (אימה חשכה גדלה)," Abram prepares the ritual and receives the benefits of the land grant, making him a party to the covenant. I will later argue that preparation for a rite is integral to the climax of the rite as well. Hence, I have no qualms depicting Abram as a ritual participant. Although the normative practice of such treaties requires two parties to be joined by full participation in the rite, this iteration is differentiated—or, ritualized—by Abram's position *off to the side*. During the land grant, YHWH enters the sacred space alone. If this is a modified land grant treaty (with or without self-maledictory elements), then its novel form here in Genesis 15 ritualizes the normative practice for the sake of highlighting what the ritual intends to do.

If we strip the story down to its most essential features, we find that the entire scene aims at answering the epistemological crisis of Abram from the opening of the passage. However, one large caveat remains. We do not have a clear instance of Abram seeing the promise differently. According to my thesis, the scripted practices should result in shaping the agent to recognize something differently. In what can only be literary irony, the very next scene opens with Sarai re-enacting the Garden narrative with Abram playing the man's role. Eve took (לקח) the fruit, ate it (אכל), and gave (נתן) it to her husband who "listened to her voice" (cf. Gen 3:6; 17). Likewise, Sarai took (לקח) her servant, gave (נתן) Hagar to her husband Abram who "listens to the voice of Sarai" (cf. Gen 16:2-3). The language is so strikingly similar in form that Gordon Wenham follows Werner Berg in understanding this passage as a re-telling of the Fall.[22]

Abram trusted in the first promise of progeny, yet the narrator portrays him and Sarai in a re-cast telling of Genesis 3, aimed at securing the desired fruition of a child-heir. His trust in God's provision of an heir is ultimately tested at Mount Moriah where he must sacrifice the long-awaited child-heir. This is to say that trust is not a one-off disposition of biblical characters. Trust waxes and wanes, evaporates and renews. The utter silence about the promise of the land ensuing this covenant ritual in Genesis 15 leaves us to conclude that whether or not Abram's trust in the land promise was fully resolved, the

---

21. See Genesis 12:7–9, 13:14–18.

22. Berg says of this story: "This leads to the conclusion. By employing quite similar formulations and an identical sequence of events in Gen 3:6b and 16:3–4a, the author makes it clear that for him both narratives describe comparable events, that they are both accounts of a fall." Werner Berg, "Der Sündenfall Abrahams und Saras nach Gen 16:1–6." *BN* 19 (1982): 7–14, quoted in Gordon J. Wenham, *Genesis 1-15*, 8.

ritualized practice was meant to aim in that direction. Since the belief about progeny was clearly not resolved, even after it is "credited to him as right-eousness," then it would not seem fruitful to assert that Abram was clearly convinced about the land after the ritual, even if that was its primary purpose.

The ritual did not instruct him to know in the way that we expect. If the goal was to dispose Abram to see the land promise differently, then the reader must be skeptical of that outcome in light of his immediate behavior concerning an heir. However, that is not an indictment of the thesis proposed here. On the contrary, pessimism about Abram as a character because his vision is not transformed strengthens the position. The stated purpose of the ritual was to dispose Abram to know and yet he acts ambiguously towards YHWH's promises. Abram is a complicated character in the narrative, avoiding some of the reader's best guesses about whom he trusts and why. However, that complication of Abram's characterization operates in contrast to what we expect of him, that he would know that YHWH will keep his promise because he has been given sufficient reason (i.e., sworn an oath through a rite).

Exodus 10: So that you will know

In Part II, I argued that because we are shaped by whatever practices we embody, we will come to know one way or the other. The Torah then prefers good knowing that avoids two kinds of error: 1) failing to recognize the authority authenticated to the knower (first-order error) and 2) failing to enact the scripted practices to the degree required (second-order error). One plot line persistent throughout Exodus 1–14 follows the story of who knows what and how. This goal of knowledge is most often set up with the formulaic: YHWH will act so that Egypt will know that X or that Israel will know YHWH is her god.[23] However, according to the knowledge plot in Exodus 1–14, both the Egyptians and Israelites come to definitive recognition. All the acts of YHWH in Egypt are specifically focused on bringing *both* Egypt *and* Israel to different epistemological goals contingent on their submission to Moses and enacting of his directives.

I would like to argue similarly here that the biblical characters of Scripture, including Israel as a monolithic character, are all performing scripted practices that actively shape them to know. Per these texts, we are epistemologically *ritualed* by our constitution and so we cannot choose whether we will practice rituals. The matter for Scripture is that we carefully consider who are the authorities scripting our practices and to what degree we are attentively performing them.

---

23. For a detailed account of this argument, see Andrew M. Johnson, "Error and Epistemological Process," (Ph.D. diss., University of St Andrews, 2011), 76–99. For a summary account, see Johnson, *Biblical Knowing*, 67–76.

As an example, God gives a queer directive to Moses in Exodus 10. Moses commands Pharaoh while God prevents Pharaoh from obeying. This defies our sense of reason. Unless, however, we understand that the scripted practice itself disposed Moses and future generations to recognize the same phenomena differently. After the seventh plague of rain and hail ceased, YHWH sends Moses to Pharaoh:

> Then YHWH said to Moses, "Go in to Pharaoh, for I have hardened his heart and the heart of his servants, that I may show these signs of mine among them, and that you may tell in the hearing of your son and of your grandson how I have dealt harshly with the Egyptians and what signs I have done among them, *that you may know* (וידעתם) *that I am YHWH.* (Exod 10:1–2)

Why would Moses go into Pharaoh with signs, presumably meant to help him recognize the significance of these events, when YHWH specifically states that Pharaoh's heart will be hardened against listening to Moses? It is absurd, if Pharaoh is the epistemological target of Moses' actions. However, he is not. The scripted practice, which Moses must embody, is for the sake of the children of Israel (Exod 10:2). Moses acts both for his own understanding, a stated concern of YHWH (cf. Exod 3:12), but more so for the generations to come.[24]

I will further discuss how signs are meant to be epistemically efficacious below. For now we must notice that in a narrative where both Pharaoh and Israel are meant to recognize discrete patterns in the world, Moses' actions are scripted so that he can bring the children to know. This kind of representative participation in ritual practices, for the sake of others, will become especially important pertaining to sacrifices. More specifically, ritual sacrifice did not always involve personal participation in order for the ritually-instilled knowing to be efficacious. Hence, the "in order that you all know" statements that accompany rituals might include a representational kind of knowing, where individuals learn, not by direct participation, but by preparing for and participating in the corporate event.

Further, in Exodus, a negative instance of recognition is patently displayed in the pharaoh. To say that the pharaoh of Exodus does not understand slightly misrepresents the text. The narrator intends to show us that Egypt and the pharaoh will come to know something by participating in the epistemological process of the plagues. There is never a question about Pharaoh's coming to know, but rather, what will he recognize by his participation? Most of the "that you may know" statements in Exodus, nine in total, are aimed at

---

24. In some sense, these actions that punish Egypt are for their sake epistemologically. Most of the "that you may know" statements in Exodus are predicated upon the plagues and directed at Pharaoh and Egypt (cf. Exod 5:2; 7:5, 17; 8:10, 22; 9:14, 29; 11:7; 14:4, 18). However, the same is true for Judah later. Jeremiah admonished Judah: "I will punish you in this place, in order that you may know (למען תדעו) that my words will surely stand against you for evil" (Jer 44:29).

Pharaoh and/or Egypt.[25] How is Pharaoh's knowledge different from Israel's? The text emphasizes the difference by noting the focus of Pharaoh.[26]

Prior to Moses' re-entry into Pharaoh's court in Exodus 10, the narrator highlights what Pharaoh is looking at when the plagues come and go. Although Pharaoh acquiesces and reneges several times on the release of the Hebrews, his skill in recognizing the grander problem is mitigated by his own obduracy toward Moses. I argued in *Biblical Knowing*:

> The plagues were meant to show (ראה) Pharaoh evidence of God's power. God kills the livestock of Egypt, "in order to show you [Pharaoh] My power" (9:16b). Yet, the narrative focuses in on Pharaoh's myopic seeing (ראה). Instead of recognizing God's power as totalizing, Exodus says, "But when Pharaoh saw (ראה) that the rain and the hail and the thunder had ceased, he sinned yet again and hardened his heart" (9:34).[27]

To say that Pharaoh did not understand is only correct insofar as we mean that he attempted to understand all these events without submitting to the correct authoritative guide. Pharaoh understands that the hail and thunder are calamitous and their cessation is better for Egypt and himself. The narrative highlights his failure to acknowledge Moses as authoritative, which leads the pharaoh to recognize *something*. However, from the omniscient narrator's perspective, that which Pharaoh recognizes is disjointed, out of sorts with the larger reality. In other words, the way in which Pharaoh participates in this scripted process determines what he recognizes through it.

In Summary

So far, my case only applies generally, that the Hebrew Bible connects together the insights (or lack thereof) of characters as contingent upon their performance of a practice. Passages such as the above also broach a larger question: What actions can we perform that do not mold our insights and form us as knowers? For instance, the forty years of wandering is posed in Deuteronomy as a test of Israel's ability to discern a pattern among particulars: "to know that which is in your heart (לדעת את אשר בלבבך)" (Deut 8:2). Likewise, Israel's lack of bread and strong wine were also epistemological practices, "that you might know (למען תדעו) that I am YHWH your God" (Deut 29:5). This question—Are all scripted practices ultimately epistemological?—confronts us more persistently as we look at the evidence for specific rituals for the sake of knowing.

---

25. Cf. Exod 5:2; 7:5, 17; 8:10, 22; 9:14, 29; 11:7; 14:4, 18.

26. For a more detailed account of Pharaoh's myopia, see Johnson, *Biblical Knowing*, 68–76.

27. Ibid., 69.

For now, I want take the above observations together as substantial reasons for asserting that the Hebrew Bible understands that scripted practices
bring us to recognize and possibly discern, seeing the same evidence differently because we have been formed by the experience. Below, I will further consider how the scripted rituals of Israel function as discretely epistemological in
the Hebrew Bible.

Israel's Epistemological Rituals: Specific Cases

Although explicit instances of ritual knowing are rare, enough cases exist to
make us question whether all prescribed rituals have an epistemological goal.
Particularly, the instances that basically instruct Israel to "do these things, so
that you will know" are of most interest. As a caveat, we cannot explore the
majority uses of "know" (ידע) in Leviticus here (i.e., the unknowing sin; Lev
5:3).[28] "Know" here means something like "be made aware of" and so it presumes that the person in question can already recognize how this sin coheres
within a larger framework of actions and responsibilities. In such cases,
"know" functions differently, presuming a process has already been enacted
that enables the sinning man to discern how his actions fit into the pattern
called "sin." Setting aside this outlier from the sin sacrifices of Leviticus, we
must now examine those overtly epistemological rites of Israel.

Sabbath

Moses instructs Israel concerning the ritualized practice of Sabbath: "Nevertheless, you must keep my Sabbaths, for this is a sign between me and you
throughout the ages, *that you may know* (לידע) that I YHWH have sanctified
you" (Exod 31:13). We do not need a detailed account of either Sabbath or
sanctification in order to see that the phrase "that you may know" is predicated on Sabbath-keeping.[29] I discuss the significance of Sabbath as a sign below,
but a more immediate concern springs to mind: Can Israelites know that
YHWH has sanctified them apart from Sabbath-keeping? If not, then merely
relating a theological fact (Proposition: "YHWH sanctified Israel") appears futile. Sabbath-keeping, whatever that may entail, disposes Israel to know some-

---

28. For instances of ידע as "made aware of," see Lev 4:14, 23, 28; 5:1, 3, 4, 17, 18.

29. While some will speculate as to what Israel knew by means of Sabbath-keeping
(e.g., Durham), Childs observes that in the Hebrew Bible as a canon, "a variety of different reasons were added [to Sabbath-keeping], but no one ever became fully normative,
as the continual fluidity demonstrates." Brevard Childs, *The Book of Exodus* (OTL; Louisville, KY: Westminster John Knox, 1974), 415. For a theologically interpreted account of
knowledge brought about by Sabbath-keeping, see John I. Durham, *Exodus* (WBC 3; Waco, TX: Word Books, 1987), 412–13.

thing about her sanctification, the Sabbath's significance within the grander scheme of theology. Sanctification might be a peripheral topic for many, but YHWH puts it at the center of Israel's calendrical practices as a weekly activity, an activity founded in the work of God Himself at creation (Gen 2:1–3). Hence, according to Exodus, we cannot truly know the significance of sanctification until we begin keeping the Sabbath.

When the question comes up to the Babylonian exiles, how will Israel "know the abominations of their fathers [which ended in their exile]," Ezekiel reifies the command to keep the Sabbath, "I gave them my statutes and made known to them my rules . . . I gave them my Sabbaths, as a sign between me and them, in order to know (לידע) that I am YHWH who sanctifies them" (Ezek 20:11–12, 20).

Sabbath-keeping appears to be a clear candidate for what we have been calling "ritualized practice." Sabbath typifies the idea of differentiation—this day is unlike all the other days because of the activities not done on that day. Sabbath forms an implicit critique of the other workdays. Because Sabbath is built into the structure of the week, it also forms the knower through habituation. It is the ritual with the highest recurrence rate in the Hebrew Bible. The Sabbath is also the basis of larger calendric cycles of rest and relief. Economically, loans and slaves are released and agriculturally, the land is left to rest on an annual Sabbath (i.e., every seventh year). Quite possibly, the seven year preparation leading up to the debt release, slave release, and living off the feral growth of the land functions to bring Israel to recognize the significance of YHWH's sanctification. However, they are logically kept from recognizing it apart from Sabbath-keeping.

Sukkot

The end of the Levitical teaching on festivals contains the only instance of Levitical ritual overtly oriented to cause recognition (i.e., "that you may know"). In the directions for celebrating Sukkot, Leviticus instructs Israel to live in booths for seven days. Why? "In order that your generations may know (למען ידעו) that I made the people of Israel to live in booths when I brought them out of Egypt" (Lev 23:43). The plain meaning of this passage presents modern readers with a problem: Why can the generations *not* know that "Israel lived in booths" merely by telling them?[30] Does not the reading of the command itself give them the very knowledge being described? If we take a strictly propositional view of knowing, we could say that Israel is meant to know an historical fact (e.g., "the table is brown," "Israel lived in booths," etc.). The

---

30. Preferring to pursue a thesis about the exilic background to the Sukkot commands—a holiday with no need for a Temple—Milgrom unfortunately ignores the epistemological instructions of the passage (Lev 23:41). Jacob Milgrom, *Leviticus 23–27* (AB; New Haven: Yale University Press, 2001), 2045–76.

epistemological goal is then to show what Israel knew (i.e., the fact) and how she could justify that knowledge. Knowledge—under a very common philosophical view—is knowing the fact itself ("Israel lived in booths") and showing how this could be true, or at least, coherent.

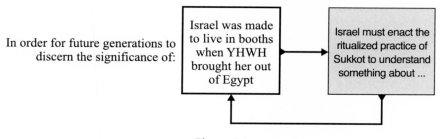

Figure 7.1

However, the Hebrew Bible does not generally appear interested in the propositional view of knowledge, and the Torah's justification mainly rests upon testimony, when push comes to shove. Although testimony, as a form of evidence, is currently being re-examined in philosophical epistemology, it has a malingering history of problems for all the reasons that one can easily suppose.[31] Nevertheless, for Leviticus the logical gap between what Israel's generations know and what they need to discern is not bridged by schemes of propositional justification or even the testimony of elders. That logical gap is bridged by ritualized practice that shapes the knower to recognize and subsequently discern what is significant about the historical reality: "Israel was made to live in booths." That logical gap is breached by scripted participation, which by the nature of the ritual itself also addresses the need to pass along this discernment to future generations (See Figure 7.1). Sukkot acts as one of many ritualized tools in Israel's toolbox for discerning novel instances of YHWH's actions and Israel's appropriate response.

Hence, Israel does not need to know a fact; rather, she must embody the practice of Sukkot to discern the significance of her own historical realities (i.e., "Israel was made to live in booths."). Deuteronomy reifies this point when teaching about Sukkot. Combining the Sabbath of years with Sukkot in the seventh year, Deuteronomy commands the Torah to be read that the "children

---

31. Although I have not explored it here, there is an emerging subsection of epistemology concerned with the problem of trust and social epistemology. While these wrestle with some of the pertinent questions raised in the biblical texts, they do so within the narrower analytic modes. Trust is a "problem" for these analyses because they mostly view trust as if it is beyond deductive inferences, as something ultimately foreign to normative epistemology. Trust as a topic "departs from traditional epistemology." Alvin Goldman, *Pathways to Knowledge: Private and Public* (New York: Oxford University Press, 2004), 139. See major works cited in *Biblical Knowing*, 177, n. 77.

who have not known, shall listen and learn (ולמדו) to fear YHWH your God"
(Deut 31:13). This constant anxiety for generational discernment is not new in
Deuteronomy. The Passover service, not to be confused with the Passover
event itself, presumes that the practice of eating a lamb is sufficiently ritualized—differentiated from other meals—to be noticed by the children themselves (Exod 12:26). Joshua's stone memorial presumes the same (Josh 4:6).

What, precisely, is meant to be known from seven days dwelling in a
booth? The phrase "dwell seven days" (ישב שבעת ימים) is unique enough in the
Hebrew Bible to draw tentative conclusions concerning the ritual. It occurs in
situations of exile for the sake of restoration. Levites are to dwell at the entrance of the Tent of Meeting for seven days as a part of their consecration
(Lev 8:35). In the finale to ritually cleansing a leper, the leper must dwell outside the camp seven more days before being restored (Lev 14:8). Job's friends
initially "sat" (ישב) with him for seven days to discuss his plight (Job 2:13).
Likewise, Ezekiel "sat" (ישב) with the exiles by the Chebar canal for seven days
(Ezek 3:15). All of these are stories of instrumental separation for the purpose
of being a transformed person or people upon restoration.

If habit, neuroplasticity, and prescribed rite are meant to craft our vision
to see something, then what can Israel's generations see from participation in
Sukkot? In chorus with the instances cited above, two of which are also Levitical rituals, it appears that the analogical constructs that this rite builds into
the participant offers a concept of holiness (i.e., separation) for the sake of
restoration. Of course, this is speculation. However, if it were on target, then
the idea that Israel's time in the wilderness booths was not aimless wandering
or mere punishment for misdeeds. Rather, sitting seven days outside of one's
house might dispose an Israelite to grasp that the wandering period was a period of consecration and restoration to a land. This narrative certainly reflects
the promise to Abram concerning the land (Gen 15:13–21). Further, these sev-
en days of separation offer Israel an embodied analogy for instrumental holiness, separation that serves a purpose. And, that *purposed separation* must be
borne in mind when reasoning about why Israel must perform the rituals.

The point cannot be missed that when the Hebrew Bible discussed discernment (sometimes called "knowing"), Israel's overtly epistemological ritualized practices often included the children. This means that the skill of discerning God's future novel acts requires a very shrewd understanding of Israel's past. Access to the vital history of Israel's past is brought about not by
hearing the facts anew, but by a ritual, which accommodates the children's
burgeoning skills of recognition as well.

Summary and Generalizing Ritual Epistemology

Thus far, I have attempted to give direct and compelling evidence that the
Hebrew Bible has within it the presumption that discerned knowing requires
its rituals to be epistemically oriented. The necessity of scripted practices has

been explored as implicit to the texts of creation (Gen 2–3), Abram's land covenant (Gen 15), and Pharaoh's negative example of recognition (Exod 1–14). One objection to this thesis could be the scarcity of explicit evidence. Outside of Sabbath and Sukkot, what other rituals state that their purpose is "in order that Israel may know X"? This objection can be turned on itself. For, in the presence of our tentative evidence, we could ask: Since some rituals are overtly epistemological (Lev 23:43) and some seem to require an implicit epistemological goal (e.g., Gen 15), then by what criteria do we determine which rites are epistemological and which are not? No categorical scheme appears to naturally distinguish why booth-living, Sabbath-keeping, and land grants all have the goal of rendering discernment, while cleanliness codes, sin sacrifices, and Pentecost (*Shavuot*) would not.

The parsimonious explanation, which must be considered, assumes that all rituals have epistemological discernment as one of several goals. One of the psalmists appears to have this in mind where he speaks of covenant-keeping and Torah practice as epistemological and for the sake of the children's discernment. Particularly, Psalm 78 focuses intently on the generational fostering of discernment. "Things known" to this generation will be "made known" (להודיעם) to the next generation. How so? "[K]eeping His commandments" is juxtaposed against "forgetting the works of God" (Ps 78:7, 10–11). Psalm 78 acts as a treatise where YHWH guides Israel through multifarious scripted actions (e.g., exodus, manna, water, conquest, etc.) which ought to result in discernment, yet end in Israel frustrating YHWH. What cannot be missed in the psalm is that logical gap between this historical trend of Israel's poor discernment and the need for future generations to break this epistemic cycle (i.e., "that the next generation might know . . ." Ps 78:6). What breaks the cycle? The testimony of the Torah and keeping God's commandments breaks it, which presumably included a fully ritualized life (Ps 78:5,7).

Psalm 106 diagnoses the same problem that "our fathers did not perceive (לא השכילו) Your wonders in Egypt," despite the intention "to make known (למען ידעו) His might" (Ps 106:8). The psalmist couples Israel's obduracy directly with her repeated false ritualization (i.e., Ps 106:10–39). In other words, covenant-keeping includes proper ritualized practices and has an inherent effect on the epistemological process of Israel's children. Failure to discern—epistemic obduracy—is directly associated with false rituals. In fact, this is the rhetoric of Isaiah's famous discourse on idolatry, that folly—a repetitive epistemological failure to discern—is intimately related with incorrect practice of rituals and false worship (Isa 44:9–20). The motif of epistemological folly and false worship is no mean trope in the Hebrew Bible. It includes the fall of Solomon himself, where the narrator of Kings makes sure that readers understand that Solomon's story veers widely away from his wisdom right at the point where he established false worship in the land. Notably, the lionization of Solomon as pious and wise (1 Kgs 8:1–10:13) ends abruptly with his egregious violation of the Deuteronomic codes for future kings (cf. Deut 17:14–20; 1 Kgs 10:14–29) and his founding of foreign religion as part of his kingdom

(1 Kgs 11). Indeed, a general indicator that biblical characters are on the path toward discernment is true worship and avoidance of false ritual practices.

There are many more texts I could point to here, but the argument can now be taken more seriously. Later in the Hebrew Bible, Israel views keeping the Torah as epistemologically efficacious, both for Israelites and their future generations. Skilled discernment is practiced through the scripted participation in the Torah in order to discern novel instances that were not addressed in the Torah. Hence, all of the Torah, from unscripted keeping of the legal intentions (e.g., showing particular kindness to a particular stranger according to the general rules of Leviticus 19) to scripted ritual participation had a totalizing epistemological effect. And thus, all practices in the life of Israel according to the Torah should lead the Israelite to ask, "What does *this practice* teach me to recognize which I can later discern elsewhere?"

What is Wrong with False Rituals?

Besides the obvious problem with worship directed toward "no gods" (לֹא אֱלֹהִים) in the Scriptures (Deut 32:17), idolatry runs askew of the contiguity and authoritative scripts of worship. Much of Israel's worship can be viewed as appropriated practices, ritualized for their specific use in YHWH worship. Circumcision is not new in Israel, but an appropriated rite from Israel's neighbors. The case might be the same for animal sacrifice, harvest festivals, and more. Even the covenant ceremony of Genesis 15 appears to be an appropriation of a land grant with self-maledictory features. YHWH commands that these known practices be ritualized and formalized, making Israel's use of them an implicit critique of that which they resemble. *True* worship does what it ought to do: worship the one real God.[32]

When Israel's idolatry causes morphological change in worship without authoritative scripts from prophets, they are essentially ritualizing Israel's true ritual practices. Changing scripted rituals damns those participants according to the later prophets. But this matter, the ritualization of Torah rituals, is of utter importance for us, especially when we approach the later ritualizations of Israel's practices found in the rites of Judaism and the New Testament. John's baptism seems to have ritualized *mikvah* cleansing, which itself was a ritualization of Levitical cleansing. Importantly, the authority and authentication of the prophet to ritualize a practice is central.

Accordingly, I suggest in chapter ten that the idea of ritual supersessionism—the replacement of Israel's rites with the Christian sacraments—is not as helpful as ritualization, because the former highlights the discontinuity while the later focuses on the continuity *and also* what is being critiqued by the dis-

---

32. "True" in terms of Yoram Hazony's understanding of biblical truth as reliability, which I have discussed in chapter four of this present work. Yoram Hazony, *The Philosophy of Hebrew Scripture* (New York: Cambridge University Press, 2012), 201.

continuity. In other words, supersessionism is a thinner term. We will later explore Jewish and Christian versions of supersessionism, which rightly focus on the all-too-radical disparities between Scriptural embodied rites and their move to the mental realm of non-action. As we consider what is wrong with false worship, and supersessionism as a possible form of false worship, the matter centers upon who has the authority to ritualize Israel's true worship.

Conclusions

As I have repeatedly claimed above, there are two cases being made here in order to eventually put the biblical view in conversation with philosophical views of science. Neither case is meant to be exhaustive, but provisional for the task. First, there is a pervasive and general connection between embodied actions and knowing, which is not merely reducible to the difference, say, between mental abstraction and muscle memory.[33] Thus, ritual knowing plays a role in a grander view of epistemology, of which scripted rituals are a subset to particularly dispose the Israelite to know something. Second, specific ritual practices are prescribed and repeated with the express outcome "in order that you all might know." In the coming chapter, I examine the extent of these premises with regard to tests and memorials, which are both expressly epistemic in their orientation. I will show that tests and memorials are also viewed as embodied activities intended to dispose Israelites to know. Finally, I must deal with what appears as several counter-examples to my claims in the prophetic critique of Israelite ritual. Are the prophets diminishing or ejecting ritual from among the practices of Israel desired by YHWH?

---

33. I argued in chapter five against the Hebrew-Greek dichotomy, where Hebrew thought is rooted in the concrete and immediate, but Greek thought is able to abstract and therefore reason.

Chapter 8

Tests and the Prophetic Indictment
of Ritual in the Hebrew Bible

If the Hebrew Bible associates the body with knowing, then how do events like tests employ the body for the purpose of knowing? First, I will examine tests as historical and embodied events that commend a discrete form of recognition. For instance, if I want to assess a person's discrete ability to recognize in cellular biology, I might give them an image and ask them to identify the parts of the cell. Second, as rituals like Sukkot mean to dispose Israelites to know something particular about their history, memorial celebrations such as Passover and artifacts such as stone monuments mean to create an encounter that must be interpreted. Hence, memorials play a vital role in Israel's epistemological process, at the level of family and nation.

Finally, what then are we to make of the prophet's repeated critique of ritual? I will contend that their attack is not premised upon the inferiority of rituals, but when taken together, they attack Israel's wrongful performance of rites precisely because those rites will not lead her to true discernment.

Tests of Recognition and Discernment

Exams intend to test our ability to recognize patterns. By "exam" I have in mind the tests which represent an examiner's goal and are designed to offer new examples of a pattern we have learned to recognize through ritualized practice. For example, the analogies exam tests our ability to recognize how the term (and its referent) "lynch" is related to "execute."

Lynch is to execute :: _____ is to _____

    a) steal:confiscate
    b) testify:subpoena
    c) interrogate:prosecute
    d) deface:kill

If we understand that "execute" is the broader category of killing, under which "lynch" is a specific mode, then we know to look for that same pattern in the ensuing word pairs where the first word represents a specific example of the larger class. In this case "steal:confiscate" is the only word pair where this is true. If we have the skill of recognizing the pattern, the test means to demonstrate our skill. The ambiguity between "recognize" and "discern" now appears more pronounced. After all, did we discern that the analogies were comparable or did we recognize it? What is the difference?

For the sake of clarity, but not out of lexical necessity, I will use *recognize* to denote instances where a pattern is learned and then can be identified in novel and comparable instances. After enough recognitions of a pattern have been identified in varying degrees of comparability, we begin to see the knower move toward integrating this particular skill into a broader framework of discernment. The *subclass:class* construct identified above can be broadened to a discussion of belonging as a natural kind (i.e., one thing belongs to another larger thing). Questions such as, "Does anything ever *belong*," involve the recognition of *subclass:class* construct in broader discussion of metaphysics and epistemology.[1] Or to ask the question, "In what way does a child *belong* to her parent," presumes the identification of a *subclass:class* concept that can be applied for fit to the question. We may decide that a child does not *belong* to a parent in the same way that a concept has subcategories, but we must be able to first recognize both instances in order to discern the differences.

In this sense, tests function to help confirm our ability to recognize. In the biblical texts, we are not obliged to adumbrate the entire framework of discernment when evaluating the epistemic use of tests. Rather, we only need to show that these tests functioned to instill confidence that a broader and coherent scheme can be discerned among the particular patterns recognized. Biblical examples of tests, therefore, do not function as an end *in se* whose goal is recognizing a pattern. The tests and corresponding recognition, then, act as waypoints toward discernment, yielding confidence in the examiner and examinee who are bound together in the epistemological process. Tests are the critical feedback needed to determine whether or not the process is working, whether the process should proceed, or whether new rites need to be scripted and old rites repeated in order to dispose the examinee toward discernment.

Noah's test to recognize the cessation of flooding serves as a rudimentary example. Noah's test is binary, attempting to recognize one simple state of affairs by releasing birds from the ark: land or no land. Recalling my discussion of cyborgic extension in chapter five (i.e., extending ourselves through a tool),

---

1. George Lakoff deems this understanding of a patterned construct (e.g., subclass:class) to be derived from embodied experience an "image-schema," which when grasped, can be recognized and used in proliferating ways. *Women, Fire, and Dangerous Things: What Categories Reveal about the Mind* (Chicago: University of Chicago Press, 1989), 363. Esther L. Meek, when explaining Michael Polanyi's view of scientific epistemology, calls this "Indeterminate Future Manifestations." The basic construct has indeterminable uses. "'Recalled to Life': Contact with Reality," *TD* 26, no. 3 (1999–2000): 72–83; Esther L. Meek, *Longing to Know: The Philosophy of Knowledge for Ordinary People* (Grand Rapids, MI: Brazos, 2003), 159.

we find Noah extending his sight through birds. Literally, the text reads: "He sent out the dove *to see* (לראות) whether the waters had decreased" (Gen 8:8). Lest we think he was not extending his sense of the world through the dove, when he sends out the second dove and it comes back with a branch, "Noah *knew* (וידע) that the waters had decreased" (Gen 8:11). How does Noah *see* and then *know* through a dove? The dove extends his sight, as it were, by his interpretation of its return. Although many inferences are loaded into his interpretation, the dove does not know or see anything at all, but acts like his blindman's cane. Every return of a bird to the ark is interpreted as representing a greater reality about the world unseen to Noah. His discernment comes after his recognition. Not only does he recognize that the waters have decreased, but he discerns the salient features of the decreased waters, made clear to the reader through his altar building. Noah appears to recognize that all these discrete events had one cause, namely YHWH. From that recognition, he discerns a reason to worship him.

Noah's bird-seeing provides an interesting example, but we must examine more profound tests of God and men in the Hebrew Bible. There are other common examples of testing, such as the angels of YHWH who visit Abraham and then go down to Sodom "to see whether they have acted altogether according to the outcry that has reached me" (Gen 18:21). In an attempt to recognize the veracity of the report, the angels go down in order to test (literally: "to know") if the report is true to reality. Unfortunately, the men of Sodom reciprocate, attempting to forcibly "know" the visitors under Lot's roof. These two messengers of God go down to assess, through an embodied process, the truth or falsity of the report.

In one of Scripture's most famous tests, the *Akedah*, YHWH explicitly seeks to test Abraham: "God put Abraham to the test (נסה)" (Gen 22:1). What was God attempting to recognize? He later says it precisely: "for now I know (ידעתי) that you fear God" (Gen 22:12). In order to avoid working over an infamously thorny passage and without ascribing epistemological motives to YHWH, we see a patent epistemological process at work, where someone attempts to recognize a pattern and a ritualized practice is employed in order to recognize. This passage makes our claim less far-fetched, where God is logically separated from knowing (in the anthropic terms used here to describe YHWH's epistemology) apart from participating in a ritual practice. Though a burnt offering is a ritualized practice, we understand that YHWH, using Isaac as the offering, ritualizes the ritual itself. This ritualization of burnt offerings differentiates this sacrifice from all other sacrifices.

Is YHWH a participant in this ritual? Akin to what I previously argued concerning Abram's participation in the land grant covenant (Gen 15), YHWH participates in this burnt offering as the recipient of the offering. The ritualized practice disposes him to know something he could not have recognized otherwise and he states the results of the practice in epistemic terms: "now I know" (עתה ידעתי). Further, the story implies an epistemological outcome for Abraham and Isaac in the continuing action after the sacrifice, which indicates that Abraham (and possibly Isaac too) knew something that they could not have known apart from their participation. In an unusually transparent view of the layers of editing, Genesis tells us that Abraham named the place "YHWH sees/provides" (יהוה יראה) and adds the historical note that "hence the saying today, 'on the mount of YHWH it will be seen/provided'" (Gen 22:14).[2] If we were to ask: What does Abraham now know by participating in this ritual? We could defend the answer: He now knows that YHWH sees/provides.

As with learning language, scientific concepts, or color, both the examiner and examinee come to recognize through the employment of tests. The disparity in tests exists in that the examiner is skilled at discerning what the examinee needs to recognize in the epistemological process, knowing how to adjust and coordinate their efforts toward discerning. For the examinee, recognizing a pattern is usually a signpost along the way, a fixed confirmation that she is on her way to discerning if she continues to embody the practice.

As an example of the former in Genesis, Joseph puts his own brothers to the test to discern their motives. His brothers are not capable of recognizing the motives behind Joseph's actions from his haphazard and incognito behavior. Nevertheless, Joseph wants to know what has happened with his younger biological sibling: "that your words may be *trued* [against reality]" (Gen 42:33). In this instance, Joseph is scripting the practices of his brothers *in order to recognize* what has happened in his father's household while he has been away.

Similarly in Genesis, Abraham sent his senior servant to his homeland in Mesopotamia (Gen 24:1–10). In attempting to recognize the future bride of Isaac, the servant established a test for YHWH—a particular phrase out of a woman's mouth: "I will also water your camels" (Gen 24:14). The goal of this test was not to recognize who said this phrase, but rather that the phrase from a woman's mouth enabled the servant to recognize the correct woman, presumably from among several possible women. The servant's own inner monologue attests to the intent, "by this [utterance] I will know" (Gen 22:14). Later, Genesis reports that a woman came and said the same utterance, while the servant "stood gazing at her in order to know" (Gen 24:21). This test, in which YHWH was the examinee, proceeded to help the servant recognize the proper woman to entreat on behalf of his master. Again, participation by both the servant and YHWH is required to bridge the logical gap of recognition.[3]

In Exodus 16, YHWH specifically tests (אנסנו) Israel using manna in order "to recognize whether they will follow my teaching or not" (Exod 16:4). Again here, the test aims both at Israel's knowledge and God's attempting to recognize something about Israel. The result is that "you all shall know (וידעתם) it was YHWH who brought you out from the land of Egypt" (Exod 16:6). Knowing

---

2. This present day saying is all the more interesting if it refers to a saying on Mount Moriah (i.e., the mount of showing/providing), which becomes the place of the Jerusalemite temple sacrifices in tradition.

3. A similar case could be made for Moses' recognizing YHWH's binding to Israel in Exodus 33:12–23.

(ידע) appears to describe recognition which leads to discernment. YHWH prescribes a practice in Exodus 16. Just like the Edenic commands to humanity and their post-deluvian reification, YHWH provides Israel with manna as food, as much as she wants, but with one condition. This time, the restriction reflects the creation account: they rest because God rested. Conspicuously, "have your fill of bread" has the consequence "and you all shall know (וידעתם) that I am YHWH your God" (Exod 16:12). The ritualized practice, eating bread and meat in differentiation, acts as a critique of all other sourced food and intends to bring them to recognize something about YHWH as their god.

Deuteronomic teaching reminds Israel that YHWH intends to test her as he did in the Sinai wilderness to recognize what she discerned regarding Israel's immediate past (Deut 8:2).

> And you shall remember the whole way that YHWH your God has led you these forty years in the wilderness, that he might humble you, *testing you to know* (לנסתך לדעת) what was in your heart, whether you would keep his commandments or not.

Deuteronomy goes on to say that the ritualized and scripted practices of manna eating and general hardship were "in order to make you all *know/recognize* (למען הודעך) that man does not live on bread alone" (Deut 8:3). Misleading prophets will speak authoritatively to Israel "*testing you ... to know/recognize* (מנסה...לדעת) whether you all really love YHWH your God" (Deut 13:4). And if this were not enough, Deuteronomy reiterates that all the hardships up to that point were "*so that you might know/recognize* (למען תדעו) that I am YHWH your God" (Deut 29:5).

These examples from the Torah lead us back again to the question of propositional and non-propositional epistemology. If the goal is to know the fact "YHWH is your God," then all of these scripted hardships appear gratuitous. The Torah seems to have something else in mind, epistemologically. Israel does not need to know facts about YHWH. Rather, she needs to recognize something *about the fact* that YHWH is her God. Even more, Israel needs to discern the significance of this relationship and its broader implications.

Examples of testing in order to recognize extend beyond the Torah as well. Judges tells us of Israelites who tested God in order to recognize something basic about his historical actions. The renowned story of Gideon and his fleece in Judges 6 captures a distinctly ritualized practice in order to recognize, but not necessarily discern. When the angel of YHWH shows up, Gideon's question demonstrates to the reader that he is one of those described in the prologue (Judg 2:10), not knowing the deeds which YHWH had done (Judg 6:13): "If YHWH is with us, why has all this befallen us? Where are all his wondrous deeds about which our fathers told us saying, 'Truly YHWH brought us up from Egypt'?"

The test scripted by Gideon was in order for him to recognize that YHWH is with him so that he will go up and fight. The angel of YHWH scripted the first ritual that helps Gideon recognize to whom he is talking (i.e., fire consuming the meat and bread, Judg 6:20–21). The result of the sign was that Gideon "saw that it was an angel of YHWH" (i.e., the messenger vanishing, Judg 6:22). Now Gideon scripts the second set of rituals, but for the same purpose. He is testing God in order to recognize a firmer grasp of his own role in Israel's history. Specifically, if the ground is dry under his fleece overnight, then "I shall know that you will deliver Israel through me" (Judg 6:37). In order to gain confidence, Gideon runs a second control experiment and asks for a dry fleece with dew on the ground under it (Judg 6:39–40). What should not be missed is that Gideon needs to recognize that YHWH is with him first before he can discern anything about YHWH's plans for Israel as a whole. And, Gideon is logically separated from recognizing any of these until they go through the scripted rituals. Notice that the reader does not need to understand the significance of the fleece, dew, or burned-up food in order to see the epistemological process at work through these rites.[4]

Although examples could multiply, I will leave it to the reader to test the hypothesis. However, I should address the issue of tests for errors, where the narrator portrays incorrect discernment of Israel's leaders, and how it is resolved. Numbers offers us three instances: one hypothetical and two historical.

First, the teaching of Numbers 5 gives opportunity for husbands to test their wives for adultery. Setting aside issues of magic and the test's efficacy, the instruction depicts a woman guilty of un-coerced adultery and/or a woman whose husband experiences unjustified jealousy. The test is only to recognize her guilt. The ceremony also acts literarily to prepare the reader for similar and wrongful accusations against Moses in the ensuing narratives of Numbers. The woman is brought before the priest with a meal offering. Water mixed with earth from the tabernacle floor is prepared for her to drink. If she is innocent, then no harm will come to her and the man's jealousy, which caused the accusation, presumably is corrected as well. This test is really about the husband's ability to recognize and stands as justification or a corrective. Again, the logical gap between recognizing the true account and not is bridged only by a ritual. This is not a regulative ritual to be recurrently practiced, but an occasional ritual, only practiced by dint of circumstance.

Numbers goes on then to tell two stories about groups who believed that they had discerned the correct position, different than Moses' understanding. More simply, Numbers portrays tests for those who think Moses has gotten it wrong somehow. In the first instance, Miriam and Aaron believe that they have discerned a perspective at odds with the unique prophetic role of Moses (Num 12). A few chapters later, Korah and others propose a view of holiness at odds with the unique holiness of Moses and the priests (Num 16).

In both cases, yet again, the narrator focuses the reader on whether or not we should recognize their ability to discern and embody what they are pre-

---

4. The same scenario without the lexical term "test" can be seen in 1 Sam 6 where the clear intention is to "know that it was not His hand that struck us; it just happened to us by chance" (6:9). Cf. 1 Sam 12:16–17; 1 Kings 18.

scribing. And in both cases, the answer is definitively "no," but only after being invited to participate in a test of their authority. In the former case, Miriam and Aaron are rebuked by being subjected to one of the unique signs of Moses' authority. Where leprosy was an object under Moses' control as a sign of his authority to speak on behalf of YHWH, Miriam was subjected to the disease (cf. Exod 3:6–7; Num 12:1–12). In the latter story, Korah et al. appear to want the spatial restrictions of the tabernacle required by YHWH's holiness to be broken down: "all the community are holy, all of them" (Num 12:3). The epistemological thrust of this text is made plain when Moses replies: "Come morning, YHWH will make known (וידע) who is His and who is holy" (Num 12:5). Like the possibly adulterous wife, Korah and his men participate in a ritual meant to definitively resolve which discerned perspective is truer to reality. They bring their fire pans and stand before YHWH. Moses epistemically prepares the congregation, saying, "By this *you shall know* (תדעון) that it was YHWH who sent me," and "*you all shall know* (וידעתם) that these men have spurned YHWH" (Num 12:28, 30). Once Korah et al. are swallowed alive into Sheol, YHWH orders their fire pans to be hammered out and displayed as plating on the altar, the place where the uniquely holy priesthood operates.

These ritual practices also act as signs, meant to bring definitive resolution and cause Israel to recognize basic facts of which they must later discern the significance. Coming back to my prior thesis, if Israelites do not recognize that Moses is the ultimate authority, authenticated to guide them, *then nothing else they do will be epistemically effective.* All knowing will end up out of sorts and a truncated version of reality. The same could be said of episodes such as Elijah and the prophets of Baal on Mount Carmel, where the central matter to be recognized was that God answers only to the name YHWH (1 Kgs 18).

I suggest that tests and signs create epistemologically veracious waypoints for those learning to discern. As with most of life, in the flux and flummox of indiscernible particulars that confront us, tests and signs enable recognition. They act as buoys in the choppy waters of discernment. The Hebrew Bible is enthralling for this reason alone, if not many more, that the signs which act as points of confident recognition lead Israel to discernment and those signs are not annexed to the sphere of religious knowing. The Torah of YHWH is to act as guiding instruction, leading Israel toward a way of being in the world that fosters discernment. *Mezuzot* (Torah on the doorposts) and prayer bindings (e.g., phylactery) are meant to act as signs to the Israelite (Deut 6:4–9). Even granting the foreigner's prayer at the temple is "so that all the peoples of the earth know (למען תדע) your name and fear you."[5] All of life, when seen through the history of Israel, is meant to lead toward discernment of transcendent properties. Even drinking water from a cistern in the land acts as a sign meant to discern YHWH's intentions for His people.[6]

---

5. 1 Kgs 8:60.

6. According to Deuteronomy, all of life in the land was to serve as a sign: cities, cisterns, houses, fruit, etc. (Deut 6:10–15).

The book of the Law,[7] the Deuteronomic Song of Moses,[8] the heavens and earth,[9] and even the Tabernacle itself serve as testimony,[10] both of what YHWH has done and how he intends for Israel to respond in ritualized practices. Just as with rituals, a scripted practice is embodied in order to dispose the participants to recognize. These tests become crucial in the movement from recognizing to discernment.

Memory and Memorials

Memorials function as an occasional ritual, demanding participation when one encounters the memorial. Some of these occasions are geographical encounters and some are calendric holidays. Prominent and by design in these memorials, the pediatric focus of their epistemology dominates the practice. These rites simultaneously address the discernment of the adult and the skill to recognize required of children. How does this memorial or rite help the adult Israelite to discern their history and how does it teach their child to recognize?

In discussing memorials, we must take care not to conflate the biblical sense of memory with what some take to be a purely mental (i.e., not physical) act of remembering. Deuteronomy is often considered the book of remembering due to the density of the term "remember" (זקר) unique to that text. Ryan O'Dowd proffers that our notion of "remembering" cannot be reduced to mental memory and still resonate with the demands of the text. Deuteronomic remembering is fully embodied, so pervasively somatic that O'Dowd summarizes it:

> Israel's access to knowledge is performative by virtue of the roles
> Deuteronomy creates for the community. Reading, hearing, writing,
> singing, remembering and obeying the Torah actualize the ontolog-
> ical realities of Israel's relationship with Yahweh.[11]

In his monograph on wisdom and Torah, O'Dowd effectively argues that knowing, for Israel in the Deuteronomic tradition, began with an ontological connection to the creation narrative and an embodied practice of memory, both of which are ethically loaded.[12] Wisdom, or what we are calling "discern-

---

7. Deut 31:26.

8. Deut 31:22.

9. Deut 30:19.

10. Re "the tent of testimony."

11. Ryan P. O'Dowd, "Memory on the Boundary: Epistemology in Deuteronomy," in *The Bible and Epistemology* (eds. Mary Healy and Robin Parry; Milton Keynes, England: Paternoster, 2007), 20.

12. "Positioned in this way, the knowledge of Yahweh prefaces and qualifies the ensuing legal discourse . . . . The implication for Israel is that the knowledge of Yahweh, of his activity in history, and of his universal uniqueness are the foundation of her knowledge of the world . . . reinforces the fact that epistemology is grounded in the

ment" in this work, is intimately connected with a Torah-oriented life, both individually and corporately.[13] Hence, in our most memory-centered biblical text, remembering is a function of the ritual practices of Israel, disposing her to discern past history and YHWH's future plans through those practices.

Performative Memorials

Passover serves as a unique rite in Israel's history because of its placement in the story of the exodus. Specifically, the memorial ceremony is given before the actual exodus happens and bifurcated into the later annual celebrations, making two events. The Passover night itself is historically unique but Israel is meant to repeat the Passover memorial annually. The historically unique rite required the lamb's blood to be spread on the doorposts "as a sign *for you*," the Israelites who survived that night (Exod 12:13). Even in the event itself, YHWH built a sign into phenomena so that survivors could recognize what was happening, but only by practicing the rite to the degree required. The Pesach meal, however, is a memorial (Exod 12:14) meant to provoke the children struggling to recognize its significance and to be interpreted to them by the adults at the meal (Exod 12:26–27). In the unique historical event, the stated purpose of this final plague is one of recognition: "*in order that you may know* (למען תדעון) that YHWH makes a distinction between Egypt and Israel" (Exod 11:7). Both the unique event and the subsequent annual feasts were scripted together to dispose participants, young and old, to recognize aspects of YHWH's historical actions in the immediate circumstance and for generations to come. The blood on their doorposts acted as a sign to the exodus generation, but the Passover celebration acts as a memorial for generations to come.

This use of ritualized practice is not unique to the Passover celebration. We find that pediatric epistemological concern reverberating in Deuteronomy, but also beyond into Joshua and its absence that is later lamented in Judges.[14]

---

ontology of divine presence and divine power and the ethics of obedience." Ryan O'Dowd, *The Wisdom of Torah: Epistemology in Deuteronomy and the Wisdom in Literature* (FRLANT 225; Göttingen: Vandenhoeck & Ruprecht, 2009), 42.

13. "Wisdom and Torah, then, share the same cosmic worldview which sets individual folly and pride alongside national pride and covenant infidelity as matters of distorting the moral structures of the created order. Folly . . . is a state of pride-induced blindness which leads to sin, death and curse. Only Torah explicitly articulates the narrative framework of Yahweh's future discipline and restoration; Torah is the means through which Yahweh renews Israel's wisdom and respect for her role in God's cosmic plans to bless the nations (Deut 30:15; 32:47; Prov 2:19, 4:23)." O'Dowd, *The Wisdom of Torah*, 174.

14. E.g., Judg 2:10–19; 3:1–4.

Memorial Artifacts

In the West, a memorial is most often associated with a physical feature: a sculpture, plaque, or some other durative artifact. This physical artifact could fool us into thinking that the headstone of a grave, for instance, is the memorial in and of itself. But the headstone ritualizes several practices, provoking us to remember. When we encounter a headstone, the stone's function is to form us in some way, to make us aware of a former ancestor or to call us back to the day that we buried a family member or friend. The point is, the artifact creates an occasional rite *through us*. The memorial resides, not just in that place, but is also embodied in us as memorial participants.

An obvious example of memorial artifact is the stone memorial set up by Joshua after crossing the Jordan (Josh 4:20). Stone memorials are described in the Hebrew Bible under four distinct uses: 1) in places of significant historical events (e.g., Gen 28:18), 2) over the bodies of significantly bad people (e.g., Achan, the King of Ai, and Amorites), 3) in remembrance of the Torah (Exod 34:4; Josh 8:30–32; 24:25–27), and 4) as boundary markers (e.g., Josh 15:6).

In Joshua, the narrative is unambiguous about the ritualization of the stones and how those exact stones create an epistemological practice that includes the children. The stones were not found slapdash, but selected smooth stones which would indicate that they were sourced from the center of the river. The number of stones indicated the tribes as a closed set. The narrator informs us of the exact function of this pile of stones:

> . . . that this may be a sign among you. When your children ask in time to come, "What do those stones mean *to you*? . . . So these stones shall be to the people of Israel a memorial forever . . . and they are there to this day.[15]

This hypothetical familial encounter with the memorial is restated (Josh 4:21–24) and extended to connect the Jordan crossing directly to the Red Sea crossing. The purpose is clear, encountering these stones as an artifact broaches the question among the memorial participants, "What do these mean *to you all*," which is resolved with "make it known (והודעתם) to your children" (Josh 4:22), which is then extended to the larger goal "in order that all the people of the earth know (למען דעת) how mighty is the hand of YHWH" (Josh 4:24).

Living briefly in Israel, I observed this with my own children. While we often have to temper the traditionally ascribed biblical locales with the words "reportedly" or "supposedly," we can be more confident about some sites. The City of David is a facile example. When we report what happened at the fall of Jerusalem in 586 B.C.E., it certainly did not firmly capture the attention of my elementary-aged children. However, when we brought them to the Ophel at the top of the City of David and pointed to the house where Jeremiah's perse-

---

15. Josh 4:6, 7, 9.

cutors' might have lived (i.e., where their personal signatory bullae were found; re Jer 38:1–6), their attention was piqued. They started processing all the same old stories differently, trying to recognize each part of the excavation in some aspect of the text or imagine what it would be like to stare down the ancient city from the palace roof toward Uriah the Hittite's roof, where his wife "reportedly" bathed. There was a palpable based-on-a-true-story effect merely from encountering the actual artifact: the locale of the story's events.

The artifact creates a nexus of the actual historical place of the event with the interpretation of Israel's history for the sake of the children's ability to discern its significance. In Joshua, the encounter is hypothetically scripted, but the epistemological intention is clear. *This* pile of stones, differentiated from all other piles of stones (and there are many in the Jordan Valley), is meant for the discernment of the generations of Israelites to come.

Summary of Tests and Memorials

I hope to have tentatively shown with the above examples that tests, signs, and memorials have explicitly epistemological goals. These goals are most coherent in an epistemological scheme utilizing ritualized practice, not propositional facts, in order to dispose persons to recognize. Not only do these texts affirm these practices as overtly epistemological, framing the practice with language like "in order that you know," but they also take the unusual step of pediatric inclusion implicit in the purpose of the practice. If rites have an implicit epistemological function, they also appear to possibly have a pediatric epistemology built in to them as well. I explore this further when my discussion of direct and representational ritual participation in the Scriptures (see chapter eleven).

Counterexamples: Knowledge versus Rituals

If the reader is at all familiar with biblical literature, you will have been wondering about those passages in the prophets that appear to directly confront my thesis, juxtaposing knowing and rituals against each other.[16] Hosea's declaration is the most direct:

---

16. Klawans cites six reasons typically offered to explain the prophetic critique of sacrifice while maintaining that the prophets still had a positive view of ritual: 1) prophets are either priests or associated with priestly cult; 2) priestly texts (e.g., Lev 19) connect ethics and ritual directly; 3) prophets object to festivals and prayers, not just sacrifices, yet no one believes prayer to be eclipsed in Israelite history; 4) eschatological visions often include priestly cult; 5) prophets used hyperbole to reprioritize, not abolish; and 6) prophets attack abuse of rites, not the proper use. Jona-

For I desire mercy and *not sacrifice*,
knowledge of God rather than burnt offerings.[17]

Or, some places appear to espouse knowing apart from ritual (e.g., Exod 18:11).[18] I must now deal with these passages and show how, when read in their context, they support my thesis. First, because these passages are occasional in nature (i.e., they deal with specific historical contexts),[19] I must consider the difference between first and second order epistemological errors in the Hebrew Bible. Second, I examine the primacy of Torah as *the script* of Israel's ritualized practices. Finally, I will be prepared to assess how the prophetic critiques of Israel's ritual practices are actually epistemologically savvy.

First and Second Order Errors

Although this appears an odd place to bring in a discussion of error, understanding precisely how Israel goes wrong in their discernment is part of recognizing the task of the prophets. For this reason, I need to differentiate between errors derived from failing to acknowledge the prophet's authority (first-order) versus errors from not participating in the specified practices to the degree required (second-order).[20] Examples of these two different errors can be found in Exodus. The pharaoh of Exodus commits a first-order error in refusing to listen to Moses, the authoritative voice clearly authenticated to him by signs. Although Moses could have guided Pharaoh to see the world *truly*, interpreting Egypt's own history through the lens of YHWH's actions (i.e., Exod 1:8), Pharaoh's blunt response to Moses is telling of the first-order error: "Who is YHWH that I should listen to his voice" (Exod 5:2). Pharaoh recognized

---

than Klawans, *Purity, Sacrifice, and the Temple: Symbolism and Supersessionism in the Study of Ancient Judaism* (Oxford: Oxford University Press, 2006), 79–82.

17. Hos 6:6. This stands apart from a pattern of prophetic critique seemingly against sacrifice itself. See also: 1 Sam 15:22; Isa 1:11; Jer 6:20; and Amos 5:21–24.

18. "Now I know that YHWH is greater than all gods, because in this affair they dealt arrogantly with the people." Although this appears to be simple statement of fact, this interpretation is clearly rooted in evaluating history. We could argue that this ability to discern "that YHWH is greater than all the gods" results from layers of practiced discernment.

19. As Klawans notes, context has been diminished for the sake of focusing on the prophetic condemnation of sacrifice. However, "It is no coincidence that Samuel calls for obedience (שמע), while Amos calls for justice (צדק), and Hosea calls for steadfast love (חסד)." *Purity, Sacrifice, and the Temple*, 79.

20. For a full exegesis of these texts regarding the two orders of error, see: Andrew M. Johnson, "Error and Epistemological Process," (Ph.D. diss., University of St Andrews, 2011), 90–93; Johnson, *Biblical Knowing*, 72–74.

neither YHWH nor Moses as an authority; hence, he sees the exodus signs out of sorts from their intended meaning.[21]

Later in Exodus, the Israelites appear to acknowledge Moses as their authority (cf. Exod 4:31; 14:31). However, immediately upon leaving Egypt, the people do not participate in the epistemological process to the degree required. In the giving of manna, the sole condition surrounding the plentiful food is violated when some go looking for it on the Sabbath. The people embodied the action of manna collection directed by Moses, which had an epistemological intent: "Then you shall know that I am YHWH your God" (Exod 16:12). However, mere performance without attentive reflection on the manner of performance brings problems, intimating that embodying the script of a practice goes beyond rote performance. These two distinct errors in the process of knowing—not acknowledging proper authority and failing to embody their directives—are requisite for us to understand the target of the prophetic critique of ritual.

Torah as Script

The efficacy of ritual becomes apparent in the prophetic indictments. We should be clear to distinguish that false rituals, aimed at foreign gods or the syncretizing of Israel's god, are not the matter of concern. Those are explicitly condemned from the Exodus forward, if not implicitly throughout the Tetrateuch. The indictments of concern regard only those Israelites who are practicing Torah ritual, yet the prophets interpret their behavior as counterproductive. For instance, Haggai metaphorically compares the post-exilic Levitical sacrifices to the defilement of touching a corpse. Whereas they presumably sought cleanliness and atonement through the ritual sacrifices of Torah, they were being systematically defiled by the very practices of cleanliness (Hag 2:10–14).

What makes the difference between proper and improper sacrifices? Or in the language offered above: How can someone who is performing a ritual as scripted in the Torah—avoiding a second-order error—still be considered erroneous? The problem appears to result from a mismatch between the purpose

---

21. Discussions of YHWH hardening Pharaoh's heart tend to focus on two facets in Christian theology. First, the verb "harden" is in the hiphil imperfect with YHWH as the subject and Pharaoh's heart as the object (Ex. 7:3). This indicates causation. But second, the actual mechanism may be more nuanced than direct causation. The mirror image of this in the Gospel narratives is the disciples of Jesus (Mk. 6:52; 8:17), the Jewish leaders (Mk. 3:5), and the crowds following him (paraphrase of Is. 6:10 in John 12:40) all being described as having "hardened hearts." Lexically, the phrase "hardened heart" is not formulaic and several verbs (קשה, חזק, אמץ + לב) are conflated to the one Septuagintal rendition that is repeated from the LXX into the NT as "hardened heart" (i.e., σκληρυνω καρδια).

of the rite in relationship to the primacy of the Torah. This means that unless Israelites consider the Torah to be instructing (i.e., scripting) a whole socio-political, economic, and ethical way of existing as a nation, the rites will not work in and of themselves. However, throughout the Hebrew Bible we see that the ritualized practices actually conjoin into a nexus of activities, including immigration policy, treatment of the poor, agricultural practices, and more (e.g., Lev 19). Isaiah 58 presumes something akin to the ethical teaching of Leviticus 19 in rejecting the ritual fasts of Israelites: "Behold, in the day of your fast you seek your own business and oppress all your workers" (Isa 58:3). I will discuss preparation as part of the ritual in chapter eleven, though one analogy is worth positing here and exploring later.

If a husband or wife brings home flowers to their spouse, that ritualized practice is not efficacious *in se* to evince that the spouse is loved. More realistically, the day-in and day-out practices of the spouse, who then ritually offers the flower gift, make the gift work for its purpose: a discrete expression of affection. I cannot violate my covenant obligations with my wife throughout the year and then honestly expect that giving her flowers in February will effectively relate my affection to her, or at least, not in the way I might intend.[22] If the analogy holds true to practices of the Torah, then we cannot consider ritual practice apart from the Torah-centric life of Israel, which appears to be the heart of the prophetic indictment at many points.

Saul's sacrifice of the sheep devoted to destruction offers a clear instance of this bisect between obedience and sacrifice (1 Sam 15). The matter of disloyalty to YHWH was broached at the beginning of 1 Samuel regarding Eli's sons. 1 Samuel portrays Eli's priestly sons negatively; primarily for treating the offerings in the Tabernacle contemptuously (1 Sam 2:17). YHWH states that he desires the opposite persona, one who is "true as to which is in my heart (נאמן כאשר בלבבי)."[23] Later, the narrative summarizes Samuel's prophetic reputation in the same terms: "Samuel was true as a prophet to YHWH (נאמן שמואל לנביא ליהוה)."[24] The positive valuation of appropriate priestly behavior—following the script set out by YHWH—as a way of understanding reality appears strong in the burgeoning kingship motif. Deuteronomy has already prepared the canonical reader of the Hebrew Bible to understand that a good king is one who follows Torah, writing a copy of it for himself in submission to the priesthood (Deut 17:18). YHWH's indictment of the people's folly when they ask for a king reiterates their departure from his ways (1 Sam 8:8–9). Samuel admonishes the people in his king-speech with that ever-present trend: "If you will fear YHWH, worship him, and listen to his voice (ושמעתם בקלו) . . . but if you do not listen to the voice of YHWH . . . YHWH will strike you down" (1 Sam 12:14–15). This phrase, "listen to the voice," high-

---

22. Jeremiah Unterman recounted this example of the flower-giving spouse, originally given by Moshe Greenberg in lectures at Hebrew University.

23. 1 Sam 2:35.

24. 1 Sam 3:20.

lights the possibility of a first-order error looming: failure to acknowledge the authority of the Torah and/or the prophet who speaks on behalf of YHWH.

The stakes are clear, and the narrator lauds to us the ones who closely associate themselves with YHWH's explicit intentions, including the ritual cult of Israel. This emphasis to avoid first-order errors—failing to listen—makes Saul's burnt offering all the more egregious, which explains the bifurcation between "listening to the voice of YHWH" (שמע בקל) on the one hand and his sacrifice on the other.

Saul is sent by Samuel to devote everything in Amalek to destruction (חרם), including animals and humans. Samuel commissions him with these words: "listen to the voice (שמע לקול) of YHWH's command" (1 Sam 15:1). Yet, Saul spares the Amalekite king and sacrifices some of their choicest livestock. The following dispute occurs when Samuel arrives and confronts Saul:

> "Why did you *not listen to the voice* (לא שמעת בקול) of YHWH?" (1 Sam 15:19)

> "I did *listen to the voice* (שמעתי בקול) of YHWH" (1 Sam 15:20)

> "Does YHWH delight in burnt offerings and sacrifices as much as in *listening to the voice* (כשמע בקול) of YHWH? Surely, *listening* (שמע) is better than sacrifice?" (1 Sam 15:22).

> "I sinned to violate the command of YHWH and your instruction because I was afraid of the people and *listened to their voice* (ואשמע בקולם)"[25]

This episode allows us to see that because Saul committed a first-order error, not listening to YHWH, he went on to commit a second-order error of not following the instruction of YHWH, especially concerning sacrifice. Sacrifice, in and of itself, cannot accomplish its task apart from a wider scheme of Torah obedience. When done outside of that broader obedience (i.e., listening), it actually becomes adversarial to the task, setting the ritual participant at odds with the people and the God meant to be enjoined through the rite.

Prophetic Indictments of Ritual

Understanding ritual as Torah listening and living, which comes to a nexus in rites, is crucial to discern the later prophetic critique of Israel's ritual behavior. Before addressing the rhetoric of Hosea, I want to advocate for a position that is fundamentally in line with the prophetic critique of ritual. Namely, one reason that the prophets indict Israel for her impoverished ritual practice is that they are not epistemically effective unless they are Torah-reverent. The pointless rites, rites that even defile Israel, are the ones performed out of synchronicity with the Torah. Hence, Amos shows no shock that the "cows of Ba-

---

25. 1 Sam 15:24.

shan" (i.e., Israelite women) are committing false worship, as false worship appears to be fully commensurable with their anti-Torah oppression of the poor, among other problems:

> because they sell the righteous for silver,
> and the needy for a pair of sandals
> those who trample the head of the poor into the dust of the earth
> and turn aside the way of the afflicted;
> a man and his father go in to the same girl,
> so that my holy name is profaned;
> they lay themselves down beside every altar
> on garments taken in pledge,
> and in the house of their God they drink
> the wine of those who have been fined.[26]

Amos chides Israel for her anti-Torah living, which dovetails with her malformed sacrifices and makes them altogether inefficacious, not prepared for YHWH by a Torah-submitted life. These are not the right rites:

> Hear this word, you cows of Bashan, who are on the mountain of Samaria, who oppress the poor, who crush the needy, who say to your husbands, "Bring, that we may drink!" YHWH God has sworn by his holiness that, behold, the days are coming upon you, when they shall take you away with hooks, even the last of you with fishhooks. . . . Come to Bethel, and transgress; to Gilgal, and multiply transgression; bring your sacrifices every morning, your tithes every three days; offer a sacrifice of thanksgiving of that which is leavened, and proclaim freewill offerings, publish them; for so you love to do, O people of Israel![27]

However, learning to discern by practicing rites is not altogether ejected from the prophetic discourse during the divided kingdom, exile, and return. Rather, the disjunct between anti-Torah society and ritual (sometimes typified by false ritual) creates a target for prophetic critique. Hence, readers can understand the logic of Jonah's prayer (Jonah 2:8–10):

> Those who pay regard to vain idols forsake their hope of steadfast love.
> But I with the voice of thanksgiving will sacrifice to you;
> What I have vowed I will pay. Salvation belongs to YHWH!
> And YHWH spoke to the fish, and it vomited Jonah out upon the dry land.

While clinging to vain idols is bad, sacrifice that corresponds to one's thanksgiving is still fundamentally good. So Klawans concludes: "The objection to sacrifice rests [*sic*] the assumption that God detests the facts of the situation

---

26. Amos 2:6–8.
27. Amos 4:1–5.

at hand. One who has taken unjustly from the poor cannot properly *give* any-thing, and therefore the 'sacrifice' offered by such a person is anathema."[28]

Micah's renowned discourse on "what is required of man" begins with the admonition to "remember [God's acts at Moab] . . . in order to know (למען דעת) the gracious deeds of YHWH" (Mic 6:5). The discourse then immediately pro-ceeds to discuss rituals: "With what shall I approach YHWH?" An escalating and exorbitant list of ritual offerings is suggested in order to approach YHWH and all are dismissed rhetorically. However, the ritual is contextualized by a Torah-centered life. The answer to "with what shall I approach YHWH" is found in the life lived according to Torah. For example, the overarching thrust of the teaching found in Leviticus 19 alone appears to be fully commensurate with doing justice, loving goodness, and walking humbly.[29]

In other words, Micah does not answer the question "with what shall I ap-proach YHWH" by suggesting that sacrifice is not needed to approach YHWH. It is a radical claim to say that Micah believes Israel can now approach YHWH empty-handed, sacrificially speaking. Instead, Micah states that when they approach with their sacrifice, they also need to bring a Torah-centered life and society, illustrative of justice, kindness, and humility. In other words, when Israelites approach YHWH *with their sacrifices*, it is their Torah-centered society and life practices which make *this* ritual practice efficacious. In light of the argument of this book, I would add that the Torah-submitted life and ritual are also efficacious in the epistemological sense to dispose the participant to see something about YHWH's reality that they could not have otherwise recog-nized apart from their participation. I maintain that the prophetic critique of pointless sacrifice might include within it one other reason: *falsely practiced rituals are futile because they cannot teach or dispose Israel to discern. These rites do not fulfill the "in order that you/your generations might know" clause that we found in rites such as Passover and Sukkot.* Micah suggests that there is a Torah prepara-tion, a disposition to embody, prior to the rite. Or, as I will later argue in chap-ter eleven, the preparation is contiguous with the rite and Israel's failure to recognize that contiguity leads to ritual practices at odds with true rites.

Hosea's Separation of Ritual and Knowing

Now we are in a position to return to Hosea's apparent bifurcation of knowledge and ritual where he says:

---

28. Klawans, *Purity, Sacrifice, and the Temple*, 87.

29. Bohdan Hrobon has tracked a similar connection between ethical life and ritu-al in Isaiah. *Ethical Dimension of Cult in the Book of Isaiah* (BZAW 418; Berlin: de Gruyter, 2010).

For I desire mercy and *not sacrifice*,
knowledge of God rather than burnt offerings.[30]

I want to suggest a rhetorical tension in Hosea between false ritualization and the inability to discern. Amazingly, the ability and inability to discern are exposed by the same teaching and practices summarized in the very last sentences of Hosea: "He who is wise (חכם) will discern (ויבן) these words . . . while sinners stumble upon them" (Hos 14:10). Hosea's teaching acts as a smooth path to the righteous and a treacherous way to the sinners. What determines the difference?

As previously observed, discernment for Hosea is directly connected with moral behavior. Hence, something about that which makes one righteous disposes them to recognize and discern Hosea's words. Conversely, the behavior of the sinner makes them blind *to the same evidence*. It behooves us to consider what is diagnosed as sin and righteousness in Hosea in order to determine whether or not this dichotomy between sacrifice and knowing opposes this book's thesis.

In the fore of Hosea's teaching, he reviews the patterns of Israel's conduct, diagramming it as a series of estrangements and returns which are directly related to Israel's epistemological abilities. "And she *did not discern* (לא ידעה) this: It was *I* who gave to her the new grain and wine and oil; *I* who lavished silver on her and gold, which they used *for Baal*" (Hos 2:10). This initial passage on Israel's faulty epistemology links our core concerns. Although it was YHWH who was giving Israel her gifts, Israel did not recognize the giver. This appears to presume that someone who was rightly disposed to see the same gifts could have pointed Israel to YHWH as her gift-giver. What made Israel indisposed to recognize, much less discern? Hosea intimates that false worship, gifts received from YHWH and given in turn to Baal, lies at the root of their inability to recognize. Hosea directly connects ritual practice and epistemology.

In the 2007 National Geographic documentary on North Korea,[31] a covert team of journalists follows a Nepalese eye surgeon who performs over one thousand cornea replacements in just ten days. This surgeon's mission is humanitarian, even creating a training opportunity for North Korean doctors to continue his work once he is gone. These thousand functionally blind persons become sighted in a matter of just a few days. When their bandages are finally removed and many of them see clearly for the first time in decades, the moment is expectedly emotional. Weeping and gratitude are on display, almost grotesquely, women and men alike are bowing down low in gratefulness. Some even sing songs of praise and lead the whole multitude of previous blind patients in chants and cheers, even farcical paeans.

---

30. Hos 6:6; This stands apart from a pattern of prophetic critique seemingly against sacrifice itself. See also: 1 Sam 15:22; Isa 1:11; Jer 6:20; and Amos 5:21–24.

31. National Geographic Explorer, "Inside North Korea," season 21, episode 14 (February 27, 2007).

However, none of this praise or thanksgiving is directed at the surgeon or his team who dedicated weeks of their lives to come perform this humanitarian mission. It was all directed at the paintings of the current and former leaders of the People's Republic of Korea (Kim Jong Il at the time of filming). Their paintings, though deaf and mute, silently received the praise that continued for hours.

It is not unfair to suggest that their religious devotion to the leaders of North Korea handicapped the once-blind Koreans' ability to recognize to whom the praise should have gone.[32] The surgeon who volunteered to come gave the gift of sight. However, the gift was used as predication, feigned in some cases and genuine in others, to worship their distant leaders. Israel's ritual adultery to Baal while simultaneously being the prodigal wife of YHWH can only be explained by an epistemological lacuna. The pressing question remains: How does worship of foreign gods hinder Israel in recognizing? Answering this question requires following out the logic of Hosea's indictment.

Hosea goes on to analogize a fornicating wife with Israel's idolatry to Baal (Hos 3:2–3). But eventually, Israel will turn back to YHWH and again, we wonder, will "turning back" to YHWH include Torah ritual practices which enable correct discernment? The problem is again diagnosed in epistemic terms. Because there is no obedience (i.e., listening), there is no knowledge (cf. Hos 4:1, 6). Lack of knowledge is destroying Israel and because she rejects knowledge, YHWH rejects her. But what does such knowledge entail? Or, if they are not listening, to whom or what are they not listening? We suggest that, as is the case with the Hebrew Bible in general, the Torah life that includes appropriate rituals and festivals is what Israel rejects, favoring instead the rituals of Baal and others (Hos 2:10). Rituals in and of themselves are not the problem. Rather the life of Israel that runs counter to the Torah and the directing of the rituals toward "unknown gods" forms the core of their moral and epistemological dysfunction. Otherwise, we have to presume that, in Micah (6:6–8) and Hosea (6:6), there exists a wholesale usurpation of the Torah, rejecting ritual writ large. Again, we must keep in mind what the return back to YHWH is meant to look like. Does Hosea's return to YHWH include ritual?

Israel's peril is both related to her lack of discernment, and then to her contortion of sin rituals (cf. Hos 4:6, 8). Yet again, the sin offering does not appear to be the target of Hosea's charge, but rather her inappropriate use of the rite, to which a long list of social and moral failures are associated (Hos 4:12–15). Hosea continues to assess that which hinders Israel from turning back: unfaithful conduct (Hos 5:1, 7), religious fornication (Hos 5:3), and Israel's *poor habits* (מעלליהם),[33] her ritualization of anti-Torah practices (Hos 5:4) which leads her to not know YHWH (לא ידעו).

---

32. We need not make a moral judgment here, but follow the story as told by the journalists, who clearly wanted the viewers to come to this conclusion.

33. Some translations render מעלליהם as "deeds," which puts it closer to morally neutral עשים. However, מעלל is associated with repetitive and negative practices, hence

Now we arrive at this problematic teaching on knowledge as opposed to sacrifice. The exhortation "Come let us turn back to YHWH" (Hos 6:1) answers the original problem of Israel's failure to discern (Hos 2:10) with a solution: "Let us pursue *knowledge* (ונדעה) *in order to know* (לדעת) YHWH" (Hos 6:3). And, "For I desire goodness and *not sacrifice* (ולא זבח), and *knowledge* (ודעת) of God than burnt offerings" (Hos 6:6). Is this a wholesale rejection of sacrifice?

First, rejecting sacrifice would mean that Hosea rejects the inter-tangled nature of sacrifice and Torah life. It is genuinely difficult to conceive of a way in which a rejection of sacrifice is not a rejection or profound critique of the Torah itself.[34] Second, the particular instances of sacrifice being indicted in Hosea are not the sacrifices themselves, but the misappropriation of sacrifice. "Ephraim has multiplied altars, for guilt" (Hos 8:11), "they present me sacrifices, but as flesh for them to eat" (Hos 8:23), and "no sacrifices *of theirs* will be pleasing to Him" (Hos 9:4). Thus Klawans's verdict, "The prophets did not, it must be clear, oppose ritual as such. The question is why they were dissatisfied with the practice of sacrifice as they knew it."[35] This is not an indictment of sacrifice, but of *their* corrupted sacrifices. YHWH later laments that he has "pampered Ephraim, . . . but they have *not recognized* (ולא ידעו) my healing care" (Hos 11:3). For the sake of parsimony, the rejection of *these wrong sacrifices* could equally be for epistemological reasons. These false rituals cannot dispose them to recognize God, much less discern. Mine is the conservative position as opposed to Hosea enticing Israel to reject large tracts of the Torah.[36]

Recalling Saul's faulty sacrifice in 1 Samuel 15, the prophet demands obedient listening over sacrifice. Samuel's dictum lexically resembles Hosea's call where he asked, "Does YHWH desire delight in burnt offerings and sacrifices as much as listening to the voice of YHWH?" (1 Sam 15:22). Framed this way,

---

"habits." "This word (עלל) speaks of relationship. It is used to indicate the exercise of power over another person, generally in a bad sense, hence meaning "to maltreat." It signifies some great achievement, generally malevolent. . . . (מעלל) Used somewhat more often with a similar range of meaning. Again the deeds of men are wicked deeds." "עלל" in *TWOT* (ed. R. Laird Harris; 2 vols.; Chicago: Moody, 1980).

34. Klawans argues that the dichotomy of ethics and ritual is false, though ever-present in scholarly assumptions about the prophetic critique. However, the economic and ethical life of Israel (e.g., Lev 19) is intimately intertwined with her ritual practices: "the prophets' 'rejection' of sacrifice was deeply connected to their belief that Israel was economically rotten to the core. . . . [W]hen it comes to sacrifice, ethics and rituals are intricately and inherently connected." *Purity, Sacrifice, and the Temple*, 87.

35. Ibid., 84.

36. Hosea 14:3 is another passage that appears to signal the irrelevance of sacrifice: "Instead of bulls we will pay [the fruit or offering] of our lips." This passage has a text-critical ambiguity, which makes it difficult to address directly, and cannot be settled here. The Qumran scroll and MT agree on "the offering (פרים שפתינו) of our lips," although 4Q78c is missing the פ in פרים. However, the Septuagint reads "the fruit of our lips (καρπὸν χειλέων ἡμῶν)," which could easily be achieved in the Hebrew by dropping the mem sofit (ם), so that פרים becomes פרי.

properly embodied rites which are prepared in the everyday moral conduct of Israel disposes Israelites to recognize and discern. But the ability of rituals to properly dispose Israelites only happens when their listening to YHWH and embodying the prescribed actions correlate. However, knowing YHWH and discerning his actions are futile goals if no prior Torah-centric life exists in the participants. If we could alter what is *said* to what is *meant*, Hosea reads:

> For I desire goodness, not sacrifice that is completely out of sorts with Torah; obedient listening that leads to discernment rather than mere burnt animals, which blind you from recognizing me and my ways.

Hosea, like other prophets, does not look toward the abolition of ritual, but the corrected conduct of Israel that enables her ritual practices to be epistemically efficacious. His critique is narrowly focused on abuse of Israel's rituals, not their proper use. Further, Hosea himself identifies the connection between the misappropriation of sacrifices and Israel's inability to recognize. In consideration of these elements of Hosea's rhetoric, the return to YHWH must include the proper (i.e., non-fornicated) used of ritual in order to know YHWH and discern his actions.

Thus, Lafferty concludes in her survey of the prophetic critique:

> [P]reexilic prophetic criticism of the cult, then, had in view neither an elimination of the cult nor merely a sympathetic care toward the widow, the orphan, and the oppressed. The feature shared by each of the Old Testament passages that contain criticism of the cult is a focus on the lack of proper attitude towards and respect for the relationship between the Israelite people and their God.[37]

So too, the Hebrew Bible depicts proper ritual not merely as worship focused toward YHWH, but also as normative of Israel's epistemological process. However, beginning with Israel's exodus wandering, inappropriate worship is condemned by Israel's arch-prophet and YHWH (e.g., Exod 32, Lev 10, Num 16). After the exile and return, post-exilic prophets focus their attention on restoring the proper ritual practices of Israel (e.g., Zechariah, Haggai, and Malachi). The target of prophetic critique is not sacrifice writ large, but failure to employ ritual to worship YHWH appropriately. In between, when Israel goes into a period of sustained syncretism and idolatry, prophets condemn the wrongful use of Israel's normative rites (e.g., Solomon, Jeroboam, Manasseh, etc.). What's so wrong about false ritual? Among other things, those rites will not dispose them to know.

---

37. Theresa V. Lafferty, *The Prophetic Critique of the Priority of the Cult: A Study of Amos 5:21–24 and Isaiah 1:10–17* (Eugene, OR: Pickwick, 2012), 84.

The Enigmatic Red Heifer

Finally, the red heifer ritual (Num 19) represents the litmus test for a ritual theory's explanatory power. This practice deals with purification of persons after touching a human corpse (Num 19:11) or killing in battle (Num 19:16) through the burning of the heifer outside the camp and dispensing its ashes. Traditionally, interpreters have been confounded by the symbolic logic of the rite. Why a red heifer? Why is it killed outside the camp? Why do even the ashes of the animal make one unclean? What are the practitioners being *purified of* by performance of the rite?

Maimonides passes along the tradition of ignorance concerning the rite. Despite Solomon knowing the reasoning behind all the instruction of the Torah, the Rambam claims, with the sages, that even Solomon did not understand the ritual of the red heifer.[38] Is this rite a *prima facie* case against rituals functioning epistemologically if the red heifer rite perplexed both Solomon and the Jewish sages?

Roy Gane's treatment of the red heifer argues that the rite is a personal purification that moves the death-contamination, "from the infected person to the ash water and to the whole cow of which the ashes are a part (*pars pro toto*), and from there to the persons involved in the ritual process of burning the red cow."[39] Like Jacob Milgrom and others, the focus on explaining the ritual through its metaphysical ability to transfer contamination neglects another aspect: how the rite shapes the participant who has just intimately experienced killing or the death of a loved one.[40]

If we consider the ritual to be pedagogical, other possibilities emerge that can dovetail with examinations like Gane's.[41] Even if it is the case that the ritual was meant to purify the Israelite from the stain of death or killing, it certainly must be the case that *the participant needed to know that too.* In other words, dispensing trite sayings (e.g., "It is all in God's hands") to those struggling with loss or the act of killing does not mitigate the existential morass caused by a family or combat-related death. Rather, the ritual gives Israelites a tangible way to begin the long walk out of the inscrutable pangs and confusion of death near to them.

---

38. Maimonides, *Guide to the Perplexed*, III/26.

39. Roy E. Gane, *Cult and Character: Purification Offerings, Day of Atonement, and Theodicy* (Winona Lake, IN: Eisenbrauns, 2005), 183.

40. Jacob Milgrom, "The Paradox of the Red Cow (Num xix.)," *VT* 31 (1981): 62–72. Nathan MacDonald walks the line between the red cow rite being a fictive invention of Second Temple Judaism—to cover logical gaps in the Priestly texts—and yet instructive to the ritual practitioners as it became an actual practice. "The Hermeneutics and Genesis of the Red Cow Ritual," *HTR* 105, no. 3 (2012): 351–71.

41. Thanks to Joshua Weinstein for helping to steer my thinking on this ritual and stimulate productive thinking.

Joan Didion describes the malaise ensuing her husband's death as, "the unending absence that follows, the void, the very opposite of meaning, the relentless succession of moments during which we will confront the experience of meaninglessness itself."[42] For those who have known the loss of close ones or the fog of combat, we often don't know what questions to ask, much less how to act.

Conversely, our bodies certainly know how to respond physiologically (e.g., the physiological effects of depression, post-traumatic stress, etc.). The red heifer ritual employs the body, showing it an unambiguous path where the living body and dead body clearly and symbolically diverge. Indeed, a recent Harvard study on grieving rituals showed that public displays of grief (e.g., funeral services, local mourning norms, obituaries, etc.) were less impacting than private and personal rituals, for instance:

> Asking participants to sit in silence after telling them that people often sit in silence after a loss neither increased perceived control nor reduced grief, whereas performing a ritual that consisted of a series of behaviors after learning that people often engage in rituals after experiencing a loss was effective.[43]

The ritual might be able to teach the Israelite the meaning behind phrases such as "It is all in God's hands" in a way unavailable through any other intellectual means:

> Rituals, which are deliberately-controlled gestures, trigger a very specific feeling in mourners—the feeling of being in control of their lives. After people did a ritual or wrote about doing one, they were more likely to report thinking that "things were in check" and less likely to feel "helpless," "powerless," and "out of control."[44]

In saying all this, I am being intentionally speculative. The red heifer reads as if it offers a means of purification from death, metaphysically speaking. Moreover, rites similar to the red heifer work because they prescribe and give structure to mourning, among other things. In sum, the red heifer rite if seen as epistemological could offer the same benefits of regulating mourning and offering confidence to mourners as seen even today.

---

42. Quoted in Emily Esfahani Smith, "In Grief, Try Personal Rituals: The psychology of rituals in overcoming loss, restoring broken order" *Atlantic* (online) March 14, 2014 (accessed July 16, 2015: http://www.theatlantic.com/health/archive/2014/03/in-grief-try-personal-rituals/284397/).

43. Michael I. Norton and Francesca Gino, "Rituals Alleviate Grieving for Loved Ones, Lovers, and Lotteries," *JEP* 143, no. 1 (2014): 266–272.

44. Smith, "In Grief, Try Personal Rituals".

Chapter 9

Continuity and Ritual Knowing
in the Early Jerusalemite Jesus Community

An overriding presumption, which must be stated up front, will carry my analysis into the New Testament texts: Unless I have reasons to suspect otherwise, silence concerning Torah ritual practices will be considered as a possible indication of continuity. Stated otherwise, because the New Testament authors and much of their audiences were Jews who lived in and around the Levant, unless I have pronounced reasons to suspect that they were overthrowing the Torah's ritualized practices, I will not presume the absence of Torah rituals.[1] Being first-century Jews, I presume that some authors—James, John, Peter, Paul, and Matthew—participated in temple-centered worship and reading of the Hebrew Bible/Septuagint as did their peers. Indeed, Luke records Paul's direct participation in Temple worship during Paul's very last days in Jerusalem for the sake of reifying his Torah-centered approach to the Gospel (Acts 21:17–26). That being said, does the New Testament as a whole have a negative or cessationist view of ritual?

Scholars such as Jonathan Z. Smith, Mary Douglas, and Jonathan Klawans have all demonstrated the anti-ritual tendency that affects large swaths of biblical interpretation.[2] Basically, Western readers are predisposed to think of ritual as rote, non-cognitive, and therefore, not epistemically helpful. Or, rituals are premised upon magic, doing something in order to get something. The-

---

1. Thus Brevard Childs focuses on the discreteness of the NT as centered in its socio-historical situatedness amongst the Jews: "Rather the New Testament has its discrete historical context, its traditions were treasured by different tradents, and its central force stems from another direction than that of the Old Testament. Thus the New Testament is not a midrash on the Old, nor is it simply the last chapter of a story . . . the decisive feature of the New Testament is the element of newness over against the past. The witness to the gospel arose from the early church's encounter with Jesus Christ and not from scholarly reflection on sacred texts." *Biblical Theology of the Old and New Testaments: Theological Reflection on the Christian Bible* (Minneapolis: Fortress, 1992), 211–12.

2. Jonathan Klawans, *Purity, Sacrifice, and the Temple: Symbolism and Supersessionism in the Study of Ancient Judaism* (Oxford: Oxford University Press, 2006), 32, 114. Mary Douglas, *Purity and Danger: An Analysis of the Concepts of Pollution and Taboo* (New York: Routledge, 1966), 18–19, 62–63.

se kinds of biases excise the epistemic function of rites and fund presumptions about the use of ritual in the political structure of Israel. Further, a palpable distaste for the killing of animals as a type of YHWH worship might have skewed decades of scholarship. Scholars predisposed against flesh and blood ritual might miss what these texts are describing and what they could have meant to the ancient practitioners apart from any political wrangling or manipulation of the rites in Israel's history.

I will continue to maintain that we need to approach the biblical texts with the presumption that rituals shape theology, as much as or more than verbal debates in the early Jewish-Christian community. If the New Testament has a positive view of ritual—that rites have an active function in this Jewish Jesus movement—can we still see the vestiges of Torah rites linked to knowing in Christian Scripture? Stated otherwise, is there a connection between embodied action and knowing in the historical and epistolary writings of the New Testament? I must pursue this question, considering how the authors of these texts thought about the epistemological process and seeking to find the role of the body and ritual, if they are indeed part of that process.

In this chapter, I begin by exploring the question of cessation of rites in the NT. Affirming their necessity in a Christian epistemology, I then examine the historical texts and epistles, focusing in two distinct corridors of the historical texts. First, because of its brevity and purported seminal role, I walk through Mark's gospel asking what role the body and ritualized practices play in knowing. Second, because it spans both the life of Jesus and the reception of Christianity among both Jews and Gentiles, Luke-Acts will be examined likewise. Because I can only make a tentative case here, some of Paul's epistles will be assessed for their fit with what was discovered in the Hebrew Bible. I will later treat the epistle to the Hebrews as a possible counter-example.

If my thesis holds, we should expect to find that knowing is still described as a process where authoritative guides are authenticated to Israel and Gentiles. When those authorities are clearly authenticated, knowers are required to embody the ritualized practices they prescribe. Submission to the authority and embodiment of prescribed rites should dispose knowers to recognize something they could not have otherwise seen, but recognition is only a point on the way toward the goal of discernment. We should also see both a value of the authoritative voice and a necessity of the body in recognizing, where the same inputs—as it were—are seen differently after characters of the text have practiced the rite to know.

With the Hebrew Scriptures as the subtext to the Gospels and epistles of early Christianity, ritual efficacy appears presumed rather than discursive in most NT stories. For instance, the Jewish practice of baptism appears without comment in the Gospels as a normative ritual act. The festivals and Sabbath appear only in the background of the central stories of the Gospels, coming to the foreground in points of conflict.[3] In the following examination, I will show why Klawans is correct when he says, "Jesus' followers did not separate themselves from the temple and its sacrificial worship."[4] With this in mind, I will make a brief case that knowing is related to scripted action and that these new Jewish NT rituals retain an explicitly epistemological goal in the Christian Scriptures.

Mark's Gospel on Ritual

My immediate purpose below is to assess whether or not the gospel account is written to wean Christianity off of its Israelite ritualism. If it is not, then does Mark depict ritual in epistemologically commensurate ways with the Hebrew Bible? Several Markan episodes, taken roughly in order, will be suggestive:

> 1) the John the Baptist narrative,
> 2) miraculous signs (signs not working, signs of the coming age),
> 3) the secret of the kingdom,
> 4) embodying the script,
> 5) the disciples' failure to understand,
> 6) continuity with Sinai,
> 7) blind disciples metaphor,
> 8) cleansing the temple,
> 9) the Passover, and
> 10) the Crucifixion.

First, Mark begins with John (the Baptist) baptizing, a ritual adapted from the Torah. Citing Isaiah, Mark's gospel frames this ritual with an epistemological purpose: preparing the people to see/recognize (ראה/גלה) the glory of YHWH being revealed (Isa 40:5). Somehow, this ritualized practice prepares them to see, which might be understood as "recognize," and not necessarily "discern" in this context. More tentatively, John the Baptist himself witnesses and recognizes something during his participation in these rituals: the secret of Jesus being the Son of God. This second link between John the Baptist's participation and recognition is too tenuous in Mark, but John's Gospel paints the same scene in stronger epistemological language. The Baptist specifically cites the ritual in epistemological terms of recognition: "I myself did not know him, but for this purpose I came baptizing with water, that he might be revealed" (John 1:31). John also seems to indicate that keeping the Torah, including its prescriptive rites, prepares Israelites to discern Jesus' actions as commensurate with God's will (John 7:16–19). Although the scene is scant of detail, Jesus patently affirms the role of the temple priesthood and Mosaic authority at the

---

3. E.g., Jesus' disciples processing grain on the Sabbath (Luke 6:1–5), delay in visiting the tomb of Jesus due to keeping Sabbath (Matt 28:1).

4. Klawans, *Purity, Sacrifice, and the Temple*, 217.

fore of Mark when he sends a healed leper to the temple to be declared clean (Mark 1:44).

Second, Mark incorporates signs for their epistemological effect, like all the New Testament authors. For our purposes, these are miraculous signs in that they are markedly beyond natural operations and they beg questions from the audience *within the narrative* (i.e., Who is this man?). Mark's Jesus explicitly instructs a lame man to walk *"that you all may know* that the Son of Man has authority on earth to forgive sins" (Mark 2:10). Yet, for those whom he deemed obstinate, Jesus refused to give a sign (Mark 8:11–13).[5] Important in all the gospels, the signs of the "age to come" center around an unknown date—a date, however, attended by recognizable signs. Recalling our prior discussion, signs are often described *as signs* because they *signal* something to the knower, enabling her to recognize. However, the "coming age" discourse requires that the disciples are recognizing the signs in order to discern the coming kingdom. In other words, the initial problem is to recognize the "signals in the signalbox." But even then, the signals must be discerned for meaning.

What precisely must one do in order to recognize? Like Mosaic teaching in Deuteronomy, Jesus focuses on maintaining orthodoxy with his own teaching. He repeatedly warns that people will come to "lead away" those who are not recognizing the signs. Many will perform signs and wonders to lead them astray (Mark 13:22). Yet, Jesus does not explicitly say how they are to interpret the signs that indicate that day to come. In fact, his only advice comes cryptically in two places. First, he commands them to "look out" or "discern" (βλέπετε) according to that which he has said before (προείρηκα) (Mark 13:23). Second, he advises them to learn the lesson from interpreting the fig tree: "as soon as its branch becomes tender . . . you know that summer is near" (Mark 13:28). Together, these appear to indicate that learning the skill of *recognizing* agricultural signs (e.g., tender branch, leaf sprouting, etc.) is imperative before one can *discern* the transcendent meaning of such agricultural signals (e.g., Summer's approach). In essence, this forces us to look at Mark more broadly

---

5. Luke's account of Jesus' pharisaic rebuke contains a parable, which indicates that theirs is a first-order error, failing to acknowledge the authenticated authority. The point of his parable on Lazarus returning from the grave (i.e., Hades): "If they do not listen to Moses and the prophets, neither will they be convinced (πεισθήσονται) if someone should rise from the dead" (Luke 16:31). Matthew's account of Pharisees demanding a sign ends with a proleptic irony: "An evil and adulterous generation seeks for a sign, but no sign will be given to it except the sign of the prophet Jonah" (Matt 12:39). So Wilson concludes: "The clear implication of both verses is that the law and the prophets were an adequate guide for those who wished to enter the kingdom. If the rich man had heard and obeyed, especially though not exclusively with respect to the use of his wealth, he would not have found himself in such dire circumstances. As in 10:25f the emphasis is on 'hearing' (ακουειν), that is obeying and doing, the law." S. G. Wilson, *Luke and the Law* (New York: Cambridge University Press, 1983), 18.

for an epistemological process that develops the former (signals) in able to discern the latter (signified).

Third, why did Jesus intuit those who would and would not be able to recognize his signs? Or, what made his signs epistemically efficacious? From the outset, when Mark recounts Jesus developing his disciples' ability to understand, we read about a process thoroughly rooted in the Hebrew Bible. I have argued extensively elsewhere about the exact lexical and conceptual connections that fund Mark's epistemology from Deuteronomy 29 and Isaiah 6.[6] In brief, the disciples are promised to know the "secret of the kingdom of God" (Mark 4:11), but for everyone else, they will be blind and deaf to the secret (cf. Isa 6:9–10; Mark 4:12). What differentiates those who will recognize the secret of the kingdom—an unseen reality that is akin to something hidden (κρυπτὸν) that ought to be revealed (φανερωθῇ)— and not?[7] According to the parable, the one who listens to the authority's instructions and "bears fruit" will then discern (Mark 4:20).[8] As long as "bears fruit" synonymously includes ritual practices, then my thesis holds.

Fourth, this instruction to "listen and do" inaugurates a fairly intensive series of interactions with the disciples. Jesus offers them instruction and their ability to recognize varies with their level of embodying the scripted actions. For example, when he sent them out to proclaim repentance and heal, the disciples appear to have followed Jesus' terse instructions with success and recognized that success as directly related to embodying the instructions (Mark 6:7–13, 30). However, the disciples seem epistemically stymied by Jesus' instructions, "You give them something to eat," when confronted by the thousands of hungry followers (Mark 6:37). Their inability to recognize, implicitly due to their failure to practice directives, is persistent. The contrast between their practicing the instructions in the first instance and failure in the second is not explored by Mark, as the story continues to paint the disciples negatively from that point onward.

However, the Markan author uses absurd irony to highlight the disciples' inability to recognize basic matters. Indeed, when Jesus later walks on the Galilean Sea, we read about the disciples' inability to recognize directly related to their prior failure to act in feeding the five thousand (Mark 6:51–52):

> But when they saw him walking on the sea they thought it was a ghost, and cried out, for they all saw him and were terrified. But immediately he spoke to them and said, "Take heart; it is I. Do not be afraid." And he got into the boat with them, and the wind ceased.

---

6. In an in-depth examination of the connections between Deut 29, Isa 6, and Mark 4–9, see Andrew M. Johnson, "Error and Epistemological Process," (Ph.D. diss., University of St Andrews, 2011), 90–93; Johnson, *Biblical Knowing*, 134–69. For a summary of that research, see Johnson, *Biblical Knowing*, 98–110.

7. Cf. Deut 29:28 LXX; Mark 4:22.

8. Submission to authority is found in the pairing of "listen/obey" (ἀκούουσιν) with "welcome/receive" (καὶπαραδέχονται).

> And they were utterly astounded, *for they did not understand about the* *loaves,* but their hearts were hardened.

Notice that a man walking on water does not confound the disciples. Rather, Mark draws the reader's attention directly back to their failure to participate in the feeding miracle. This leads us to a distinct feature of Mark's account: the disciples' perplexity.

Fifth, the disciples' failure to understand is more profound in Mark than in other gospel accounts,[9] causing the reader to scramble for clues as to why they are so obdurate while others seem to discern the kingdom clearly.[10] After having carried the leftover bread in the second miraculous feeding of 4,000, the disciples argue about not having enough bread themselves. Jesus presumes that their bodily participation in the miracle should have led them to recognize basic matters and chastises them according to the language of Deuteronomy 29 and Isaiah 6 (Mark 8:17–21):

> "Why are you discussing the fact that you have no bread? Do you not yet perceive or understand? Are your hearts hardened? Having eyes do you not see, and having ears do you not hear? And do you not remember? When I broke the five loaves for the five thousand, how many baskets full of broken pieces did you take up?" They said to him, "Twelve." "And the seven for the four thousand, how many baskets full of broken pieces did you take up?" And they said to him, "Seven." And he said to them, "Do you not yet understand?"[11]

Morna Hooker perceptively notes that the relevant question at hand in this passage is how we separate the epistemological process of the Pharisees from the disciples: "[F]or what the Pharisees and the disciples share in common in Mark's view, to greater or lesser degree, is obtuseness, a lack of under-

---

9. The negative view of the disciples in Mark is so caustic that Thompson reads Mark as a fundamentally negative ground where Jesus is the sole positive figure. Mary R. Thompson, *The Role of Disbelief in Mark: A New Approach to the Second Gospel* (Mahwah, NJ: Paulist Press, 1989), 33–59.

10. Outsiders do appear to recognize something in Jesus which the disciples are blind to and are commended for their recognizing (e.g. the Syrophonecian woman; Mark 7:24–30). In tragic contrast, the disciples appear to be lost, or worse, hardhearted, seeming to confirm Tolbert's diagnosis that Mark's gospel takes a fundamentally negative of the disciples. Mary Ann Tolbert, *Sowing the Gospel: Mark's World in Literary-Historical Perspective* (Minneapolis: Fortress Press, 1989), 176, 206. Collins, in her conclusion to Mark 8, offers that the disciples' incomprehensibility is itself incomprehensible: "Despite their 'being with him' (3:14), their 'having the mystery of the kingdom' (4:11), their being given private instruction by Jesus (4:10–20; 7:17–23), their authority over unclean spirits (6:7, 13), their proclamation of the need for repentance (6:12), and their ability to heal the sick (6:13), the disciples do not yet understand who Jesus is or the significance of his mighty deeds." Adela Yarbro Collins, *Mark* (ed. Harold W. Attridge; Hermeneia; Minneapolis: Fortress, 2007), 388.

11. Cf. Deut 29:4 (29:3 MT) and Isaiah 6:9–10.

standing which renders them incapable of comprehending the evidence which is placed before them."[12]

Immediately following this, Peter appears to *recognize* that Jesus is the Messiah, but then he is incapable of *discerning* anything meaningful about his own statement: "You are the Christ" (Mark 8:27–38).

A similar insensitivity to recognize persists and forms the source of Jesus' upbraid to his disciples and Jewish leadership. When requests for political power spring from his disciples' mouths, Jesus reprimands James and John for their inability to even recognize the nature of their request: "You do not know what you are asking" (Mark 10:38). I want to suggest that the failure of the disciples and Jewish leadership to perform prescribed action marks one traceable reason for Jesus' epistemological ire throughout Mark's gospel.[13]

Taken together, these begin to make the case that the ability to recognize is acculturated through embodied and scripted participation. But because of the extreme doltishness of the disciples, purportedly self-ascribed by the most ancient sources, their ability to discern is not yet on the table for discussion.[14]

Sixth, and important to Jesus' relationship with Torah, the Transfiguration acts to establish Jesus as the prophet of Israel. Mark casts this scene in Deuteronomic depictions of the Sinai event (Deut 4:36–37 LXX) and Deuteronomy's teaching on future prophets (Deut 18:15 LXX).[15] Most of the Gospels' narratives focus on the disciples' inability to recognize the secret of the kingdom of God, which is the explicit purpose of their time with Jesus (cf. Mark 4:10–12; Matt 13:11; Luke 8:9). Jesus, in a transfigured state and coupled with God's abrupt command on the mountain, is the prophet whom they should be obeying in order to see what he is showing them.

Seventh, the problem of the disciples' inability to recognize appears to be metaphorically and literarily framed by the healing of two blind men at Bethsaida (Mark 8:22–26) and Jericho (Mark 10:46–52) respectively. Some Markan scholars see the Bethsaida double-event healing as representative of the disciples' blindness. Although they are currently blind, by practicing the scripted actions of Jesus, the disciples will move to fuzzy recognition: "I see men walking like trees" (Mark 8:24). Ultimately, they are meant to have discerning sight: "and he saw everything *clearly*" (Mark 8:25).

After Peter's hollow confession of Jesus as the Christ, we have our first indication that he might recognize something like a messianic figure in Jesus.

---

12. Morna Hooker, "Isaiah in Mark's Gospel" in *Isaiah in the New Testament* (eds. Steve Moyise and Maarten J.J. Menken; London: T&T Clark, 2005), 49.

13. Johnson, *Biblical Knowing*, 97–109.

14. Though now disputed, this is in reference to the Papias fragments retained in Eusebius, which described Peter's public teaching as the majority source of Mark's gospel. Joanna Dewey, "The Survival of Mark's Gospel: A Good Story?" *JBL* 123, no. 3 (Autumn 2004): 495–507.

15. For a comparison of the Exodus, Deuteronomy, and Mark Sinai accounts, see Johnson, "Error and Epistemological Process," 164–68.

However, Peter cannot clearly discern the larger pattern associated with Jesus' version of "Messiah." After the trip up the mountain, an experience meant to remedy Peter's blurry vision, readers encounter the Sons of Zebedee on the other side of the mountain story still conceiving of the messiah solely in terms of power.

> Following the Transfiguration, we observe a blind request for power ensuing Jesus' question to James and John, "What do you want me to do for you (10:36)?" Then Jesus responds to Blind Bartimaeus with the identical question: "What do you want me to do for you (10:51)?" In short, sight qua understanding is a faculty being developed in the disciples *despite their resistance.* But it is their responsibility to acknowledge Jesus as their prophet by enacting his instruction in order to see what he is showing them. Their incomprehensibility is mitigated by either their failure to listen or their failure to participate.[16]

Concerning this sequence, Kelly Iverson concludes that recognition is meant to open the way toward discernment:

> The two-stage healing of the blind man (8.22-26) symbolizes the possibility for the restoration of the disciples' vision. They are no longer blind as Peter's confession makes clear but neither do they have full sight. . . . The two-stage healing of the blind man suggests that the movement from blindness to sight, from misunderstanding to understanding, is possible, but the disciples must await a second restorative touch that brings clarity of vision.[17]

The blind seem to recognize what the sighted disciples cannot. Notably, embodied processes mean to make the sighted men recognize like the blind men.

Eighth, not only is Jesus the prophet *par excellence,* but like many of the prophets, his critique is sharpened against the abuse of temple worship. After entering the temple complex, his rage fixes on what he sees happening in the courts: the sale of animals and money changing. Despite the attempts to set this scene in the Court of the Gentiles, which would make further sense of his quotation of Isaiah ("My house shall be called a house of prayer for all peoples ('the nations' LXX)," Isa 56:7), Jesus did not comment on the ritual practices of the temple at all. He does affirm Isaiah's note on prayer in the temple. However, Isaiah envisions prayers and sacrifice by the nations that are conjoined with animal sacrifices at the temple: "their burnt offerings and their sacrifices will be accepted" (Isa 56:7). Jesus only goes after what appears to be parasitic profiteering in the temple courts. In the same vein of prior prophetic critiques, Jesus makes no attempt to usurp Torah worship in the temple, but only the abuse of it—affirming Isaiah's vision of acceptable sacrifice.

---

16. Johnson, "Error and Epistemological Process," 154.

17. Kelley R. Iverson, *Gentiles in the Gospel of Mark: 'Even the Dogs Under the Table Eat the Children's Crumbs'* (ed. Mark Goodacre; LNTS 339; London: T&T Clark, 2007), 121.

Klawans offers a superb review of the proffered motivations for Jesus' attack on the temple:

1) exacting of the half-sheqel temple tax
2) use of foreign currency (Tyrian sheqel) for the tax
3) the image of the eagle on the foreign sheqel
4) the placement of the trading within the temple courts
5) the sale of animals not owned by the offerers
6) the temple commerce inordinately affected the poor

Of these options, Klawans believes Bruce Chilton's view of ownership makes best sense of what we know from contemporaneous archaeology, literature, and history. Namely, there was a dispute about whether one could offer an animal which they had recently purchased.[18] Although Klawans eventually cannot support Chilton's view in its details, he commends the idea that Jesus was upset by the abuse of sacrifice on the grounds of ownership. I will also pursue this idea further in coming chapters explaining why ownership creates a unique ritual preparation that merely purchasing animals cannot.

Despite these various reasons offered, Klawans finally concludes that the most likely explanation of Jesus' behavior is revealed by the details contained in accounts of Matthew, Mark, and John: money-changing and pigeon sales. These odd details are actually significant within the context as pigeons are the most inexpensive animals that can be purchased for sacrifice, reserved for those without means. As well, "The money changers have their impact on the impoverished because only the poor would feel pinched by the small surcharge assessed at the temple."[19] Citing Jesus' special consideration of the poor that marked his public life and the behavior of the early Jerusalemite church, Klawans argues that this factor alone explains his actions in the temple. However, he neglects another aspect of the same argument: that Jesus saw himself as the Prophet of Israel,[20] and therefore, *this ire for the sake of the poor stands in long tradition of prophetic critique focused on the disparity between sacrifice and the treatment of the poor.*

Ninth, as John did with baptism, Jesus ritualized the ritual of the Passover meal.[21] From our previous examination of Passover as a means to knowing his-

---

18. See Bruce Chilton, *Rabbi Jesus: An Intimate Biography* (New York: Doubleday, 2000), 213–30.

19. Klawans, *Purity, Sacrifice and the Temple*, 237.

20. N.T. Wright has demonstrated in Part II of *Jesus and the Victory of God* that Jesus both saw himself as a prophet and was received that way as well: "[T]he best initial model for understanding this praxis is that of a prophet; more specifically, that of a prophet bearing an urgent eschatological and indeed apocalyptic, message for Israel." And, "All the evidence so far displayed suggests that he was perceived as a prophet." N.T. Wright, *Jesus and the Victory of God* (COQG; Minneapolis: Fortress, 1996), 150, 196.

21. Although a great debate exists as to the univocity of the gospel narratives on the giving of the Lord's Supper (cf. Matt 26:17–25, Mark 14:12–25, Luke 22:7–23, John 13:1), even if its immediate context was not the Passover meal, the meal described in

tory (Exod 10:2; 12:26), we are now in the position to affirm that the gospels portray the Lord's Supper as an epistemologically oriented rite. Even in Mark's account, Passover is a day full of ritual: they slaughtered a lamb (Mark 14:12), they prepared a special meal (Mark 14:17f), Jesus ritualized the meal as a Passover for the new covenant (Mark 14:22–25), they sung hymns (Mark 14:26), and they ended with prayer in preparation for the coming sacrifice of Jesus (Mark 14:32–42).

Mark employs two epistemological paths: 1) the Isaianic path which is defined by epistemic deafness and blindness and 2) the Deuteronomic path which begins with epistemic obduracy, but ends in God's circumcision of the heart which enables Israel to recognize and discern.[22] Although the disciples most often appear to be on the Isaianic path, blind to what Jesus is doing, (even how suffering and death could be part of the kingdom for which they are hoping; re Mark 8:31–9:1), Mark holds out Deuteronomy's hope for disciples who remember through embodied participation.[23]

Assembling these two emphases found in the Torah—the epistemological impetus of Passover and Deuteronomy's ritualized remembrance—the difficulty with asserting the Communion imperative "do this in remembrance of me" outside of ritual epistemology is almost absurd. The very institution of Communion reifies Deuteronomy's ritualized sense of remembering: "do this" in order to remember. In the Lord's Supper, Deuteronomy's sense of embodying

---

the gospels was directly associated with Passover itself. Paul's call to "remember" in his received ceremony of Communion also adds weight to associating it with the Passover's epistemological features that we have previously reviewed. Klawans surmises that Paul's account offers not a metaphor, but an appropriation of temple cult (or what we have been calling a ritualization): "We must equally accept from Paul that those overtones need not be understood as an outright rejection of the Jerusalem temple. To the contrary, we are to understand Jesus' sacrificial metaphors as we understand Paul's: not as a spiritualization of, or a critique of, the cult but as an appropriation of, a borrowing from, the cult." Klawans, *Purity, Sacrifice and the Temple*, 222. Although, I would qualify that "a borrowing from" will always have an implicit critique. Brant Pitre's work is a good example of how biblical themes and the ritual of Passover itself are ritualized by Jesus. *Jesus and the Jewish Roots of the Eucharist: Unlocking the Secrets of the Last Supper* (New York: Doubleday, 2011).

22. I have previously argued that Mark's gospel explicitly seeks to show a process that prepares the disciples to discern the crucifixion as necessarily constituent of the secret of the kingdom of God promised in Mark 4. Johnson, "Error and Epistemological Process," 134–69. Many have noticed the difficulty in cohering crucifixion with the kingdom theme for the disciples. "Only in the passion narrative does Mark appeal to the general or particular authority of the scripture as explaining *the events that were difficult to accept and understand, such as the betrayal, arrest, and crucifixion of Jesus and the desertion of the disciples.*" Italics mine. Richard A. Horsley with Jonathan A. Draper, *Whoever Hear You Hears Me: Prophets, Performance, and Tradition in Q* (Harrisburg, PA: Trinity Press International, 1999), 143.

23. Cf. Deut 10:12–22; 29:1–3, 28; 30:6 (MT).

to remember means to cohere the concept of the new covenant by ritualizing Israel's known rite—Passover—with the coming events *that very evening*.

A comprehensive review of the epistemological process present in Mark would likely reveal a more nuanced relationship to ritual. I have attempted to establish a minimally sufficient case that ritual and knowing are part and parcel for the Markan author. To know is to acknowledge Jesus as the authoritative prophet of Israel who is scripting ritualized practices for his disciples. Mark depicts normative participation in Israel's rites, ritualized rites (i.e., baptism and Communion), and *ad hoc* scripting of actions (i.e., "You give them something to eat.") as pointing the disciples toward recognizing. These various instructions meant to dispose them to discern the mystery (μυστήριον) of the kingdom of God, which includes his crucifixion.

Tenth and finally, given the above argument, the fact that none of the disciples actually recognize the big picture within Mark's gospel demands explanation. Indeed, if we take the shortest ending of this gospel (i.e., Mark 16:8), no one ever sees Jesus resurrected. This has funded no small amount of scholarship attempting to understand the negative tone of Mark's gospel that ends so abruptly.[24] However, one plain act of recognition does occur at the crucifixion itself. The centurion, seeing (ἰδὼν) Jesus as he cried out and then "breathed his last breath," concluded, "Truly this man was a/the son of God" (Mark 15:39). The passage is too cryptic to draw strong conclusions about the centurion's participation in the crucifixion as a type of sacrifice ritual that leads to his recognition, however, one could understand the temptation to draw such a conclusion. At the least, we can see that Mark's gospel has an extenuating narrative comparing the disciples' incomprehensibility with this conspicuously placed centurion who does recognize at the very end of the Passion narrative. In contrast to those we care most about—the disciples—this centurion at the outermost fringe of the story recognized the most basic pattern apparent to the reader all along.

Mark's gospel maintains a persistent focus on the epistemological process of its characters. I want to suggest that in doing so, the gospel account sews ritual participation into the fabric of that process, presuming it to be the normative and necessary practice in order to recognize the prophet of Israel and discern the kingdom that he brings. In order to know who is the Messiah and discern what that means for Israel, the disciples must according to Jesus' in-

---

24. Tolbert and Kelber prefer to see the gospel as a negative account. Mary Ann Tolbert, *Sowing the Gospel*, 176, 206; Werner H. Kelber, *The Kingdom in Mark: A New Place and a New Time* (Minneapolis: Fortress, 1974), 62. But even on the most optimistic reading, the accounts are quite brutal on the disciples and Jewish leaders. Confounded by the evidence, Kermode contends that an honest reading of Mark suggests that the Markan author might be repeating stories that he/they did not even understand: "All this is very odd . . . .. It gives rise to suggestions that Mark did not understand the parable, that its original sense was already lost." Frank Kermode, *The Genesis of Secrecy* (The Charles Eliot Norton Lectures, 1977–1978; London: Harvard University Press, 1979), 11.

struction. Failure to act logically separates them from that which this process intends for them to know.

Ritual Knowing and Torah Temple Continuity in Luke-Acts

Among the chief advantages of including Luke in our study is that we can examine a gospel account self-reflective about its position among the several gospel accounts (πολλοί).[25] From its own prologue, this distinction means that Luke is offering *something else*, which some see as its orderliness based on a multi-perspective account.[26] We do not need to speculate here, other than to note this helpful peculiarity. Another advantage, previously mentioned, is that the Lukan author continues the account into the life of the early church. This distinction of Luke-Acts gives us the ability to see, through the Lukan lens, how the ritualized practices of Israel and the new ritualizations of baptism and Communion are incorporated into the early church.

The thesis will persist to the Jesus-sect within Israel, namely that it still views rituals as part of their normative Torah-centered life, disposing them to know the mystery of the kingdom of God as it is freshly discerned by the disciples of Jesus.

Since the Markan source shares an affinity with the Lukan source, from which they gain their status as synoptic gospels, we do not need to review the same ten aspects from above.[27] Luke makes very similar and discernible connections as Mark between both the temple rites and Jesus' disposing his disciples to discern the mystery of the kingdom of God. While Luke's gospel represents a significant expansion over Mark's terse narrative, the nodal points remain the same, some of which more indelibly link knowing with ritual in Luke. Below, I examine Luke and Acts for affirmation of ritual as efficacious. Second, I consider if ritual has an epistemological aspect beyond what we have already discovered in Mark.

---

25. It might be the case that Luke presumes Mark's gospel is already known in his prologue statements (Luke 1:1; the διήγησιν of the πολλοί), and according to Papias' comments about Mark's account, makes a more properly ordered account based on multiple perspectives rather than Peter's alone.

26. For more on the epistemological thrust of Luke-Acts, see: Thomas D.J. Stegman, "'The Spirit of Wisdom and Understanding': Epistemology in Luke-Acts," in *The Bible and Epistemology: Biblical Soundings on the Knowledge of God* (eds. Mary Healy and Robin Parry; Milton Keynes: Paternoster, 2007).

27. For points of direct continuity between Mark and Luke: 1) the John the Baptist narrative (Luke 3:1–22), 2) miraculous signs (Luke 5:17–26; 11:29–32), 3) the secret of the kingdom (Luke 8:4–18), 4) embodying the script (Luke 9:1–6, 13), 5) the disciples' failure to understand (Luke 18:34), 6) continuity with Sinai (Luke 9:28–36), 7) blind disciples metaphor (no parallel in Luke), 8) cleansing the temple (Luke 19:45–48, 9) the Passover (Luke 22:7–23), and 10) the crucifixion (Luke 23:44–47).

Ritual Continuation in Luke-Acts

Luke's gospel depicts the characters of its narrative as full participants in the ritualized practices of Israel. Likewise, the seminal event of Acts is an Israelite pilgrimage ritual—the feast of Pentecost (*Shavuot*). However, as the Gentiles become part of the plan of the kingdom of God, the relationship between Israelite ritual and the new covenant rituals is complicated. Without following the multitudinous complexities of Jewish ritual in the early church, a debatable topic amongst the apostles themselves (Acts 15), we merely want to show that Luke-Acts portrays temple ritual as central to the lives of the early church.

First, in Luke, the temple is the place of divine communication. John the Baptist's father is a Levite serving on rotation in the temple when he has a vision (ὀπτασίαν) in the Holy Place (Luke 1:5–25). John the Baptist is later circumcised and Jesus presented at the temple for Mary's post-birth purification "according to the law of Moses" (Luke 2:22–24). Luke even quotes the passage from Exodus (Exod 13:2, 12) and Leviticus (Lev 12:8) concerning the precise animal sacrifice brought on behalf of her purification: two birds. Anna, the prophetess, is described as a woman of the temple, fasting and praying there night and day (Luke 2:36–38). The summary of the birth narrative in Luke ends with a full affirmation of their rituated life: "And when they had performed everything according to the law of the Lord, they returned to Galilee" (Luke 2:39). The one slice of Jesus' life completely obscured in the other gospels—Jesus' childhood—is fleetingly depicted in reference to the pilgrimage and temple worship of Passover (Luke 2:41–51).

Second, in Jesus' adult life, we see the continuation of a positive view of Torah and Israelite ritual. Luke-Acts expressly and repeatedly affirms the positive role of Torah. Luke predicates the parable of the good Samaritan on a proper understanding of Deuteronomy 6 and Leviticus 19 as the center of Torah (cf. Luke 10:25–37; 18:18–20). Jesus subdues the idea of replacing the Torah (Luke 16:16–17)—where his parable of Lazarus in Hades ends in the problem of not obeying Moses and the Prophets (Luke 16:31). The Transfiguration account later cited by the apostles in Acts depicts Jesus as the fulfillment of Deuteronomic prophecy (Deut 18:15): "I will raise up a prophet . . . listen to him" (cf. Luke 9:35; Acts 3:22). When the resurrected Jesus explains the necessity of the crucifixion, Luke notes, "and beginning with Moses and all the prophets, he interpreted (διερμήνευσεν) to them in the Scriptures the things concerning himself" (Luke 24:27).

Third, Luke recounts John's baptism in epistemic terms. In recalling John's prophetic authority, Luke notes that those who understood John were the ones who discerned John's actions as evidence that "God is just." Even more, Luke's gospel continues on to tell the reader that those who discerned were the very ones whom John had previously baptized. However, those who were undiscerning (i.e., the Pharisees and the lawyers), "rejected the purpose of God not having been baptized by him" (Luke 7:29–30). At the very least, some connection between discernment based upon prior baptism exists in Luke, even if only to denote the ones who "get it" apart from those who do not.

As for rituals themselves, Luke does nothing to discourage the reader from thinking about this new Jewish sect in terms of Israelite ritual practices. At the inauguration of Jesus' public ministry with John the Baptist, water rituals have been moved to the Jordan as preparation for the messiah (Luke 3:1–21). Upon healing the ten lepers, Jesus sends them to the priests to perform their sacrifices and rites of purification, which would include Levitical baptism (Luke 17:11–19). Upon "cleansing" the temple courts of commerce, Luke notes that Jesus then begins to teach in the temple, which is where he was instructed as a child (cf. Luke 2:41–52; 19:45–48). Although Jesus prophesies the destruction of the temple, he appears to consider that a sad but necessary event (cf. Luke 21:5–9; 19:41–44). Finally, in Luke, Jesus participates in animal sacrifice during Passover (Luke 22:7).[28] Luke makes no effort to hide the fact that Jesus and his family are full participants in the rituals of Israel with positive descriptions of the rites and the Torah throughout. Like the prophets, Jesus singles out the abuse of rituals for critique, but continues to pursue their proper use.

The narrative of Acts continues the trend of Luke's positive treatment of Torah ritual. While it certainly creates a perplexing relationship between Israelite rituals and their necessity amongst the Gentiles (e.g., circumcision), Luke does not downplay the centrality of the temple rites for the early church as long as the temple is still standing. The seminal event of Acts—the Holy Spirit at Pentecost—is predicated by the Pentecost sacrifices and ends with mass baptism (Acts 2). After Pentecost, Peter and John go to the temple at the hour of prayer (Acts 3:1). The first believers gathered bravely at Solomon's portico in the temple and the first apostolic healings after the resurrection were performed at the Temple (Acts 5:12–16). This temple-centered Jesus sect also serves to explain why "many of the priests became obedient to the faith" (Acts 6:7). Stephen's fatal rebuke includes a lengthy discussion as to how rejecting Moses leads to an abuse of ritual (Acts 7:35–43). Taken together, these support Klawans's conclusion: "Jesus' followers did not separate themselves from the temple and its sacrificial worship."[29]

Moving out from the location of the Temple, the Ethiopian who is returning from ritual practices at the temple in Jerusalem is baptized, a rite of the new covenant (Acts 8:26–40). Although an argument from silence, there is no sense in Acts that his temple worship is fruitless. Rather, along with other God fearers, their ritual participation acts a sign of their preparedness for the gospel. Cornelius, the centurion who brings Peter to teach the Gentiles, is commended to the reader as a man (and his household) considered "devout" (εὐσεβὴς) among the Jews (Acts 10:1–2; cf. 10:22; 13:16, 26). Though not a con-

---

28. To what extent he directly participates is unknown, but whether or not he personally killed the Passover lamb is immaterial for our purposes. I will discuss direct and representative participation in rituals in chapter eleven.

29. Klawans, *Purity, Sacrifice and the Temple*, 217.

vert to Judaism, Luke demonstrates the meaning of "devout" in God's response to Cornelius' prayers and alms-giving, which are then depicted in terms of Levitical altar sacrifices: "Your prayers and your alms have ascended as a memorial before God" (Acts 10:4). Cornelius' household is then baptized in the same way and for the same reasons as the Jewish Pentecost-celebrants of Acts 2 (Acts 10:44–48).

A theological problem caused by the inclusion of Gentiles brings the Torah and Israelite rituals to the fore of Acts in chapter fifteen. The question surrounded the parts of the Torah Gentiles should practice was stated as, "What must one do to keep the Law of Moses?" (Acts 15:5). The Torah does not appear to be on the verge of abrogation, but is rather re-contextualized for the Gentiles. The Torah, as interpreted by Jesus, now appears to point Israel outwards, rather than to bring the stranger/foreigner in to perform temple rites.[30]

Notably, abuse of worship is one of the three central warnings from the Torah commended to the Gentiles (Acts 15:19). Although Peter observed that the Torah created a burden on the Jews that is unfair to place onto the Gentiles, no negative sense of the Torah-obedience bleeds through the apostle's letter to the Gentiles (Acts 15:10). The commendation to the Gentiles could be just as easily interpreted as a *freedom to* this practical exegesis of Torah, rather than a *freedom from* the Torah rites. Either way, Gentiles still must have a cognizance of their personal practices in keeping with the Jerusalem council's decision—maintaining the sexual ethos of Torah and abstaining from abuse of rituals, which implies a proper use.

Finally, Paul partook in the Israelite ritual of Nazarite vows specifically for the sake of settling rumors that he was instructing Jews to "forsake Moses, telling them not to circumcise their children or walk according to our customs" (Acts 21:21). Paul agrees to practice the Nazarite vow with four others at the temple in order to confirm that he was not forsaking the Torah or its rites (Acts 21:26). While many will debate the theological significance of the scene, we only need to observe that toward the end of his time of apostolic teaching, Paul sees no deficit in practicing sacrificial rites *in the Temple*. As well, Luke portrays Paul's actions directly with no moral or narratival critique.

With a review of Luke's content now in front of us, we can recognize that the gospel and story of the early church in Luke-Acts has a fundamentally positive orientation towards the Torah in general, Israelite rituals in particular, and their continued use in the life of the early church so long as the temple exists. Luke does not turn the reader off from the idea of ritual at the temple, but considers the temple a foundational place—the locale of Jesus' ministry in Jerusalem and the meeting place of the early Jerusalemite church. This does not abrogate its functions, but rather associates the Gospel's scenes strongly with the temple's special, geographical, and ritual role in the life of Israel.

---

30. E.g., Exod 12:48–49; Lev 18:26.

Ritual Knowing in Luke

Having established the positive view of Torah and ritual in Luke-Acts, I must now show that embodied practices and rituals are presumed to maintain their epistemological function, disposing Israelites to recognize that which is being shown to them. First, I examine the birth and child narratives. Second, I turn to the public life of Jesus and Passion Week. Third, the efficacy of rites meant to enable recognizing in Acts gives impetus to pursue ritual epistemology in the epistolary material of the New Testament.

Practice and Knowing in Luke. First, Luke's narratives concerning Jesus' formative years center mainly in two locales: Jerusalem and Nazareth.[31] In a scene that recalls the promises to Abraham (cf. Gen 15), the angel appears to an elderly Zechariah while he is servicing the Holy Place of the temple with a message of improbable birth through his barren and elderly wife (cf. Luke 1:7, 8–17). Luke describes this child in terms of Malachi's returning Elijah (cf. Luke 1:16–17; Mal 4:5–6).[32] The direct allusion to Malachi must be considered alongside Malachi's own rebuke, which is permeated with a care for proper ritual practices (Mal 1:6–14) and the pursuit of Torah living (Mal 4:4; 3:22 [MT]).[33]

Another similarity to the Abrahamic promise of progeny is Zechariah's response: "How shall I know this (κατὰ τί γνώσομαι τοῦτο)" (Luke 1:18).[34] The response to Zechariah's questioning is not a defined ritual, as it was with Abraham (Gen 15:9–10; 17–18), but a definitively unnatural muteness that served as a sign to Zechariah and Elizabeth concerning the promise (Luke 1:20). It was a sign because Zechariah did not trust (οὐκ ἐπίστευσας). In other words, Zechariah's "how shall I know" is answered with an embodied process (i.e., temporary muteness) which means to confidently dispose him to recognize who is responsible for both Zechariah's muteness and Elizabeth's pregnancy. The effect of these signs, vision, and muteness is public, known to Elizabeth (Luke 1:24–25) and the other priests as well (Luke 1:21–22). Luke, through Zechariah's prophecy at John's birth, also presents us with John the Baptist's epistemological goal: "to give knowledge of salvation to his people *in the forgiveness of their sins*" (Luke 1:77). Here, we have the first direct link in Luke-Acts between John's baptism and disposing Israel to recognize, apart from which the knowledge of salvation presumably might not occur (cf. Luke 1:77; 3:3, 6).

---

31. With the brief exception of the birth in Bethlehem (Luke 2:1–21).

32. Mal 3:23–24 (MT).

33. Malachi opens with a critique of the abuse of proper rituals (Mal 1:6–14) and the rituals to foreign gods (Mal 2:10–11).

34. Cf. Gen 15:8 (LXX): κατὰ τί γνώσομαι ὅτι κληρονομήσω αὐτήν. Mary's response shares similar incredulity: "How can this be since I haven't known a man (πῶς ἔσται τοῦτο, ἐπεὶ ἄνδρα οὐ γινώσκω)?" (Luke 1:34).

Jesus' birth and childhood also evince knowing as embodied process. Mary herself is given signs similar to Zechariah about progeny. Since she was a virgin (Luke 1:34; ἐπεὶ ἄνδρα οὐ γινώσκω), her greatest sign was the pregnancy itself, which was followed by a string of other signals to reiterate that the initial pronouncement of the angel was indeed true to life (Luke 1:35). Dealing with Mary's epistemic concerns is part of the narrative strategy for Luke.

Elizabeth becomes pregnant as predicted (Luke 1:36, 39–41). Elizabeth then prophesied about Mary's child in the womb in accordance with the angel's statements (Luke 1:42–45). Signs and witnesses to whom God revealed the event attend the birth itself (Luke 2:8–18). But concerning Mary's epistemological process, Luke is careful to show the reader that Mary recognizes the pattern developing and discerns its significance. Luke relates this to the reader in poetic language: "But Mary treasured up (συνετήρει) all these things [signs reiterating the angels message], pondering (συνβάλλουσα) them in her heart" (Luke 2:19).[35]

Related to this, although not directly relevant, the actions of Jesus' parents indicate a positive epistemic relationship with the temple presumed by Luke. If ritual were actually a false form of worship extinguished for the sake of something superior, then participating in temple ritual could blind Jesus' family to reality. As seen in Amos and Micah, false worship makes Israel insensitive—unable to recognize or discern patterns before her. Jesus' family circumcised him, offered meager sacrifices for Mary's impurity, and "performed everything according to the *Torah of the Lord* (νόμον κυρίου)" (Luke 1:39). This statement is immediately ensued by the only record of Jesus' pediatric development in the gospels, which acts as an opening inclusio: "And the child grew and became strong, filled with wisdom (σοφία)" (Luke 2:40). Adjacent to this summary, Jesus' family goes back down to Jerusalem for the Passover festival where they lose track of young Jesus and later find him learning from teachers in the temple courts. This story is concluded with the inclusio: "And Jesus increased in wisdom (σοφία) and stature and in favor with God and man" (Luke 2:52). Apart from this being the Septuagint's same description of Samuel as a young man devoted to tabernacle service (1 Sam 2:26), the blunt association of the temple and festival rites with Jesus' wisdom does not create a conclusive argument for my thesis. Nevertheless, it shows an atmosphere in Luke that presumes positive association between ritual practices and wisdom.

Witnesses to these rites in the childhood narrative are also described in epistemic terms of "seeing," where sight is the metaphor for "discerning." Before "all flesh shall see the salvation of God" (cf. Isa 40:5; Luke 3:6), Simeon is

---

35. The term translated "pondering" (συνβάλλουσα) is rare in the NT, occurring only six times and all of which are in Luke-Acts. The word most often means "to meet with" (e.g., Luke 14:31; Acts 20:14) or "to confer/converse" (e.g., Acts 4:15; 17:18). The connotation is that of deliberation, hence the English Standard Version's "pondering" (also, King James Bible, New American Standard Bible, New International Version, Revised Standard Version, and New Revised Standard Version).

uniquely disposed to recognize Jesus: "for my eyes have seen your salvation" (Luke 2:30). Simeon recognized Jesus as the promised salvation in infant form and discerned the significance of his presence in the temple (Luke 2:34–35). A prophetess named Anna follows directly after Simeon, immediately recognizing this family and the significance of their participation in the ritual acts: "She did not depart from the temple, worshiping with fasting and prayer night and day" (Luke 2:37–38). What disposed these two persons to uniquely recognize Jesus according to Luke?

Simeon is "devout," a term ripe with associations to ritual practices of prayer and giving.[36] Anna practiced rites in the temple as preparation for what she saw. Both appear to deem their own ritual practices as preparation, waiting to recognize the Lord's Messiah and not departing for the sake of prayer and worship (Luke 2:26, 37). Individually, these references to temple and ritual are not significant. Taken together, they form a pattern that supports a particular Lukan understanding of the role of Torah rites in understanding Israel and Jesus as her messiah.

Recognition and Discernment in Luke. Several instances of recognition and discernment during Jesus' public ministry are worth considering. First, when John's disciples seek to know if Jesus is indeed the one they are expecting, Jesus does not answer the question (Luke 7:18–23). Rather, he challenges them to recognize—looking at his works and the testimony of healings—a pattern from which they could presumably discern the answer. However, this offers weak support for my thesis because this passage does not deal directly with what John's disciples must do in order to be disposed to recognize. I could argue, if pushed, that Jesus scripts the ritualized practice of observing—looking with attentive focus beyond the miracle itself and toward its transcendent significance, which disposed them to recognize. But this all seems too thin to sustain the point.

Second, Jesus sends out of the seventy-two disciples, which yields clearer indications of the relationship between scripted practices and recognition. Jesus sent these out with clear instructions: pray (Luke 10:2); rely absolutely on others for subsistence (10:4); look for the "son of peace" (10:6); do not go house to house (10:7); eat, heal, and preach in a town that receives you (10:8–9); and warn the town that does not receive you of judgment (10:8–9). When the seventy-two return from their expedition, they recount its success (Luke 10:17). Jesus' thankfulness at their report reveals that they followed the scripted practice. And hence, embodying his instructions enabled them to see something they could not have otherwise recognized. Moreover, Jesus himself indicates the intentionally epistemic nature of the process: "You have hidden these

---

36. Luke exclusively uses this term "devout" (εὐλαβής) four times in Luke-Acts, three of which appear to link their devoutness with their performance of Torah (cf. Acts 2:5; 8:2; 22:12).

things from the wise and . . . Blessed are the eyes that see what you see" (Luke 10:21–23).

Third, the extensively chronicled conflict between Jesus and Jewish leadership provides some negative examples, where Israelites should have discerned, but did not for cited reasons. In one poignant incident, Jesus argues with a Pharisee and lawyer about the confusion of customs from Torah. Although they still practice scripted acts, tithing spices and giving alms (Luke 11:39–41), these acts load burdens upon the people (Luke 11:46). Jesus metaphorically depicts this as creating tombs, which they then fill with prophets whom they have killed (Luke 11:47–48). Unfortunately, the prophets were the exclusive voice of Wisdom, now dead and buried (Luke 11:49). Hence, Jesus summarized the burden, not of Torah, but of following customs and eschewing of the prophets: "For you have taken away the key of knowledge. You did not enter yourselves and you hindered those who were entering" (Luke 11:52). Jesus plays the prophetic role, the one he just identified as deadly, and critiques them for false practices, which lead away from knowing. His critique is noticeably not aimed at proper temple ritual, but *ad hoc* customs of tithing. Just as with the prophetic critique of false worship, we see Jesus associating abuse of ritual with the inability to discern.

Fourth, Jesus addresses the motivation to understand in his example of the interpretation of meteorology (Luke 12:54–56): agrarian subsistence farmers needed to know how to read the skies. Israelites understood the process of discernment, recognizing (δοκιμάζειν) patterns in the sky and cohering them into a transcendent weather forecast. Even though they are motivated to interpret the skies,[37] Jesus chastises them, focusing on the fact that they do not transfer the skill to this "present time": "You know how to interpret (οἴδατε δοκιμάζειν) the heavens . . . but you do not interpret (οὐ δοκιμάζετε) the present season" (Luke 12:56). Here, we have a paradigmatic example where someone was taught through an embodied practice to recognize certain patterns in the skies and discern their transcendent meaning. Jesus chides his hearers, essentially, because they have the skill, yet they do not apply it presently. The lingering question—what precise embodied practices would have disposed them to discern this present messianic season—remains unanswered.

Fifth, and likewise with his own disciples, Jesus attempts to get his audience to recognize the necessity of his own death and resurrection; but without success (Luke 18:31–34). While he teaches about what will eventually happen in the Passion narrative, Luke notes the disciples' insensitivity to the instruction: "But they understood (συνῆκαν) none of these things" (18:34).[38] It must

---

37. The need to interpret the skies is most pressing due to the immediate consequences of not properly interpreting weather in an agrarian culture.

38. Contrast this with the disciples on the road to Emmaus, where Luke reports: "Then he [Jesus] opened their minds to understand (συνιέναι) the Scriptures" (Luke 24:45). In that narrative, these two disciples have experienced the Crucifixion, walked along the road, listened, and then break bread, which ultimately leads to the

be asked: why did the disciples not understand? Was it a failure of their rational faculty or powers of deduction? Were they simply not paying attention?
I have argued elsewhere that the ability to recognize, as it is described in the
Torah and Gospels, appears to occur when persons 1) submit to the authority
guiding them and 2) embody the scripts they assign in order to know. Amazingly, the failure of the disciples to recognize the mystery of the kingdom as
promised is rooted in a first-order error: failure to fully acknowledge Jesus as
the authoritative prophet whose instructions they must practice.[39] This failure
to embody the prescribed practices results in not being disposed to recognize.[40] Conversely, when they perform as prescribed (e.g., sending out the seventy-two), hidden things are revealed (Luke 10:21–23).

Sixth, as for Israel's rituals, Luke connects false practices not prescribed
by Moses with the inability to recognize. Jesus laments over the coming destruction of Jerusalem, which he ties to their epistemic negligence. "Would
that even you had known on this day the things that make for peace. But now
they are hidden from your eyes . . . *because you did not know/recognize*
(οὐκ ἔγνως) *the time of your visitation*" (Luke 19:42, 44). Why were they not able
to recognize the "visitation"? Luke shows Jesus in the immediately ensuing
text driving out inappropriate practices from the temple. Moreover, Luke
quickly moves us to what happens next, where Jesus sets up shop and begins
teaching daily in the temple courts. We cannot miss Jesus' lamentation over
Jerusalem's epistemic insensitivity (Luke 19:41–44), followed by Israel's temple
gone awry (Luke 19:45–46), and the solution found in Jesus then teaching daily
in those same temple courts (Luke 19:47–48)—all in quick narratival succession. A large part of how we understand Jesus' epistemic use of ritual depends
on how we imagine this precise scene unfolding. Of course, while Jesus is
teaching in the temple, we cannot imagine that the ritual practices were suspended. Animal and vegetal offerings for sacrifice and prayer must have still
continued and surrounded the teaching of Jesus. Do we imagine that he scowls
at practices that might be mere outward acts of piety? Whatever we imagine,
Luke offers no clues.

Seventh, Luke's Jesus offers praise for outward practices in appropriate
circumstances. Does he see such ritual practices, when properly employed, as
preparing Israel for the new covenant in his body and blood? Luke's Jesus considers the spoken prayers of a sinner (Luke 18:9–14), the gifts of a widow (Luke
21:1–4), and the actions of a Samaritan (Luke 10:25–37) as fundamentally good,
all of which could be considered outward acts. Actions, even public practices,
cannot be fundamentally anti-kingdom, but there appears to be ways in which

---

opening of their minds. (Luke 24:16, 31). These actions are not a prescribed ritual, but
they certainly appear to be a guided process.

39. Johnson, *Biblical Knowing*, 97–109.

40. We will not address here the problem that God Himself is often described as
the one who allows and disallows the disciples to recognize (cf. Luke 18:34; 24:16, 31).

practices can either correctly form disciples to recognize or warp them into confoundedness.

Ritual Knowing in Acts

Rituals in Acts are expressly connected to the knowledge of Israel. The Holy Spirit's descent synchronized with the Feast of Weeks, a Torah festival with sacrifices. When Peter interprets what the masses are witnessing, and misinterpreting as drunkenness, his concluding words home in on the epistemic nature of the event: "Therefore, let all the house of Israel *know confidently* (ἀσφαλῶς . . . γινωσκέτω) that God has made him both Lord and Christ, this Jesus whom you crucified" (Acts 2:36).

In other words, the gathering of the Israelite diaspora into Jerusalem to practice the temple rituals of Pentecost is the context that led up to Peter's climactic words "therefore, . . . know confidently" with the immediate response of "Brothers, what shall we do" (Acts 2:35–37). The answer to that question, which implies that it will resolve Peter's imperative to "know confidently," is a ritualized ritual: "Repent and be baptized" (Acts 2:38). Stated otherwise, if they want to "know confidently" all that Peter has just interpreted, repentance *and* baptism form part of the process to dispose them thusly.

Again, the reader can observe that temple rituals do not end at Pentecost, but persist, positively portrayed all the way through to Paul's sacrifices prior to his arrest (Acts 21:26). An epistemological plot drives Paul's sacrifice as well. The Jerusalemite church's concern turns on whether or not Paul trusts the Torah rituals and encourages Gentiles to do the same. The problem is not Paul's ability to recognize or discern, but the Jerusalem elders' ability to recognize Torah faithfulness in Paul. This pertains to Paul's internal disposition towards the Torah and testimony of others to the opposite: "that you teach all the Jews who are among the Gentiles to forsake Moses" (Acts 21:21). The Jerusalemite community is disturbed by something they cannot know about Paul—his internal disposition toward the Torah—and that which they have heard about Paul among the Gentiles. Hence, they script a ritual practice for the sake of helping them to recognize whether or not Paul has indeed forsaken Moses' instruction: "Thus all will know that there is nothing in what they have been told about you [Paul]" (Acts 21:24). In this instance, the ritual practice acts as a test, performed in order to recognize something otherwise indiscernible and internal to Paul.

The persistence of water baptism also acts as a noticeable rite that attends epistemic sequences. In Acts 8, Philip arrives upon an Ethiopian courtier who has just returned from his rituals at the temple and reads Isaiah's scroll. Philip's question, "Do you know what you are reading (γινώσκεις ἃ ἀναγινώσκεις)," sets the epistemological tone of the passage (Acts 8:30). Aside from Philip "enlightening" (εὐηγγελίσατο) the Ethiopian about the Messiah from the Hebrew Bible, we cannot miss the fact that baptism resolves the initial narratival conflict posed by Philip's question, "Do you understand?" The courtier essentially answers, "No, I do not understand," but also, "How can I understand unless someone guides me?" (Acts 8:31). Again, the answer is "enlightening" (εὐηγγελίσατο) by Philip's use of the historical texts of Israel *plus* the new ritualized rite of baptism.

In a similar vein, Acts premises Paul's teaching at Athens upon the Athenians' request, "We wish to know what these things mean (γνῶναι τίνα θέλει ταῦτα εἶναι)" (Acts 17:20). After Paul's words of explanation that begin with their religious impulse evident from Athenian statuary, he ends at the resurrection (Acts 17:31). Most mocked him, but a few "joined him and trusted (ἐπίστευσαν)" (Acts 17:34). Although Acts does not explicitly mention baptism, it appears implied by the pattern of the text.[41] In short, the request "to know what these things mean" is ultimately answered by Paul's speech and the baptism of the few who "believed."

Later, when Paul addresses the violent crowd in Jerusalem after his arrest, he recounts his own reorientation citing an epistemological transformation as its basis. While Paul is temporarily blinded, Ananias comes to Paul to restore his sight, saying, "The God of our fathers appointed you to know (γνῶναι) his will" (Acts 22:14). The immediate action that Paul is to take, presumably enabling him "to know his will," is baptism: "And now why do you wait? Rise and be baptized" (Acts 22:16).

Despite the instances cited above, there is a noticeable paucity of temple ritual in Acts. This is most easily explained by the nature of the narrative, that it moves out of Jerusalem early on and follows the apostles to the Gentiles. The minimally sufficient case made here includes 1) that the early church did not reject the Torah rituals, 2) that embodied practices were still seen as epistemological, and 3) that ritual practices persisted in disposing Israelites to recognize a particular facet of God's plan. If this is correct, then we should find a corresponding disposition toward ritualized practices not centered on the temple in the epistles, which by their occasional and geographical nature would not lend themselves to conversations about temple-centered ritual.

The Hebrews Epistle and Ritual Knowing

The epistle to the Hebrews marks the most natural teaching to consider when making the case for ritual and knowing.[42] If ritual is necessary in order to

---

41. Acts establishes a pattern of "believing" (πιστεύω) which ends in baptism. In this way, "believed" becomes a shorthand report for baptism as well and joining a local assembly of Jews and/or Gentile Christians. Cf. Acts 13:12, 48; 14:1, 23; 16:15, 33–34; 17:4, 12, 34; 18:8.

42. For a summary of the current debate on the rhetoric and *Sitz im Leben* of the Hebrews epistle, see Jared C. Calaway *The Sabbath and the Sanctuary: Access to God in the Letter to the Hebrews and Its Priestly Context* (WUNT 2/349; Tübingen: Mohr Siebeck, 2013).

know, then the epistle renowned for expositing Levitical law ought to reveal the same impetus. Building up to Hebrews 11:1, one of the more widely known epistemological statements in Christian Scripture, the author sews the language of assuredness, hope, and belief into the rhetoric of the letter. The author roots the reason for that assuredness, hope, and trusting belief in the history of Israel through participation in her rituals. In fact, Israel's rituals act as the presumed background to discerning the death of Jesus as a type of sacrifice (Heb 10)—something not entirely obvious without the author's interpretation.

Beginning in Hebrews 6, the readers are expected to know (Heb 6:4, φωτίζω; lit. "enlightened") about mature Christian teaching because they have experienced it for themselves (i.e., "tasted" and "drank"; Heb 6:5–8). The author then reviews the history of epistemic assurance from Abraham forward: "So when God desired to *show more convincingly* to the heirs of the promise the unchangeable character of his purpose, he *guaranteed* it with an oath" (Heb 6:17). This assurance building through ritual is what validates Jesus' own actions: "This makes Jesus the guarantor of a better covenant" (Heb 7:22). The ensuing chapters of the letter contend that Israelites performing rituals in the tabernacle/temple mirrors the worship in the heavens (Heb 8–9). Finalizing the argument, (Heb 9:11–28) the author seeks to show that the blood of the new covenant fulfills the old covenant, which is the basis for the epistemological confidence being demanded in the next two chapters. Hence, "Therefore, we have confidence (παρρησία)," which in turn yields clinging to the God of Israel (Heb 10:19).

Although many have taken Hebrews to be an anti-ritual treatise of the Christian church, that cannot flatly be the case.[43] The rituals act as the analogical basis of understanding. Hebrews is not anti-ritual; rather, it eschews the blood of the Mosaic covenant as sufficient for the new covenant. However, ritualized blood practices are fully contiguous from Moses to the first century Jewish church, and up until today, in Communion. Arguing that the blood ritual is still metaphorically in view, Klawans contends:

> It is indeed nearly impossible to conceive of a plausible Jewish teacher of the first century c.e. who advocates the eating of human flesh, or the drinking of blood of any species. Yet, as has been often pointed out, neither human flesh nor blood of any species was consumed by Jesus, his followers, members of the early church, or even, for that matter, by Catholics after the fourth Lateran Council in 1215. Even when performed by Christians with a firm belief in the doctrine of transubstantiation, no violation of Jewish purity codes is taking place in any enactment of eucharistic traditions.[44]

---

43. "Within the New Testament, this perspective [supersession of the temple sacrifices] is laid out most clearly in the epistle to the Hebrews." Klawans, *Purity, Sacrifice, and the Temple*, 7–8.

44. Ibid., 216.

Although Klawans has a thin view of metaphor in mind, his point remains. Early Christianity to the present teaches Communion as a blood and flesh ritual, ritualized on the basis of Mosaic rites. Therefore Klawans concludes regarding the Luke-Acts depiction of the rite: "Luke did not interpret the Last Supper event as an unambiguously antitemple action: if he had, then he would have depicted the disciples as abandoning the temple immediately thereafter."[45]

The build up to Hebrews 11 is important because it shows that an embodied knowledge of Israel's rites, her festival calendar, and lived grasp of the Torah provides the analogical basis of the confidence of Jewish believers who followed Jesus as the Messiah. Stated otherwise, the section of Hebrews that rehearses Israel's famous league of those who trusted God begins with a foundation in the ritual life of Israel (Heb 11:1):

> Now *trusting belief* (πίστις) is the *foundational confidence* (ὑπόστασις) of those things for which we *hopefully expect* (ἐλπιζομένων), the *testing* (ἔλεγχος) of the not-seen-things.

If we could plot the confidence of Israel to know that she has correctly recognized God's plan, according to Hebrews, her confidence is founded in 1) creation, 2) the Abrahamic covenant, 3) participation in the Torah rites and ethical life of Israel, and 4) the continuing participation in the ritualed life of the new covenant.[46]

---

45. Ibid., 217. His surprisingly thin account of the Hebrews epistle as "antitemple, antisacrifical, and antipriestly" is jarring given Klawans's insightful commentary throughout the rest of his work. While I am sympathetic to most of what he argues, Klawans does make a few substantive oversights in his all-too-brief review of antitemple polemics in the NT. First, in support of his case, he never mentions one of the most pro-temple arguments from Luke-Acts where Paul goes to the temple and offers sacrifices for purity on his very final trip to Jerusalem. In fact, his purpose in being purified is to show that he is not antitemple and he is arrested for the last time during those sacrificial rites at the temple (Acts 21:17–26). Second, Klawans does not consider the idea that Mosaic' rites are being ritualized by a Jewish prophet, John the Baptist, and later by Jesus. Third, he mistakenly argues that the eschatological vision of Revelation ends with no temple in the new Jerusalem. He stops short at John's statement, "And I saw no temple in the city [new Jerusalem]. However, Klawans ignores the second half of the sentence entirely, "for its temple is the Lord God the Almighty and the Lamb" (Rev 21:22). Whatever one makes of God Himself being the temple, it is an oversimplification to say "Clearly, in this vision of the future, the temple holds no place, and the Jerusalem of the future will not suffer from its absence." Klawans, 243. One could more rigorously argue the opposite: that the temple is so utterly central in the eschaton that God Himself is the only thing to take up its place and function, as it were.

46. Thanks to Carol Anne Kemp, Ruth Janzen, Kelsey Heinz, and Gabrielle Campbell for pointing out the epistemological thrust of Hebrews 6–10 to me in a seminar at The King's College (New York City), Spring 2012.

Conclusions

No doubt, this chapter is a truncated conversation about ritual and knowledge in the New Testament. Each section of this chapter could serve as an introduction to a thesis in its own right. I know that many readers would expect me to engage Paul's epistles, another book-length project in-and-of itself.[47] My goal here is only to give a minimally sufficient reason to think that the Scriptures of that early Jerusalemite Jewish Jesus sect often discussed vital knowledge in light of embodied process, and sometimes in light of embodying rituals in order to know.

Beyond ritual knowing, the matter of supersessionism will occupy coming chapters. And so, identifying the relationship of NT authors to the primacy of embodied practice, ritual, and temple rites is an initial step in that direction.

---

47. A very tentative case could be made to show that Paul has a similar construct in mind through his epistles. For instance, Paul repeatedly claims that through Torah practice (in which I would include ritual), Israelites come to know sin (Rom 3:19–20; 6:1–6; 7:7).

Chapter 10

Ritualization:
A Better Construct than Supersessionism

Now that I have made a tentative case for considering biblical rituals as epistemological, a brief discussion regarding the diminution of ritual will prepare us to think about its current role in theological discourse. For instance, it might strike us as odd that the apostles baptize in response to epistemological concerns. We might be leery of a theologian who suggests that prayer and fasting are the preferred ways to rationalize through thorny theological dilemmas. Despite our hesitation to acknowledge the body involved in our thinking, we must ask ourselves why it is that we hesitate. I have argued that scientific practices are rife with scripted ritual behaviors requiring the body's involvement in discrete mental processes. Yet, we do not view a scientist as unreasonable if she wants to "stare at the data" for a few hours to see if a pattern emerges. Why would we hesitate in realms outside of science to embody practices? The short answer is that we often do not hesitate, but translate the way we speak of rituals so that they do not seem like rituals.[1] *But why would we want to avoid the appearance of ritual in the first place?*

Two reasons spring to mind: cultural supersessionism and practical traceability. First, it is no secret that the West has culturally embraced a rationalist construct about mentality, where thoughts occur in the mind *a priori* and embodied actions are expressed *a posteriori*. We receive no cock-eyed looks if we claim that thinking happens in the brain or that knowledge is in our mind. Not only do we tacitly value *a priori* thought, we have a general sentiment averse to rituals involving rote, but also anything to do with animal sacrifice.

Rote is problematic for the aforementioned reason: rote practices presumably cease to engage the mind after they are learned. Hence, in the tritest understanding of rote practices, thinking is not involved. Howard Wettstein apprises us about prayer—rote and spontaneous—according the thoughts that attend each:

---

1. As a simplistic example, I often take a walk when I am perplexed about a particularly complex issue. The walk is meant to help me get away and re-process—to see the same information differently than I have been. Indeed, this is an embodied ritualized practice—a walk different from my other walks and meant to dispose me to see something that I could not have otherwise seen.

> Ritualized prayer does indeed present challenges of its own. The
> challenge is presented not by the repetition, but rather by the diffi-
> culty, the sheer hard work, involved in summoning up the thoughts
> and feelings appropriate to such literary magnificence.[2]

Prayer of all forms, however, is culturally benign as compared to the idea
of animal sacrifice, which has a whole other connotation in the Americas.
Where something akin to prayer is linked to all religions, sacrifice is almost
uniquely associated with the occult practices of minority religions today (e.g.,
voodoo, Satanism, Africanist religions, etc.). Even the Mormon Church's baptism for the dead antagonizes the orthodox line within Christianity because
death is intermingled with the sacrament of the church. Recently, I was able to
attend a mass animal sacrifice at Mount Gerizim in Israel. At this Samaritan
Passover, a small enclave of a few hundred surviving Samaritans follow the
Samaritan Torah of Moses and slaughter their family lambs together in a large
public celebration. Either by nature or nurture, the thought of attending an
animal sacrifice made me feel a bit uneasy.

To my surprise, the ritualized killing and butchering of the animals did
not seem as bizarre as I had anticipated. As far as I can judge, this was aided by
the fact that I have helped to slaughter large animals before, so I was basically
familiar with the mechanics of killing, bleeding, and butchering from a herd.
For many Americans, although less so for Europeans and the majority world,
the sight of an actual butchered animal in their supermarkets would cause
averted eyes. In much of the world, large parts and whole animals are com-
monly on display at the butcher's shop. For reasons we cannot explore here
(but are worth considering further), American supermarkets generally go to
great lengths to separate the packaged meat from any notion that it once came
from a living animal. Both the packaging and sequestering the butchering
away from prying eyes of consumers might ensure that no animal seems to
have ever been harmed in the production of *this meat*. This to say, we cannot
have a frank discussion about animal sacrifice without acknowledging this
mitigating factor regarding our connotations of sacrifice derived from our
Western and hermetic encounters with meat.

After several hours on Mount Gerizim—watching the killing, butchering,
offering the fatty parts on YHWH's altar, and the cooking of the meat over
large pit fires—the event did not even seem strange to me. If I am to be honest,
the ritual felt mostly like an American barbeque (or, more like a Brazilian *chur-
rasco*), but starting with longer prayers from a high priest and live animals
rather than previously butchered meat and shorter prayers (e.g., "Rub-a-dub-
dub, let's get to the grub. Amen!").

Despite our cultural reservations with ritual, a second more profound
epistemological problem haunts our understanding in the West. Namely we

---

2. Howard Wettstein, *The Significance of Religious Experience* (New York: Oxford University Press, 2012), 207.

have a problem with *traceability*, where the connection between the event and outcome must be transparent to all who understand.

Through rigid rules and careful judging, organized sports attempt to make the outcome (i.e., winner) unmistakably traceable throughout the event (i.e., the game/match). The same could be said of elections, judiciary decisions, and well-crafted arguments in academia. In ritual, many contemporary practitioners are rightfully faulted by asserting the strict traceability of their rituals and the outcome. We need only to mention football players (of all three sorts: American, rugby, and association) who attribute their victories to their prayers. Or, we could cite the popularity of the prosperity gospel within Christianity, which attempts to directly connect economic success with individual giving rites performed. The rites of the Hebrew and Jewish Scriptures strike us as more mysterious than these. While many will cite instances in Scripture where magic might be presumed, the overarching message throughout the canon about the traceability of ritual is inscrutable. Where magic is, by definition, directly traceable (i.e., I do *this* rite in order to get *that* outcome), the rites of Scripture do not cleanly fall under such a contract.

As we move forward to discuss the problem of ritual cessationism in the Judaic and Christian understanding of Scripture, we need to bear in mind that we too have been formed and shaped by our own ritual practices and the culture of ritual participation in which we reside today. We are what Gadamer broadly terms "historically-situated consciousnesses" (*wirkungsgeschichteliches Bewußtseinen*), but more specifically, I want to argue that we are "ritually-situated consciousnesses" (*wirkungsrituell Bewußtseinen*), both for good and inevitably for ill.

Supersessionism

We ought to consider a distinct line in the study of ritual, which might help to explain why ritual supersessionism has been neglected in theology. The term supersessionism refers to the broad belief that the ancient Israelite religion has been replaced by rabbinic Judaism and then later by Christianity. But the term itself is not sufficient for our purposes, as it most often emphasizes replacement rather than continuity.[3] Klawans's work on purity and ritual help-

---

3. A deep well of literature on "supersessionism" goes far beyond what I can discuss here. Instead, I only want to use the concept to show its limited functional utility. Kendall Soulen's recent work has proposed three types of supersessionism: punitive, economic, and structural. What I argue here has more to do with the structural aspects, if rituals structurally guide Israel to salvation. R. Kendall Soulen, *The God of Israel and Christian Theology* (Minneapolis: Fortress, 1996). David Novak speaks of the Christian Scriptures as either adding into the covenant with Israel ("soft supersessionism") or replacing it ("hard supersessionism"). "The Covenant in Rabbinic Thought," in *Two Faiths, One Covenant: Jewish and Christian Identity in the Presence of the Other* (eds. Eugene B.

fully points out that the cessation of ritual and its intellectual supersessionism can be found within Judaism itself.[4]

While not original to Maimonides (1135–1204 C.E.), his analysis of the epistemological matters surrounding Israel's temple rituals is telling. Regarding the traceability of rituals and their intended meaning, the Rambam asserts that they must have *a meaning,* even if *that* meaning cannot be traced by us:

> All of us, the common people as well as the scholars, believe that there is a reason for every precept, although there are commandments the reason of which is unknown to us, and in which the ways of God's wisdom are incomprehensible . . . even these ordinances have a cause, and are certainly intended for some use, although it is not known to us; owing either to the deficiency of our knowledge or the weakness of our intellect.[5]

Maimonides not only believes that rites ought to be logically traceable in principle, but that Jews specifically should not endeavor to trace every last reason behind the rites: "Those who trouble themselves to find a cause for any of these detailed rules, are in my eyes void of sense."[6] Why should they not look for reasons behind their ritual actions? First, according to Maimonides, sacrifices are an accommodation to the primitive tendencies of Israel due to their time in Egypt. Hence, in God's graciousness, He weans Israel off of Egyptian rituals and into tabernacle/temple rituals: "it is therefore according to the nature of man impossible for him suddenly to discontinue everything to which he has been accustomed."[7] The Rambam clarifies this instrumental use of Torah sacrifice:

> [P]eople are allowed to continue the kind of worship to which they have been accustomed, in order that they might acquire the true faith, which is the chief object. . . . As the sacrificial service is not the primary object [of the commandments about sacrifice], whilst supplications, prayers, and similar kinds of worship are nearer to the primary object, and indispensable for obtaining it.[8]

Korn and John T. Pawlikowski; New York: Rowman & Littlefield, 2005). This present work would be sympathetic with the view of soft supersessionism, but not hard for the reasons outlined below.

4. Because Klawans's work is insightful and overlaps with my current thesis, sans epistemology, we will interact heavily with him on points of convergence and departure.

5. Maimonides, *Guide to the Perplexed,* III/26.

6. Although he goes on to trace some of the meaning in the Temple rituals, a charitable reading would indicate that he means those who think that they have exhausted the meaning of a rite by their explanation of it. Ibid., III/26.

7. Ibid., III/32.

8. Maimonides, *Guide to the Perplexed,* III/32. Later, Rambam discusses why Passover is still practiced and concludes that the epistemological function "that we may remember what was done in those days" makes it eternally efficacious for its purpose. III/46.

According to Maimonides, sacrifices appear to be an accommodation to Israel's primitive religious impulse, while prayer is the ultimate goal.

Second, sacrifices cannot be durative for the Rambam because they are a temporary accommodation and too localized. Prayer, on the other hand, is the goal of their ritual weaning so that Israel could "serve Him in *thought* and not by any *action*," which is necessarily restricted to a place.[9] In this sentiment, we find the seeds of rationalism: *mental prayer apart from physical ritual.* Supersession is an apt term for Maimonides' view, and he clearly sees Israel's rituals being purposely replaced by God. Namely, ritual exists in the world of action, where the superior world of thought has always been the desired aim.

Third, for Maimonides, this hidden goal of replacing sacrifice with prayer explains the prophetic critique of sacrifice. It was not that Samuel or Hosea critiqued the abuse of proper ritual, as I have previously argued (1 Sam 15: 22–23; Hos 6:6). Rather, the prophets saw the futility of all sacrifice which would eventually be usurped anyway:

> [T]he Prophets in their books are frequently found to rebuke their fellow men for being over-zealous and exerting themselves too much in bringing sacrifices; the prophets thus distinctly declared that the object of the sacrifices is not very essential, and that God does not require them.[10]

To identify a progenitor of ritual supersession within medieval Judaism, we need go no further than Maimonides. However, the Rambam's explanations have a common-sense appeal, ferreting out how we should feel about the persistence of sacrificial worship shot throughout the Torah that cannot be lived far away from the land of Israel—not to mention the fact that no temple exists in the land itself. In the vein of Franz Overbeck's critique regarding the early church's theologizing in the void of the promised *paraousia* (i.e., the second coming of Jesus), Judaism has a long history of theologizing about ritual life without the Second Temple and the pronounced absence of a Third Temple. This to say that Maimonides' program concerning the Torah rituals is unsurprising, given the prominence of Aristotelian thought, the concern for the

---

9. Ibid., III/32. He goes on to say, "By this Divine plan it was effected that the traces of idolatry were blotted out, and the truly great principle of our faith, the Existence and Unity of God, was firmly established; this result was thus obtained without deterring or confusing the minds of the people by the abolition of the service to which they were accustomed and which alone was familiar to them. I know that you will at first thought reject this idea and find it strange; you will put the following question to me in your heart: How can we suppose that Divine commandments, prohibitions, and important acts, which are fully explained, and for which certain seasons are fixed, should not have been commanded for their own sake, but only for the sake of some other thing: as if they were only the means which He employed for His primary object [i.e., prayer]?"

10. Ibid., III/32.

diaspora, and the absence of a Third Temple for those Jews who did live in the land and for diaspora pilgrims.

If Maimonides represents a principled bias against temple rituals, Douglas, Klawans, and others have critiqued a less defensible trend in the scholarship that also carries an unnecessary bias against ritual. Klawans identifies the progressive tendency, which he calls "evolutionism," as the root of biblical scholars' avoidance of rituals. Distinguishing this "evolutionism" from the biological variety, he conjectures:

> Yet on the whole, evolutionist theories posit broad, definitive, and positive development of human civilization. The theories, moreover, exhibit the presumption of intellectual and ethical superiority of the author's position. Typically, the highest rung on the evolutionist ladder is occupied by whatever perspective the author advocates, be it monotheism, Christianity, or science.[11]

Klawans sees a primitivism in scholarship, where the discussion of ritual focuses almost entirely on the anthropological origins of the rites described in the biblical texts.[12] This aversion to examine sacrifice beyond its origins is hindered by progressivism, which in turn is averse to violence. The Christian narrative, so says Klawans, grounds that violence (and shores it up) in Jesus' crucifixion. The progressivist's narrative of sacrifice goes something like this:[13]

> In primitive society, sacrifices literally feed the gods.

> Hebrews revolutionized this concept by making ritual food metaphorical so that the "feeding of YHWH" language is retained, but without the absurd metaphysical beliefs attached. Thus, the language (e.g., sacrifice as "a pleasing aroma before YHWH") becomes a "fossilized vestige" of former practices.

> Progressing beyond these, sacrificial food now simply feeds humans.

For Klawans, this progressivist meta-narrative blinds scholars in two ways. First, "The problem with such schemes is that by nature they preclude the possibility that sacrifice was understood symbolically by those Israelites who practiced it."[14] Second, this view assumes that sacrifices involved violence *and* that violence is a fundamentally negative feature that needs to be reconciled. Despite the specious nature of viewing sacrifice as violent in a negative sense only, "There is even less evidence that today's post-sacrificial humanity

---

11. Ironically, he fails to add Maimonides' Judaic supersessionism to his short-list of interfering constructs. Klawans, *Purity, Sacrifice, and the Temple,* 7.
12. Ibid., 6, 34.
13. I am following Klawans's discourse fairly closely here. Ibid., 30–32.
14. As well, he notes the peculiar bifurcation between rituals and sacrifices on this understanding and asks, "why is it that ritual purity becomes a symbolic system [in the scholarship] while sacrifice does not?" Ibid., 32.

is any less violent than it was before sacrifice began. . . . This is the claim that sacrifice is inherently violent and immoral."[15]

If one takes the progressive view that violence and sacrifice are necessarily intertwined, then the natural desire to root the origins of violence in sacrifice, as some have done, will create a negative or supersessionist view of all sacrifices. René Girard's renowned work serves as an example of reconciling this negative view of sacrifice. Because violence must be dealt with, it is transferred to the scapegoat of the society. Sacrifice then becomes a way of diverting and converting violence, unfortunately requiring a victim, a scapegoat.

> [H]uman culture is predisposed to the permanent concealment of its origins in collective violence. Such a definition of culture enables us to understand the successive stages of an entire culture as well as the transition from one stage to the next by means of a crisis similar to those we have traced in myths.[16]

> This drama [the sacrifice of Jesus] is needed to give birth to new myths, to present the perspective of the persecutors. But this same drama is also needed to present the perspective of a victim dedicated to the rejection of the illusions of the persecutors.[17]

Despite Girard's admirable insights, his desire to root violence in sacrifice forces him to reconcile violence in myth. The assumption that there must be progressive stages of ritual in history means that *sacrifices must contribute to progress more than mean anything in and of themselves.* And so, the scholarly neglect of the pedagogy of rituals is instantiated in the very models of ritual explanation being employed.

Rituals Prior to Supersessionism

I would like to suggest that there are several reasons why an anti-ritual bias combined with supersessionist exegesis can cause an unnecessary crux in understanding the biblical texts. First, if United Kingdom (ca. 1000 B.C.E.) Israelites were to travel through time and sit under the teaching of Maimonides, what would change when they returned to the Iron Age? In other words, how would United Kingdom Israelites live if they could prophetically see into a future without sacrifice? Presumably, their entire attitude would look forward to a day when they no longer had to go through the hassle of temple rituals. Giving up valuable food, animal or vegetal, would certainly seem pointless to agrarian Israelites, or naïve at best. But ancient Israelites, per the Hebrew Bible, did not view ritual this way. In fact, as I will demonstrate below, the

15. Ibid., 9.
16. René Girard, *The Scapegoat* (trans. Yvonne Freccero; Baltimore: Johns Hopkins Press, 1986), 101.
17. Ibid., 102.

prophets repeatedly called the people back to proper ritual practices and cast an eschatological vision that included temple worship. Maimonides appears to be out of sorts with the Hebrew Bible's own view of sacrifices, trying to reconcile the former practice with a progressivist view of sacrifices because rituals had long since ceased in his day.

Second, sacrifice does not necessarily entail animal death, and sacrificial killing is not mere violence—it is possibly not violent at all. Regarding the term "sacrifice" (קרבן), Christian Eberhard argues persuasively that scholarship has had an inordinate focus on animal killing qua sacrifice. But this simply does not do justice to the construct of sacrifice found in the Hebrew Bible or New Testament. Regarding the various laws requiring non-animal sacrifice, he asks, "Yet how can a theory that focuses on animals and blood application rites provide the rationale for the ritual of offering grain, oil, and frankincense?"[18] Hubert and Mauss had previously argued that "sacrifice" could not be solely focused on any single motive.[19] More recent treatments have gone further to argue that the construct of "sacrifice" discovered throughout the Hebrew Bible can equally apply to animals as it can to vegetal offerings. And hence, contrary to Girard and others, sacrifice cannot be narrowly viewed as an act of violence. Not only is grain an acceptable sacrifice (קרבן) for atonement of sin (Lev 5:11–13), grain sacrifices (קרבן מנחה) are a discrete form of sacrifice in and of themselves. So Katherine McClymond says: "[I]t is important to emphasize that these vegetal offerings are not just substitutes for animal offerings but act as distinct offerings in their own right."[20]

In short, the metaphor of *sacrifice as violence* may not do justice to the totality of what is prescribed in the Hebrew Bible. Other metaphors could replace violence; some have suggested *sacrifice as consumption*.[21] I only need to admit that violence, and all the prejudice that it connotes, does not need to fund a global view of Israel's rituals. Rather, the tension that grain is as sacrificially viable as an animal's life should equally cause me to question the meaning of the rite in light of its purpose.

Other views also militate against the cessation of sacrifice rites. For instance, the rabbis often conceived of the temple as representing the cosmos. Klawans argues that if this rabbinic notion of cosmos-temple has any merit, then the rituals prescribed in the temple fit into the fabric of the cosmos itself and cannot be merely removed without directly affecting the structure of the

18. Christian A. Eberhard, *The Sacrifice of Jesus: Understanding Atonement Biblically* (Minneapolis: Fortress, 2011), 28.

19. "Moreover, it is an amorphous rite; it is not orientated in a fixed direction, but nay serve the most diverse ends." Henri Hubert and Marcel Mauss, *Sacrifice: Its Nature and Function* (trans. W. D. Halls; Chicago: University of Chicago Press, 1898), 19–25.

20. Katherine McClymond, *Beyond Sacred Violence: A Comparative Study of Sacrifice* (Baltimore: Johns Hopkins University Press, 2008), 65.

21. Bruce Chilton, *The Temple of Jesus: His Sacrificial Program Within a Cultural History of Sacrifice* (University Park, PA: Pennsylvania State University Press, 1992), 41.

cosmos. Unless we presume that the cessation of sacrifice is progressive, which I have argued against, then we cannot merely remove sacrifice as a negative, naïve, or primitive function within Israelite religion. If sacrifice is part of Israel's theological fabric, then tugging on the thread unravels the garment.

Summary

The general bias against ritual can stem from various biases: progressivism, evolutionism, cultural formation, metaphors of violence, and more. However, none of these need to act as the basis of this study. For reasons I have previously discussed, epistemic efficacy need not be traceable in sacrifice.[22] The lack of traceability in ritual actually makes it fit with other epistemic rituals in science and elsewhere. We do not need to know *why* we do *what* we do in order to recognize what is being shown to us. In short, the epistemic power of ritual need not be gauged by our mental grasp of it.

First, the supersessionist's assumption—that animal sacrifice must eventually transmogrify for the sake of theological or humanistic progress—appears to put us at odds with the biblical teaching. Israelites and their prophets appear to believe that rituals are meaningful despite their eventual change. This includes, as I have shown in the previous chapter, the apostles and the early church—all of whom practiced temple rites after the "sacrifice" of Jesus. We do not need to treat Israelite ritual as if it must be superseded, *but realize that the ritualizing of Israel's rites in the New Testament* (e.g., baptism, prayer, Communion, etc.) *is predicated upon the proper practice of those rituals in the first place.* I want to suggest that the notion of *ritualizing Israel's rites*, adapted from Catherine Bell, better captures the intended continuity of the early Jerusalemite church. That "church" consisted of Jewish leaders and scholars according to the New Testament's historical texts. Jewish and Christian versions of supersession will eventually develop. However, the *etic* assumptions of those later views need not coerce us to take the texts of *emic* ritual practitioners less seriously for the sake of an *etic* progressivist meta-narrative.

Second, the metaphor of sacrificial violence might do conceptual violence to the practices described in the Hebrew Bible and New Testament. Moreover, for Christian theologians the consequences have profound implications for understanding the purpose of Jesus' death itself. For instance, Eberhard claims that merely equating sacrifice with death does metaphorical violence to the sacrifice of Jesus—what is meant by the rite and how it is to be understood?[23]

This entire discussion returns our attention to the eschaton. After all, the supersessionist's assumption must deal with the temple and ritual nature of

---

22. See "Oversight" in chapter two of this book.

23. Eberhard shows that the gospel writers and the epistles do not presume a sacrifice-death conflation but intentionally overlap them at key points. Eberhard, *The Sacrifice of Jesus*, 103–30.

eschatological depictions strewn throughout the prophetic vision of days to come.

Eschatological Epistemology

Cultic supersession is made even more difficult to accept considering that the temple appears so often in eschatological visions in both the Hebrew Bible and New Testament. In those visions, knowledge continues to be part of the ritual discourse. For instance, Jeremiah's vision of the eschatological new covenant is flatly epistemological (Jer 31:31–34). Because the Torah will be written "upon their hearts," no long will people need to compel others saying, "'Know YHWH (דעת את יהוה),' for they shall all know (ידעו) me from the least of them to the greatest" (Jer 31:34). Two aspects of this vision stand out. First, we notice that implicit to Jeremiah's description, the Torah and its rituals function to teach Israel to know YHWH. Second, Jeremiah depicts the Torah written onto their "hearts" (minds) as the sole reason why they no longer need to instruct one another.[24] Does this mean that Jeremiah moves Israel's external worship to internal knowledge in the eschaton? When the prophets' eschatological visions are taken together, they do not appear to form a rejection of external ritual.

Deuteronomy also describes a future circumcision of the heart required by YHWH (Deut 10:16) and eventually promised as a gift of YHWH (Deut 30:6). This description of a heart-circumcised Israel and her offspring reminds the reader of Jeremiah's Torah that will be written on their hearts in the new covenant. Unless we intend to see Jeremiah as critiquing those prophets before him, we must reconcile his eschatological vision with others. As a consequence, we will see that temple ritual is a persistent theme of the eschaton in both the Hebrew Bible and New Testament. More specifically, if embodying the Torah constitutes Israel's "wisdom and discernment," which is centered around Israel's cult (Deut 4:5–6), then can the eschaton genuinely picture such wisdom apart from some kind of ritualized version of that cult?

Eschatological Epistemology in the Prophets

Isaiah's and Micah's picture of the eschaton centers upon Israel's temple for the purpose of the people's knowledge. The people are marked by their knowledge, eschewing the learning of war for the instruction of YHWH's ways (וירנו מדרכיו).[25] Notably, all of this epistemic activity takes place in the temple, receiving the nations in order to instruct them (Isa 2:3; Mic 4:2). Regarding

---

24. "לבב," in BDB (eds. Francis Brown, S. Driver and C. Briggs; Peabody, MA: Hendrickson Publishers, 1996), 523.

25. On learning war (לא ילמדו עוד מלחמה), cf. Isa 2:4; Mic 4:3; Judg 3:2.

their eschatological vision of the temple (Isa 2:1–4; Mic 4:1–5), Klawans asks, "Is it really conceivable that an exclusively non-sacrificial form of worship is imagined here?"[26] While I can only speculate, Isaiah's heavenly temple might offer clues. First, Isaiah promises punishment because of Israel's failure to know (Isa 5:12–13), though they consider themselves "wise in their own eyes" (Isa 5:21). Second, Isaiah describes their folly. Knowing, for Isaiah, is not knowledge of facts that could have precluded their punishment, but rather their failure to discern, "Those who call evil good and good evil, who present darkness as light and light as darkness" (Isa 5:20).

Third, in the call of Isaiah, he has a vision of the throne of God, which is depicted in icons of the temple (Isa 6:1–6). Indeed, a fire on the altar indicates ritual practices in whatever cosmos this vision takes part (Isa 6:4, 6). The call itself then contrasts the current scene of a temple with the epistemologically obstinate nation of Israel, to whom Isaiah is called. His commission itself is given in terms of blunting their ability to know and serves as the only other text in the Hebrew Bible where heart, eyes, and ears are put together in this epistemological relationship (cf. Deut 29:3 [MT]).[27] The contrast is starkly set between the visionary temple of Isaiah 6 and the street-level reality of Israel's blind and deaf epistemic condition. Whether or not this is a proleptic or eschatological vision of the temple is another matter altogether. Nevertheless, we later find the nations gathered again in another post-exilic visionary temple (Isa 56), where Sabbath-keeping brings happiness and the sacrifices of foreigners are acceptable (Isa 56:2–8). But as for those who do not attach themselves to YHWH, their epistemic ability is chided: "The watchmen are blind . . . they know nothing (לא ידעו)" (Isa 56:9).

Likewise, Ezekiel is both dense with epistemological discourse[28] and visions of future worship conjoined together. Ezekiel as a text is worthy of an entire treatment on Torah living and its role in epistemology; however, I will restrict this treatment to the role of worship depicted beyond Israel's current failures. Ezekiel diagnoses Israel's current problem of detestable worship (i.e., child sacrifice, among others) as rooted in their lack of discernment (Ezek 20:7–8). His resolution requires that they restore proper worship so that they can properly know YHWH (Ezek 20:19–20): "I am YHWH your God; walk in my statutes, and be careful to obey my rules, and keep my Sabbaths holy that

---

26. Klawans, *Purity, Sacrifice, and the Temple*, 80.

27. "These three terms [heart, eyes, ears] do not form a perfect triplet as in Deuteronomy 29:4 or Isaiah 6:9–10, but they do provide a near parallel." Michael A. Grisanti, "Was Israel Unable to Respond to God? A Study of Deuteronomy 29:2–4," *BS* 163 (April–June 2006): 176–196; See also J. Ross Wagner, *Heralds of the Good News: Isaiah and Paul in Concert in the Letter to the Romans* (Leiden: Brill, 2003), 243–45.

28. By my count, there are 74 instances of "know" (ידע) used throughout Ezekiel in consequential construction (e.g., thus they will know, so that you might know, etc.). Although there are three Hebrew constructions at work in Ezekiel, the consequential sense of the verb is equal between them (וידע, לדעת, למען ידע or).

they may be a sign between me and you, *that you may know* that I am YHWH your God." Again, Ezekiel twice more identifies Sabbath-keeping as enabling their ability to know (Ezek 20:12, 20) and false ritualized practices as misguiding them epistemically.

Despite these connections, what are we to make of this difficult passage that ensues, seemingly identifying God's laws as negative? Is YHWH abrogating ritual in this teaching where it says: "Moreover, I gave them statutes that were *not good* and rules by *which they could not have life*, and I defiled them through their very gifts in their offering up all their firstborn that I might devastate them. I did it *that they might know* (למען אשר ידעו) that I am YHWH" (Ezek 20:25–26). The question surrounds the matter of which statutes (חקים) are being defined as not good (לא טובים). Are these YHWH's statutes or does this intimate that he is handing them over to the rules and rites of the nations (Ezek 20:18)? We do not need to solve that interpretive question, as the point remains unchanged for us. The rules given (or the rules to which they are handed over) intend to dispose them to recognize something: "that they might know that I am YHWH."

Ezekiel then goes on to decry Israel's syncretism: "And what you have in mind shall never come to pass—when you say, 'We will be like the nations, like the families of the lands, worshiping wood and stone'" (Ezek 20:32). After a time of exile meant to purge them of this desire, the prophet envisions a future when proper sacrifice is restored in the temple (Ezek 20:40–41) that "you will know (וידעתם) that I am YHWH" (Ezek 20:42). Thus, this closes the pericope that aptly began with the giving of Sabbath "that they might know (לדעת) that it is I YHWH who sanctifies them" (Ezek 20:12). At a minimum, Ezekiel indicates that rites dispose Israel to know and that the antidote to epistemological blindness—caused by false worship—is proper worship.

There are other passages, of course, that suggest or state directly the view that Israel's rituals are durative and will not be superseded by a disembodied spiritualization of those rites (e.g., Jer 33:18). I argued in the preceding chapter and above that the Christian sect in Judaism did not see itself as superseding the embodied ritualization of Torah either. Indeed, the disembodying of knowledge is precisely what causes some later sects of Christianity to be condemned as heretical (e.g., the Gnostics).

Christian Eschatological Visions

We now consider if the New Testament authors carried forward the idea of eschatological knowing by means of ritual. Maintaining the principle of textual silence as an indicator of continuity, the New Testament authors, in general, presume that ritualized practices persist in Christianity and that they still serve an epistemological function. My only task here then is to show that the eschatological vision of the New Testament includes the same temple worship described by the prophets, even if they are a ritualized form of Israelite rituals.

First, in Paul's letters to Thessalonica, a unique concern exists in that early Christian community about the return of Jesus. Paul addressed the nature of the resurrection in the day of visitation in his first letter. In Paul's second letter, he describes a coming "man of lawlessness" whom the Thessalonians should be able to discern as separate from the returning Jesus. One of the recognizable features of this lawless figure is that "he takes his seat in the temple of God" and deems himself god in opposition to other "objects of worship" (2 Thess 2:4). Paul then concludes his precautions about this man in the temple saying that following this man has an epistemological effect: "Therefore God sends them a strong delusion ['man of lawlessness'], so that they may trust what is false" (2 Thess 2:11). Again, we see Paul emphasizing the same prophetic critique of the Hebrew Bible—that false worship has an epistemically deleterious effect—blinding them to the truth and condemning them.

Second, although we have already discussed the letter to the Hebrews, which posits that Torah rituals enable knowledge, it is briefly worth mentioning the eschatological vision of the epistle. In order to make the point that Torah rituals persist *through* Jesus, the omniscient narrator describes for us the priestly duties of Jesus (Heb 8–9) that are predicated upon his own self-sacrifice (Heb 9:11–10:18). Even more, the author roots Jesus' non-Levitical credibility in Melchizedek, the ancient and mysterious Jebusite priest from Jerusalem (Heb 7). As I have previously argued, the rhetoric behind the entirety of this heavenly vision of the temple is pointed toward the epistemological assurance the audience had by means of their participation in these earthly Torah rituals (Heb 10:19–39).

Third and less directly, Peter maintains a positive view of temple in the eschaton. He depicts Christians in his first letter as the very stones of a spiritual temple (οἶκος πνευματικὸς), a holy priesthood offering spiritual sacrifices (πνευματικὰς θυσίας), a royal priesthood (βασίλειον ἱεράτευμα), and holy nation (ἔθνος ἅγιον).[29] These overlapping metaphors of priesthood and temple mean to compel their holy conduct in anticipation of the eschaton's day of visitation (i.e., the day of judgment).

Finally, Revelation offers multitudinous images of the eschaton, of which we will only focus on two. First, when John goes up to the heavens, he sees a bizarrely opulent scene centered on a throne to which all were bowing down in worship (Rev 4:1–11). On that throne is a sacrificed animal, "a lamb standing as though it had been slain" (Rev 5:6). While a jewel-laden throne, the sea of glass, and the queer creatures might not remind us of Jerusalem's temple, the white garments, the fires, and the sacrificed lamb do. I raise this episode because the scene clearly contains elements of Israelite temple ritual. Also, at the end of Revelation, we will see that John's vision involves the Third Temple, reminiscent of Isaiah's vision (Isa 6:1–5), when this opulent scene is brought down as the new Jerusalem.

29. 1 Peter 2:4–10.

John describes the eschaton of the eschaton at the very end of the book—the new heavens and new earth. The spectacle of Revelation 4 in the heavens is now brought down (Rev 21:9–21). Remarkably, the author states, "And I saw no temple" (Rev 21:22). As it turns out, God Himself along with the lamb *are* the temple (Rev 21:22). There is almost certainly an epistemological figuration being employed here, as the main purpose of the temple is to provide light so that nations can metaphorically see, and hence walk.[30] Even still, there persists the slain lamb in the new temple (Rev 22:3) and a distinction between clean and unclean (Rev 21:27), intimating that supersessionism is an insufficient concept, where ritualization of Israel's temple cult is clearly in mind. Hence, this new cult is continuous with, but unlike the other in cardinal matters. And finally, the oracle ends with the blessed, those "who wash their robes [do his commands]" and thus are able to eat from "the tree of life" (Rev 22:14).

Revelation ends where Genesis 2–3 appeared to be headed before rebellion and exile interrupted: toward the tree of life. As I previously contended, the tree-eating practices in the Garden were rituals to be embodied in order to know. Jeremiah's new covenant describes a ubiquitously knowing people, and the New Testament account of the eschaton ends with the people of God being re-cleansed in the new earth at the new temple in order to have the right/authority (ἐξουσία) to eat of the tree of life, previously denied to them because of their improperly attained *knowledge* (Gen 3:22–23).

Conclusions

I have attempted to argue in this chapter counter to the most basic challenges presented by an anti-ritual bias, whether it is funded by a cultural or theological disposition. The progressive tendency to see ritual as a means of dealing with violence leaves us wanting in the broader context of Israelite ritual, which does not conflate sacrifice with animal killing. The logic of the rite does not need to be found in its primitive origins, its magical efficaciousness, or its symbolic traceability. If rites have an epistemic function, then cognizance of the rite's discrete logic will not be necessary at each performance, though mastery might enable such a cognizance.

Further, the presumption that these ancient Hebrew rites were or will be superseded by Christian spiritualization of the rites simply does not hold true under the lights of the practices described in the New Testament. Neither is it

---

30. Light in opposition to dark is the paradigmatic epistemological language of the Johannine corpus. Cf. John 1:6–13; 3:19–21; 8:12; 9:5; 11:9–10; 12:35–36, 46; 1 John 1: 5, 7; 2:8–10. See Cornelius Bennema, "Christ, the Spirit and the Knowledge of God: A Study in Johannine Epistemology," in *The Bible and Epistemology: Biblical Soundings on the Knowledge of God* (eds. Mary Healy and Robin Parry; Milton Keynes, England: Paternoster, 2007), 109–14.

a helpful rubric for understanding the ritualed life of the early Jewish Jesus community in Jerusalem as described by Luke-Acts.

Finally, this supersessionist assumption does not equip us to make sense of the eschatological descriptions of temple cult. The ritualism of Israel is either superseded by a non-embodied practice or it is not. I have shown that in the texts of these Hebrew and later Jewish authors, these rites are not replaced. We must have a more robust idea of ritual that can account for the ritualizing of Israelite rituals, maintaining the embodiment and practice without usurping the rite. Did the prophets see a vision of ritual practices in the eschaton? Yes. Did the ritual practices include animal sacrifice? Yes, they centered on the slain lamb ritualized from a temple's altar to its throne (cf. Rev 5:6; 21:22).

Part IV

Theological Implications
of Ritual Knowing

Chapter 11

Ritual as an Ethically Prepared Process

In Part I, I surveyed the landscape of epistemological theories and the problems posed through their engagement with Scripture. Arresting the Scripture's *emic* epistemological structures requires more than a simple combination of current epistemological theories. It requires careful analysis of the texts and their way of depicting regulative knowing through the disparate voices of the prophets. As well, we looked to ritual theory, which is not as concerned with a particular theology or religion, but the human practices that become ritualized in order to form knowers. My methodology, then, revolves around an attentive reading of ritual structures in the Scriptures that attempts to understand how those texts can assume that Israel's rites function epistemically. Additionally, I proposed that the analog of scientific epistemology is one venue that allows fresh insight into current ritualized knowing as commensurable with that ancient Semitic epistemology.

In Part II, I concentrated on differentiating some of the conceptual framework that was explored in previous work on biblical epistemology and the long-neglected matter of the body. The Scriptures appear to presume the body as required for normative knowing. As well, current work in metaphor, analogical reasoning, and neuroscience offered support for my suggestions about ritual knowing. Wider problems with neglecting the body's fundamental role in reasoning were considered, giving greater momentum to examine why the Scriptures connect knowing with rituals at key junctures in Israel's history. Part II ended by attending to why scientific training and discovery makes an exceptionally good counterpart to this discussion about ritual.

In Part III, I focused all attention on the texts of Scripture. While I cannot treat all the relevant texts, the sample of texts and seeming counter-examples were meant to create a core collection that clearly has the epistemological function of rituals in mind. This provides a minimally sufficient Scriptural case that requires me to consider the broader assumption about ritual's role in knowing.

And now in Part IV, I examine the problems of disparity in ritual participation, considering it an advantage to a discovering community, as is the case with the scientific enterprise. I will investigate the implications of our central findings. Because epistemological process in Scripture requires embodied processes, Israel must perform particular actions in order to know. In essence, this gives credence to John Frame's claim that all of epistemology is a subset of ethics.[1] Moreover, in the coming chapters, it is now impossible to avoid suggestions for the implication of our view upon Christian sacramental theology.

More immediately in this chapter, I examine the variety of ritual experience and distinguish disparate types of participation. Not everyone in ancient Israel participated in ritual practices in the same way or to the same extent. We moderns, who tend to be tacitly egalitarian, might unduly import notions of power and fairness into these disparate types of participation. However, I want to caution against such assumptions unless compelled by the texts to think that power structures are attempting to create an unfair system by control of ritual practice. I hope to show that even if they had the chance, most rational Israelites would not have wanted to participate directly in rituals because of danger protocols. In this chapter, I re-engage scientific epistemology and the anthropology of scientific ritual in order to show kinship between Israel's practices, scientific knowledge, and contemporary laboratories.

Preparation for Practice

"Ancient Israel was a culture that not only lived with animals
but thought and theologized with them too."[2]

In Part III, I suggested that the killing of animals in sacrifice had an inordinate gravitational pull in the anthropological study of rituals. As a consequence, the preparation for rites has sometimes been left to the side of the ritual theories and biblical treatments on the topic too, to the deficit of those studies. As we saw in previous chapters, the Israelite's connection to the animal, grain, or fruits being offered might have had as much to do with the ritual practice as the butchering and/or burning of the sacrifice itself. To explore this notion of preparation, we could ask probing questions, such as: "Would a Levite priest be within his rights to ask an offerer if his grain was harvested in a field whose fringes were left for the poor to reap?" If we think he ought to be able to ask such a question, then the Levitical stipulations requiring an intentional care for those on the boundary of subsistence might have direct implications for our ritual practice. If we think the Levite has no business asking about the condition of the sacrifice, then what do we make of the Levite's responsibility

---

1. Although from a slightly different angle than what Frame intended. John M. Frame, *The Doctrine of the Knowledge of God* (Phillipsburg, NJ: Presbyterian & Reformed, 1987), especially Appendix 1.

2. Jonathan Klawans, *Purity, Sacrifice, and the Temple: Symbolism and Supersessionism in the Study of Ancient Judaism* (Oxford: Oxford University Press, 2006), 73.

to judge a blemished animal or the "prostitute's wages" as an offering?[3] Why would we presume that he must assess the historical preparation of the offering in one case and not the other?

The point is that sacrifices began in the attentive domain of the homestead well before they came to a climax in the temple sacrifice. The failure to attend to this single reflection has led many anthropologists to scrutinize studies that myopically focus on the ritual actions apart from their preparation. First, Anne Porter relates the danger of studying rites purely as a clinical outsider. Porter reminds her fellow anthropologists that the *etic* study of ritual can fail in certain aspects—believing one has understood the rite with the strong possibility she has not: "The raw power of sacrifice is something that we who deal with only uninflected descriptions of it, or the meager, bare-boned remains of it, find hard to imagine in our envisioning of its significance, let alone its performance."[4] The outside *etic* study of the ritual has an injurious effect because it does not seek to understand the theology, motivations, and lived logic of the rituals being studied.[5]

Gillian Goslinga attempts an *emic*-sensitive approach to contemporary Hindu sacrifice only to find out that she had unduly focused on the wrong cluster of events. She suggests that a Christian crucifixion-centered understanding of sacrifice has distracted anthropologists with the killing event without enough understanding of what all leads up to the event.

> This Judeo-Christian bias makes the sacrificial act the "center of gravity" of all analyses because it is assumed that the violence in the victims' immolation is what separates what "has wrongly been united" (or wrongly separated in so-called rites of propriation [sic]). For this reason, the sacrifice itself is typically read as the moment of greatest symbolic significance in the anthropological literature and the animal appears structurally as the "victim" because it "naturally" bears on its body the violence that should accrue to the "guilty" patron.[6]

---

3. Hosea goes further to suggest that their reaping of fruit and grain are like a "prostitute's wages," which would indicate that there must be some kind of Levitical discernment for the various blemishes that could stain the sacrifice, seen and unseen. Cf. Deut 23:18; Hos 1:12; 9:1.

4. Gillian Goslinga, "On Cakti-Filled Bodies," in *Sacred Killing: The Archaeology of Sacrifice in the Ancient Near East* (eds. Glenn M. Schwartz and Anne Porter; Winona Lake, IN: Eisenbrauns, 2012), 33.

5. "In focusing on sociopolitical ramifications of sacrifice, the human manipulations of animal and human bodies in the accomplishment of human goals, we ignore at our peril the very realness of the agency of the divinity and the religious framework in which sacrifice is constituted." Ibid., 34–35.

6. Ibid., 43. It is unclear to me whether "propriation" is a typographical mistake or if Goslinga is employing a technical phrase source I could not discover.

I would argue that the gospel accounts in the New Testament spend a fair amount of time focusing the reader's attention on that which led up to the crucifixion. Fair or not, the point remains: how well can we claim to understand a rite at a clinical distance and apart from understanding the narrative of which the rite is a climax? Goslinga proposes a new view of rites, seen in seminal form in Hubert and Mauss' work,[7] which encompasses multiple concentric circles leading up to the rite and then ensuing it as well.

> A ritual's "center of gravity" must be understood as plotted along a multitude of centers of gravity, on either side of the act itself, and in and around the humans, converging on the ritual from the past and the future and many dispersed points in the present. These centers of gravity taken together express, quite literally through the everyday biographies of humans and ritual objects, one particular instantiation or perhaps orchestration of the relationship between the collective of devotees and the divinity.[8]

Goslinga seems to be after something like ritual-as-narrative, where the sacrifice has "everyday biographies" (setting and conflict) that come to a climax and resolution. No matter what metaphor we construct, Goslinga wants us to think of a rite as a nexus of events contiguously construed together. And yet, we normally gravitate to what happens *at the temple*, for instance. But what happens at the temple is predicated upon a series of events and biographies that *culminate at the temple*. Below, I argue why Goslinga's biographical view of studying ritual is necessary in order to make sense of the Torah's teaching, the prophetic critique, and even Jesus' critique in the temple. The pressing question then, in light of the fact that we have no access to Israel's rituals themselves, asks whether the biblical texts relate a sense of preparation as necessary for the rite. In other words, is the sacrifice's at-home preparation part of the setting to the story of sacrifice, or the conflict?

Torah Requirements for Preparation

> This regulation [unblemished animals] requires of all offerers of sacrifice, priestly and otherwise, to remain keenly aware of the familial relationships among the animals to be offered as sacrifices.[9]

---

7. "Sacrifice is a religious act that can only be carried out in a religious atmosphere and by means of essentially religious agents. But, in general, before the ceremony neither sacrifier nor sacrificer, nor place, instruments, or victim, possess this characteristic to a suitable degree. The first phase of the sacrifice is intended to impart it to them." Henri Hubert and Marcel Mauss, *Sacrifice: Its Nature and Function* (trans. W. D. Halls; Chicago: University of Chicago Press, 1898), 19–20.

8. Goslinga, "On Cakti-Filled Bodies," 43.

9. Cf. Lev 22:17–30. Klawans, *Purity, Sacrifice, and the Temple*, 63.

We do not have any extant biblical commands about how to regulate preparation for rituals. Although the rabbis will take up the project in detail,[10] we do not have biblical rules answering a question like the one posed above: Can an Israelite offer grain from a field intentionally harvested to its edges for the sake of cutting out the poor and sojourner? The question reveals the interpenetrating nature of Torah commandments. According to the Torah, must Israelites follow the ethical teaching as preparation for their sacrifices?

I want to contend that Israel's sacrifices are premised upon the explicitly moral codes in the Torah, a fact which—if it were not patently obvious in the Torah itself—is clarified repeatedly in the later prophetic critique. However, does the Torah suggest that which the prophets thought to be obvious, that ethical treatment of plants, animals, fellow Israelites, and foreigners is precisely what they brought with their sacrifice? Is their ethical life an invisible feature of sacrifice?

First, and most obvious, the Torah contains within it a consistent expectation of moral behavior for Israelites towards the land and people. Moral impurity such as sexual sins, idolatry, or murder, does not just pollute an individual's sacrificial offering. Rather, moral sins pollute the land itself.[11] In commanding ritual practices central to Israel's livelihood, moral dynamics are directly relevant. Hence, Leviticus and Deuteronomy can aver without explanation that Israel is not to prostitute her daughters (Lev 19:29) nor bring the wages of prostitution into the temple (Deut 23:17–18).[12] Considering the practice of temple prostitution in the Ancient Near East more generally, the connection between prostituting one's daughter and making offerings at the temple cannot be neglected altogether.[13]

Leviticus 19 famously expounds upon the commands given on Sinai, including practical visions of loving one's neighbor as oneself (Lev 19:18) and loving the resident aliens in Israel (Lev 19:33–34). After all, what does loving the alien look like? This is partly answered in the equivalent treatment that begins within Israel between the poor and great (Lev 19:15–16) and extended in the market to the alien (Lev 19:33–36).

---

10. For example, on the issue of a burnt offering given by an impenitent Israelite, Raba says in the Babylonian Talmud, "For how is it possible? If there is no repentance, then the sacrifice of the wicked is an abomination." This comes amid an extended discussion of how preparation of particular animals could be misappropriated for the wrong sacrifices, already evincing the idea that what happens before the animal arrives for sacrifice is of consequence. *b. Zebaḥ.* 7b.

11. Klawans, *Purity, Sacrifice, and the Temple*, 53–56.

12. Immediately ensuing, we read about not creating a financial burden of interest on loans, and a reification of the laws requiring a field's periphery produce to be left, but from the neighbor's perspective.

13. Morris Silver, "Temple/sacred prostitution in ancient Mesopotamia revisited: religion in the economy," *UF* 38 (2006): 631–63.

Does the Torah teach that these two areas of law, ceremonial and moral, are actually intertwined so that one affects the other?[14] In other words, must a sacrifice be morally prepared in order to be ceremonially acceptable? Beginning with the priesthood, it is uncontroversial to insist that moral behavior directly pertains to the Levite's participation in ceremonies. Aaron and the Levites must be specially consecrated, specifically so that Israel's offerings can be accepted (Exod 28:38). Indeed, one of the few stories found in the Levitical code concerns the Levite failure to obey the ceremonies so that offerings could be accepted, leading to the death of Nadab and Abihu (Lev 10). Similarly, YHWH kills Hophni and Phinehas for conniving the food offerings for themselves (1 Sam 2:12–17) and for sexual promiscuity surrounding the tabernacle (1 Sam 2:22–25). Samuel's reaction to his sons' behavior reveals that their failure as morally prepared mediator condemns them (1 Sam 2:24–25).

Returning to the Torah, the challenge to the Levites' exclusive access to YHWH results in the death of Korah and his multitude (Num 16:1–40). Notice that despite Korah's attack on the ritual control of the Levites, Numbers characterizes their transgression in more moralistic terms: "then you shall know that these men have despised YHWH" (Num 16:30).

As it pertains to the Levites, moral and ceremonial conduct appears to be directly related. Because Levites must make Israel's ritualized offerings acceptable, they must be ritualistically and morally prepared for their service as mediators. What about the moral preparation of the other tribes of Israel?

Concerning the Israelite in general, a phenomenological approach will help to consider how families living across the land prepared to make their sacrifices acceptable. Consider some of the more intimate laws, those which would have been taxing on the family unit. The Torah supposes all sorts of circumstances where one is ritually and morally impure, but that impure status can only be known or determined within the family unit. For instance, how many people would actually know whether or not someone:

> had a bodily discharge (Lev 15)?
> had sex during menstruation (Lev 18:19)?
> had a strategically located leprous condition (Lev 14:1–32)?
> had mold growing in a house (Lev 14:33–54)?

To a greater or lesser degree, all of these statutes required individuals to attend to their bodies and relations *and* self-report items that would have financial and functional ramifications for their family. In other words, implicit within the Torah is an expectation that ceremonial commands are moral, demanding a sober reflection and the integrity to act upon discovery of a breach, *all of which prepare the Israelite for the temple ritual.*

---

14. The popular tripartite division of the law—ceremonial, civil, and moral—is an artifice for the sake of comparison and helpful at a point like this where some might want to divide them. However, the Torah makes no such distinction between different laws.

I am arguing here that the Torah is not schismatic on this front. The Torah supposes that individual Israelites have moral culpability. As such, a matrix of self-diagnosing laws—which had no financial advantage to the individual— was deemed functional. If Israelites understood and followed such exclusively private domain laws out of moral compunction alone, then we are merely extending that ideal of Torah observance to the entirety of the law. Hence, the way Israelites raise crops, reap fields, husband livestock, and treat others, regardless of their national status, all prepare their sacrifices to be acceptable.

To re-employ a prior illustration, we imagine a spouse participating in the ritualized practice of flower-giving on Valentine's Day. But in this instance, we must imagine a spouse who steals money from her office in order to buy flowers for her husband whom she has mistreated week after week and month after month. The background makes it plain that she brings home more than the flowers in the ritualized practice. Or, from her husband's perspective, he does not merely receive flowers, but the gift of flowers has been prepared—for good or ill—by the behavior of his wife in the weeks and months prior to the rite. We do not need to detail how the preparation works, but only see that it cannot be divorced from the ritual act, and is indeed itself part of the ritual act.

Prophetic Critique of Preparation

The divorce of sacrifice from ethical preparation is the stated grounds for the rejection of Israel's rituals in the prophetic literature, specifically concerning the poor. By way of reminder, the Torah stipulates specifics for an outward-looking life *of the nation and the individual* that actively accommodates others.[15] For instance, agrarian fruitfulness should not be reaped with perfect efficiency, but a remainder left for the poor and sojourner (Lev 19:9–10). We see the benefits of this later depicted in Ruth 2, where David's ancestry is dependent upon such hospitality.

Further, not only is stealing forbidden outright (Exod 20:15; Lev 19:11), but even holding onto wages overnight, possibly putting an employee in a bind, is singled out as an example of theft (Lev 19:13). Judicial decisions cannot favor the great in reverence or poor in pity, but judge by the rule of "righteousness" instead (Lev 19:15). These ideals and practical implications in Leviticus 19 resemble the core of the prophetic critique. However, we must not tire of the common observation that Israel's sacrifices are specifically targeted, at times, for being incongruous with these ethical norms. In other words, Israel's prepa-

---

15. Thanks to Jeremiah Unterman for reminding me how remarkable this ethical innovation is in the Ancient Near East. The presumption that the individuals and the collective are morally responsible as the state is a unique feature of the Israelite ethical legacy. This feature certainly has had obvious and discrete implications for republics ever since.

ration for sacrifice not only includes attending to livestock, harvest, and personal purity *as an individual*, but also to the treatment of others *as a society*.

First, the book of Isaiah opens and closes with the theme of rites apart from ethical preparation. In the opening volley concerning Judah, he decries:

> What to me is the multitude of your sacrifices? says YHWH;
> I have had enough of burnt offerings of rams
> and the fat of well-fed beasts;
> I do not delight in the blood of bulls,
> or of lambs, or of goats.[16]

Judah's offerings are futile because Judahites "do evil." The prophet prescribes that they "learn to do good, seek justice, correct oppression, bring justice to the orphan, defend the widow" (Isa 1:17). At the very end of Isaiah, the prophet directly identifies the personal attributes of the prepared worshiper, the one "who is humble and contrite in spirit and *trembles at my word*" (Isa 66:2). Isaiah begins a familiar pattern where ritual sacrifices are identified as part of the normative lives of Israel, but their sacrifices are like flowers to the mistreated husband: counterproductive.

> He who slaughters an ox is like one who kills a man;
> he who sacrifices a lamb, like one who breaks a dog's neck;
> he who presents a grain offering, like one who offers pig's blood;
> he who makes a memorial offering of frankincense, like one who
> blesses an idol.[17]

Second, Jeremiah's chastisement identifies Judah's pernicious greed and ubiquitous deceit as reasons that their sacrifices were ill-prepared (Jer 6:20):

> What use to me is frankincense that comes from Sheba,
> or sweet cane from a distant land?
> Your burnt offerings are not acceptable,
> nor your sacrifices pleasing to me.

Why is deceit so injurious? Of interest to us, Jeremiah cites the communal and epistemological effect, where they cannot discern peace from danger (Jer 6:14). Their inability to discern, seemingly caused by a downward spiral that begins with greed and injustice, makes their sacrifice beside the point.

Third, Amos' critique of Israel cites her oppression of the poor as indicative of her waywardness (Amos 2:6–7; 4:1–5):

> [B]ecause they sell the righteous for silver, and the needy for a pair
> of sandals—those who trample the head of the poor into the dust of
> the earth and turn aside the way of the afflicted.

> Hear this word, you cows of Bashan [Israel], who are on the mountain of Samaria, who oppress the poor, who crush the needy, . . .

---

16. Isa 1:11.
17. Isa 66:3.

> Come to Bethel, and transgress; to Gilgal, and multiply transgression; bring your sacrifices every morning, your tithes every three days; offer a sacrifice of thanksgiving of that which is leavened, and proclaim freewill offerings, publish them; for so you love to do.

In this indictment, the affliction of the poor and abuse of rituals makes Israel's sacrifices worthy only of Amos' mockery.

Fourth, Micah makes similar proclamations based on stealing property and oppression of the poor (Mic 2:1–2), which we have already discussed concerning the prophet's discourse on sacrifice. In the face of being indicted with oppressing the poor, Israel rhetorically asks, "With what [sacrifice] shall I come before YHWH?" (Mic 6:6), Micah's answer points directly to preparation. As previously argued, Micah does not usurp the Torah, but insists that their sacrifices are prepared correctly by doing justice, walking humbly, and loving kindness (Mic 6:8).

Remarkably, these indictments of Israel as an entity seem to override any one individual's ethical performance. Instead, a presumption of a national ethical preparation for ritual exists in the vision of the prophets. Israel was always meant to process the rites communally, preparing them together through their actions in the home, region, tribe, and nation.[18]

Having briefly surveyed the Torah and prophets, we are now in position to see that a divorce of the full-orbed Torah life from ritual is both entirely artificial and ultimately fatal for many Israelites. Preparation of one's sacrifices begins with an attentive eye to their own body (emissions and conditions), their family and house, their fields and livestock, their tribe, and their nation as a whole. The prophets also diagnose the source of Israel's persistent problem: oppressing those on the fringe. False worship blinds Israel so that she can no longer discern YHWH's actions from her false gods' actions. Oppression of the social periphery ensues this blindness and the prophetic critique focuses on the disparity between the sacrifice and their moral corruption. The sacrifice, as it would now appear, was meant to be ethically prepared at every layer of society—the entirety of Israel's life.

Prophetic Critique in the New Testament

Returning to the episode of Jesus in the temple, we have already tipped our hat toward the impetus of Jesus' anger: failure to prepare and endangering the poor by the temple authorities. I am employing both Chilton's and Klawans's understanding of the temple episode. Although Klawans acknowledged the ripe nature of Chilton's suggestions about animal ownership, he leaves the matter undeveloped. However, if I can expand the notion of ownership to in-

---

18. E.g., the Benjaminite predicament, Judg 20.

clude preparation as we have described it above, then we can simultaneously include Klawans's observation about treatment of the poor.

The suggestion is this: ethical preparation includes attention to the animals that one brings for sacrifice as well as the individual and corporate treatment of society's fringe. This includes radical Torah commands such as caring for your enemy's animal, when it struggles under a burden, for the sake of your enemy and the animal (Exod 23:4–5). This expansive ethical preparation intimates that owning the sacrificial animal is not merely a legal convention, which can be solved by legally purchasing an approved animal in the temple courts. Rather, the problem of not owning the sacrificed animal indicates a lack of ethical preparation.

What the temple courts purportedly offered were "temple-ready" animals that had the guarantee of being acceptable for sacrifice.[19] This, effectively, removed the risk of bringing an animal that may have been unworthy or fell sick during the pilgrimage. But more importantly, it removed the attentiveness required in selecting a proper animal from cradle to grave, as it were. The temple court system could be guilty of enabling learned-helplessness, but more injurious to Israelites, it removed the sacrificed animal from a broader fabric of ethical preparation.

No doubt, the cries of Malachi can be heard in bringing acceptable sacrifices: "When you offer blind animals in sacrifice, is that not evil" (Mal 1:8). *However, Malachi's point is that they are being attentive to the flock, and yet choosing to bring in the blemished animal,* which indicates "evil" within them: "Cursed be the cheat who has a male in his flock, and vows it, and yet sacrifices to YHWH what is blemished" (Mal 1:14). If Israel will not bring the proper animals from her flock, that problem is not remedied by forfeiting the requirement to attend to the livestock and fruits of the fields. By the logic of the indictment, Israel's problem is resolved by attending to the flock in order to present the correct sacrifice *from one's own flock.* In forfeiting the risk with temple-ready sacrifices, they have already ceded the ethical preparation in its most basic form.

So Klawans observes in the fostering of proper ritual practice:

> Before any animal can be sacrificed, it must first be protected when born, fed, and then finally guided to its place of slaughter. What is more, because maimed animals are unfit for the altar (Lev. 22:18–25), the careful shepherd will keep an eye toward protecting the animals that are fit for sacrifice. Because Israelites are prohibited from offering an animal and its offspring on the same day (Lev. 22:28), shepherds cannot lose track of the familial relationships within their herds and flocks. Because the art of herding is selective breeding—choosing which males will be allowed to reproduce with which

---

19. Klawans, *Purity, Sacrifice, and the Temple,* 234.

females—shepherds will, therefore, as a matter of course, make the "life-and-death" decisions for their herds and flocks.[20]

If one cannot be trusted to provide an acceptable sacrifice, then how would they be capable of looking out for those people on the fringe as required by the Torah? I am suggesting that the Torah creates an ethical cosmos, which includes everything from attention to bodily emissions all the way up to systemic corruption in society—personal sin (as we say) to organizational sin. Removing a key aspect, attentiveness to animal rearing and sacrificial selection, will necessarily create ethical ramifications elsewhere in the cosmos. This would be especially true if the reason is to remove the risk for the sake of priestly acceptance.

Taking this view of ethical preparation, ownership becomes a subsumed point, because ownership and selection from the flock or harvest indicates a broader participation in the Torah's requirements. In this sense, the desire to buy a risk-free sacrifice not only rejects the notion of ownership. Even more, the lack of ownership and hence, lack of selection, possibly indicates a more systemic cancer upon one's ability to live the Torah, including care for the poor. Stated otherwise, if one cannot be trusted to care for and select a proper sacrifice, then how can he be responsible for systematic care for the periphery within a stable society? But this neglect is exactly what the prophets hold Israel accountable for.

If Jesus wants to be seen as a prophet of Israel, apart from messianic tropes in his teaching, then his actions in the temple follow the familiar prophetic critique. The failure to require ownership of animals and the standard tax that inordinately affected the poor are both commensurate with the broad prophetic chastisement of Israel. When there is systemic oppression of society's fringe, the prophets routinely attack the sacrifices of Israel and specifically how they are incongruous with the basic ethical standards required by the Torah. Specifically, Israel's ethical cosmos has been schismatized so that Israelites have come to believe that treatment of the poor has nothing to do with their sacrifices, which they continue to offer.

Concerning ethical preparation and ritualized practices, Jesus even teaches that a sacrifice ought to be suspended if the sacrificer was aware of a dispute or grudge with a fellow Israelite. Intimating that one is not ethically prepared to sacrifice if offense against a brother persists. He instructs, "Leave your gift there before the altar and go. First be reconciled to your brother, and then come and offer your gift" (Matt 5:23–24).

Although we must be careful about constructing theology based on chastisement alone, Paul also famously critiques the Corinthians on their ritualized meal. Remarkably, Paul teaches that the Corinthians may eat food sacrificed to false gods on a theological technicality (1 Cor 8). However, for the sake of their community, it might be an unwise action and Paul concludes: "Therefore, if

---

20. Klawans, *Purity, Sacrifice, and the Temple*, 60–61.

food makes my brother stumble, I will never eat meat [sacrifices to idols], lest I make my brother stumble" (1 Cor 8:13). Nevertheless, when it pertains to the ritualized meal of Communion, Paul insists that ethical behavior apart from the meal mediates one's participation in the meal: "But in the following instructions I do not commend you, because when you come together [for the Communion meal] it is not for the better but for the worse" (1 Cor 11:17).[21] Why is their ritual meal counterproductive? Because of the divisions and strife (1 Cor 11:18), sexual immorality (1 Cor 5:1–13), and abuse of the sacrifice (i.e., bread and wine) itself (1 Cor 11:20–22). For Paul, their ritual preparation begins in an individual ethic (i.e., sexual immorality and idol food) that extends through the community (i.e., divisions and strife).

Finally, James the purported brother of Jesus, writes sharply in his epistle about vain religion. As long as we allow for the concept of religion to include sacrifice, we can see that James also indicts the divorce of ritual preparation from the religion (James 1:26–27):

> If anyone thinks he is religious and does not bridle his tongue but deceives his heart, this person's religion is worthless. Religion that is pure and undefiled before God, the Father, is this: to visit orphans and widows in their affliction, and to keep oneself unblemished from the world.

Moreover, the connection between religious behavior and ethical preparation is distinguished, once again, by the disparity. James presumes that visiting the afflicted must jibe with the ritualized practices *because visiting the sick is part of the ritualized practice itself.* [22]

Scientific Ritual Preparation as Epistemological

If ritual is a process that begins in the ethical fabric of Israelite society, climaxes in the scripted rite, and then transforms the way a person discerns something (i.e., brings her to see something she could not have otherwise seen), *preparation must have an epistemological function as well.* In the past decades, there has been a collection of anthropological studies seeking to reconcile Mary Douglas' work on purity and ritual with the actual practice of science. Several are worth considering more closely, not in order to confirm Douglas' theoretical work with empirical studies, but because they describe for us the

---

21. Paul has previously cited their corrupt sexual behavior (1 Cor 5:1–5), which mitigates their participation in Communion. He directly relates Communion to the Passover festival where he says, "Christ is our Passover Lamb" (1 Cor 5:6–8).

22. Although it might not be apparent, the reference to Christ as "a lamb without blemish (ασπιλος)" draws upon the sacrificial language used in Peter's epistles (1 Pet 1:19). Cf. 2 Pet 3:14; 1 Tim 6:14.

rituals of science which are specifically meant to dispose the participants to know.

The natural question arises about preparation: How does caring for and selecting an animal sacrifice ultimately dispose an Israelite to know something? In the same vein, we could ask: How does preparing an experiment dispose a scientist to know something? Even further, is there an ethical structure in which scientists participate that must cohere with the knowledge wrought by the experiment?

Methodologically, scientific epistemology provides an apt analog for our examination. As we have seen, science is an explicitly epistemological endeavor that relies upon tightly scripted experimentation. Experiments are intent on disposing the scientist to see something they could not have seen apart from the scripted practice. As well, the scientist's seeing through participation in the experiment is not an observation of brute evidence, but rather a skilled discernment that has been developed through years of training. After all, most experimentally significant revelations are not due to observing an event, but emerge by sloughing through tables of numerical data. Discerning what is significant requires a high degree of fostered skill. Without flatly equating religious ritual with scientific experiments, we can notice the significant points of contact between the two that will assist us in thinking about the epistemological efficacy of ritual.

Concerning the ethical matrix within which experimental practices operate, Michael Lynch noticed the similarities between Levite and laboratory preparation of animal sacrifices.[23] In his study of practices in a medical laboratory, Lynch observed the language and behavior surrounding animals to be used for medical experiments. These practices require the animal to be killed in a very precise format. To the uninitiated, it is difficult to read these accounts passively, especially the way in which the animals *must* die as a necessity of the experimental data capture.

Though the death of the animal is not the only aspect that Lynch saw as congruous with Levitical rites, the lab's preparation of the animal, however, commanded his attention. Just as Leviticus conceives of a "naturalistic animal" being converted through ritual into a sacred object, one worthy of being offered to God, the lab converts the "naturalistic animal" into an "analytic" object, one worthy of study.[24] Hence, the *preparation* of the "victim" played as large a role in scientific understanding as the actual sacrifice.

> Through a series of practices (sometimes including the breeding
> and rearing of the animal) that prepare the animal for experimenta-

---

23. Michael E. Lynch, "Sacrifice and the Transformation of the Animal Body into a Scientific Object: Laboratory Culture and Ritual Practice in the Neurosciences," *SSS* 18, no. 2 (May 1988): 265–89.

24. "While the 'analytic animal' is a creature in a generalized mathematical space, the 'naturalistic animal' is a phenomenon in the commonsense life world." Ibid., 267.

tion, the lab worker begins with the naturalistic animal in order to supersede it.[25]

The ethical matrix within which such preparation occurs was not lost on Lynch either: "a researcher . . . confided that experimental success depended, in part, on his abilities to monitor the 'emotions' of his ant subjects."[26] The connection made between the attentiveness of the experimenter and the subjects of the research (e.g., ants, rats, primates, etc.) reveals a more complex fabric of ethical thinking than merely commitment to the experiment.

The reason for all this ritualized language and practice in the lab, Lynch surmises, surrounds the transcendent significance of the animal. A rat, in its natural estate, is limited in what it can offer the scientist concerning its neurology. Most everything about a "naturalistic" rat's neurological states must be found out by maze experiments or other such tasks. However, when converted into an "analytic" object (i.e., a rat who has died in a precise neurological state and has been preserved in that state), it can now reveal what was previously invisible to the outside observer. The lab ethos involves a reverence for the tightly scripted procedures that prepare the animal, the participants' roles, and the practices that convert the rat into that analytic object. Thus, Lynch reckons:

> While the "scientific world" is not a world of gods and spirits, it is a world of abstract relationships never concretely experienced, but iconically represented through concrete residues and traces.[27]

Lynch avers that scientific knowledge of this sort cannot be understood when scientists are considered "intelligentsia with privileged access to truth, but as occupational subcultures sharing specialized techniques and understandings."[28] Thus he concludes:

> The "analytic animal" therefore becomes the real animal in a scientific system of knowledge while tacitly depending upon the "naturalistic animal" for its practical foundation. This is to say not simply that the abstract representations of animal tissue produced in the laboratory necessarily refer to an animal that once lived; it is to raise the question of how scientific knowledge is produced on the basis of pre-scientific praxis. Though commonsense knowledge of animals is a form of "subjugated knowledge", with little or no foundation in positive science, laboratory practitioners rely upon such knowledge in order to produce scientific findings.[29]

---

25. Lynch, "Sacrifice and the Transformation," 280.
26. Ibid., 280.
27. Ibid., 279.
28. Ibid., 266.
29. Ibid., 267.

According to Lynch, scientific knowledge is built up through skilled participation in the rituals of experimentation, which requires a nexus of preparations in order to dispose the scientist to know. Although we cannot pursue it in full, other analyses such as Cyrus Mody's have shown similarities in preparation practices where matters of purity and lethal equipment are used.[30] In both Lynch's and Mody's studies, the ethical preparation of the experiment takes center stage, impossible to divorce what is practiced from what is meant to be known.

Briefly, when it comes to matters of ritual purity, Mody observed the metaphorical employment of "dirty" constructs: "There is no one thing uniting these and other disparate laboratory phenomena: rather, they are overlapping strands making up an analytically interesting thread around themes of purity, cleanliness and contamination."[31] And:

> Dirt *as a means to control behaviour* is a critical fact in many laboratory sciences; but I hope to show that pollution and contamination are often sought out by scientists as ways to expand the boundaries of their knowledge, as solutions to problems and anomalies, and as guides in their local logic of practice.[32]

And in matters of safety in practices which involve equipment that could kill the experimenters, Sims remarks about how the lethality must be accounted for in what can be known:

> [S]afety appears as an object of epistemological concern, as a central organizing principle of group culture, and as a resource for defining the relationship between the research group and the larger institution in which it is situated. Safety can pose epistemological problems in a laboratory setting in part because safety efforts are not easily abstracted from the processes that produce scientific knowledge itself.[33]

Sims concludes that the experimenters' care for each other (i.e., general concern for others) and discernment based on competence—both requiring persistent ethical attentiveness and preparation—were central in explaining the laboratory's scripted practices that enabled scientific knowing: "Watching the procedure enacted is like watching a morality play in which the actors, through gesture and attitude, very literally demonstrate the concept of 'ultimate respect' toward pulsed-power equipment."[34]

---

30. Cyrus C. M. Mody, "A Little Dirt Never Hurt Anyone: Knowledge-Making and Contamination in Materials Science" *SSS* 31, no. 1 (February 2001): 7–36. Regarding lethal equipment, see: Benjamin Sims, "Safe Science: Material and Social Order in Laboratory Work," *SSS* 35, no. 3 (June 2005): 333–66.

31. Mody, "A Little Dirt," 8.

32. Ibid., 8–9.

33. Sims, "Safe Science," 334.

34. Ibid., 350.

Before moving into a discussion of types of participation, it was necessary to make a bare case for the dangers of divorcing preparation from ritual in the practice of science. As we look to degrees of ritual participation, we will also see that recognizing and discerning happen within the scientific community, not due to direct observation, but participation in the community.

Disparate Ritual Participation

Since ethical preparation is part of the ritual act, both in the Torah and the laboratory, I now must clarify how participation varies in Israel. Not all persons perform the rites of Israel to the same degree. From the children who may (or may not) have accompanied the father to the temple courts to the high priest who alone put both hands on the head of the goat, degrees of participation varied. If we are to make the case that these rituals function epistemologically, then we need to differentiate how this variegated participation can still allow for knowing among the participants. We will continue to pursue these distinctions using some phenomenological aspects of the practice, imagining what it would have been like to embody these rites as we find them in the text. As well, I will draw again on scientific epistemology to explain how a practice can be epistemologically viable both for those who participate directly and representatively.

Varying Roles of Participation

Until now, I have spoken about ritual monolithically, as if everyone in Israel practiced all rituals equally. However, depending on who we are (e.g., tribe), what station we have (e.g., high priest), what member of the family (i.e., father), and/or what gender we are, we will be more or less directly associated with different ritual practices. For instance, girls are not circumcised, a rite of boys acted out by the parents and community. Mothers have lengthier impurity after the birth of a girl (Lev 12:5). The priest presents the offerings on behalf of Israelites, so that in some aspects, the offerer merely observes. Presumably, the male head of household would represent the family for certain offerings. In Passover, the children are clearly in a different epistemic position than the parents. And most obvious of all, the High Priest is the only human who can represent Israel to God on Yom Kippur, the Day of Atonement (Lev 16).

If rituals dispose Israelites to know, then must they dispose them disparately? A child in the crowd at Yom Kippur is disposed to know something differently than the High Priest. The ritual shapes the husband whose wife offers impurity sacrifices, but surely the rite impresses him differently than it does his wife who offers. Moreover, the one laying the hand on the head of sacrificial animals must be disposed distinctly from those who watch. What I am attempting to draw out in these examples is the presumption of disparity in the text itself. Like our cultural biases against ritual, these disparities might grate against egalitarian sensibilities. Although most all countries in the West grasp the necessity of representation, hence the proliferation of representational democracies, our sense of fairness might impose itself at this juncture.

It might be that fairness is not a stake in the rites of Israel, and likewise with scientific ritual. As with any good epistemological community—a community that discerns well—the development of skilled knowing is direct and representational, embodied and analogical. Scientists simply do not have direct access to the totality of observations that undergird their research agendas. Some are more skilled than others and some have better access to the observations than others. Because of a given scientist's location, citizenship, habituated skill, and colleagues, her insights and analogical reasoning she brings to her observations will vary from her colleagues. She, on behalf of her similarly skilled colleagues around the world, will act as a representative to be trusted when she participates in the rituals of scientific observation. Her carefully honed bias as a scientist, in the traditions and techniques of her culture, allow her access to the small wedge of observable reality of which she testifies among her peers in their adjacent wedges of observation.

Arguing against the current of scientific thinking in his day, Kuhn contends that scientific knowledge is not built brick by brick, where the bricks are data provided by individual scientists:

> [A] discovery like that of oxygen or X-rays does not simply add one more item to the population of the scientist's world. Ultimately it has that effect, but not until the professional community has re-evaluated traditional experimental procedures, altered its conception of entities with which it has long been familiar, and, in the process, shifted the network of theory through which it deals with the world.[35]

In the same way, Grinnel asserts that the goal of objectivity does not contradict personal biography and cannot be found in the mind of an individual scientist, but the community of science:

> In practice, biography and personality never really disappear. Intersubjectivity can be achieved only partially. Because *the objectivity of science depends on the community* rather than the individual, the influence of personality and biography on the researcher's scientific judgments becomes an asset to science rather than an impediment.[36]

What we face is the conflict of ideals, the objective and discretely logical observer on the one hand, and the historically situated and practiced discerner

---

35. Thomas Kuhn, *The Structure of Scientific Revolutions* (3rd ed.; Chicago: University of Chicago Press, 1996), 7.

36. Italics mine. Frederick Grinnel, *Everyday Practice of Science: Where Intuition and Passion Meet Objectivity and Logic* (New York: Oxford University Press, 2009), 17.

on the other. Kuhn, Grinnel, and Polanyi put the former in the realm of myth and pose the latter as reality. The implication of *the reality* of scientific knowing is that I, as a scientist, cannot know what I need to know directly, but only through participation in the community of scientists and scripted ritual practices of experimentation. Through the ritualized development of skills and the ritual practices of experimentation, I build up paradigms, theory-laden constructs that act as lenses through which all researchers observe: "According to this way of thinking, the researcher's understanding of things is not simply given. Rather, understanding requires interpretation of experience."[37]

Even the scientist herself struggles to see that this is true of her own thinking, that it is nestled in a biographical history of scientific practices:

> A scientist can accept, therefore, the most inadequate and misleading formulation of [her] own scientific principles without ever realizing what is being said, because [s]he automatically supplements it by [her] tacit knowledge of what science really is, and thus makes the formulation ring true.[38]

Moreover, these practices tacitly inform her interpretation within the community. No scientist knows *scientifically* apart from the community. Indeed, repeatability and confirmation are the hallmarks of the experimental sciences. So Kuhn reminds us: "Both normal science and revolutions are, however, community-based activities. To discover and analyze them, one must first unravel the changing community structure of the sciences over time."[39]

What the scientist knows herself must be considered representative knowing because a single scientist in a lab is only performing a role in community. The community shares the paradigms and the ability to confirm, which is the interpretive lens for our scientist in a lab. Considering the social structure of scientific knowledge, Stephen Shapin claims likewise, "No one individual keeps the whole of a discipline's knowledge in his or her head, and even the technical knowledge involved in the conduct of a single experiment in modern physics or biology is typically distributed across a range of specialist actors."[40]

Not only is the scientist's understanding a token representative of a community, but within the practice of experimentation, the scientist is not always the direct observer. Much experimentation relies on a field of trained actors and observers, not all of whom are directly involved in the experiment's goal

---

37. Grinnel, *Everyday Practice of Science,* 10.

38. Polanyi, *Personal Knowledge,* 169.

39. Kuhn, *The Structure of Scientific Revolutions,* 179.

40. Stephen K. Shapin, "Here and Everywhere: Sociology of Scientific Knowledge," *ARS* 21 (1995): 302. This seems to rehearse Polanyi's point: "Indeed, nobody knows more than a tiny fragment of science well enough to judge its validity and value at first hand. For the rest he has to rely on views accepted at second hand on the authority of a community of people accredited as scientists." Polanyi, *Personal Knowledge,* 163.

of understanding. As an undergraduate, I was a confederate in a fairly elaborate social-psychology experiment of negotiation behaviors.[41] As a confederate, I pretended to be just another undergraduate subject in the experiment. When the research assistant paired us off, we confederates would go into rooms with the actual subject and negotiate the sale price of a fictional car with fictional money and fictional information. Unknown to the subject, I was actually walking them through a very precise script that we confederates had memorized. Although it appeared to the subjects to be an impromptu negotiation regarding a fictional car, it was actually a carefully manipulated scenario where I had to track the variables and controls closely to ensure that there would be a measurable result.

In this experiment, who is the observer? We were in private rooms and no recording equipment was used. Hence, the primary data (i.e., the record of prices and personal self-report of the confederate and subject) was dependent upon me: an undergraduate helper. I observed the negotiation. However, I did not know or have a sense of the experimental results until months later after the experiment was complete and confederates were debriefed. The research assistant, a Ph.D. student at the time, ran all the experimental sessions and ensured coaching and consistency were maintained, but she did not observe the negotiations either. The psychologist in charge of the experiment conceived the research design and worked with his research assistant to craft the study. However, he did not attend the negotiation sessions, being even further removed from direct observation. Yet, in the end, he was the one who knew what happened in those negotiations according to his experimental hypothesis and the statistically significant results garnered by the experiment.[42] Many scientists of varying fields have affirmed to me that such practices are normative, where students observe and collect measurements and the experimenter analyzes the data.

To say that a scientist "observes the phenomenon" might often entail a representational observation, testified by the networks of trust built up in a lab. However, I am not supposing that because the scientist did not kill the animal herself, or perform each observation at each iteration, she therefore does not know scientifically. Just as the confederates, the research assistant, and the senior researcher all came to know something about bargaining strategies through our communal participation with disparate roles, so too I can advocate that Israel's participation in ritual *as a community* is sufficient to maintain their epistemological features. If the direct or representational participation does not diminish a scientist's use of ritual in order to know, then I

41. Paul W. Paese and Debra A. Gilin, "When an Adversary is Caught Telling the Truth: Reciprocal Cooperation Versus Self-Interest in Distributive Bargaining," *PSPB* 26, no. 1 (2000): 79–90.

42. From anecdotal evidence, this experimental scenario—a professor and graduate student working together with assistants who perform the direct observation—is repeated in the halls of most research institutions.

see no substantive reason that the epistemological efficacy of ritual would be diminished through diverse participation.

I would suggest instead that diverse participation creates a polyphonic understanding of the phenomena, which requires an attentive community in order to understand. And it appears that the scientific community offers us a contemporary view of what that kind of attentive community, diversely participating in experimental practices, *could have* looked like in Israel.

In ancient Israel, we cannot presume that diverse means of ritual participation would have been viewed as unfair. Although Korah and his men fought this very point, their end seems to also have shaped Israel's thinking about who can approach God and how. Indeed, we later find a reverent (or terrified) Israel demanding disparate participation (Deut 5:24–25). One significant role of a prophet, as I have argued elsewhere, is to act as a privileged seer asking Israel the question, "Do you see what I see?"[43] Although this prophetic task is often lamentable,[44] its premise is that skilled seeing comes from disparate views engaging the community from within and without.

Finally, if scientific epistemology is communal in nature, then the veracity of trust bonds ultimately determines the veracity of that knowledge. Recently, there has been a renewed focus on integrity in publishing experimental results, now being monitored mostly by independent watchdog groups.[45] Like other communal endeavors, the erosion of fidelity directly ensnares the fabric of knowledge in the community. Just as in the Scriptures, so it goes in science that ritual is epistemologically connected with ethical preparation, participation, and reporting of findings.

Scientific Ritual

Without rehearsing our prior section on scientific ritual, we return to the idea of experiment as ritual. This analogous understanding is most helpful because it is uncontroversial to assert that experiments intend to dispose the scientist to discern. The scripting of embodied actions, the attentiveness to significant details in observations, and the reflection upon what happened are directly intended to dispose the scientist to see something from which she is logically separated apart from participation. As Michael Lynch described it, scientists are in the business of designing very discrete ritualized practices and embodying them in order to see something otherwise transcendent or invisible to them. A natural rat cannot confer what a neurologist could see unless it is ritualized for the sake of seeing the transcendent neurological properties.

These scripted rites create traditions, biographically-connected ways of disposing oneself to see. Scientists with revolutionary constructs did not gen-

---

43. See Johnson, *Biblical Knowing*, 52–59.
44. E.g., Jer 20: 7–18; Hos 1.
45. E.g., "Retraction Watch," http://retractionwatch.wordpress.com/.

erate those revolutionary ideas *ex nihilo*, but critiqued the ideas of their community (e.g., Einsteinian versus Newtonian mechanics). Therefore, they ritualized the previous practices in order to see if their revolutionary construct actually transcends to novel instances of known phenomena.

To study how humans regain their balance, for instance, a researcher must trip her subjects to observe the transcendent constructs being discerned. The tripping of her subjects is a practice, but ritualized from accidental to purposeful.[46] Because few would assert that science suffers from problems associated with mystery or fideism, science is helpful in thinking about ritual epistemology. The whole enterprise unashamedly ritualizes and scripts embodied practices for the sake of recognizing and then discerning transcendent patterns. The practices of science appear immanently rational to us. The reason for this *prima facie* rationale is based in part on the traceability of its rites. If we asked the experimenter, "Why are you tripping your subjects," we presume that she could give reasons ultimately traceable to her hypothesis.

What we miss in such a discussion of traceability is that her reasons are not necessarily traceable to the person being tripped or other researcher who have yet to conduct such experiments. It might be the case that the quickest and most logical route to understand the practice of experimental tripping is to get onto the tripping treadmill itself and then hear the explanation of the experiment. The embodiment of tripping makes sense of the experiment's traceable logic in a way that mere observation does not. Hence, it is not necessarily the case that the logic of experimentation must be traceable apart from the subjects' practice of the scripted rite. We can imagine that the experimental constructs could be explained to the subjects, but apart from their repeated participation in being tripped, the logic might still be untraceable to them. Or there might be a sense of "Oh, I see what you mean" once the subject has been tripped. However, the subject does not need to be aware of or able to trace the exact logic of the rite in order to eventually benefit from what is discerned through it.

But the biblical logic on rituals is clearer than this. It espouses, "Do this in order to know." In this sense, the comparison is not between what the experimenter and the subject (i.e., the *tripee)* know. Rather, the comparable relationship is between one successful experimenter who has recognized through this ritual (i.e., experiment) commending the same experiment to another researcher so that they can recognize it too. Upon such commendations and rites, the researchers come to discern a construct about balance that goes beyond their local observations of it.

Here, we are focused on the diverse epistemological goals of an experiment, whose primary epistemological audience is not typically the subjects themselves. The disparate community required by the ritual creates a polyphonic perspective on the invisible kinematic construct called "tripping," pre-

46. Karen L. Troy and Mark D. Grabiner, "Asymmetrical ground impact of the hands after a trip-induced fall: Experimental kinematics and kinetics," *CB* 22, no. 10 (2007): 1088–1095.

sumed to transcend individual observations, which is discerned through ritualized attention to visible actions.

If what I have said here maps in any way onto the actual practice of scientific discernment, then Israel's ritualized practices can be clearly distinguished by the authority of her scripts. Israel, according to the Torah, is not primarily writing her own scripted practices in order to recognize some feature of reality. Rather God, who already knows what Israel needs to know, prescribes her disparate rites that will dispose her to see through the polyphonic knowledge of the community.

Chapter 12
Knowledge as a Subset of Ethics

Before addressing the implications of knowledge as ethics, I will summarize my central findings from Parts I–III for the sake of clarity below. In describing this polyphonic community of knowers who are pointed toward wisdom (i.e., discernment), I begin with the community and work my way toward the individual who's learning to discern through ritual participation. All the while, I must maintain awareness that just as knowing is inextricably embodied, the human body is inextricably bound within the social body, even the political body of the community which acts as the soil of the rite. Bell succinctly points out: "political rituals do not refer to politics . . . they *are* politics. Ritual is the thing itself. It *is* power; it acts and actuates."[1] Hence the disparately participating community provides a fertile social body in which scripted and practiced rites dispose individuals to first recognize a pattern, and then discern its transcendent features (Figure 12.1). All of these elements enmesh together as a social body forming an individual's ritual body (or "habit-body" as Merleau-Ponty called it) toward the central goal of discernment.

Communal

The fact that Scripture prescribes a social dynamic to the epistemological process should not alarm us. Only with the most naïve reading can one assume that the enscripturated guidance of Israel means to shape only one's individual ethical behavior, an individual's beliefs, or how one individual knows apart from the community. In being disposed to know objects, constructs, or God Himself, more than one person is required. If knowing requires guidance, *even if only to learn the knack which can be individually extended*, then epistemological process is social. Two aspects are central here. First, polyphonic knowing is a strength of this view. Second, Israelite knowing is pediatrically focused, but not pedia-centric.

---

1. Catherine Bell, *Ritual Theory, Ritual Practice* (New York: Cambridge University Press, 2009), 195.

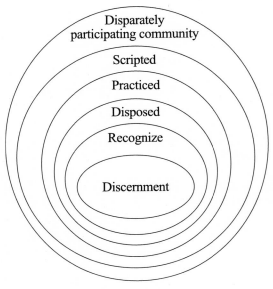

Figure 12.1

First, not only is knowing a social process, but there is an intentional disparity in the performance of rites, which means that by its constitution, the Torah does not construct an egalitarian epistemology, where everyone has access to the same knowledge—a caricatured ideal of rationalism. Rather, because different roles in Israelite society will necessarily dispose persons to be variously discerning, they must rely upon each other in order to know well. In other words, the man was required to rely upon God in Eden in order to come to know his mate (Gen 2). The woman must rely upon the man to understand the creation mandates given to the man alone. The disparity of epistemological roles actually necessitates covenantal relationship. Israelites of all statuses are disposed to see the cosmos from various positions and their interdependence creates the possibility for a profoundly communal understanding of the world. Again, science provides us with a good analog of what this could have looked like, where the very nature of discovery evident in these ancient texts has developed into the scientific community. That course to discovery requires disparate access to the reality being discovered, which strengthens the confidence of discovery. By saying that knowing is communal, *I assert that it is polyphonic and therefore multi-vantaged, which is its advantage.*

Second, the rituals that were explicitly epistemological often focused on the children coming to recognize. This intense interest to maintain a living memory of Israel's history means that history for Israel is hermeneutics: how the generations know what happened and how they interpret its significance. Of interest to us, the manner in which young Israelites studied history centers upon ritualized practices: doing in order to recognize and discern. While most of us are generally familiar with the use of memorials in order to remember (e.g., headstones at a grave, holidays of commemoration, etc.), in the West we can be easily estranged from a larger and systematized life of ritual practices. This system values rituals within which memorials do not merely cause mental memories, but somatically situate the knower, orienting her to discern novel and future occurrences.[2]

Remarkably, the inclusion of Israel's children is not merely for the children's sake. The process is not pedia-centric, but pediatrically inclusive because the children force the adults to become guides, helping to lead them to the waters of discernment. Stated otherwise, the role of children is different than that of the adult for the obvious reasons. But in the Hebrew Bible, the less obvious advantage is that the presence of youth creates an ethical imperative for the adults: your generations must be disposed to discern. The children's questions, generated by ritual participation, make the adults accountable to guide them. In other words, Israel's future discernment is predicated upon their current discernment.

Scripted

First, the fact that ritualized practices are scripted points to the matter of authority. Given the financial burden that rituals placed on families, good reasons beyond piety must have existed to motivate such practices. In other words, these practices must be scripted by an authority, who is authenticated to that community. In most all cases, Moses is that authenticated authority.

Second, the scripted nature of ritual does not make it unique to Israel, but evinces that an authoritative guide is requisite. This also helps us to distinguish religious ritual from practices. I occasionally take my family camping and this could be considered a ritual in our family. However, seeing it as a practice that can be ritualized helps us to discern the purpose of the practice *and* some possible reasons for ritualizing that practice. No one has ever said, "You must go camping." We camp as a family for various reasons. However,

---

2. I would make the case that we do understand this; however, the scripted nature of such practices makes them difficult to enforce outside of a strictly religious practicing community. Hence, we remember the independence of the United States on July fourth, but we remember it loosely as an event. We do not have scripted practices that force us to re-enact the event or make us to feel the tragic and embattled sense of the event, though the symbology of battle surrounds the ritualized practices of Independence Day. The practices do not embody the memory, but almost reduce it to a mental acknowledgment of the fact that happened. Conversely, Sukkot begins with acknowledging what happened and then scripts the practice in order to bring Israel to know something, by embodying the practice, about the event.

the scripting of camping for epistemological reasons ritualizes the practice, making it requisite for the prescribed purpose.

Ritualizing practices, as Bell forcefully contends, helps us to distinguish the practice from the rite, as the rite forms a critique and heightened continuation of the practice. This may seem like a benign point, but the discussion of ritual supersession in Judaism and Christianity often fails to heed this point. Judaic and Christian ritual practices are both critiques *and continuations* of Israel's rituals. They are, in all actuality, *ritualized* rituals. Indeed, Moses himself, on the authority of YHWH, prescribes *ritualized* rituals to Israel. Circumcision, animal and grain sacrifice, and more were already known rites in the ancient Near East that were ritualized for Israel. According to the earliest Jewish texts within the Jesus community, which included Jewish scholars, these ritualizations of Torah rites (e.g., baptism, Communion, etc.) were legitimate.

Viewing rites as ritualized practices offers a more fruitful and nuanced examination of the texts as it highlights the continuation of ritual that appeared centrally important to the early Jewish church and notably did not focus on the discontinuity. In other words, the early church considered itself to be continuous with the people of Israel and this explains their belief that Jesus had the requisite authority to ritualize Israel's rites.[3]

Practiced

Not only are the rites prescribed, they must be practiced. I have attempted to show throughout that the ideal of knowing apart from one's embodied practices transgresses the biblical view of anthropology and epistemology. In contemporary philosophy, strong arguments suggest that all of our constructs, mathematical to scientific to religious, are embedded in and imbued by our embodied existence. If this is even remotely correct, then knowing is always embodied in and derivative of our practices.

Therefore, the most reasonable and parsimonious way to think of good knowing requires that practiced rites, which have proven to be epistemologically efficacious, form the core of our knowing. Classroom rites of repetition and prompting (i.e., testing) have been shown to be effective in developing certain areas of abstract reasoning. Practices are systematized and prescribed, not for the sake of transferring knowledge, but for shaping the knower to discern. All of these require embodied participation. Listening, writing, thinking, questioning, and more are all embodied and personal practices to which one must commit in order to recognize and discern.

---

3. N. T. Wright argues for the Jesus-as-prophet model as his primary identity: "The best initial model for understanding this praxis is that of a prophet; more specifically, that of a prophet bearing an urgent eschatological and indeed apocalyptic, message for Israel." And, "All the evidence so far displayed suggests that he was perceived as a prophet." *Jesus and the Victory of God* (COQG; Minneapolis: Fortress, 1996), 150, 196.

Disposed

The commitment of the guide to the learner who is practicing the prescribed rites does not transfer knowledge, but rather disposes the knower to recognize, and later discern. That the process of knowing is not only embodied; embodying rites actually transforms the knower. The rites dispose her to recognize something she is logically separated from apart from the ritual. In other words, ritual participation does not give her knowledge. Rather, it ritualizes her body—her entire person—disposing her to see and offering her an otherwise unattainable vista of reality. This is "another shore of reality" implicit to Polanyi's scientific epistemology, where the rituals dispose scientists to be illuminated: "'Illumination' is then the leap by which the logical gap is crossed. It is the plunge by which we gain a foothold at another shore of reality. On such plunges the scientist has to stake bit by bit his entire professional life."[4]

Similarly, a community of researchers must embody the scripted practices of experimentation. Through the practices, the knowers are formed to see through the lens of the experiment, disposed to discern that which they observe. They are not, however, given data as the output to an experiment.

Recognize and Discern

Finally, the difference between qualities of insight appears on a continuum of knowing, so as to avoid flattening the construct. The variety of contexts within which the Scripture uses "see," "know," "discern," and "understand" requires that we distinguish insensitivity to a construct from recognizing it and then discerning its significance. There is a logical space between being insensitive and recognizing, bridged solely by ritual participation. However, there is a gradation between knowing (i.e., Aha! recognizing), which can be tested for, and discernment, which is a more subjective but profound grasp of the transcendence of a pattern.

The importance of this distinction revolves around the goals of ritual knowing. If one is insensitive to the pattern, then the rite must bridge that gap, making one basically aware and able to recognize its order. However, once we can recognize, then discernment becomes the task of the rite. Discernment is most often conveyed in Scripture by the notion of wisdom (חכמה/σοφία). As I have argued elsewhere, biblical wisdom is portrayed throughout Scripture as skilled discernment, analogous to a craftsman's knowledge of a trade.[5]

---

4. Michael Polanyi, *Personal Knowledge: Towards a Post-Critical Philosophy* (Chicago: University of Chicago Press, 1974), 123.

5. Dru Johnson, *Biblical Knowing: A Scriptural Epistemology of Error* (Eugene, OR: Cascade, 2013), 137–40.

Epistemology as Ethics

If our epistemological goals shape our practices, then epistemology is ethical. In order to know cellular tonicity, the proper interpretation of an X-ray, family systems behavior, or attributes of God, we must perform distinct practices, which require us to relate to persons while embodying rites. However, our disposition toward our guides and how we act with our bodies is determined by the epistemic goal. *What we want to know determines how we will act, and thus knowing, as a process, is ethical.*

Deontology, a rules-based view of ethics, does not help to explain this type of behavior as it seeks to find universal and principled rules which, if followed, will produce the best ethical behavior. Immanuel Kant's categorical imperative is the paradigmatic example of such thinking. Avoiding consequentialist ideas of ethics, Kant sought to base all ethics in the *a priori* world of reasoning: "[T]he ground of obligation here must not be sought in the nature of the human being or in the circumstances of the world in which he is placed, but a priori simply in the concepts of pure reason."[6] A well-formed rule based in pure reason means to steer us ethically in all circumstances. The categorical imperative means to be such a rule, basically asking us, "If everyone did what I am doing, would the underlying reasons for this behavior be upheld or diminished?" For instance, if I lied about my age in order to seem younger, my lie is premised upon a general sense of how old people are as judged by their physical appearance. However, if everyone lied about their ages, then the ability to judge age by looking at someone's physical appearance would presumably be lost. There would be no sense of age based on appearance and there would be no reason to trust someone's statements about her age. The very principle upon which I am playing my lie would be diminished, not to mention that lying in general diminishes any sense of veracity.

Likewise, utilitarianism and other consequentialist schemes of ethics presume that our knowledge is front-loaded, and that we understand the possible ramifications of our actions in advance. John Stuart Mill's famous version of this is captured in his phrase, "actions are right in proportion as they tend to promote happiness." Pleasures must be assessed for their intellectual value and ability to properly educate. The central critique of consequentialist ethics has been epistemological. We must be able to recognize and discern the discrete and wide ranging outcomes of our behavior *in advance*, weighing those outcomes to determine *in advance* which route best serves happiness for the most people. As it turns out, this sort of ethical prognosticating is tricky. More obviously, the Hebrew Bible is advocating something radically *other* than deontological and consequentialist ethics. We are not disposed to know in advance by a priori reasoning, though discernment might eventually help us here.

---

6. Immanuel Kant, *Groundwork for the Metaphysics of Morals* (trans. Mary Gregor; New York: Cambridge University Press, 1997), 3.

The Platonic tradition does offer us some kinship to the biblical nexus of ethics and knowing. First, Plato was keen to make us aware that knowing is a process guided by one who has already come to know. This process has a narratival structure: a problem is posed, questions progressively prod the learner, and then the knowledge is delivered, like an infant in birth. For Plato the teacher is the midwife (μαιευτικός),[7] not inculcating knowledge, but rather coaxing the knowledge that is already there within the learner, inseminated from pre-life contact with the true reality of forms in the heavenlies.

Second, Aristotle's ethics center upon the development of the person through their reasoning. Ethical obligations are not divorced, in Aristotle, from habituation. To be ethical is to be practiced, reflecting deeply on what virtues ought to be esteemed. And once virtuous goals are recognized, how do people habituate themselves in the most excellent (ἀρετή) practice? In Aristotle's treatment, we find an ethic that must be instantiated through the body and reflected upon in relationship to virtue, as it is understood in his tradition.

Aristotle's ethical sensibilities have been revived in the field of virtue epistemology. Namely, habituating the virtues through practice is the best way to know with veracity. The ability of a virtue-focus to produce justifiable beliefs, which can be called knowledge, is an admirable appropriation of the Hellenistic tradition. As Ernest Sosa wrote in his seminal essay on the matter:

> The important move for our purpose is the stratification of justification. . . . Here primary justification would apply to *intellectual* virtues, to stable dispositions for belief acquisition, through their greater contribution toward getting us to the truth.[8]

As an ensuing development in virtue epistemology, Linda Zagzebski combines the motivation to pursue excellence with its epistemological outcomes:

> It requires the knower to have an intellectually virtuous motivation in the disposition to desire truth, and this disposition must give rise to conscious and voluntary acts in the process leading up to the acquisition of true belief (or cognitive contact with reality), and the knower must successfully reach the truth through the operation of this motivation and those acts.[9]

What is gained through this reclamation of the Hellenistic tradition is a re-emphasis on knowing as a process, which demands that we form our habit-bodies through good practice. The intellectual pursuit of excellence with reference to classic virtues then becomes the disposition to acquire the right kinds of beliefs in order to know truth. The esteem showed toward process,

---

7. Plato, *Theaetetus*, 148c–151d.

8. Ernest Sosa, "The Raft and the Pyramid: Coherence versus Foundations in the Theory of Knowledge," *MSP* 5, no.1 (September 1980): 23.

9. Linda Trinkaus Zagzebski, *Virtues of the Mind: An Inquiry into the Nature of Virtue and the Ethical Foundations of Knowledge* (Cambridge: Cambridge University Press, 1996), 273.

habit, and being rightly disposed to know makes this version of epistemology attractive for what I have proposed here. There are, however, some significant losses for taking on such a view. First and foremost, the development of concern is "intellectual virtues," which means that we are still dealing with a form of the thinking-acting dichotomy. The goal of virtue epistemology, in the end, is not to accredit an embodied process that disposes knowers to see, but an intellectual process that yields true belief acquisition. In essence, this is still a propositional take on the problem of knowing.

Despite this, what the Platonic tradition indicates to us is that even with very strong metaphysical and propositional beliefs about knowledge, the fathers of Western philosophy commended knowing as an embodied process that disposes one to better or worse types of knowing.[10] In other words, the lived experience of knowing was aptly reflected in their epistemologies. This alone warrants considering the Greek tradition to be an aid to our cause, as much of contemporary epistemology actively neglects the participation in a process as constitutive of the disposition to know.

Scriptural and Ethical Knowing

What ethical guidelines do the epistemological goals of Scripture dictate? Whatever answer we arrive at, we can already see that homing in on just the scripted rituals themselves (e.g., the burnt offering) will be insufficient. Because Israel is meant to know through ritual practices *and* her ritual participation includes preparation, *then* the ethics of Israelite epistemology encompasses every aspect of life.

If this analysis of preparation is correct, then what Israel brings along with her sacrifices are her ethical preparations. Those preparations, both in an Israelite's general ethical concern for others,[11] attentive concern for her private sphere of body and home,[12] specific attentiveness to what sacrifices are worthy to bring as an offering,[13] etc., are part of the sacrifice itself and cannot be divorced from it without detrimental consequences to the process (Figure 12.2). Because ritual is epistemological, then the general ethical concerns that constitute preparation for ritual also prepare one to know.

---

10. Unfortunately with Plato, the body is the very thing that disrupts the process of knowing.

11. E.g., "You shall love him [the alien] as yourself, for you were once aliens in the land of Egypt." Lev 19:34.

12. E.g., Lev 12–14.

13. E.g., "Your lamb shall be without blemish, a yearling male; you may take it from the sheep or from the goats." Exod 12:5.

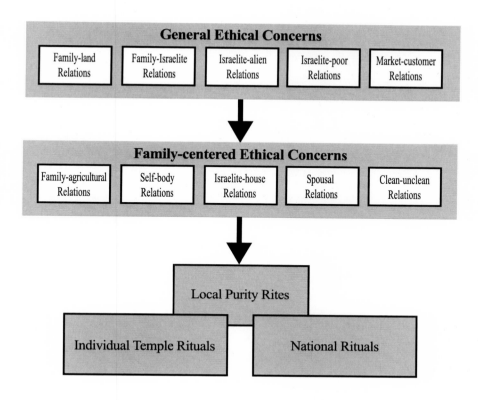

Figure 12.2

The Scriptures make an odd claim for modern ears, that concern for the resident alien, consideration of food rationing in light of the poor, and the inclusion of children in the ritualized life of Israel all work together to enable knowing.[14] Epistemology is not an intellectual activity in an amoral space called the mind, but intimately integrated with our treatment of others in the social body and our own bodies. To put it in biblical terms, discerning the significance of the exodus event begins in an Israelite's ability to follow ritual purity. That purity demands attentiveness to body, relationships, and the pertinent rites of cleansing, *even when no other human would ever know about instances of impurity.* The prophets judge an Israelite's morality based on his attentiveness to her fields and flocks, families, fellow brothers and tribesmen, strangers, the poor, and her enemies. The prophetic assessment then extends to organizational versions of justice and charity, how Israel as a whole carries

14. Bohdan Hrobon has tracked a similar connection between ethical life and ritual in Isaiah. *Ethical Dimension of Cult in the Book of Isaiah* (BZAW 418; Berlin: de Gruyter, 2010).

out the Torah that requires systemic justice. Remarkably, the Torah's totalizing view of ritual participation sweeps across every aspect of Israelite life.

Summary

How does an Israelite prepare for a ritual? Everything they do, the entirety of their ethical cosmos, prepares them to practice rites, which dispose them to know, for good or for ill. Good preparation means that the ethical nexus of the Torah is never annexed, for instance, from the animals and grains offered to the priests.

Chapter 13

Implications for Constructing
Sacramental Theology

The implications of my proposal will now appear more controversial as we consider the sacraments as Christian ritual. I want to briefly show why my analysis provides a fruitful route to examine sacramental theologies, thinking about them in terms of epistemology: What do rites dispose us to know?

What follows below are suggestions, prodding questions that rise to the surface if we take seriously this notion that rituals dispose us to know. I suspect that just as the rites of Israel would have been expressed differently in the various contexts of the Tabernacle, the Solomonic Temple, and the Herodian Temple, so too the rites of Christianity will evince aspects that reflect the diverse contexts in which they occur. Below, I pose questions pregnant in the preceding analysis which must be answered in those diverse contexts.

I do have a general concern that analyses of the meaning of rituals can suffer from an overdetermination of meaning within differing theological traditions. It is not the goal of this work to find out *what God knows* about these rites, as it were. Rather, my best reflections will aim at glimpses of *what the prophets discerned* through their textual communications, the Scriptures. However, Christian practitioners are in a unique position in that the meaning of the biblical rites is not necessarily lost to us. While the ancient Israelite religion centered upon the temple is gone (sans a third temple or something like it), Christians have practiced their canonical rites continuously since the first century. For instance, Christians have ritualized their own rites as well. For instance, Communion is sometimes performed in a Protestant wedding by only the couple being married. The wedding guests then become spectators during this part of the service. In this appropriation of the practice, Communion is ritualized to mean and do something other than its normative function in the church. What this ritualized rite means to do is less important than the fact that Christians sometimes practice the rite in a fundamentally new way. However the new strategic use of the rite still maintains continuity with the biblical rite. The elements, bread and wine, and the words of institution scripted by Jesus and Paul identify this act directly with the same rite practiced by Paul.

Despite such ritualizations of the rites that might vary from the early Jerusalemite church, Christian theology has a direct inroad to understand what the biblical rites of the New Testament dispose us to discern. Because both Judaism and Christianity do not maintain continuity with the ancient Israelite religion of Jesus, both are incapable of a phenomenological understanding of the Torah's rites afforded by their performance. However, both religions ritualize those rites—in some cases, even viewing their Judaic or Christian ritualization as supersession of Mosaic Law. And so we can examine the contemporary practices accordingly. In the case of Christianity, its rites directly reflect the New Testament practices, though the particulars of the practices were hammered out in the ensuing centuries. For Judaism, with its protracted Talmudic tradition, Levitical practices were ritualized into Judaic practices, while still reflecting the rites.

Regarding the New Testament Rites

Should we pursue the symbolic meaning of New Testament rites? I want to argue that decoding the symbolism of rites ought not to be our primary task. Jesus announced in the inauguration of Communion that the wine "is" his blood (τοῦτό ἐστιν τὸ αἷμά μου)[1] and the bread "is" his body (τοῦτό ἐστιν τὸ σῶμά μου).[2] Is not the mystery of symbolic meaning therefore informed by his instruction? Likewise, Mary Douglas' analysis of the symbolism in Yom Kippur seeks to answer this exact type of correlation. She argues persuasively what she thinks the release of the goat into the wilderness symbolizes. However, I have tried to show that the meaning of release might not be what is in view of the one who prescribes such a practice. Though the epistemological goal of Yom Kippur need not exclude symbolic meaning, it may take priority.

But in the Gospel accounts, Jesus says quite clearly what the symbols are and exactly what they stand for. Just as the author of Revelation interprets the symbols in the fore of the letter (Rev 1:20: "the seven lampstands are the seven churches"), Jesus interprets the elements of the ritual. So any pursuit of symbolic meaning is pursuing a different question, some like: In what way is wine Jesus' *blood* and bread Jesus' *body*? Answering this question might presumably answer the question that Maimonides broached in our previous discussion: why do we do this?

The fact that Maimonides cannot know the "why" apart from participating in temple rituals should now appear to be the most controversial front of my proposal. I would suggest that, although these questions ought to be pursued in due time, we risk neglecting another more basic question if we are too distracted by exegesis of the symbols. Just as the novice biologist cannot understand why she is doing the discrete actions required to adjust a microscope *while she is doing them*, a ritual practitioner can discern the logic and meaning

---

1. Mark 14:24
2. Luke 22:19

of the rite only after being mastered by it. Studying the meaning of the ritual symbols in advance, or thinking that we understand the secret meaning by study of such symbols, could be akin to the biologist studying "microscope looking" and "knob turning" in order to understand "tonicity in a cell." The object of study is not the knobs or ways of looking, rather the knobs and looking enable her to see the proper object of study.

The appropriate route for understanding rituals, given this proposal, centers on questions such as: how is this ritualized practice an act of remembrance (e.g., Luke 22:19)? Further, how does remembering serve to develop discernment? Below, I suggest that Jesus' ritualization of Israel's rites will provide a fruitful way to understand both the rite and its contemporary practice.

Returning to methodological implications for sacramental theology, the submission to authorities and what Catherine Bell calls "oversight" must feature prominently. Essentially, if a rite means to shape us as knowers, we do not have to understand *how it shapes us* in order for it to do so. We do not have to see clearly how the rite disposes us to know in order to thus be disposed.

> Specifically, its relationship of seeing to not-seeing is the production of agents embodying a sense of ritual constituted by and expressed in particular schemes of ritualization. These schemes act as instruments for knowing and appropriating the world.[3]

The matter, then, revolves around our trust of those providing the ritual scheme. As Polanyi also argued regarding rites that train the scientist, the apprentice needs to trust her master more than be able to trace the logic of the practice. The failure to do the former excludes her from grasping the latter.

> To learn by example is to submit to authority. You follow your master because you trust his manner of doing things even when you cannot analyse and account for its effectiveness. . . . A society which wants to preserve a fund of personal knowledge must submit to tradition.[4]

To answer the question regarding Communion and its function in remembrance, we must submit our bodies to the practice within a social body (i.e., the church), even though we cannot account for its meaning beyond the bare symbolism of blood, flesh, and their relationships to the Passion and Passover events and celebrations.

The problem with pursuing symbolic meaning first is that it risks flattening out the rich and *condensed symbology*[5] of Israel's rites to a linguistic matrix merely needing to be decoded for its meaning. Even worse, it reveals that the

3. Catherine Bell, *Ritual Theory, Ritual Practice* (New York: Cambridge University Press, 2009), 115.

4. Michael Polanyi, *Personal Knowledge: Towards a Post-Critical Philosophy* (Chicago: University of Chicago Press, 1974), 53.

5. Mary Douglas, *Natural Symbols* (2nd ed.; New York: Routledge, 1996), 8–11.

thinking-acting dichotomy unnecessarily constrains our ritual constructs: as words express our thinking, ritual symbols express our thoughts. This dichotomy, as Bell argued, blinds us to ritualized practices as formative. How so? Instead of seeing ourselves as participants who practice the rite to know under guidance and in community, we attempt to trace and master its internal logic.

Suppose our father is a speed enthusiast—he goes fast in cars, boats, and all things that go. When attempting to understand what it is about speed that our father loves so much, he might tell us, "Learn to ride a bike and you'll see!" But imagine that we attempt to understand our father by mounting a bicycle and then meditating upon the formula for balance and motion (i.e., "for a given angle of unbalance the curvature of each winding is inversely proportional to the square of the speed at which the cyclist is proceeding"). The analysis becomes destructive to the process of understanding our father's passion for motion.[6] Riding the bicycle was meant to dispose us to see something about the ability to go faster than our running speed that is intoxicating. Yet, the attempt to decode the act defeats the very purpose of the act.

The logic of the ritual process that I spelled out in the introductory chapters can only be grasped by embodying the process. Similarly, the logic of narrative is not coherent apart from hearing the whole story (i.e., embodying the process of listening). It also does me no good to deconstruct the deductive logic of a syllogism in order to understand what the syllogism is attempting to conclude (i.e., what is the metaphysical relation of *Premise 1* to *Premise 2* and the conclusion).[7]

Premise 1:	All cats are mammals.
Premise 2:	Fluffles is a cat.
Conclusion:	Fluffles is a mammal.

Trying to grasp how a deductive inference "works" has created an inimitable mound of scholarly debate. Yet, even without access to that debate, I can learn from a guide how to follow the ritual process of the syllogism and reap the benefits of that skill. So too, a sacramental analysis of the traceable logic of the ritual might be in order, but not until after the rite has done its epistemological forming of me as a submitted participant.

Ritualization as Continuity and Critique

Beyond the meaning of symbols, how is the rite's continuity with the Israelite religion also a critique of the practice? Legitimate questions under this heading would include those directed toward the functional role of epistemic ritu-

---

6. Polanyi, *Personal Knowledge*, 50.

7. Forgiving the anthropomorphism here, syllogisms do not attempt to conclude anything. Rather it is the human effort to follow well-coordinated premises to their conclusion that makes a syllogism "work."

als in Israel and the narratives in which they belong. For instance, Jesus inaugurates the Communion rite in the context of Passover, which we have discussed in light of its two-fold instantiation: the unique historical event (Exod 12:28–32) and the memorial ritualization to be practiced throughout Israel's generations (Exod 12:1–27). Likewise, there is a dual instantiation with Communion on the night of the unique historical event (i.e., the night prior to the crucifixion) and the memorial rite scripted by Jesus and practiced regulatively by the early church.

In other words, we cannot merely ask what the symbols of wine and bread mean, but must further distinguish *to whom* and *when?* When I once asked what the symbols of Communion meant in a group of Christians, a discerning woman said that the symbols meant to her what they meant on the night of Jesus' betrayal. Clearly, she said, the disciples could see the difference between Jesus' blood and the wine, Jesus' body and the bread being consumed. This folk analysis, which was as much a reaction to the doctrine of transubstantiation as it was her own exegesis, reveals a layer of savvy, showing that the meaning is constrained by its context in the biblical narrative. In just as many ways, the bread and wine could not mean the same things to her as the first century disciples celebrating Pesach in Jerusalem.

In the same way, we could ask if the waters of baptism have just one symbolic meaning. It is difficult to make sense of baptismal water being merely a symbol of purification considering its practice in Mosaic law (Lev 14:8), for proselyte Jews,[8] Jews under John the Baptist (Luke 3:7), Jesus' baptism (Mark 1:9–11), and then the baptisms performed by the apostles in Acts (Acts 2:38). The symbolic meaning of water could be an endless fount of interpretive distraction if the narratives and epistemological purposes of the rite are neglected for the sake of symbolic meaning. If ritualization is a feature of all rites, then baptism's continuity from Torah to New Testament has just as much to teach us as its discontinuity with circumcision due to its ritualization in baptism (cf. Col 2:11–12).

Which Rites "are" Sacraments?

As a matter for Christian theology, the number of sacraments has been a long-standing disagreement in the catholic church, though less so in the Catholic church.[9] While the dispute over what constitutes a sacrament cannot be hashed out here, we must consider what makes a particular rite a sacrament.

---

8. *b. Yebam.* 46b–47b.

9. The Roman Catholic Church has maintained the seven sacraments: baptism, communion, penance, confirmation, marriage, ordination, and healing the sick (the so-called "last rites"). Eastern Orthodoxy holds to the same seven, but includes almost any activity properly done by the church. Protestants, on the other hand, have maintained only those two explicitly instituted by Jesus: Communion and baptism.

Regarding the thesis thus far, a rite begins in the ethical nexus of home-community relations and culminates in the practice itself. However, we cannot therefore conclude that raising a goat, harvesting a field, or checking one's body for disease are sacred rites.

Many make a three-part division of the Torah's teaching, which clarifies what parts of the Law are to be kept and what makes for sacraments. The Torah, under this heuristic, consists of civil, ceremonial, and moral laws. The Torah's civil and moral laws need to be re-contextualized apart from the theocracy of Israel to our current circumstance in order for Jews and Christians to follow them. For instance, most of us no longer have an ox that is in the habit of goring people (Exod 21:28). However, we do understand that if we own something capable of lethal force (e.g., a car) and we do not properly restrain it (e.g., we do not set the brakes when parked on a hill), then we ought to be held liable. The ceremonial laws of the New Testament, under the Protestant understanding, are all ritualized into the two ordinances instituted specifically by Jesus: Communion and baptism.[10]

This division of the law might be a helpful heuristic for those trying to recognize basic features of the Torah, but too vague to serve as a way of thinking about Israel's rites as a whole. If Israelites bring their ethical behavior with their sacrifice to the temple, a web of relationships that encompasses all of life, then in what sense can we make a useful distinction between the moral and ceremonial laws? This distinction is precisely what the prophets chastised and so we must handle the division carefully.

If first century Jews such as John the Baptist and Jesus were ritualizing the Torah's rites, then the presumption of ritual continuity into the New Testament's theology must be more highly regarded. For instance, two fundamental ritual practices appear to be basic throughout the Hebrew Bible: Sabbath and marriage, in that order.

---

10. For instance, questions 92 and 93 of the *Westminster Confession of Faith*'s Shorter Catechism: "What is a sacrament? A sacrament is a holy ordinance instituted by Christ; wherein, by sensible signs, Christ, and the benefits of the new covenant, are represented, sealed, and applied to believers. Which are the sacraments of the New Testament? The sacraments of the New Testament are, baptism, and the Lord's Supper." Article 33 of the *Belgic Confession* follows a similar line, but admits to the "invisible" quality of rites to do something to the participant: "We believe that our good God, mindful of our crudeness and weakness, has ordained sacraments for us to seal his promises in us, to pledge his good will and grace toward us, and also to nourish and sustain our faith. He has added these to the Word of the gospel to represent better to our external senses both what he enables us to understand by his Word and what he does inwardly in our hearts, confirming in us the salvation he imparts to us. For they are visible signs and seals of something internal and invisible, by means of which God works in us through the power of the Holy Spirit. So they are not empty and hollow signs to fool and deceive us, for their truth is Jesus Christ, without whom they would be nothing. Moreover, we are satisfied with the number of sacraments that Christ our Master has ordained for us. There are only two: the sacrament of baptism and the Holy Supper of Jesus Christ."

Sacred Rites not Considered Sacraments?

The Sabbath is clearly one of the most discussed rites in the Hebrew Bible, sewn into every Levitical holiday (Lev 23) and premised upon creation (Gen 1). The prophets of Israel viciously attack its absence as the reason for epistemic blindness.[11] Sabbath constitutes one of the most patent instances of ritual to be kept by Israel, imbued with meaning from the creation of the cosmos itself. The rite is so obvious that it gets little attention in and of itself in the New Testament. If Paul truly depicts Jesus as being present and active in the creation (Col 1:15–20), then Jesus himself theologically instituted Sabbath without it ever being ritualized in the New Testament.

Similarly, marriage is presented in the biblical literature as a rite fundamental to creation itself. The rite is so basic that no script is ever given for the rite. Outside of a few glimpses such as Jacob's sham wedding to Leah (Gen 29:21–25), we do not know what ancient Patriarchal or Hebrew weddings consisted of. From this glimpse, we see a wedding party, a feast, and a wedding bed.[12] The actual ceremony is completely obscured to us throughout the Torah. However, the Torah considers marriage to be a normative ritual practice, so structurally basic to the cosmos that even the event in creation goes without comment. Both Sabbath and marriage present a problem in that they are foundational rites for Israel, instituted at creation and presumed by every biblical author, yet neither rite has a script to follow. However, the Hebrew Bible and New Testament's silence on a marriage ceremony does not indicate its absence from ritual practices. Rather, their silence tends to presume continuity of practice and the flexibility of ritual script. This to say, that everyone who scripts a marriage ceremony or Sabbath day's activities is doing constructive biblical theology. I assert here that we ought to think of marriage and Sabbath scripting as epistemological tasks as well, disposing us to know.

Preparation for ritual practice ought to count as well. What is clear from Scripture, in this treatment, is that a rite brings the visible elements to bear on the practitioner and the practitioner brings his invisible preparation to the rite. Like an examinee brings her invisible preparative studies to the exam, the ritual is epistemically efficacious only if training in the larger ethical nexus of Torah occurs.

If the term "sacrament" is meant to capture the sacred notion surrounding particular practices, we can certainly grant that some moments in life appear to us as more sacred than others. Surely the rites of Israel drew upon that abundance of the sacred, where it was most often related to the spatial loca-

---

11. E.g., Isa 56:2; 58:13; Jer 17:17–21; Hos 2:13; Amos 8:5.

12. There are varying views of marriage even as a ritual. In some states in America, persons become common law married by merely living together for more than a few years. Their life together, more specifically their sexual life together, acts as the rite. When in western Kenya, I was informed that if a man and woman live together for more than a week, they are considered married.

tion in reference to YHWH. In the temple, the closer to the Holy of Holies one got, so too purification, atonement, and representative rites intensified (i.e., Yom Kippur). However, the fact that Christian rites are ritualizations of Israel-ite rites must bear on any discussion about what is considered a sacrament and what is not. The traditional Protestant measuring stick for sacraments— whether or not Jesus instituted the rite—appears insufficient, as this ignores the practice of ritualization—how the rite appropriates and critiques the for-mer practice. As well, Sabbath and marriage as instituted at creation are left to the side of the discussion.

A productive solution to this disparate treatment of rites might be found in pursuing the epistemology of Christian ritual alongside these other aspects. Avoiding the dual errors of overdetermining symbolic meaning and attempt-ing to discern the meaning apart from the practice, the questions of sacramen-tal theology might have to change. The question might not be: What does this ritual mean in and of itself (betraying the thinking-acting dichotomy)? Rather, Christian rites must be approached with a different set of questions in mind:

> How must we prepare for this rite?
> How is this rite a continuation and critique of the former rite?
> Who is scripting our participation and upon what understanding?
> What are we disposed to know through this practice?
> How does this rite dispose a community of discerning voices to know that which the rite can point them toward?

Communion as Ritual Knowing

I want to briefly examine how our embodied practice can be assessed accord-ing to the findings of this work. First, I consider how we cyborgically extend into the rite. And second, I pursue some basic critical framework for evaluat-ing our disposition to know.

How do we extend ourselves into a ritual and what does it dispose us to recognize? Only the former question is answerable, but we must always criti-cally evaluate the latter in our practices. It is not my wish to espouse an object of knowledge garnered through rites. However, if I cannot subjectively point to critically engaged learning through those practices, then I should rightly suspect the epistemic efficacy of the ritual.

For instance, it might not be entirely clear how we cyborgically extend ourselves through the tool of Communion. I offer here a supposal of what that might be. In the practice pictured to us in the New Testament, Communion is described most basically as 1) a communal meal and 2) a remembrance prac-tice. The practice, of course, on the night of the Passover is a specially prepared meal.[13] It is not that the food items are ritualized (e.g., lamb's flesh, bread, water, wine, etc.), but that the communal meal itself is ritualized, imbued with new meaning. And so the epistemologically oriented ritual of Passover is itself ritualized by Jesus in the instantiation of Communion. The Last Supper, a ritualization of Passover, inaugurates a regular meal that came to be known as the Lord's Supper.

How do we cyborgically extend ourselves into this rite? Though I can only conjecture, an internal and external cyborgic connection can be explored. Internally, I do not think it is fair to rule out the gruesomeness of the ritual as a means of consumption. John's Gospel certainly plays up this exact facet of the Lord's Supper in Jesus' early discourses. Jesus even scares away most of his followers with the prospect of cannibalistic consumption, using it as a test to discern those who genuinely trusted him (John 6:53–56):

> Truly, truly, I say to you, unless you eat the flesh of the Son of Man and drink his blood, you have no life in you. Whoever feeds on my flesh and drinks my blood has eternal life, and I will raise him up on the last day. For my flesh is true food, and my blood is true drink. Whoever feeds on my flesh and drinks my blood abides in me, and I in him.

John's gospel clearly portrays Jesus' teaching of cannibalism as gruesome, *without any reference to a symbolic version of it* (i.e., Communion). The direct result of these eternal-life-via-cannibalism sayings is that all but the twelve disciples stop following Jesus (John 6:60, 66): "When many of his disciples heard it, they said, 'This is a hard saying; who can listen to it?' . . . After this many of his disciples turned back and no longer walked with him." And Jesus acknowledges that the grotesque descriptions were meant to test, to weed out those who God meant as disciples from the pretenders. In the end, whatever else we desperately want to affirm about the Lord's Supper, there is some way in which practitioners are meant to eat Jesus as if they are eating an animal used in Passover's sacrificial offering.

When Jesus later inaugurates the ritual, it cannot be missed that he conceives of Communion as a sort of fleshy consumption with which Torah-keeping Jews would have been directly familiar. Having participated in such real flesh-eating rituals as Passover in the home and peace offerings in the temple, the cyborgic connection is not an extension, but a type of internalized consumption. This is all to say that whatever the consumption of flesh was meant to do for Israelites in Passover, it is meant to do in Communion.

Certainly we could draw links of remembrance to consumption. While eating the flesh, our thinking and discernment are being shaped. For instance, consuming the animal's flesh at Passover reminds me of the sacrificial killing, which leads me to remember the divine judgment of death that would have

---

13. John's Gospel records the Last Supper on the night before Passover (John 13:1), while the synoptic gospels record it as the Passover meal.

otherwise come to my household. Not only does the lamb die for my household's sake, but we are nourished from its death. The blood that saves me from the wrath of God is a signifier to my household that we have been saved, but also signals to the Angel of Death to spare us.

The above thoughts represent a type of reasoning that could be shaped by the practice of Communion. Further, this kind of reasoning makes deep points of contact between the Passover event and the crucifixion event. We cannot miss that the act of consumption and the historical understanding of its context means that we are cyborgically employing these physical elements in order to reason and therefore recognize something. The rite disposes us to know. Moreover, the constant contact within the rite reasons with the practitioner by placing her between historical understanding, social body, and the embodied actions themselves. These form her, disposing her to see something otherwise unavailable to her.

Externally, Communion is practiced like Passover in a social body: the church. In this sense, we extend ourselves into that social body through this rite. I can only offer my subjective speculations at this point by my contemporary practice of Communion. The function of the ritual enables me to recognize myself as a part of this social body, shaped by the ritual. Whatever the rite disposes me to know, it must somehow cohere to the polyphonic sense of discernment collected in the social body called the church. Similarly, a single scientist cannot have "scientific knowledge." That kind of knowing is not considered properly "scientific" until the wisdom and experience of the scientific community deem it so through the appropriate channels and processes. And so Communion, as a ritual that shapes the knower, simultaneously allows her to grasp her extension into and participation within the social body.

What do I recognize and then discern through this rite? The nature of the body metaphor (i.e., a group of people united to one organism) is palpably recognized through the ritual. Also, how does God work through these people in this location and on what basis? The Lord's Supper seems to direct us in answering such a question by ritualizing our gathering and our focus. The implications of that construct, invisible to the naked eye of the observer, can be discerned through repeated practice of communion. Many things are possible here and I require the disparate voices of participants to help me discern more profound patterns from learned by the sacrament.

Implications for a Theological Reading of Scripture

If the theological reading of Scripture shows any deference to what Scripture seems to be advocating, then the implications of my thesis both affirm and indict the practice of theologians. The embodied and rituated life of the theologian has as much to do with the traditions and intellectual practices that she brings to the task of reading Scripture as anything else. Three results of this focus on sacramental epistemology moderate how we read Scripture theologically: the relation of embodied practices to our understanding of Scripture, the import of ritualed life for the sake of understanding Scripture, and the ritual practice of reading Scripture.

First, the ritualed life of the reader shapes her reading of Scripture. This manifests in at least three ways: the habituation of the individual, embodying specific rituals in order to know, and participation in the social body.

Presuming that all of our embodied life shapes us in some way, no matter how subtle, it is inconceivable to excise that formative practice from our reading. Even more, returning to the matter of analogical reasoning, our embodied life often, and possibly always, provides the very analog from which we conceptualize the world. If theology is a form of pattern-finding and conceptualizing the world of the text, then the necessary connection between our embodied life and our reading of Scripture appears obvious and direct.

As an example, though not an indictment, it is difficult for us to read Paul Tillich's theology at its more radical points without any consideration of what his wife Hannah described as Tillich's "slide down the ladder to pornography, using women for his peculiarities."[14] The infamy of his womanizing, the paces he habitually put his body through, seem to weigh heavily on our minds when considering his version of theological anthropology. We might be flippant about it or unfairly distracted by it, but his embodied life certainly does not appear to be extraneous to his reading of Scripture. The same could be said of John Howard Yoder's reported sexual misconduct. These extreme cases only clarify that the embodied life of the theologian matters, and matters to how we understand their reading of Scripture, especially if she seeks to justify her actions according to Scripture (which neither Tillich nor Yoder did).

Second, and despite instances of inconsistency, we should consider ritual practice informing our reading of Scripture in a positive sense. Practicing rituals *in order to know* inextricably pervades our understanding of Scripture. As is so often said in many disciplines, rites dispose us to know no matter what. Hence, Scripture focuses on practicing the right rites in order to understand Scripture. Let me offer two examples. Sukkot, as I have previously argued, is meant to change Israel's view of the same known exodus story (Lev 23:42–43). There is something about the practice of Sukkot that will craft their view of the exodus event, known through the Scriptural story itself, that can only be known by the practice.

In the New Testament, Paul's admonition to the church of Colossae begins with a charge to combat false frameworks with a particular ritualed life that they have received (Col 2:6–7).[15] This way of living is so that they "may be

14. Hannah Tillich, *From Time to Time* (New York: Stein and Day, 1973), 103.

15. It is a broader task than mine to piece together precisely what that early church's ritual life consisted of. Nevertheless, we only need to permit that Paul had some particular ritual life in mind when he refers to living the life they have "received." For the particular ritual life of the early church, see Jonathan Schwiebert,

filled with the knowledge of God's will in all spiritual *wisdom and understanding*" (Col 1:9). Their ritual life also acts as an antidote to the false philosophies of this world and distracting ritual practices of angel worship, new moon festivals, and Sabbath (Col 2:6–7). Further, notice that the false ritual practices lead to "the appearance of wisdom through self-imposed piety, humility, and severe treatment of the body" (Col 2:23).[16] *In other words, rituals will either lead to the appearance of wisdom or the true wisdom of being revealed in Christ.*

This to say, Paul is writing to instruct the Colossians and appears to presume that their embodied and ritual life will affect how they hear his words. Moreover, those Jewish interpreters of Torah practice (e.g., the ones advocating new moon festivals and restrictive Sabbath; cf. Ps 81:3; Amos 8:5) distract them with practices that alter their view of Scripture, only offering "the appearance of wisdom." A properly rituated life acts as *the way* they can understand Paul's words and the gospel that they have received (Col 1:5, 23).

Additionally, ritual participation as an individual is clearly insufficient to understand our reading of Scripture. One of the primary rites of the New Testament, Communion, intentionally ritualizes a collective meal. It may seem obvious by now, but the rite of Communion as a communal ritual must have an effect on our reading of the Last Supper, but other less obvious texts too. Genesis 3 focuses in on the woman's distorted vision of the trees under the serpent's sway. Hence, she *takes* and *eats* from the tree of prohibition, along with the man, and they *know* of their nakedness.

These very actions of *giving, taking,* and *eating*—δίδωμι, λάβετε and φάγετε respectively, in the LXX and NT—are sacramentally reversed in Matthew's depiction of Communion. If we compare Genesis 3:6 (LXX) with Matthew 26:26, we find that we can no longer hear the words "he *gave* . . . *take* and *eat*" free from our reading of Genesis 3 and our practice. Further, our ritual practice reveals that Genesis 3 is fundamentally a problem for the community, not merely an individual's sin. We can no longer read Matthew's account of the Last Supper without thinking about our participation in the community: "after blessing it [he] broke it and *gave* (δίδωμι) it to the disciples, and said, '*Take* (λάβετε), *eat* (φάγετε); this is my body'" (Matt 26:26). The fact that Jesus' death and resurrection feed, and therefore, shape the knowledge of the Christian community is known through the symbiotic relationship between ritual participation and reading Scripture in light of that participation.

Third, reading Scripture is a ritualized practice. The way we read it—how we ritualize the act of reading—determines what we will know. I was a bit sur-

---

Knowledge and the Coming Kingdom: The Didache's Meal Ritual and its Place in Early Christianity (LNTS 373; New York: T&T Clark, 2008).

16. "The appearance of wisdom" is the translators' rendering of σοφιας in rhetoric of Paul's argument in Colossians 2, or taking λογον to be related to "wisdom" (as in "the report of wisdom"). The phrase "the appearance of" is found, inter alia, in the following modern English translations: New American Standard Bible, New Revised Standard Version, English Standard Version, and New International Version.

prised when I began working with some religious Jewish scholars who were brilliant and devout, yet did not seem familiar with some of the content of the Torah. This was even more surprising when I realized that they had been reciting the Torah every single week in their Kabbalat Shabbat synagogue service. How could it be that they could sing the Torah to me, but sometimes be unfamiliar with the content of the biblical texts? This was not true for everyone, but certainly a few scholars appeared to know the Talmud better than the Torah and sometimes had to remember parts of the Torah by where it shows up in the Talmudic debates.

One explanation that I have heard for this phenomenon is that the ritual of reading is different in Kabbalat Shabbat services than in the typical expositional sermon of Protestant tradition. It is not that one is superior to the other. However, some religious Jews (like some Protestants who might read disproportionate amounts of systematic theology rather than Scripture) simply do not engage Scripture reading as an expositional task, and hence, they do not see the same things as those who do. Indeed, a large sector of religious Judaism does not believe there can be such a thing as theology in Judaism, a position that must be formed to some extent by their rituals of reading. The same could be said of devotional Scripture reading practiced by many Evangelical Christians. The daily ritual of reading very small passages of Scripture and attempting to discern transcendent principles for everyday life certainly shapes the reading and the theology that issues from it.

It is not my task to describe biblically advocated models for ritual reading, another book in itself, but only to suggest that reading is a rite. Thus, the position of our bodies, the translations we read, the amount read, and what is expected to happen because of the ritual of reading all shape our theological understanding of the content of Scripture.

Aims and Claims

Finally, the goal of this work has been to show the philosophical confluence regarding the epistemic function of rituals in scientific inquiry, ritual theory, and the biblical literature. To demonstrate their commensurability, the philosophical examination of embodied knowing was brought to bear. This analysis included the constructs of phenomenology, neural plasticity, habituation, cyborgic extension, and analogical reasoning. Essentially, I argued for knowing as a type of movement: an embodied process that 1) began with insensitivity to a present pattern, 2) came to a distinct recognition of that pattern, and 3) persisted through to discernment of the transcendence of the pattern.

The radical claim of this book is that a similar presumption about knowledge appears both explicitly and presumptively throughout the biblical literature. In fact, the biblical authors force modern readers to rethink thin contemporary accounts of propositional epistemology in order to reckon the body's primary role in biblical accounts of knowing.

Consequently, any attempt at a sacramental theology that regards the authority of Scripture must reckon with this principle: *we practice rites to know.* Moreover, it is not that rituals imbue knowledge. Rather, human knowing is ritualed, inaugurated in embodied practices and extended through the skilled of discernment within a community. Although popularists pit science against religion, I have attempted to show that their epistemological processes profoundly resemble one another. Likewise, Christian theology respects ritual knowing not by commanding identical practices for all Christians uniformly. Israel's theology of rites resists egalitarian approaches to participation. Rather, the biblical literature esteems the cultivation of polyphonic discernment through disparate participation in community. This disparate practice of rites need not be viewed as elitist or oppressive, but just as it was shown to strengthen confidence within scientific understanding, diverse involvement in rites strengthens the community's discernment.

Hence, the epistemic function of ritual ought to cause a reappraisal of not just theology, but all endeavors to know. Nevertheless, any system of Christian theology begins on specious footing if its epistemological tenets are not grounded in the embodied, social, and ritual nature of knowing found throughout the biblical texts.

Bibliography

Audi, Robert. *Epistemology: A Contemporary Introduction To the Theory of Knowledge*. 3rd ed. New York: Routledge, 2011.

Avrahami, Yael. *The Sense of Scripture: Sensory Perception in the Hebrew Bible*. LHBOTS 545. New York: T&T Clark International, 2012.

Azuma, Hideki, Shiro Hori, Masao Nakanishi, Shinji Fujimoto, Norimasa Ichikawa, and Toshiaki A. Furukawa. "An intervention to improve the interrater reliability of clinical EEG interpretations." *PCN* 57, no. 5 (October 2003): 485–89.

Baadsgaard, Aubrey, Janet Monge, and Richard L. Zettler. "Bludgeoned, Burned, and Beautified: Reevaluating Mortuary Practices in the Royal Cemetery of Ur." Pages 125–58 in *Sacred Killing: The Archeology of Sacrifice in the Ancient Near East*. Edited by Anne Porter and Glenn M. Schwartz. Winona Lake, Ind.: Eisenbrauns, 2012.

Bakhtin, M. M. *The Dialogic Imagination: Four Essays*. Edited by Michael Holquist. Translated by Caryl Emerson and Michael Holquist. Austin: University of Texas Press, 1981.

Barr, James. *The Concept of Biblical Theology: An Old Testament Perspective*. London: S. C. M., 1999.

_____. *The Garden of Eden and the Hope of Immortality*. London: S. C. M., 1992.

_____. *The Semantics of Biblical Language*. Oxford: Oxford University Press, 1967.

Barth, Karl. *Church Dogmatics*. 4 vols. Edinburgh: T&T Clark, 1936–77.

Bartholomew, Craig and Michael W. Goheen. "Story and Biblical Theology." Pages 144–71 in *Out of Egypt: Biblical Theology and Biblical Interpretation*. Edited by Mary Healy, Karl Möller, Robin Parry, Craig Bartholomew, and Anthony C. Thiselton. SHS. Grand Rapids, MI: Zondervan, 2004.

Bartholomew, Craig. *Where Mortals Dwell: A Christian View of Place for Today*. Grand Rapids, MI: Baker Academic, 2012.

Beattie, Geoffrey. *Visible Thought: The New Psychology of Body Language*. New York: Routledge, 2003.

Bell, Catherine. *Ritual Theory, Ritual Practice*. New York: Cambridge University Press, 2009.

Bennema, Cornelius. "Christ, the Spirit and the Knowledge of God: A Study in Johannine Epistemology." Pages 107–33 in *The Bible and Epistemology: Biblical Soundings on the Knowledge of God*. Edited by Mary Healy and Robin Parry. Milton Keynes, England: Paternoster, 2007.

Berg, Werner. "Der Sündenfall Abrahams und Saras nach Gen 16:1–6." *BN* 19 (1982): 7–14.

Bergen, Wesley. "Studying Ancient Israelite Ritual: Methodological Considerations." *RC* 1, no. 5 (2007): 579–86.

Bibb, Brian D. *Ritual Words and Narrative Worlds in the Book of Leviticus.* LHBOTS 480. New York: T&T Clark, 2009.

Biederman, Irving and Eric E. Cooper. "Size invariance in visual object priming." *JEPHPP* 18 (February 1992): 121–33.

Black, Max. "The Identity of Indiscernibles." *Mind* 61 (April 1952): 153–64.

Boman, Thorleif. *Hebrew Thought Compared with Greek.* LHD. London: SCM, 1960.

Bourget, David and David J. Chalmers. "What Do Philosophers Believe?" *PS* 170, no. 3 (September 2014): 465–500.

Brown, Francis, S. R. Driver, and Charles A. Briggs, eds. *A Hebrew and English Lexicon of the Old Testament.* Oxford: Clarendon Press, 1906.

Bruce, F. F. *This Is That: The New Testament Development of Some Old Testament Themes.* Exeter, England: Paternoster, 1968.

Buber, Martin. *The Legend of Baal-Shem.* Translated by Maurice Friedman. New York: Routledge, 2005.

Bynum, Caroline. "Why All The Fuss about the Body? A Medievalist's Perspective." *CI* 22 (Autumn 1995): 1–33.

Calaway, Jared C. *The Sabbath and the Sanctuary: Access to God in the Letter to the Hebrews and Its Priestly Context.* WUNT 2/349. Tübingen: Mohr Siebeck, 2013.

Calvin, Jean. *Institutes of the Christian Religion.* Translated by Henry Beveridge. Edinburgh: Calvin Translation Society, 1845–46.

_____. *Commentaries on the First Book of Moses, Called Genesis.* 2 vols. Translated by Henry Beveridge. Edinburgh: Calvin Translation Society, 1847.

Carasik, Michael. *Theologies of the Mind in Biblical Israel.* SBibLit 85. Oxford: Peter Lang, 2005.

Carter, Elizabeth. "On Human and Animal Sacrifice." Pages 237–90 in *Sacred Killing: The Archeology of Sacrifice in the Ancient Near East.* Edited by Anne Porter and Glenn M. Schwartz. Winona Lake, Ind.: Eisenbrauns, 2012.

Cassuto, Umberto. *A Commentary on the Book of Genesis.* Jerusalem: Magnes, The Hebrew University, 1961.

Cavallin, Clemens. *Ritualization and Human Interiority.* Copenhagen: Museum Tusculanum Press, 2013.

Childs, Brevard. *Biblical Theology of the Old and New Testaments: Theological Reflection on the Christian Bible.* Minneapolis: Fortress, 1992.

_____. *The Book of Exodus.* OTL. Louisville, KY: Westminster John Knox, 1974.

Chilson, Richard. *Catholic Christianity: A Guide to the Way, the Truth, and the Life.* New York: Paulist Press, 1987.

Chilton, Bruce. *Rabbi Jesus: An Intimate Biography.* New York: Doubleday, 2000.

_____. *The Temple of Jesus: His Sacrificial Program Within a Cultural History of Sacrifice.* University Park, PA: Pennsylvania State University Press, 1992.

Clark, Andy. *Natural-Born Cyborgs: Minds, Technologies, and the Future of Human Intelligence.* Oxford: Oxford University Press, 2003.

Clark, Malcolm. "A Legal Background to the Yahwist's Use of 'Good and Evil' in Genesis 2–3." *JBL* 88 (1969): 266–78.

Collins, Adela Yarbro. *Mark*. Edited by Harold W. Attridge. Hermeneia. Minneapolis: Fortress, 2007.

Crisp, Oliver D. "On Analytic Theology." Pages 33–53 in *Analytic Theology: New Essays in the Philosophy of Theology*. Edited by Oliver D. Crisp and Michael C. Rea. New York: Oxford University Press, 2009.

Crownfield, David R. "Consciousness and the Voices of the Gods: An Essay Review." *JAAR* 42, no. 2 (1978): 193–202.

Cuneo, Terence. "Ritual Knowledge," *FP* 31 (2014): 365–85.

Dewey, Joanna. "The Survival of Mark's Gospel: A Good Story?" *JBL* 123, no. 3 (Autumn 2004): 495–507.

Dorman, Ted M. "The Future of Biblical Theology." Pages 250–66 in *Biblical Theology: Retrospect and Prospect*. Edited by Scott J. Hafemann. Downer's Grove, IL: IVP Academic, 2002.

Douglas, Mary. *Leviticus as Literature*. New York: Oxford University Press, 2000.

——————. *Natural Symbols: Explorations in Cosmology*. 2nd ed. New York: Routledge, 1996.

——————. *Purity and Danger: An Analysis of the Concept of Pollution and Taboo*. New York: Routledge, 1966.

Dumbrell, William J. *Covenant and Creation: An Old Testament Covenantal Theology*. Exeter, England: Paternoster, 1984.

Durham, John I. *Exodus*. WBC 3. Waco, TX: Word Books, 1987.

Eberhard, Christian A. *The Sacrifice of Jesus: Understanding Atonement Biblically*. Minneapolis: Fortress, 2011.

Einstein, Albert. "To Max Born." 3 March 1947, Letter 84 in *The Born-Einstein Letters: Friendship, Politics, and Physics in Uncertain Times*. Edited by Diana Buchwald and Kip S. Thorne. Translated by Irene Born. New York: Macmillan, 2005.

Feldman, Richard. *Epistemology*. FPS. Upper Saddle River, NJ: Prentice Hall, 2003.

Foer, Jonathan Safran. *Eating Animals*. New York: Bay Books, 2010.

Fortes, Meyer. "Ritual and Office in Tribal Society." Pages 53–88 in *Essays On the Ritual of Social Relations*. Edited by Max Gluckman. New York: Manchester University Press, 1966.

Fox, Michael. *Proverbs 1-9: A New Translation With Introduction and Commentary*. AB. New York: Doubleday, 2000.

Frame, John M. *The Doctrine of the Knowledge of God*. Phillipsburg, NJ: Presbyterian & Reformed, 1987.

Gadamer, Hans Georg. *Truth and Method*. Translated by Joel Wensheimer and Donald G. Marshall. 2nd ed. New York: Continuum, 2012.

Gane, Roy E. *Cult and Character: Purification Offerings, Day of Atonement, and Theodicy*. Winona Lake, Ind.: Eisenbrauns, 2005.

Geller, Stephen. *Sacred Enigmas: Literary Religion in the Hebrew Bible*. New York: Routledge, 1996.

Girard, René. *The Scapegoat.* Translated by Yvonne Freccero. Baltimore, MD: John Hopkins University Press, 1986.

Goldman, Alvin. *Pathways to Knowledge: Private and Public.* New York: Oxford University Press, 2004.

Gonzalez, Justo L. *A History of Christian Thought: From the Beginnings to the Council of Chalcedon.* 3 vols. Nashville, TN: Abington, 1970.

Gorman, Frank H., Jr. *Ideology of Ritual: Space, Time and Status in the Priestly Theology.* LHBOTS 91. Sheffield, England: JSOT Press, 1990.

Goslinga, Gillian. "On Cakti-Filled Bodies and Divinities: An Ethnographic Perspective on Animal Sacrifice and Ritual in Contemporary South India." Pages 33–56 in *Sacred Killing: The Archeology of Sacrifice in the Ancient Near East.* Edited by Anne Porter and Glenn M. Schwartz. Winona Lake, Ind.: Eisenbrauns, 2012.

Green, Joel B. *Body, Soul, and Human Life: the Nature of Humanity in the Bible.* Grand Rapids, MI: Baker Academic, 2008.

Grene, Marjorie. *The Knower and the Known.* London: Faber & Faber, 1966.

Grinnell, Frederick. *Everyday Practice of Science: Where Intuition and Passion Meet Objectivity and Logic.* New York: Oxford University Press, 2009.

Grisanti, Michael A. "Was Israel Unable to Respond to God? A Study of Deuteronomy 29:2–4." *BS* 163 (April-June 2006): 176–96.

Gruenwald, Ithamar. *Rituals and Ritual Theory in Ancient Israel.* Atlanta: Society of Biblical Literature, 2003.

Haivry, Ofir. "Act and Comprehend." *Azure* 1 (5756/1996): 5–42.

Hanson, Norwood. *Observation and Explanation: A Guide to Philosophy of Science.* London: Allen and Unwin, 1972.

Harris, R. Laird, ed. *Theological Wordbook of the Old Testament.* 2 vols. Chicago: Moody, 1980.

Hasel, Gerhard. "The Meaning of the Animal Rite in Genesis 15." *JSOT* 19 (1981): 61–78.

Hazony, Yoram. *The Philosophy of Hebrew Scripture: an Introduction.* New York: Cambridge University Press, 2012.

Hebert, A. G. "'Faithfulness' and 'Faith'." *RTR* 14 (June 1955): 33–40.

Hempel, Carl Gustav. "Studies in the Logic of Confirmation (I.)." *Mind* New Series 54, no. 213 (1945): 1–26.

Heschel, Abraham Joshua. *God in Search of Man: A Philosophy of Judaism.* New York: Farrar, Straus & Giroux, 1955.

Hesse, Brian, Paula Wapnish, and Jonathan Greer. "Scripts of Animal Sacrifice in Levantine Culture-History." Pages 217–36 in *Sacred Killing: The Archeology of Sacrifice in the Ancient Near East.* Edited by Anne Porter and Glenn M. Schwartz. Winona Lake, Ind.: Eisenbrauns, 2012.

Hicks, Peter. *Evangelicals and Truth: A Creative Proposal for a Postmodern Age.* Leicester, England: Apollos, 1998.

Hooker, Morna. "Isaiah in Mark's Gospel." Pages 35–50 in *Isaiah in the New Testament.* Edited by Steve Moyise and Maarten J.J. Menken. London: T&T Clark, 2005.

Horsley, Richard A. with Jonathan A. Draper. *Whoever Hear You Hears Me: Prophets, Performance, and Tradition in Q.* Harrisburg, PA: Trinity Press International, 1999.

Hrobon, Bohdan. *Ethical Dimension of Cult in the Book of Isaiah.* BZAW 418. Berlin: de Gruyter, 2010.

Hubert, Henri and Marcel Mauss. *Sacrifice: Its Nature and Function.* Translated by W. D. Halls. Chicago: University of Chicago Press, 1898.

Iverson, Kelley R. *Gentiles in the Gospel of Mark: 'Even the Dogs Under the Table Eat the Children's Crumbs'.* Edited by Mark Goodacre. LNTS 339. London: T&T Clark, 2007.

Jacobs, Struan. "Michael Polanyi and Thomas Kuhn: Priority and Credit." *TD* 33, no. 2 (2006–2007): 25–36.

Jaynes, Julian. *The Origin of Consciousness in the Breakdown of the Bicameral Mind.* Toronto: University of Toronto Press, 1976.

Jeeves, Malcolm and Warren S. Brown. *Neuroscience, Psychology, and Religion Illusions, Delusions, and Realities about Human Nature.* West Conshohocken, Ind.: Templeton Foundation, 2009.

Johnson, Andrew M. "Error and Epistemological Process in the Pentateuch and Mark's Gospel: A Biblical Theology of Knowing from Foundational Texts." Ph.D. diss., University of Saint Andrews, 2011.

Johnson, Dru. *Scripture's Knowing: A Companion to Biblical Epistemology.* CCS. Eugene, OR: Cascade, 2015.

_____. *Biblical Knowing: A Scriptural Epistemology of Error.* Eugene, OR: Cascade, 2013.

Johnson, Mark. *The Body in the Mind: The Bodily Basis of Meaning, Imagination, and Reason.* Chicago: University of Chicago Press, 1987.

Jonte-Pace, Diane. Foreword to *Ritual Theory, Ritual Practice*, by Catherine Bell. New York: Oxford University Press, 2009.

Kant, Immanuel. *Groundwork for The Metaphysics of Morals.* Translated by Mary Gregor. New York: Cambridge University Press, 1997.

Kelber, Werner H. *The Kingdom in Mark: A New Place and a New Time.* Minneapolis: Fortress, 1974.

Kermode, Frank. *The Genesis of Secrecy.* The Charles Eliot Norton Lectures, 1977–1978. London: Harvard University Press, 1979.

Klawans, Jonathan. *Purity, Sacrifice, and the Temple: Symbolism and Supersessionism in the Study of Ancient Judaism.* Oxford: Oxford University Press, 2006.

Kline, Meredith. *By Oath Consigned: A Reinterpretation of the Covenant Signs of Circumcision and Baptism.* Grand Rapids, MI: Eerdmans, 1975.

Klingbeil, Gerald A. *Bridging the Gap: Ritual and Ritual Texts in the Bible.* Edited by Richard S. Hess. BBRS. Winona Lake, Ind.: Eisenbrauns, 2007.

Kuhn, Thomas. *The Structure of Scientific Revolutions.* 3rd ed. Chicago: University of Chicago Press, 1996.

Kvanvig, Jonathan L. *The Intellectual Virtues and the Life of the Mind: On the Place of the Virtues in Epistemology.* SECT. Savage, MD: Rowman & Littlefield, 1992.

Lafferty, Theresa V. *The Prophetic Critique of the Priority of the Cult: A Study of Amos 5:21-24 and Isaiah 1:10-17*. Eugene, OR: Pickwick, 2012.

Lakoff, George, and Mark Johnson. *Metaphors We Live By*. Chicago: University of Chicago Press, 1980.

Lakoff, George. *Women, Fire, and Dangerous Things: What Categories Reveal about the Mind*. Chicago: University of Chicago Press, 1989.

Legare, Cristine H. and André L. Souza. "Evaluating Ritual Efficacy: Evidence from the Supernatural." *Cognition* 124 (2012): 1–15.

Levelt, Willem J. M. and Stephanie Kelter. "Surface Form and Memory in Question Answering." *CP* 14 (1982): 78–106.

Loader, William. *The New Testament on Sexuality*. Grand Rapids, MI: Eerdmans, 2012.

Longenecker, Bruce W. "The Narrative Approach to Paul: an Early Retrospective." *CBR* 1, no. 1 (October 2002): 94–103.

Lynch, Michael E. "Sacrifice and the Transformation of the Animal Body into a Scientific Object: Laboratory Culture and Ritual Practice in the Neurosciences." *SSS* 18, no. 2 (May 1988): 265–289.

McClymond, Katherine. *Beyond Sacred Violence: A Comparative Study of Sacrifice*. Baltimore: Johns Hopkins University Press, 2008.

McKeown, James. *Genesis*. THOT. Grand Rapids, MI: Eerdmans, 2008.

Mac Lane, Saunders. "Mathematical Models: A Sketch For the Philosophy of Mathematics." *AMA* 88, no. 7 (1981): 462–72.

MacDonald, Nathan. "The Hermeneutics and Genesis of the Red Cow Ritual." *HTR* 105, no. 3 (2012): 351–71.

—————. *Deuteronomy and the Meaning of "Monotheism"*. FAT 2/Reihe 1. Tubingen: Mohr Siebeck, 2003.

Maimonides, Moses. *Guide to the Perplexed*. Translated by M. Friedländer. Skokie, IL: Varda Books, 2002.

Meek, Esther L. *Longing To Know: The Philosophy of Knowledge for Ordinary People*. Grand Rapids, MI: Brazos, 2003.

—————. "'Recalled to Life': Contact with Reality." *TD* 26 (1999–2000): 72–83.

Mehrabian, Albert and Morton Wiener. "Decoding of Inconsistent Communications." *JPSP* 6 (1967): 109–114.

Merleau-Ponty, Maurice. *Phenomenology of Perception*. Translated by Colin Smith. New York: Routledge, 1962.

—————. *The Primacy of Perception*. Edited by James Edie. Evanston, IL: Northwestern University Press, 1964.

Milgrom, Jacob. *Leviticus 23–27*. AB. New Haven: Yale University Press, 2001.

—————. "The Paradox of the Red Cow (Num xix.)." *VT* 31 (1981): 62–72.

Moberly, R. W. L. *The Theology of the Book of Genesis*. Edited by Brent A. Strawn and Patrick D. Miller. OTT. Cambridge: Cambridge University Press, 2009.

—————. "Did the serpent get it right?" *JTS* 39 (April 1988): 23–24.

Mody, Cyrus C. M. "A Little Dirt Never Hurt Anyone: Knowledge-Making and Contamination in Materials Science." *SSS* 31, no. 1 (February 2001): 7–36.

Moser, Paul K. *The Elusive God: Reorienting Religious Epistemology.* New York: Cambridge University Press, 2008.

Moseley, A. M. and M. C. Yapp. "Interrater Reliability of the TEMPA for the Measurement of Upper Limb Function in Adults with Traumatic Brain Injury." *JHTR* 18, no. 6 (2003): 526–31.

Moses, Sharon. "Sociopolitical Implications of Neolithic Foundation Deposits and the Possibility of Child Sacrifice: A Case Study at Çatalhöyük, Turkey." Pages 57–78 in *Sacred Killing: The Archeology of Sacrifice in the Ancient Near East.* Edited by Anne Porter and Glenn M. Schwartz. Winona Lake, Ind.: Eisenbrauns, 2012.

Nagel, Thomas. "What Is It Like To Be A Bat?" Pages 391–402 in *The Mind's I: Fantasies and Reflections on Self and Soul.* Toronto: Bantam Books, 1982.

Nietzsche, Friedrich. *Nietzsche: Writings From the Late Notebooks.* Edited by Rüdiger Bittner. Translated by Kate Sturge. CTHP. New York: Cambridge University Press, 2003.

_____. *Thus Spoke Zarathustra: A Book for All and None.* Edited by Adrien del Caro and Robert B. Pippin. Translated by Adrien del Caro. New York: Cambridge University Press, 2006.

Norton, Michael I. and Francesca Gino. "Rituals Alleviate Grieving for Loved Ones, Lovers, and Lotteries." *JEP* 143, no. 1 (2014): 266–272.

Novak, David. "The Covenant in Rabbinic Thought." Pages 65–80 in *Two Faiths, One Covenant: Jewish and Christian Identity in the Presence of the Other.* Edited by Eugene B. Korn and John T. Pawlikowski. New York: Rowman & Littlefield, 2005.

O'Dowd, Ryan. *The Wisdom of Torah: Epistemology in Deuteronomy and the Wisdom in Literature.* FRLANT 225. Göttingen: Vandenhoeck & Ruprecht, 2009.

_____. "Memory on the Boundary: Epistemology in Deuteronomy." Pages 3–23 in *The Bible and Epistemology.* Edited by Mary Healy and Robin Parry. Milton Keynes, England: Paternoster, 2007.

Overbeck, Franz. *On the Christianity of Theology.* Translated by John Elbert Wilson. Eugene, OR: Pickwick, 2002.

Paese, Paul W. and Debra A. Gilin. "When an Adversary is Caught Telling the Truth: Reciprocal Cooperation Versus Self-Interest in Distributive Bargaining." *PSPB* 26, no. 1 (2000): 79–90.

Pedersen, Johannes. *Israel, Its Life and Culture.* 2 vols. London: Geoffrey Cumberledge, 1959.

Perrin, Nicholas. "Dialogic Conceptions of Language and the Problem of Biblical Unity." Pages 212–24 in *The Practice and Promise of Biblical Theology.* Edited by Scott J. Hafemann. Minneapolis: Fortress, 1991.

Pitre, Brant. *Jesus and the Jewish Roots of the Eucharist: Unlocking the Secrets of the Last Supper.* New York: Doubleday, 2011.

Plantinga, Alvin. *Warranted Christian Belief.* Oxford: Oxford University Press, 2000.

Polanyi, Michael. *Personal Knowledge: Towards a Post-Critical Philosophy.* Chicago: University of Chicago Press, 1974.

Polanyi, Michael and Amartya Sen. *The Tacit Dimension*. Chicago: University of Chicago Press, 2009.

Polzin, Robert M. "Deuteronomy." Pages 92–101 in *The Literary Guide to the Bible*. London: Collins, 1987.

Popper, Karl. *The Logic of Scientific Discovery*. New York: Routledge, 2005.

Porter, Anne. "Mortal Mirrors: Creating Kin through Human Sacrifice in Third Millennium Syro-Mesopotamia." Pages 191–216 in *Sacred Killing: The Archeology of Sacrifice in the Ancient Near East*. Edited by Anne Porter and Glenn M. Schwartz. Winona Lake, Ind.: Eisenbrauns, 2012.

Quartz, Steven R. and Terrence J. Sejnowski. "The Neural Basis of Cognitive Development: A Constructivist Manifesto." *BBS* 20, no. 4 (1997): 537–96.

Quine, W. V. O. "Epistemology Naturalized." Pages 15–32 in *Naturalizing Epistemology*. Edited by Hilary Kornblith. 2nd ed. Cambridge, MA: MIT Press, 1997.

_____. "Natural Kinds." Pages 114–38 in *Ontological Relativity and Other Essays*. New York: Columbia University Press, 1969.

Rad, Gerhard von. *Genesis: a Commentary*. Louisville, KY: Westminster John Knox, 1972.

Ramachandran, V. S. and Sandra Blakeslee. *Phantoms in the Brain: Probing the Mysteries of the Human Mind*. New York: William Morrow, 1998.

Rappaport, Roy A. *Ecology, Meaning, and Religion*. Richmond, CA: North Atlantic Books, 1979.

_____. *Ritual and Religion in the Making of Humanity*. Edinburgh: Cambridge University Press, 1999.

Rea, Michael C. "Introduction." Pages 1–32 in *Analytic Theology: New Essays in the Philosophy of Theology*. Edited by Oliver D. Crisp and Michael C. Rea. New York: Oxford University Press, 2009.

Russell, Nerissa. "Hunting Sacrifice at Neolithic Çatalhöyük." Pages 79–96 in *Sacred Killing: The Archeology of Sacrifice in the Ancient Near East*. Edited by Anne Porter and Glenn M. Schwartz. Winona Lake, Ind.: Eisenbrauns, 2012.

Sailhammer, John H. *Genesis*. EBC. Grand Rapids, MI: Zondervan, 1990.

Sallustius. *On the Gods and the World*. Translated by Thomas Taylor. London: Jeffery & Mall, 1793.

Schillebeeckx, Edward. *Christ the Sacrament of The Encounter with God*. New York: Rowman & Littlefield, 1963.

Schmemann, Alexander. *For the Life of the World: Sacraments and Orthodoxy*. New York: Saint Vladimir's Seminary, 1973.

Schultz, Richard. "What is 'Canonical' about a Canonical Biblical Theology? Genesis as a Case Study of Recent OT Proposals." Pages 83–99 in *Biblical Theology: Retrospect and Prospect*. Edited by Scott Hafemann. Downer's Grove, IL: IVP Academic, 2002.

Schwartz, Glenn M. Introduction to *Sacred Killing: The Archeology of Sacrifice in the Ancient Near East*. Edited by Anne Porter and Glenn M. Schwartz. Winona Lake, Ind.: Eisenbrauns, 2012.

Schwiebert, Jonathan. *Knowledge and the Coming Kingdom: The Didache's Meal Ritual and its Place in Early Christianity*. LNTS 373. New York: T&T Clark, 2008.

Seow, Choon Leong. "Textual Orientation." Pages 21–24 in *Biblical Ethics and Homosexuality: Listening to Scripture.* Edited by Robert Lawson Brawley. Louisville, KY: Westminster John Knox, 1996.

Shapin, Stephen K. "Here and Everywhere: Sociology of Scientific Knowledge." *ARS* 21 (1995): 289–321.

Sherwood, Stephen K. *Leviticus, Numbers, Deuteronomy.* Edited by David W. Cotter. BO. Collegeville, Minn.: Liturgical, 2002.

Shils, Edward. "Ritual and Crisis." Page 733–49 in *The Religious Situation.* Edited by Donald R. Cutler. Boston: Beacon, 1968.

Silver, Morris. "Temple/sacred prostitution in ancient Mesopotamia revisited: religion in the economy." *UF* 38 (2006): 631–663.

Sims, Benjamin. "Safe Science: Material and Social Order in Laboratory Work." *SSS* 35, no. 3 (June 2005): 333–66.

Sklar, Jay. *Sin, Impurity, Sacrifice, Atonement: The Priestly Conceptions.* HBM. Sheffield, England: Sheffield Phoenix, 2005.

Smith, Emily Esfahani. "In Grief, Try Personal Rituals: The psychology of rituals in overcoming loss, restoring broken order." *The Atlantic.* Cited July 16, 2015. Online: http://www.theatlantic.com/health/archive/2014/03/in-grief-try-personal-rituals/284397/.

Smith, James K. A. *Desiring the Kingdom: Worship, Worldview, and Cultural Formation.* 3 vols. CL. Grand Rapids, MI: Baker Academic, 2009.

Sosa, Ernest. "The Raft and the Pyramid: Coherence versus Foundations in the Theory of Knowledge." *MSP* 5 (1980): 3–26.

Soulen, R. Kendall. *The God of Israel and Christian Theology.* Minneapolis: Fortress, 1996.

Staal, Fritts. "The Meaninglessness of Ritual." *Numen* 26 (1975): 2–22.

Stegman, Thomas D. "'The Spirit of Wisdom and Understanding': Epistemology in Luke-Acts." Pages 88–106 in *The Bible and Epistemology: Biblical Soundings on the Knowledge of God.* Edited by Mary Healy and Robin Parry. Milton Keynes, England: Paternoster, 2007.

Stump, Eleonore. *Wandering in Darkness: Narrative and the Problem of Suffering.* New York: Oxford University Press, 2010.

Taylor, Charles. *Philosophical Arguments.* Cambridge, MA: Harvard University Press, 1995.

Thompson, Mary R. *The Role of Disbelief in Mark: A New Approach to the Second Gospel.* Mahwah, NJ: Paulist Press, 1989.

Tillich, Hannah. *From Time to Time.* New York: Stein and Day, 1973.

Toews, Brian G. "Genesis 1–4: The Genesis of Old Testament Instruction." Pages 38–52 in *Old Testament Theology: Retrospect & Prospect.* Edited by Scott J. Hafemann. Leicester, England: Apollos, 2002.

Tolbert, Mary Ann. *Sowing the Gospel: Mark's World in Literary-Historical Perspective.* Minneapolis: Fortress, 1989.

Torrance, Alan J. "What Is A Person?" Pages 199–222 in *From Cells To Souls—and Beyond: Changing Portraits of Human Nature.* Edited by Malcolm Jeeves. Grand Rapids, MI: Eerdmans, 2004.

Torrance, T. F. "One Aspect of the Biblical Conception of Faith." *ET* 68 (January 1957): 111–14.

Trible, Phyllis. *God and the Rhetoric of Sexuality*. Minneapolis: Fortress, 1986.

Troy, Karen L. and Mark D. Grabiner. "Asymmetrical ground impact of the hands after a trip-induced fall: Experimental kinematics and kinetics." *CB* 22, no. 10 (2007): 1088–95.

Vroom, Victor Harold. *Work and Motivation*. New York: Wiley, 1964.

Wagner, J. Ross. *Heralds of the Good News: Isaiah and Paul in Concert in the Letter to the Romans*. Leiden: Brill, 2003.

Watson, Francis. *Text and Truth: Redefining Biblical Theology*. Grand Rapids, MI: Eerdmans, 1997.

Watts, James W. *Ritual and Rhetoric in Leviticus: From Sacrifice to Scripture*. New York: Cambridge University Press, 2009.

Wenham, Gordon J. *Genesis 1–15*. WBC 1. Waco, TX: Word Books, 1987.

Westermann, Claus. *Genesis: An Introduction*. Minneapolis: Fortress, 1992.

_____. *Genesis 12–36*. CC. Minneapolis: Augsburg Publishing, 1985.

Wettstein, Howard. *The Significance of Religious Experience*. New York: Oxford University Press, 2012.

Wilson, S. G. *Luke and the Law*. New York: Cambridge University Press, 1983.

Wood, William. "On The New Analytic Theology, or: The Road Less Traveled." *JAAR* 77, no. 4 (December 2009): 941–60.

Wright, N. T. *Jesus and the Victory of God*. COQG. Minneapolis: Fortress, 1996.

Yoder, Douglas. "Tanakh Epistemology: A Philosophical Reading of an Ancient Semitic Text." Ph.D. diss., Claremont Graduate University, 2007.

Zagzebski, Linda Trinkaus. *Virtues of the Mind: An Inquiry into the Nature of Virtue and the Ethical Foundations of Knowledge*. Cambridge: Cambridge University Press, 1996.

Scripture Index

Author and Subject Index